PHILOSOPHY OF SPORT

Core Readings

PHILOSOPHY OF SPORT

Core Readings

edited by Jason Holt

broadview press

Library and Archives Canada Cataloguing in Publication

Philosophy of sport : core readings / [edited by] Jason Holt.

Includes index.
ISBN 978-1-55481-146-5 (pbk.)

1. Sports—Philosophy. I. Holt, Jason, 1971-, editor of compilation

GV706.P445 2013   796.01   C2013-902825-0

Broadview Press is an independent, international publishing house, incorporated in 1985.

We welcome comments and suggestions regarding any aspect of our publications—please feel free to contact us at the addresses below or at broadview@broadviewpress.com.

North America
PO Box 1243, Peterborough, Ontario, Canada K9J 7H5
2215 Kenmore Ave., Buffalo, New York, USA 14207
Tel: (705) 743-8990; Fax: (705) 743-8353
email: customerservice@broadviewpress.com

UK, Europe, Central Asia, Middle East, Africa, India, and Southeast Asia
Eurospan Group, 3 Henrietta St., London WC2E 8LU, United Kingdom
Tel: 44 (0) 1767 604972; Fax: 44 (0) 1767 601640
email: eurospan@turpin-distribution.com

Australia and New Zealand
NewSouth Books
c/o TL Distribution, 15-23 Helles Ave., Moorebank, NSW, Australia 2170
Tel: (02) 8778 9999; Fax: (02) 8778 9944
email: orders@tldistribution.com.au

www.broadviewpress.com

Copy-edited by Robert R. Martin

Broadview Press acknowledges the financial support of the Government of Canada through the Canada Book Fund for our publishing activities.

This book is printed on paper containing 100% post-consumer fibre.

PRINTED IN CANADA

CONTENTS

Acknowledgements • VII
Preface • IX

Part I: The Nature of Sport
A. Playing Games • 1
  1. Johan Huizinga, "The Nature and Significance of Play" • 3
  2. Bernard Suits, "The Elements of Sport" • 19
B. Defining Sport • 35
  3. John W. Loy, Jr., "The Nature of Sport: A Definitional Effort" • 37
  4. Klaus V. Meier, "Triad Trickery: Playing With Sport and Games" • 55
C. Sport Epistemology • 81
  5. Margaret Steel, "What We Know When We Know a Game" • 83
  6. Jason Holt and Laurence E. Holt, "The 'Ideal' Swing, the 'Ideal' Body:
     Myths of Optimization" • 93
D. Exploring Physicality • 107
  7. Dennis Hemphill, "Cybersport" • 109
  8. Iris Marion Young, "Throwing Like a Girl: A Phenomenology of Feminine
     Body Comportment, Motility, and Spatiality" • 127

Part II: Rules and Values
E. Sport Aesthetics • 153
  9. David Best, "The Aesthetic in Sport" • 155
  10. Peter J. Arnold, "Sport, the Aesthetic and Art: Further Thoughts" • 179

F. Banning Drugs · 201

    11. Robert L. Simon, "Good Competition and Drug-Enhanced Performance" · 203

    12. W.M. Brown, "Paternalism, Drugs, and the Nature of Sports" · 215

G. Breaking Rules · 229

    13. Craig K. Lehman, "Can Cheaters Play the Game?" · 231

    14. Simon Eassom, "Playing Games With Prisoners' Dilemmas" · 239

H. Beyond Rules · 261

    15. Leslie A. Howe, "Gamesmanship" · 263

    16. Randolph M. Feezell, "Sportsmanship" · 281

Permission Acknowledgments · 299

Index · 301

ACKNOWLEDGEMENTS

Thanks to everyone at Broadview Press for making this book possible, in particular Stephen Latta for supporting this project from the very beginning. Special thanks to Robert Martin for invaluable editorial suggestions, including many of the explanatory footnotes. Thanks also to Merilee Atos for securing reprint permissions, to Shirley Wheaton for help preparing the manuscript, and to my philosophy of sport students—past, present, and prospective.

PREFACE

This is a book of core readings in the philosophy of sport, and is intended as a primary text in undergraduate courses in the area. Most philosophy of sport texts fall into one of two categories: fat anthologies or skinny monographs. The anthologies are by and large comprehensive but too thick, not only lacking concision but, for their size and expense, leaving hardly any room for creative supplementation, sometimes even having as much sociology as philosophy proper. Single-author books are usually more concise but, for equally obvious reasons, narrower in perspective than anthologizing allows. There is a need in the philosophy of sport to challenge both the endomorphic anthologies and the ectomorphic monographs—a need, in other words, for a mesomorphic text. The intent here is to provide one.

Given this niche, it should be no surprise that the book does not go as deep as the thick anthologies: they do that well enough already. But this text does not really sacrifice depth so much as anchor it in a choice selection of readings that exhibits core breadth. The readings are deemed core for being either among the most important readings available (generating or encapsulating great swaths of literature), or more modestly, covering usually underrepresented areas (as, for example, in the sport epistemology section). Each of the following specialties in the philosophy of sport finds representation here: the nature of play and games, the definition of sport, sport epistemology, the concept of physicality, sport aesthetics, doping ethics, cheating and rationality, and finally, going beyond the rules (sportsmanship, etc.). Since there are many excellent books on sport ethics, some of which might usefully supplement this text, this text deliberately underemphasizes that subject, without marginalizing it, so as to present a more balanced view of the philosophy of sport as a whole. Rather than comprehensive coverage, then, this book aims to provide a selective solid grounding.

The book is divided into two parts: the first on the nature of sport, the second on rules and values. This division is a natural one, reaching out from a grasp of what sport is toward an understanding of what it ought to be. The first section tackles the phenomena of play and games, concepts which prefigure, and provide useful context for, definitions of sport, the focus of the second section. Then we shift from an understanding of what sport essentially is to look at the different types of knowledge (first- and third-person) in and of sport. This sets the stage for the fourth section, in which we explore the types and dimensions of physicality and embodiment. It is in the second half of the book that we broach issues pertaining to rules and values, starting the fifth section by addressing sport aesthetics, moving then to moral and ethical issues: whether or not to preserve the bans on performance-enhancing drugs (the sixth section), how rule-breaking and rationality interrelate when it comes to rules generally (seventh section), and, as befits a final (eighth) section, going beyond rules. The book's natural twofold division thus reflects a rational progression of topics.

Readers should come away from this book with a broad exposure to the deep questions comprised by the philosophy of sport, a basic understanding of major attempts to answer these questions, and a grasp of where these theories are located in the conceptual terrain. Students will sharpen their capacity for critical, creative, and abstract thinking, and may come to a sense of how they might find their own place in the conceptual landscape, and perhaps make their own contribution to the philosophy of sport. Ultimately readers will glean a richer understanding of what sport is and why it matters, so much and in so many ways, across so many cultures and subcultures, to so many people.

The book features a unique selection of core readings with balance between descriptive and normative issues: matters of fact ("is" questions like "What is sport?") counterbalanced by matters of value ("ought" questions such as "Why play fair?") The book also features suggestions for not only further reading but also, more importantly, further inquiry. It is directed, then, toward the future as a kind of vector. Whether you, the reader, choose to follow it is entirely your call.

Part I

THE NATURE OF SPORT

Section A

Playing Games

W e begin in this first section with classic accounts of play and games, respectively, in part because philosophers often try to locate sport in the conceptual terrain, to triangulate it, by appeal to these related, more basic concepts. Sport may be characterized, for instance, as a species of play, or as a certain type of game.

In his important analysis of play, from which our first reading is excerpted, Johan Huizinga aims not only to understand what play is but also to show how it figures into all culture, even in those serious domains that seem to have nothing at all to do with play. In characterizing play, Huizinga stresses that such activity is free, voluntary, and transcends ordinary life, from which it is distinct, special. To be at play is to be absorbed in it, to be motivated to so engage for its own sake. Play is limited in a variety of ways, by rules for instance, and is orderly, tending to reinforce bonds among players into social groups both cohesive in themselves and excluding non-players.

When we think of 'play' as a transitive verb, the direct object that comes to mind is inevitably 'game,' and our second reading, from Bernard Suits, offers the gold standard for theories of games in the philosophy of sport. Suits emphasizes how games impose artificial constraints on behaviour directed toward achieving a certain specific goal (the object of the game). These constraints are, of course, the rules, and in Suits's view the rules do not simply distinguish acceptable (or legal) from unacceptable (illegal) play; they actually define (that is, constitute) the game, what it means to play at all. Because these constraints, though artificial, make the game possible, they are voluntarily accepted by people who want to play the game, precisely for that reason. As a bonus, Suits defends a provocative theory of sport itself, as a subset of games, which dovetails nicely with the next section.

1. THE NATURE AND SIGNIFICANCE OF PLAY*

JOHAN HUIZINGA

Play is older than culture, for culture, however inadequately defined, always presupposes human society, and animals have not waited for man to teach them their playing. We can safely assert, even, that human civilization has added no essential feature to the general idea of play. Animals play just like men. We have only to watch young dogs to see that all the essentials of human play are present in their merry gambols. They invite one another to play by a certain ceremoniousness of attitude and gesture. They keep the rule that you shall not bite, or not bite hard, your brother's ear. They pretend to get terribly angry. And—what is most important—in all these doings they plainly experience tremendous fun and enjoyment. Such rompings of young dogs are only one of the simpler forms of animal play. There are other, much more highly developed forms: regular contests and beautiful performances before an admiring public.

Here we have at once a very important point: even in its simplest forms on the animal level, play is more than a mere physiological phenomenon or a psychological reflex. It goes beyond the confines of purely physical or purely biological activity. It is a *significant* function—that is to say, there is some sense to it. In play there is something "at play" which transcends the immediate needs of life and imparts meaning to the action. All play means something. If we call the active principle that makes up the essence of play "instinct," we explain nothing; if we call it "mind" or "will" we say too much. However we may regard it, the very fact that play has a meaning implies a non-materialistic quality in the nature of the thing itself.

Psychology and physiology deal with the observation, description and explanation of the play of animals, children and grown-ups. They try to deter-

---

* From Johan Huizinga, *Homo Ludens: A Study of the Play-Element in Culture* (Boston: Beacon, 1950), pp. 1-16.

mine the nature and significance of play and to assign it its place in the scheme of life. The high importance of this place and the necessity, or at least the utility, of play as a function are generally taken for granted and form the starting-point of all such scientific researches. The numerous attempts to define the biological function of play show a striking variation. By some the origin and fundamentals of play have been described as a discharge of superabundant vital energy, by others as the satisfaction of some "imitative instinct," or again as simply a "need" for relaxation. According to one theory play constitutes a training of the young creature for the serious work that life will demand later on. According to another it serves as an exercise in restraint needful to the individual. Some find the principle of play in an innate urge to exercise a certain faculty, or in the desire to dominate or compete. Yet others regard it as an "abreaction"—an outlet for harmful impulses, as the necessary restorer of energy wasted by one-sided activity, as "wish-fulfilment," as a fiction designed to keep up the feeling of personal value, etc.[1]

All these hypotheses have one thing in common: they all start from the assumption that play must serve something which is *not* play, that it must have some kind of biological purpose. They all enquire into the why and the wherefore of play. The various answers they give tend rather to overlap than to exclude one another. It would be perfectly possible to accept nearly all the explanations without getting into any real confusion of thought—and without coming much nearer to a real understanding of the play-concept. They are all only partial solutions of the problem. If any of them were really decisive it ought either to exclude all the others or comprehend them in a higher unity. Most of them only deal incidentally with the question of what play is *in itself* and what it means for the player. They attack play direct with the quantitative methods of experimental science without first paying attention to its profoundly aesthetic quality. As a rule they leave the primary quality of play as such, virtually untouched. To each and every one of the above "explanations" it might well be objected: "So far so good, but what actually is the *fun* of playing? Why does the baby crow with pleasure? Why does the gambler lose himself in his passion? Why is a huge crowd roused to frenzy by a football match?" This intensity of, and absorption in, play finds no explanation in biological analysis. Yet in this intensity, this absorption, this power of maddening, lies the very essence, the primordial quality of play. Nature, so our reasoning mind tells us, could just as easily have given her children all those useful functions of discharging superabundant energy, of relaxing after exertion, of training for the demands of life, of compensating for unfulfilled longings, etc., in the form of purely mechanical exercises and reactions. But no, she gave us play, with its tension, its mirth, and its fun.

. Now this last-named element, the *fun* of playing, resists all analysis, all logical interpretation. As a concept, it cannot be reduced to any other mental category. No other modern language known to me has the exact equivalent of the English "fun." The Dutch "aardigkeit" perhaps comes nearest to it (derived from "aard" which means the same as "Art" and "Wesen"[2] in German, and thus evidence, perhaps, that the matter cannot be reduced further). We may note in passing that "fun" in its current usage is of rather recent origin. French, oddly enough, has no corresponding term at all; German half makes up for it by "Spass" and "Witz" together. Nevertheless it is precisely this fun-element that characterizes the essence of play. Here we have to do with an absolutely primary category of life, familiar to everybody at a glance right down to the animal level. We may well call play a "totality" in the modern sense of the word, and it is as a totality that we must try to understand and evaluate it.

Since the reality of play extends beyond the sphere of human life it cannot have its foundations in any rational nexus, because this would limit it to mankind. The incidence of play is not associated with any particular stage of civilization or view of the universe. Any thinking person can see at a glance that play is a thing on its own, even if his language possesses no general concept to express it. Play cannot be denied. You can deny, if you like, nearly all abstractions: justice, beauty, truth, goodness, mind, God. You can deny seriousness, but not play.

But in acknowledging play you acknowledge mind, for whatever else play is, it is not matter. Even in the animal world it bursts the bounds of the physical existent. From the point of view of a world wholly determined by the operation of blind forces, play would be altogether superfluous. Play only becomes possible, thinkable and understandable when an influx of *mind* breaks down the absolute determinism of the cosmos. The very existence of play continually confirms the supra-logical nature of the human situation. Animals play, so they must be more than merely mechanical things. We play and know that we play, so we must be more than merely rational beings, for play is irrational.

In tackling the problem of play as a function of culture proper and not as it appears in the life of the animal or the child, we begin where biology and psychology leave off. In culture we find play as a given magnitude existing before culture itself existed, accompanying it and pervading it from the earliest beginnings right up to the phase of civilization we are now living in. We find play present everywhere as a well-defined quality of action which is different from "ordinary" life. We can disregard the question of how far science has succeeded in reducing this quality to quantitative factors. In our opinion it has not. At all events it is precisely this quality, itself so characteristic of the form of life we call "play," which matters. Play as a special form of activity, as a "significant form," as a social function—that is our subject. We shall not look for the natural impulses and habits conditioning play in general, but shall consider play in its manifold concrete forms as itself a social construction. We shall try to take play as the player himself takes it: in its primary significance. If we find that play is based on the manipulation of certain images, on a certain "imagination" of reality (i.e., its conversion into images), then our main concern will be to grasp the value and significance of these images and their "imagination." We shall observe their action in play itself and thus try to understand play as a cultural factor in life.

The great archetypal activities of human society are all permeated with play from the start. Take language, for instance—that first and supreme instrument which man shapes in order to communicate, to teach, to command. Language allows him to distinguish, to establish, to state things; in short, to name them and by naming them to raise them into the domain of the spirit. In the making of speech and language the spirit is continually "sparking" between matter and mind, as it were, playing with this wondrous nominative faculty. Behind every abstract expression there lie the boldest of metaphors, and every metaphor is a play upon words. Thus in giving expression to life man creates a second, poetic world alongside the world of nature.

Or take myth. This, too, is a transformation or an "imagination" of the outer world, only here the process is more elaborate and ornate than is the case with individual words. In myth, primitive man seeks to account for the world of phenomena by grounding it in the divine. In all the wild imaginings of mythology a fanciful spirit is playing on the border-line between jest and earnest. Or finally, let us take ritual. Primitive society performs its sacred rites, its sacrifices, consecrations and mysteries, all of which serve to guarantee the well-being of the world, in a spirit of pure play truly understood.

Now in myth and ritual the great instinctive forces of civilized life have their origin: law and order, commerce and profit, craft and art, poetry, wisdom and science. All are rooted in the primeval soil of play.

The object of the present essay is to demonstrate that it is more than a rhetorical comparison to view culture *sub specie ludi*.* The thought is not at all new. There was a time when it was generally accepted, though in a limited sense quite different

---

* Under the aspect of—from the perspective of—play.

from the one intended here: in the seventeenth century, the age of world theatre. Drama, in a glittering succession of figures ranging from Shakespeare and Calderon to Racine, then dominated the literature of the West. It was the fashion to liken the world to a stage on which every man plays his part. Does this mean that the play-element in civilization was openly acknowledged? Not at all. On closer examination this fashionable comparison of life to a stage proves to be little more than an echo of the Neo-platonism* that was then in vogue, with a markedly moralistic accent. It was a variation on the ancient theme of the vanity of all things. The fact that play and culture are actually interwoven with one another was neither observed nor expressed, whereas for us the whole point is to show that genuine, pure play is one of the main bases of civilisation.

To our way of thinking, play is the direct opposite of seriousness. At first sight this opposition seems as irreducible to other categories as the play-concept itself. Examined more closely, however, the contrast between play and seriousness proves to be neither conclusive nor fixed. We can say: play is non-seriousness. But apart from the fact that this proposition tells us nothing about the positive qualities of play, it is extraordinarily easy to refute. As soon as we proceed from "play is non-seriousness" to "play is not serious," the contrast leaves us in the lurch—for some play can be very serious indeed. Moreover we can immediately name several other fundamental categories that likewise come under the heading "non-seriousness" yet have no correspondence whatever with "play." Laughter, for instance, is in a sense the opposite of seriousness without being absolutely bound up with play. Children's games, football, and chess are played in profound seriousness; the players have not the slightest inclination to laugh. It is worth noting that the purely physiological act of laughing is exclusive to man, whilst the significant function of play is common to both men and animals. The Aristotelian *animal ridens*† characterizes man as distinct from the animal almost more absolutely than *homo sapiens*.

What is true of laughter is true also of the comic. The comic comes under the category of non-seriousness and has certain affinities with laughter—it provokes

---

* Christian philosophical movement dating from the third century CE, emphasizing the soul's rise above the imperfect physical world, through virtue and contemplation of the Divine.

† = the laughing animal. This definition of 'human' was embraced as early as Rabelais in the sixteenth century, though it had been considered and rejected much earlier by Aristotle. Aristotle proposed that the distinguishing essence of humanity was reason—we are the rational animal. '*Homo sapiens*' is the biological classification of modern humans, distinguished by sapience ('*sapiens*'—wise, or *knowing*).

laughter. But its relation to play is subsidiary. In itself play is not comical either for player or public. The play of young animals or small children may sometimes be ludicrous, but the sight of grown dogs chasing one another hardly moves us to laughter. When we call a farce or a comedy "comic," it is not so much on account of the play-acting as such as on account of the situation or the thoughts expressed. The mimic and laughter-provoking art of the clown is comic as well as ludicrous, but it can scarcely be termed genuine play.

The category of the comic is closely connected with *folly* in the highest and lowest sense of that word. Play, however, is not foolish. It lies outside the antithesis of wisdom and folly. The later Middle Ages tended to express the two cardinal moods of life—play and seriousness—somewhat imperfectly by opposing *folie* to *sense*, until Erasmus in his *Laus Stultitiae* showed the inadequacy of the contrast.

All the terms in this loosely connected group of ideas—play, laughter, folly, wit, jest, joke, the comic, etc.—share the characteristic which we had to attribute to play, namely, that of resisting any attempt to reduce it to other terms. Their rationale and their mutual relationships must lie in a very deep layer of our mental being.

The more we try to mark off the form we call "play" from other forms apparently related to it, the more the absolute independence of the play-concept stands out. And the segregation of play from the domain of the great categorical antitheses does not stop there. Play lies outside the antithesis of wisdom and folly, and equally outside those of truth and falsehood, good and evil. Although it is a nonmaterial activity it has no moral function. The valuations of vice and virtue do not apply here.

If, therefore, play cannot be directly referred to the categories of truth or goodness, can it be included perhaps in the realm of the aesthetic? Here our judgement wavers. For although the attribute of beauty does not attach to play as such, play nevertheless tends to assume marked elements of beauty. Mirth and grace adhere at the outset to the more primitive forms of play. In play the beauty of the human body in motion reaches its zenith. In its more developed forms it is saturated with rhythm and harmony, the noblest gifts of aesthetic perception known to man. Many and close are the links that connect play with beauty. All the same, we cannot say that beauty is inherent in play as such; so we must leave it at that: play is a function of the living, but is not susceptible of exact definition either logically, biologically, or aesthetically. The play-concept must always remain distinct from all the other forms of thought in which we express the structure of mental and social life. Hence we shall have to confine ourselves to describing the main characteristics of play.

Since our theme is the relation of play to culture we need not enter into all the possible forms of play but can restrict ourselves to its social manifestations. These we might call the higher forms of play. They are generally much easier to describe than the more primitive play of infants and young animals, because they are more distinct and articulate in form and their features more various and conspicuous, whereas in interpreting primitive play we immediately come up against that irreducible quality of pure playfulness which is not, in our opinion, amenable to further analysis. We shall have to speak of contests and races, of performances and exhibitions, of dancing and music, pageants, masquerades and tournaments. Some of the characteristics we shall enumerate are proper to play in general, others to social play in particular.

First and foremost, then, all play is a voluntary activity. Play to order is no longer play: it could at best be but a forcible imitation of it. By this quality of freedom alone, play marks itself off from the course of the natural process. It is something added thereto and spread out over it like a flowering, an ornament, a garment. Obviously, freedom must be understood here in the wider sense that leaves untouched the philosophical problem of determinism. It may be objected that this freedom does not exist for the animal and the child; they *must* play because their instinct drives them to it and because it serves to develop their bodily faculties and their powers of selection. The term "instinct," however, introduces an unknown quantity, and to presuppose the utility of play from the start is to be guilty of a *petitio principii*.* Child and animal play because they enjoy playing, and therein precisely lies their freedom.

Be that as it may, for the adult and responsible human being play is a function which he could equally well leave alone. Play is superfluous. The need for it is only urgent to the extent that the enjoyment of it makes it a need. Play can be deferred or suspended at any time. It is never imposed by physical necessity or moral duty. It is never a task. It is done at leisure, during "free time." Only when play is a recognized cultural function—a rite, a ceremony—is it bound up with notions of obligation and duty.

Here, then, we have the first main characteristic of play: that it is free, is in fact freedom. A second characteristic is closely connected with this, namely, that play is not "ordinary" or "real" life. It is rather a stepping out of "real" life into a temporary sphere of activity with a disposition all of its own. Every child knows perfectly

---

* = begging the question—a fallacious form of argument in which the conclusion is already assumed in the premises.

well that he is "only pretending," or that it was "only for fun." How deep-seated this awareness is in the child's soul is strikingly illustrated by the following story, told to me by the father of the boy in question. He found his four-year-old son sitting at the front of a row of chairs, playing "trains." As he hugged him the boy said: "Don't kiss the engine, Daddy, or the carriages won't think it's real." This "only pretending" quality of play betrays a consciousness of the inferiority of play compared with "seriousness," a feeling that seems to be something as primary as play itself. Nevertheless, as we have already pointed out, the consciousness of play being "only a pretend" does not by any means prevent it from proceeding with the utmost seriousness, with an absorption, a devotion that passes into rapture and, temporarily at least, completely abolishes that troublesome "only" feeling. Any game can at any time wholly run away with the players. The contrast between play and seriousness is always fluid. The inferiority of play is continually being offset by the corresponding superiority of its seriousness. Play turns to seriousness and seriousness to play. Play may rise to heights of beauty and sublimity that leave seriousness far beneath. Tricky questions such as these will come up for discussion when we start examining the relationship between play and ritual.

As regards its formal characteristics, all students lay stress on the *disinterestedness* of play. Not being "ordinary" life it stands outside the immediate satisfaction of wants and appetites, indeed it interrupts the appetitive process. It interpolates itself as a temporary activity satisfying in itself and ending there. Such at least is the way in which play presents itself to us in the first instance: as an intermezzo, an *interlude* in our daily lives. As a regularly recurring relaxation, however, it becomes the accompaniment, the complement, in fact an integral part of life in general. It adorns life, amplifies it and is to that extent a necessity both for the individual—as a life function—and for society by reason of the meaning it contains, its significance, its expressive value, its spiritual and social associations, in short, as a culture function. The expression of it satisfies all kinds of communal ideals. It thus has its place in a sphere superior to the strictly biological processes of nutrition, reproduction and self-preservation. This assertion is apparently contradicted by the fact that play, or rather sexual display, is predominant in animal life precisely at the mating-season. But would it be too absurd to assign a place *outside* the purely physiological, to the singing, cooing and strutting of birds just as we do to human play? In all its higher forms the latter at any rate always belongs to the sphere of festival and ritual—the sacred sphere.

Now, does the fact that play is a necessity, that it subserves culture, or indeed that it actually becomes culture, detract from its disinterested character? No, for the purposes it serves are external to immediate material interests or the individual satisfaction of biological needs. As a sacred activity play naturally contributes to the well-being of the group, but in quite another way and by other means than the acquisition of the necessities of life.

Play is distinct from "ordinary" life both as to locality and duration. This is the third main characteristic of play: its secludedness, its limitedness. It is "played out" within certain limits of time and place. It contains its own course and meaning.

Play begins, and then at a certain moment it is "over." It plays itself to an end. While it is in progress all is movement, change, alternation, succession, association, separation. But immediately connected with its limitation as to time there is a further curious feature of play: it at once assumes fixed form as a cultural phenomenon. Once played, it endures as a new-found creation of the mind, a treasure to be retained by the memory. It is transmitted, it becomes tradition. It can be repeated at any time, whether it be "child's play" or a game of chess, or at fixed intervals like a mystery. In this faculty of repetition lies one of the most essential qualities of play. It holds good not only of play as a whole but also of its inner structure. In nearly all the higher forms of play the elements of repetition and alternation (as in the *refrain**), are like the warp and woof of a fabric.

More striking even than the limitation as to time is the limitation as to space. All play moves and has its being within a play-ground marked off beforehand either materially or ideally, deliberately or as a matter of course. Just as there is no formal difference between play and ritual, so the "consecrated spot" cannot be formally distinguished from the play-ground. The arena, the card-table, the magic circle, the temple, the stage, the screen, the tennis court, the court of justice, etc., are all in form and function play-grounds, i.e., forbidden spots, isolated, hedged round, hallowed, within which special rules obtain. All are temporary worlds within the ordinary world, dedicated to the performance of an act apart.

Inside the play-ground an absolute and peculiar order reigns. Here we come across another, very positive feature of play: it creates order, *is* order. Into an imperfect world and into the confusion of life it brings a temporary, a limited perfection. Play demands order absolute and supreme. The least deviation from it "spoils the game," robs it of its character and makes it worthless. The profound affinity between play and order is perhaps the reason why play, as we noted in passing, seems to lie to such a large extent in the field of aesthetics. Play has a tendency to be beautiful. It may be that this aesthetic factor is identical with the

---

*   In certain songs and poems, usually at the end of verses.

impulse to create orderly form, which animates play in all its aspects. The words we use to denote the elements of play belong for the most part to aesthetics, terms with which we try to describe the effects of beauty: tension, poise, balance, contrast, variation, solution, resolution, etc. Play casts a spell over us; it is "enchanting," "captivating." It is invested with the noblest qualities we are capable of perceiving in things: rhythm and harmony.

The element of tension in play to which we have just referred plays a particularly important part. Tension means uncertainty, chanciness; a striving to decide the issue and so end it. The player wants something to "go," to "come off"; he wants to "succeed" by his own exertions. Baby reaching for a toy, pussy patting a bobbin, a little girl playing ball—all want to achieve something difficult, to succeed, to end a tension. Play is "tense," as we say. It is this element of tension and solution that governs all solitary games of skill and application such as puzzles, jig-saws, mosaic-making, patience,* target-shooting, and the more play bears the character of competition the more fervent it will be. In gambling and athletics it is as its height. Though play as such is outside the range of good and bad, the element of tension imparts to it a certain ethical value in so far as it means a testing of the player's prowess: his courage, tenacity, resources and, last but not least, his spiritual powers—his "fairness"; because, despite his ardent desire to win, he must still stick to the rules of the game.

These rules in their turn are a very important factor in the play-concept. All play has its rules. They determine what "holds" in the temporary world circumscribed by play. The rules of a game are absolutely binding and allow no doubt. Paul Valéry once in passing gave expression to a very cogent thought when he said: "No scepticism is possible where the rules of a game are concerned, for the principle underlying them is an unshakable truth...." Indeed, as soon as the rules are transgressed the whole play-world collapses. The game is over. The umpire's whistle breaks the spell and sets "real" life going again.

The player who trespasses against the rules or ignores them is a "spoil-sport." The spoil-sport is not the same as the false player, the cheat; for the latter pretends to be playing the game and, on the face of it, still acknowledges the magic circle. It is curious to note how much more lenient society is to the cheat than to the spoil-sport. This is because the spoil-sport shatters the play-world itself. By withdrawing from the game he reveals the relativity and fragility of the play-world in which he had temporarily shut himself with others. He robs play of its *illusion*—a pregnant

---

*   = solitaire.

word which means literally "in-play" (from *inlusio, illudere* or *inludere*). Therefore he must be cast out, for he threatens the existence of the play-community. The figure of the spoil-sport is most apparent in boys' games. The little community does not enquire whether the spoil-sport is guilty of defection because he dares not enter into the game or because he is not allowed to. Rather, it does not recognize "not being allowed" and calls it "not daring." For it, the problem of obedience and conscience is no more than fear of punishment. The spoil-sport breaks the magic world, therefore he is a coward and must be ejected. In the world of high seriousness, too, the cheat and the hypocrite have always had an easier time of it than the spoil-sports, here called apostates, heretics, innovators, prophets, conscientious objectors, etc. It sometimes happens, however, that the spoil-sports in their turn make a new community with rules of its own. The outlaw, the revolutionary, the cabbalist or member of a secret society, indeed heretics of all kinds are of a highly associative if not sociable disposition, and a certain element of play is prominent in all their doings.

A play-community generally tends to become permanent even after the game is over. Of course, not every game of marbles or every bridge-party leads to the founding of a club. But the feeling of being "apart together" in an exceptional situation, of sharing something important, of mutually withdrawing from the rest of the world and rejecting the usual norms, retains its magic beyond the duration of the individual game. The club pertains to play as the hat to the head. It would be rash to explain all the associations which the anthropologist calls "phratria"—e.g., clans, brotherhoods, etc.—simply as play-communities; nevertheless it has been shown again and again how difficult it is to draw the line between, on the one hand, permanent social groupings—particularly in archaic cultures with their extremely important, solemn, indeed sacred customs—and the sphere of play on the other.

The exceptional and special position of play is most tellingly illustrated by the fact that it loves to surround itself with an air of secrecy. Even in early childhood the charm of play is enhanced by making a "secret" out of it. This is for *us*, not for the "others." What the "others" do "outside" is no concern of ours at the moment. Inside the circle of the game the laws and customs of ordinary life no longer count. We are different and do things differently. This temporary abolition of the ordinary world is fully acknowledged in child-life, but it is no less evident in the great ceremonial games of savage societies. During the great feast of initiation when the youths are accepted into the male community, it is not the neophytes only that are exempt from the ordinary laws and regulations: there is a truce to all feuds in the tribe. All retaliatory acts and vendettas are suspended. This temporary suspension of normal social life on account of the sacred play-season has numerous traces in the more advanced civilizations as well. Everything that pertains to saturnalia and carnival customs belongs to it. Even with us a bygone age of robuster private habits than ours, more marked class-privileges and a more complaisant police recognized the orgies of young men of rank under the name of a "rag." The saturnalian* licence of young men still survives, in fact, in the ragging at English universities, which the *Oxford English Dictionary* defines as "an extensive display of noisy and disorderly conduct carried out in defiance of authority and discipline."

The "differentness" and secrecy of play are most vividly expressed in "dressing up." Here the "extra-ordinary" nature of play reaches perfection. The disguised or masked individual "plays" another part, another being. He *is* another being. The terrors of childhood, open-hearted gaiety, mystic fantasy and sacred awe are all inextricably entangled in this strange business of masks and disguises.

Summing up the formal characteristics of play we might call it a free activity standing quite consciously outside "ordinary" life as being "not serious," but at the same time absorbing the player intensely and utterly. It is an activity connected with no material interest, and no profit can be gained by it. It proceeds within its own proper boundaries of time and space according to fixed rules and in an orderly manner. It promotes the formation of social groupings which tend to surround themselves with secrecy and to stress their difference from the common world by disguise or other means.

The function of play in the higher forms which concern us here can largely be derived from the two basic aspects under which we meet it: as a contest *for* something or a representation *of* something. These two functions can unite in such a way that the game "represents" a contest, or else becomes a contest for the best representation of something.

Representation means display, and this may simply consist in the exhibition of something naturally given, before an audience. The peacock and the turkey merely display their gorgeous plumage to the females, but the essential feature of it lies in the parading of something out of the ordinary and calculated to arouse admiration. If the bird accompanies this exhibition with dance-steps we have a performance, a *stepping out of* common reality into a higher order. We are ignor-

---

* Pertaining to a wild and unrestrained party—named for the ancient Roman *saturnalia*, an annual festival featuring such behaviour.

ant of the bird's sensations while so engaged. We know, however, that in child-life performances of this kind are full of imagination. The child is *making an image* of something different, something more beautiful, or more sublime, or more dangerous than what he usually *is*. One is a Prince, or one is Daddy or a wicked witch or a tiger. The child is quite literally "beside himself" with delight, transported beyond himself to such an extent that he almost believes he actually is such and such a thing, without, however, wholly losing consciousness of "ordinary reality." His representation is not so much a sham-reality as a realization in appearance: "imagination" in the original sense of the word. *

Passing now from children's games to the sacred performances in archaic culture we find that there is more of a mental element "at play" in the latter, though it is excessively difficult to define. The sacred performance is more than an actualization in appearance only, a sham reality; it is also more than a symbolical actualization— it is a mystical one. In it, something invisible and inactual takes beautiful, actual, holy form. The participants in the rite are convinced that the action actualizes and effects a definite beatification,† brings about an order of things higher than that in which they customarily live. All the same this "actualization by representation" still retains the formal characteristics of play in every respect. It is played or performed within a play-ground that is literally "staked out," and played moreover as a feast, i.e., in mirth and freedom. A sacred space, a temporarily real world of its own, has been expressly hedged off for it. But with the end of the play its effect is not lost; rather it continues to shed its radiance on the ordinary world outside, a wholesome influence working security, order and prosperity for the whole community until the sacred play-season comes round again.

Examples can be taken from all over the world. According to ancient Chinese lore the purpose of music and dance is to keep the world in its right course and to force Nature into benevolence towards man. The year's prosperity will depend on the right performance of sacred contests at the seasonal feasts. If these gatherings do not take place the crops will not ripen.³

The rite is a *dromenon*, which means "something acted," an act, action. That which is enacted, or the stuff of the action, is a *drama*, which again means act, action represented on a stage. Such action may occur as a performance or a contest. The rite, or "ritual act" represents a cosmic happening, an event in the natural process. The word "represents," however, does not cover the exact meaning of the

---

*   The sense intended here is that of forming an image, which need not be concerned with representing reality.

†   The affirmation and declaration of the holiness of someone—here, some *thing*.

act, at least not in its looser, modern connotation; for here "representation" is really *identification*, the mystic repetition or *re-presentation* of the event. The rite produces the effect which is then not so much *shown figuratively* as *actually reproduced* in the action. The function of the rite, therefore, is far from being merely imitative; it causes the worshippers to participate in the sacred happening itself. As the Greeks would say, "it is *methectic* rather than *mimetic*."[4] It is "a helping-out of the action."[5]

Anthropology is not primarily interested in how psychology will assess the mental attitude displayed in these phenomena. The psychologist may seek to settle the matter by calling such performances an *identification compensatrice*, a kind of substitute, "a representative act undertaken in view of the impossibility of staging real, purposive action."[6] Are the performers mocking, or are they mocked? The business of the anthropologist is to understand the significance of these "imaginations" in the mind of the peoples who practise and believe in them.

We touch here on the very core of comparative religion: the nature and essence of ritual and mystery. The whole of the ancient Vedic* sacrificial rites rests on the idea that the ceremony—be it sacrifice, contest or performance—by representing a certain desired cosmic event, compels the gods to effect that event in reality. We could well say, by "playing" it. Leaving the religious issues aside we shall only concern ourselves here with the play-element in archaic ritual.

Ritual is thus in the main a matter of shows, representations, dramatic performances, imaginative actualizations of a vicarious nature. At the great seasonal festivals the community celebrates the grand happenings in the life of nature by staging sacred performances, which represent the change of seasons, the rising and setting of the constellations, the growth and ripening of crops, birth, life and death in man and beast. As Leo Frobenius puts it, archaic man *plays* the order of nature as imprinted on his consciousness.[7] In the remote past, so Frobenius thinks, man first assimilated the phenomena of vegetation and animal life and then conceived an idea of time and space, of months and seasons, of the course of the sun and moon. And now he plays this great processional order of existence in a sacred play, in and through which he actualizes anew, or "recreates," the events represented and thus helps to maintain the cosmic order. Frobenius draws even more far-reaching conclusions from this "playing at nature." He deems it the starting-point of all social order and social institutions, too. Through this ritual play, savage society acquires its rude forms of government. The king is the sun, his kingship the image of the sun's

---

* Designating the period during which the Vedas (sacred writings of the Hindu religion) were written: perhaps beginning as early as 1700 BCE and continuing to as late as 150 BCE.

course. All his life the king plays "sun" and in the end he suffers the fate of the sun: he must be killed in ritual forms by his own people....

NOTES

1. For these theories see H. Zondervan, *Het Spel Bij Dieren, Kinderen en Volwassen Menschen* (Amsterdam, 1928), and F.J.J. Buytendijk, *Het Spel van Mensch en Dier als openbaring van levensdriften* (Amsterdam, 1932).
2. Nature, kind, being, essence, etc. Trans.
3. M. Granet: *Festivals and Songs of Ancient China; Dances and Legends of Ancient China; Chinese Civilization* (London, 1932).
4. Jane Harrison: *Themis: A Study of the Social Origins of Greek Religion* (Cambridge, 1912), p. 125.
5. R.R. Marett, *The Threshold of Religion* (London, 1912), p. 48.
6. Buytendijk, *Het Spel van Mensch en Dier als openbaring van levensdriften* (Amsterdam, 1932), pp. 70-71.
7. *Kulturgeschichte Afrikas, Prolegomena zu einer historischen Gestaltlehre; Schicksalskunde im Sinne des Kulturwerdens* (Leipzig, 1932).

2. THE ELEMENTS OF SPORT[*]

BERNARD SUITS

I would like to advance the thesis that the elements of sport are essentially—although perhaps not totally—the same as the elements of game. I shall first propose an account of the elements of game-playing, then comment on the relation of game to sport, and finally suggest that the resulting view of sport has an important bearing on the question as to whether sport is or is not serious.

The Elements of Game

Since games are goal-directed activities which involve choice, ends and means are two of the elements of games. But in addition to being means-end oriented activities, games are also rule-governed activities, so that rules are a third element. And since, as we shall see, the rules of games make up a rather special kind of rule, it will be necessary to take account of one more element, namely, the attitudes of game-players *qua* [†] game-players. I add "*qua* game-players" because I do not mean what might happen to be the attitude of this or that game player under these or those conditions (e.g., the hope of winning a cash prize or the satisfaction of exhibiting physical prowess to an admiring audience), but the attitude without which it is not possible to play a game. Let us call this attitude, of which more presently, the *lusory* (from the Latin *ludus*, game) attitude.

My task will be to persuade you that what I have called the lusory attitude is the element which unifies the other elements into a single formula which successfully states the necessary and sufficient conditions for any activity to be an instance of game-playing. I propose, then, that the elements of game are (1) the

---

[*]   Bernard Suits, "The Elements of Sport," in *The Philosophy of Sport: A Collection of Essays,* ed. Robert Osterhoudt (Springfield, IL: Charles C. Thomas, 1973), pp. 48-64.

[†]   = insofar as they are considered as.

goal, (2) means for achieving the goal, (3) rules, and (4) lusory attitude. I shall briefly discuss each of these in order.

The Goal

We should notice first of all that there are three distinguishable goals involved in game-playing. Thus, if we were to ask a long distance runner his purpose in entering a race, he might say any one or all of three things, each of which would be accurate, appropriate, and consistent with the other two. He might reply (1) that his purpose is to participate in a long distance race, or (2) that his purpose is to win the race, or (3) that his purpose is to cross the finish line ahead of the other contestants. It should be noted that these responses are not merely three different formulations of one and the same purpose. Thus, winning a race is not the same thing as crossing a finish line ahead of the other contestants, since it is possible to do the latter unfairly by, for example, cutting across the infield. Nor is participating in the race the same as either of these, since the contestant, while fully participating, may simply fail to cross the finish line first, either by fair means or foul. That there must be this triplet of goals in games will be accounted for by the way in which lusory attitude is related to rules and means. For the moment, however, it will be desirable to select just one of the three kinds of goal for consideration, namely, the kind illustrated in the present example by crossing the finish line ahead of the other contestants. This goal is literally the *simplest* of the three goals, since each of the other goals presupposes it, whereas it does not presuppose either of the other two. This goal, therefore, has the best claim to be regarded as an elementary component of game-playing. The others, since they are compounded components, can be defined only after the disclosure of additional elements.

The kind of goal at issue, then, is the kind illustrated by crossing a finish line first (but not necessarily fairly), having x number of tricks piled up before you on a bridge table (but not necessarily as a consequence of playing bridge), or getting a golf ball into a cup (but not necessarily by using a golf club). This kind of goal may be described generally as *a specific achievable state of affairs*. This description is, I believe, no more and no less than is required. By omitting to say *how* the state of affairs in question is to be brought about, it avoids confusion between this goal and the goal of winning. And because any achievable state of affairs whatever could, with sufficient ingenuity, be made the goal of a game, the description does not include too much. I suggest that this kind of goal be called the *pre-lusory* goal of a game, because it can be described before, or independently of, any game of which it may be, or come to be, a part. In contrast, the goal of winning can be described only in terms of the game in which it figures, and winning may accordingly be called the *lusory* goal of a game. (It is tempting to call what I have called the pre-lusory goal the goal *in* a game and the lusory goal the goal *of* a game, but the practice of philosophers like J.L. Austin has, I believe, sufficiently illustrated the hazards of trying to make prepositions carry a load of meaning which can much better be borne by adjectives and nouns.) Finally, the goal of participating in the game is not, strictly speaking, a part of the game at all. It is simply one of the goals that people have, such as wealth, glory, or security. As such it may be called a lusory goal, but a lusory goal of life rather than of games.

Means

Just as we saw that reference to the goal of game-playing was susceptible of three different (but proper and consistent) interpretations, so we shall find that the means in games can refer to more than one kind of thing; two, in fact, depending upon whether we wish to refer to means for winning the game or for achieving the pre-lusory goal. Thus, an extremely effective way to achieve the pre-lusory goal in a boxing match—viz., the state of affairs consisting in your opponent being *down* for the count of ten—is to shoot him through the head, but this is obviously not a means to winning the match. In games, of course, we are interested only in means which are permitted for winning, and we are now in a position to define that class of means, which we may call *lusory* means. Lusory means are means which are permitted (are legal or legitimate) in the attempt to achieve pre-lusory goals. Thus a soccer player may use foot or head, but not hand, in his efforts to achieve that state of affairs wherein the ball is in the goal. And a player who does not confine himself to lusory means may not be said to win, even if he achieves the pre-lusory goal. But achievement of the lusory goal, winning, requires that the player confine himself to lusory means, so that confinement to lusory means is a necessary (but of course not a sufficient) condition for winning.

It should be noticed that we have been able to distinguish lusory from, if you will, illusory means only by assuming without analysis one of the elements necessary in making the distinction. We have defined lusory means as means which are *permitted* without examining the nature of that permission. This omission will be repaired directly by taking up the question of rules. But we may provisionally acknowledge the following definition: *lusory means*, means permitted in seeking pre-lusory goals.

Rules

As with goals and means, two kinds of rule figure in games, one kind associated with pre-lusory goals, the other with lusory goals. The rules of a game are, in effect, proscriptions of certain means useful in achieving pre-lusory goals. Thus, it is useful but proscribed to trip a competitor in a foot race. This kind of rule may be called constitutive of the game, since such rules together with specification of the pre-lusory goal set out all the conditions which must be met in playing the game (though not, of course, in playing the game skillfully). Let us call such rules *constitutive* rules. The other kind of rule operates, so to speak, *within* the area circumscribed by constitutive rules, and this kind of rule may be called a rule of skill. Examples are the familiar injunctions to keep your eye on the ball, to refrain from trumping your partner's ace, and the like. To break a rule of skill is usually to fail, at least to that extent; to play the game well, but to break a constitutive rule is to fail to play the game at all. (There is a third kind of rule in games which appears to be unlike either of these. This is the kind of rule for which there is a fixed penalty, such that violating the rule is neither to fail to play the game nor [necessarily] to fail to play the game well, since it is sometimes tactically correct to incur such a penalty [e.g., in hockey] for the sake of the advantage gained. But these rules and the lusory consequences of their violation are established by the constitutive rules, and are simply extensions of them.)

Having made the distinction between constitutive rules and rules of skill, I propose to ignore the latter, since my purpose is to define not well-played games, but games. It is, then, what I have called constitutive rules which determine the kind and range of means which will be permitted in seeking to achieve the pre-lusory goal.

What is the nature of the restrictions which constitutive rules impose on the means for reaching a pre-lusory goal? The effect of constitutive rules is to place obstacles in the path leading to a pre-lusory goal. I invite the reader to think of any game at random. Now identify the pre-lusory goal, being careful to remember that the pre-lusory goal is simply any specific achievable state of affairs. I think you will agree that the simplest, easiest, and most direct approach to achieving such a goal is always ruled out in favour of a more complex, more difficult, and more indirect approach. Thus it is not uncommon for players of a new and difficult game to agree among themselves to *ease up* on the rules, that is, to allow themselves a greater degree of latitude than the official rules permit. This means removing some of the obstacles or, in terms of means, permitting certain means which the rules do not really permit. But if no means whatever are ruled out, then the game ceases to exist. Thus, we may think of the gamewright, when he invents games, as attempting to draw a line between permitted and prohibited means to a given end. If he draws this line too loosely there is danger of the game becoming too easy, and if he draws it with utter laxity the game simply falls apart. On the other hand, he must not draw the line too tight or, instead of falling apart, the game will be squeezed out of existence. For example, imagine a game where the pre-lusory goal is to cross a finish line, with an attendant rule that the player must not leave the track in his attempt to do so. Then imagine that there is a second rule which requires that the finish line be located some distance from the track.

We may define constitutive rules as rules which prohibit use of the most efficient means for reaching a pre-lusory goal.

Lusory Attitude

The attitude of the game-player must be an element in game-playing because there has to be an explanation of that curious state of affairs wherein one adopts rules which require him to employ worse rather than better means for reaching an end. Normally the acceptance of prohibitory rules is justified on the grounds that the means ruled out, although they are more efficient than the permitted means, have further undesirable consequences from the viewpoint of the agent involved. Thus, although the use of nuclear weapons is more efficient than is the use of conventional weapons in winning battles, the view still happily persists among nations that the additional consequences of nuclear assault are sufficient to rule it out. This kind of thing, of course, happens all the time, from the realm of international strategy to the common events of everyday life; thus one decisive way to remove a toothache is to cut your head off, but most people find good reason to rule out such highly efficient means. But in games, although more efficient means are—and must be—ruled out, the reason for doing so is quite different from the reasons for avoiding nuclear weaponry and self-decapitation. Foot racers do not refrain from cutting across the infield because the infield holds dangers for them, as would be the case if, for example, infields were frequently sown with land mines. Cutting across the infield is shunned solely because there is a rule against it. But in ordinary life this is usually—and rightly—regarded as the worst possible kind of justification one could give for avoiding a course of action. The justification for a prohibited course of action that there is simply a rule against it may be called the *bureaucratic* justification; that is, no justification at all.

But aside from bureaucratic practice, in anything but a game the gratuitous introduction of unnecessary obstacles to the achievement of an end is regarded as a decidedly irrational thing to do, whereas in games it appears to be an absolutely essential thing to do. This fact about games has led some observers to conclude that there is something inherently absurd about games, or that games must involve a fundamental paradox.[1] This kind of view seems to me to be mistaken.[2] The mistake consists in applying the same standard to games that is applied to means-end activities which are not games. If playing a game is regarded as not essentially different from going to the office or writing a cheque, then there is certainly something absurd, or paradoxical, or simply stupid about game-playing.

But games are, I believe, essentially different from the ordinary activities of life, as perhaps the following exchange between Smith and Jones will illustrate. Smith knows nothing of games, but he does know that he wants to travel from A to C, and he also knows that making the trip by way of B is the most efficient means for getting to his destination. He is then told authoritatively that he may *not* go by way of B. "Why not," he asks, "are there dragons at B?" "No," is the reply. "B is perfectly safe in every respect. It is just that there is a rule against going to B if you are on your way to C." "Very well," grumbles Smith, "if you insist. But if I have to go from A to C very often I shall certainly try very hard to get that rule revoked." True to his word, Smith approaches Jones, who is also setting out for C from A. He asks Jones to sign a petition requesting the revocation of the rule which forbids travellers from A to C to go through B. Jones replies that he is very much opposed to revoking the rule, which very much puzzles Smith.

> Smith: But if you want to get to C, why on earth do you support a rule which prevents your taking the fastest and most convenient route?
>
> Jones: Ah, but you see I have no particular interest in being at C. *That* is not my goal, except in a subordinate way. My overriding goal is more complex. It is "to get from A to C without going through B." And I can't very well achieve that goal if I go through B, can I?
>
> Smith: But why do you want to do that?
>
> Jones: I want to do it before Robinson does, you see?
>
> Smith: No, I don't. That explains nothing. Why should Robinson, whoever he may be, want to do it? I presume you will tell me that he, like you, has only a subordinate interest in being at C at all.
>
> Jones: That is so.
>
> Smith: Well, if neither of you wants, really, to be at C, then what possible

difference can it make which of you gets there first? And why, for God's sake, should you avoid B?

Jones: Let me ask you a question. Why do you want to get to C?

Smith: Because there is a good concert there, and I want to hear it.

Jones: Why?

Smith: Because I like concerts, of course. Isn't that a good reason?

Jones: It's one of the best there is. And I like, among other things, trying to get from A to C without going through B before Robinson does.

Smith: Well, *I* don't. So why should they tell me I can't go through B?

Jones: Oh, I see. They must have thought you were in the race.

Smith: The what?

I believe that we are now in a position to define *lusory attitude*: the knowing acceptance of constitutive rules just so the activity made possible by such acceptance can occur.

Summary

The elements may now be assembled into the following definition. To play a game is to attempt to achieve a specific state of affairs (*pre-lusory goal*), using only means permitted by rules (*lusory means*), where the rules prohibit use of more efficient in favour of less efficient means (*constitutive rules*), and where such rules are accepted just because they make possible such activity (*lusory attitude*). I also offer the following only approximately accurate, but more pithy, version of the above definition: Playing a game is the voluntary attempt to overcome unnecessary obstacles.

Games and Sport

As I indicated at the outset, I believe that sports are essentially games. What I mean by this is that the difference between sports and other games is much smaller than the difference between humans and other vertebrates. That is to say, sport is not a species within the genus *game*. The distinguishing characteristics of sport are more peripheral, more arbitrary, and more contingent than are the differences required to define a species.

I would like to submit for consideration four requirements which, if they are met by any given game, are sufficient to denominate that game a sport. They are: (1) that the game be a game of skill, (2) that the skill be physical, (3) that the game have a wide following, and (4) that the following achieve a certain level of stability. If I can persuade you that these features or something very much like them are at least the *kind* of differentiating marks we are seeking, I will be satisfied. I have no theory to support the list, except the theory that the features are more or less arbitrary, since they are simply facts about sport. Finally, I have little to say about them aside from presenting them, except as regards the question of skill, which I am interested in taking up on its own account.

Skill in Games

One may agree with my account of what it is to play a game and still find unanswered the rather pressing question why anyone would want to do such a thing (aside from professionals who do so for money and prestige). Smith was no doubt puzzled about this question even after Jones' explanation. Let me propose the following general answer. People play games so that they can realize in themselves capacities not realizable (or not readily so) in the pursuit of their ordinary activities. For example, some people enjoy running competitively, but the opportunities for this are severely limited in ordinary life. One can run for a bus, but even this small range of operations is further limited by the fact that one does not always have the good fortune to arrive tardily at a bus stop. One can, of course, intentionally allow less than enough time for getting punctually to the point of departure, in the hope that a race with the time table will then be necessary. But such a move is precisely to create a game where there was no game before by virtue of the constitutive rule requiring you to leave your home or office late. Some kinds of game—such as racing games—have this rather obvious affinity with actions performed aside from games. But most games do not have such a clear counterpart in ordinary life. Ball games which are at all elaborate have affinities with ordinary life only piecemeal; in life, too, one throws and runs and strikes objects, but there is nothing in life which much resembles baseball or football or golf *in toto.** Board games provide similar examples of the hiatus between games taken as wholes and the kinds of structured activities which characterize the rest of life. Thus, with the invention of games far removed from the pursuits of ordinary life, quite new capacities emerge, and hitherto unknown skills are developed. A good golf swing is simply useless in any other human pursuit. And despite the literary mythology which frequently represents superior military and political strategists as being (it is almost presumed to go without saying) master chess players as well, there is

---

*   = considered in its entirety.

as much similarly between those two skills as there is between the skills of golf and wood chopping. Purely topological problems are just vastly different from political and military problems. So people play games not only because ordinary life does not provide enough opportunities for doing such and such, but also (and more interestingly) because ordinary life does not provide any opportunities at all for doing such and such.

Games are *new* things to do, and they are new things to do because they require the overcoming of (by ordinary standards) *unnecessary* obstacles, and in ordinary life an unnecessary obstacle is simply a contradiction in terms.

Although I believe, as I have said, that people play games in order to realize capacities not otherwise realizable (or not readily realizable), and although in most games these capacities are, or intimately involve, specific skills, there are certain activities called games which almost conform to my definition but which do not involve skill. I mean games of chance; that is, games of *pure* chance. Draw poker is not such a game, nor, perhaps, is standard roulette (perhaps a debatable point), but show-down is, and so is Russian roulette. These games do not involve the capacity to exercise a specific skill because no skill is required to play them. Instead of skills, what is put into operation by such games is, I suggest, hope and fear. Bored people are deficient in these feelings, it seems safe to say, since if they were not they would not be bored. But hope and fear can be artificially induced by games of pure chance. (They also appear in games of skill, to be sure, but people to whom games of chance especially appeal are too bored to learn new skills.) What games of chance provide for their players may be described in almost the same words that Jan Narveson has used to describe paranoia: a false sense of insecurity. However, for games of chance the word *false* should be replaced by the word *invented*, for there is nothing false about the capacities which games bring forth, just something new.

All sports appear to be games of skill rather than games of chance. I suggest that the reason for this is that a major requirement in sports, for participants and spectators alike, is that what the participants do must be admirable in some respect. The exercise of virtually any skill—even the skills involved in goldfish swallowing or flag pole sitting—will elicit *some* degree of admiration. But the spectacle of a person sweating in hope and fear as the chamber slowly turns in the revolver evokes not admiration but morbid fascination or clinical interest.

Physical Skill

It is not difficult to draw a line between games which require physical skill and games which do not. It is not necessary first to decide very grave metaphysical issues, such as the relation between mind and body. It is a plain fact that how chess pieces are moved has nothing whatever to do with manual dexterity or any other bodily skill. One can play chess, bridge, and any number of other games solely by issuing verbal commands, as is the case when chess is played by mail. "Physical games" designates a quite definite class of objects, and the term "sport" is confined to this class (though it is not necessarily coterminous with it). The issue is thus wholly terminological; that is, the question "Why do sports have to involve physical skills?" is not a well formulated question. The question should be, "What kind of skill do we find in the class of activities we call sport?" And the answer is "Physical skill." Thus, chess and bridge appear to have all the features requisite for something to qualify as a sport, except that they are not games of physical skill. They do involve skill, and of a high order; they have a wide following and their popularity is of sufficiently long standing so that each of them may be characterized as an institution rather than a mere craze. Each can boast international tournaments, a body of experts, teachers, coaches—all the attendant roles and institutions characteristic of the most well-established sports. It is just that physical skill is not involved. (The chess match between Boris Spassky and Bobby Fischer took place after the preparation of this manuscript. Since accounts of the match appeared regularly in the sports pages of the press I am happy, consistently with my view of the fairly arbitrary distinction between sport and other games, to retract, or at least substantially to qualify, my observations here about the relation of physical skills to sport.)

A Wide Following

I have perfected the following game originally created by Kierkegaard. A high ranking official of my university has the constitutional peculiarity that when angry his anger is manifested solely by the appearance of a bead of perspiration at the centre of his forehead which then rolls slowly down his nose, clings for an instant to its tip, and finally falls. If the official's ire continues or recurs, the same steps are repeated. Whenever I have a conference with him I adopt as a pre-lusory goal that state of affairs wherein three separate beads of perspiration shall have progressed through their appointed stages inside of fifteen minutes. And I adopt the constitutive rule that I will refrain from employing as a means to this goal either threats of violence against the person of the official or aspersions on his personal and professional reputation. Although this is, I flatter myself, a pretty good game, I readily admit that it is not a sport. It is too private and too personal to quality for that status. Imagine my being asked by a colleague in the Faculty of Physical Education what sports I participate in, and my responding that I am very keen on Sweat-Bead.

Still, though Sweat-Bead is not now a sport, it could conceivably become one. If there were a great many people who shared the constitutional peculiarity of my official, and if there were a great many people equipped with the kind of sadism to which this game appeals, and if the rules were clearly laid out and published, and if there were to grow up a body of experts whose concern it was to improve the game and its players, then Sweat-Bead would become a sport. But short of these much to be hoped for developments I must accept the reality that it is simply a highly idiosyncratic game.

Stability

That a game is one of physical skill and that it is very popular is not quite enough to quality it as a sport. Hula-Hoop, in its hey-day, met these requirements but it would be proper to call Hula-Hoop a craze rather than a sport. The popular following which attends sports must have a stability which is more than mere persistence through time. Even if Hula-Hoop had lasted for fifty years it would still be a craze, only a very tiresome craze.

What is required in addition to longevity is the birth and flowering of a number of attendant roles and institutions which serve a number of functions ancillary to a sufficiently popular game of physical skill. The most important of these functions appear to be the following: teaching and training, coaching, research and development (Can the sport be improved by making such and such changes?), criticism (sports pundits), and archivism (the compilation and preservation of individual performances and their statistical treatment). Not all sports, of course, require all of these ancillary functions in order to be accepted as sports, but at least some of them will be associated to some degree with every game worthy to be called a sport.

Sport and Seriousness

The conventional wisdom about fun and games which, with brief and infrequent counter-tendencies, has prevailed from classical antiquity to the very recent past is well expressed by the following observation of Aristotle: "… to exert oneself and work for the sake of playing seems silly and utterly childish. But to play in order that one may exert oneself seems right." Play, games, and sport are seen, on this view, as subordinate to other ends, so that they may be taken seriously only if the ends to which they are subordinate are taken seriously. Thus, sports are regarded as serious insofar as they promote, for example, health, which is accepted as a serious matter; but sport unjustified by some such serious purpose is just frivolity. In a "work" ethic, work is the serious pursuit which gives play (and indeed health) what derivative seriousness it possesses. But in a leisure ethic, of the kind which much of the world appears now to be assuming, these old priorities are rapidly changing. For a person in whom the protestant ethic is quite firmly established it is difficult, if not impossible, to ask the question, "To what further interests is work itself subordinate?" and in times and societies where human and material resources are exceedingly scarce it is perhaps as well for the survival of the human race that such questions are not asked. For under conditions where unremitting labour is necessary for the bare preservation of life, the answer to the question "What are we working for?" is "Just to live." And since the life whose preservation requires continuous toil is just that toil itself, the toiler might well wonder whether the game is worth the candle.

But in a leisure ethic we have not only the leisure to ask why we are working, but the fact of leisure itself provides us with an answer which is not too bleak to bear. The industrial unionist of today who makes a contract demand for shorter working hours is not prompted to do this by Aristotelian considerations. He does not want more time for fishing, bowling, the ball park, or television so that, renewed and refreshed, he can increase his output on the assembly line on Monday. (In any case, that output will also be fixed by the new contract, and cannot be increased.) The attitude of the contemporary worker about work may be expressed as the exact inversion of Aristotle's dictum: "To play so that one may work seems silly and utterly childish; but to work in order that one may play seems right."

I do not think it is too great an overstatement to say that whereas for the Puritan it was work which gave play (as, e.g., exercise) what derivative seriousness it was accorded, it is now play—or at least leisure activities—which gives work a derivative seriousness. Another way to put this is to acknowledge that work is good because it provides us with leisure as well as the means to enjoy leisure. Work is good chiefly because it is *good for* something much better. The things for which it is finally good are good in themselves. They are intrinsic goods. This is not, as a general view, at all novel. It, too, goes back to Aristotle. The only difference in Aristotle's view (and in the view of many others who are in this respect like him) is that for him just a very few things count as intrinsically good, things like virtue and metaphysics. Partisans of this kind have typically managed to get a kind of monopoly on the notion of intrinsic good and have tried, with some success, to persuade the rest of us that only such and such pursuits were worthy of the name. Sometimes it has been holiness, sometimes art, sometimes science, sometimes love. But it seems perfectly clear that any number of things can be intrinsic goods to someone, depending upon his interests, abilities, and other resources, from philately to philosophy (including work itself, if you happen to be Paul Goodman). This view has quite wide, even if tacit, acceptance, I believe, outside of churches and universities.

The new ethic, then, is not only one of greatly increased leisure, it is also one of pluralism with respect to the goods we are permitted to seek in the new time available. It has been some time since our Sabbaths were confined to theological self-improvement with the aid of the family bible, of course, but recent changes in our views of leisure activity are just as striking as was our emergence from puritanism. Thus, the view no longer prevails (as it did in the quite recent past) that although leisure was a good thing it was wasted if one did not devote most of it to the pursuit of Culture with a capital C. Today people with the most impeccable cultural credentials may without impropriety savour jazz (even rock) and motor racing.

Although we recognize a class of things which are serious just because they are intrinsically worthwhile, there seems some reason to believe that sports (and games in general) cannot be among these things. It is as though there were something built into the very structure of games which rendered them non-serious. This view is conveyed by the expression, "Of course, such and such is just a game," as though there were something inherently trifling about games. And by the same token, if we find that someone takes a sport or some other game with extraordinary seriousness, we are inclined to say that the pursuit in question has ceased to be a game for him.

This view, though incorrect, may be made quite plausible, I believe, by the following example. Consider The Case of the Dedicated Driver. Mario Stewart (the dedicated driver in question) is a favoured entrant in the motor car race of the century at Malaise. And in the Malaise race there is a rule which forbids a vehicle to leave the track on pain of disqualification. At a dramatic point in the race a child crawls out upon the track directly in the path of Mario's car. The only way to avoid running over the child is to leave the track and suffer disqualification. Mario runs over the child and completes the race.

One is inclined to say that for Mario motor racing is not a sport at all (and certainly not a game!), but a kind of madness. Games (and sports) require a limitation on the means their players may employ, but Mario is obviously the kind of driver who would do anything to win the race. By his insane refusal to stay within proper limits he is no longer playing a game at all. He has destroyed the game.

I submit, however, that we now know what it takes to destroy a game, and that the behaviour of Mario is not what it takes. If Mario had cut across the infield in his efforts to get ahead of the other drivers, or if he had earlier violated a rule governing engine capacity in the construction of his vehicle, then his behaviour would cease to be game-playing, for he would have broken a constitutive rule. It is thus true to say that there is a limitation imposed in games which is not imposed in other activities, and it is also true that the limitation has to do with the means one can legitimately employ. Hence the plausibility of concluding that Mario was not playing a game, since there appeared to be absolutely no means he would not adopt. But it will be recalled that we earlier discovered that more than one kind of goal is associated with games, and more than one kind of means. The plausibility of the claim that racing for Mario had ceased to be a game rests on a confusion between two of these goals. It is perfectly correct to say that not any means whatever may be used to achieve a *pre-lusory* goal, but this limitation in no way entails a quite different kind of limitation, namely, a limitation on the means for *playing* the game (i.e., attempting to achieve what I earlier called the lusory goal of life).

The point of the story, of course, is not that Mario did a terrible thing, but that it is possible to make a game or a sport the over-riding concern of one's life without falling into some kind of paradox. That extreme dedication to a pursuit should somehow destroy the pursuit would be the real paradox. But that a person will do anything to continue playing a game does not destroy the game, even though it may destroy the person. So saying to Mario that motor racing is just a game is very much like saying to the Pope that Catholicism is just religion, to Beethoven that the quartets are just music, or to Muhammad Ali that boxing is just a sport.

I therefore conclude that sports are precisely like the other interests which occur prominently as leisure activities. They are a type of intrinsic good which, along with many others, make up the class of goals to which we ascribe that primary seriousness which provides such things as factories, armies, and governments with the derivative seriousness to which they are entitled.

Author's Note

The section of the paper titled *The Elements of Game* is a restatement of the substance of the thesis advanced in "What Is a Game?"[3] However, the language used here is different from the language of that version, and the definition of game-playing that I propose has been somewhat altered. The strategies of the two versions also differ. In "What Is a Game?" I attempted to produce an adequate definition by successively modifying a series of proposed definitions. Here, assuming the adequacy of that definition, I explain and illustrate the elements of game-playing which the definition designates. I should also note that some of the examples used in the present paper were originally used in "What Is a Game?"

NOTES

1.   Kolnai, A.: "Games and Aims," *Proceedings of the Aristotelian Society* (1966).
2.   Suits, Bernard: "Games and Paradox," *Philosophy of Science* (1969).
3.   Suits, Bernard: "What Is a Game?" *Philosophy of Science* (1967).

QUESTIONS

1.   Do you agree with Huizinga's analysis of play? What are the most important parts of this analysis?
2.   How should we understand the difference(s) between play in children and in adults? How about when children and adults play together?
3.   Can you think of examples that would challenge the claim that play is always present in culture, even in cases where the play element is unapparent and has "receded"?
4.   Are there games for which it is hard to specify a prelusory goal? How does this affect the plausibility of Suits's position?
5.   Could it be argued that morality in particular, or life in general, is a Suitsian game? Why, or why not?
6.   What do you think of Suits's definition of sport? Can you think of any sports that might not fit that definition, or activities it would count as sports that should be discounted?

FURTHER READING

Fink, Eugen (1960): "The Ontology of Play," *Philosophy Today* 4, pp. 95-110.

Meier, Klaus V. (1980): "An Affair of Flutes: An Appreciation of Play," *Journal of the Philosophy of Sport* 7, pp. 24-45.

Pieper, Joseph (1952): *Leisure: The Basis of Culture* (New York: Mentor-Omega).

Schneider, Angela J. and Robert B. Butcher (1997): "Pre-lusory Goals for Games: A Gambit Declined," *Journal of the Philosophy of Sport* 24, pp. 38-46.

Suits, Bernard (2005): *The Grasshopper: Games, Life and Utopia* (2nd edition) (Peterborough, ON: Broadview P).

Wittgenstein, Ludwig (1953): *Philosophical Investigations*, ed. G.E.M. Anscombe and R. Rhees. Trans. G.E.M. Anscombe (Oxford: Blackwell), especially sections 55-56.

FURTHER INQUIRY

Whether play is distinct from ordinary life or rather continuous with it seems a question not yet definitively settled. The similarity between Huizinga's view of the play element in culture and Pieper's view of leisure as the basis of culture also merits exploration, as does consideration of how play and leisure (plausibly defined as intrinsically motivated elective activity) overlap and diverge. The related, more general question of how to characterize intrinsic motivation, for fun or rather in mere recognition of some objective (e.g., moral) quality, is also germane. Consider how easy or difficult it is to specify the prelusory goal of various sports and other games—does the chess convention of laying down a checkmated king constitute, or gesture at, the notion of a prelusory goal? Might a Suits-style approach dispense with the idea that the objective of a game *must* be prelusorily describable? Do games constitute a key point of debate between essentialists like Suits (who believe that substantive theoretical definitions are both possible and of value) and anti-essentialists like Wittgenstein (who deny as much about such definitions)?

Defining Sport

The point of definition varies according to use and context. Dictionaries, for instance, report on words' common use and so provide standards of correct usage. More technical definitions often are sought by philosophers and others for a variety of reasons: to avoid ambiguity in subsequent discussion, to have a criterion for classification, and so help resolve disputes about how to apply the term (what it includes in and excludes from its scope), and—most importantly—as a theory expressing knowledge of the essence of the kind in question (here, sport). 'Sport' is ambiguous, meaning anything from fun itself or an activity done for fun's sake to someone who is pursuing leisure or who is generally easy-going or fair-minded. Here, however, we have in mind athletic competition, related to but clearly distinct from these other meanings.

John W. Loy, Jr. forwards the notion that sports are games, sometimes involving both strategy and chance, but requiring the demonstration of physical prowess. Not just any pickup game will do. As Loy has it, sports are rather *institutionalized* games, with different "spheres" (organizational, technical, symbolic, educational), their "order" with different levels of social organization (primary, technical, managerial, corporate). Some philosophers define art in terms of the "artworld"—that is, as whatever the institutions of art creation, sale, collection, criticism, and so on happen to be interested in. In a similar way, we might define sport in terms of the "sportworld" (not Loy's term): think NHL hockey rather than shinny, though the latter may perhaps count as sport in a derivative sense. Loy treats sport, in turn, as a game occurrence, as an institutional game, as a social institution, and as a social situation or social system.

By contrast, Klaus V. Meier rejects institutional approaches to defining sport, opting to understand sports as games of physical skill. Meier supports his position from the platform of a thorough appraisal of Suits's theoretical development. Arguing that there are non-institutional cases of sport, as well as pointing out the difficulty in specifying an institutional condition (for example, exactly how wide and stable a following a sport must have), Meier defends Suits's earlier claim that all sports are games from Suits's later reappraisal of certain sports (the so-called aesthetic sports) as performances rather than games. Meier also offers a useful threefold distinction of rule types: constitutive rules (*what* a sport is), regulative rules (*how* it is played), and auxiliary rules (*who* is eligible to play).

3. The Nature of Sport: A Definitional Effort*

John W. Loy, Jr.

Sport is a highly ambiguous term having different meanings for various people. Its ambiguity is attested to by the range of topics treated in the sport sections of daily newspapers. Here one can find accounts of various sport competitions, advertisements for the latest sport fashions, advice on how to improve one's skills in certain games, and essays on the state of given organized sports, including such matters as recruitment, financial success, and scandal. The broad yet loose encompass of sport reflected in the mass media suggests that sport can and perhaps should be dealt with on different planes of discourse if a better understanding of its nature is to be acquired. As a step in this direction we shall discuss sport as a game occurrence, as an institutional game, as a social institution, and as a social situation or social system.

Sport as a Game Occurrence

Perhaps most often when we think of the meaning of sport, we think of sports. In our perspective sports are considered as a specialized type of game. That is, a sport as one of the many "sports" is viewed as an actual game occurrence or event. Thus in succeeding paragraphs we shall briefly outline what we consider to be the basic characteristics of games in general. In describing these characteristics we shall continually make reference to sports in particular as a special type of game. A game we define as any form of playful competition whose outcome is determined by physical skill, strategy, or chance employed singly or in combination.[1]

---

*   John W. Loy, Jr., "The Nature of Sport: A Definitional Effort," *Quest* 10 (1968), pp. 1-15.

Playful

By "playful competition" we mean that any given contest has one or more elements of play. We purposely have not considered game as a subclass of play,[2] for if we had done so, sport would logically become a subset of play and thus preclude the subsumption of professional forms of sport under our definition of the term. However, we wish to recognize that one or more aspects of play constitute basic components of games and that even the most highly organized forms of sport are not completely devoid of play characteristics.

The Dutch historian Johan Huizinga has made probably the most thorough effort to delineate the fundamental qualities of play. He defines play as follows:

> Summing up the formal characteristics of play we might call it a free activity standing quite consciously outside "ordinary" life as being "not serious," but at the same time absorbing the player intensely and utterly. It is an activity connected with no material interest, and no profit can be gained by it. It proceeds within its own proper boundaries of time and space according to fixed rules and in an orderly manner. It promotes the formation of social groupings which tend to surround themselves with secrecy and to stress their differences from the common world by disguise or other means. (Huizinga, 1955, p. 13)

Caillois has subjected Huizinga's definition to critical analysis (Caillois, 1961, pp. 3-10) and has redefined play as an activity which is free, separate, uncertain, unproductive, and governed by rules and make-believe (ibid., pp. 9-10). We shall briefly discuss these qualities ascribed to play by Huizinga and Caillois and suggest how they relate to games in general and to sports in particular.

Free. By free is meant that play is a voluntary activity. That is, no one is ever strictly forced to play, playing is done in one's free time, and playing can be initiated and terminated at will. This characteristic of play is no doubt common to many games, including some forms of amateur sport. It is not, however, a distinguishing feature of all games, especially those classified as professional sport.

Separate. By separate Huizinga and Caillois mean that play is spatially and temporally limited. This feature of play is certainly relevant to sports. For many, if not most, forms of sport are conducted in spatially circumscribed environments, examples being the bull-ring, football stadium, golf course, race track, and swimming pool. And with few exceptions every form of sport has rules which precisely determine the duration of a given contest.

Uncertain. The course or end result of play cannot be determined beforehand.

Similarly, a chief characteristic of all games is that they are marked by an uncertain outcome. Perhaps it is this factor more than any other which lends excitement and tension to any contest. Strikingly uneven competition is routine for the contestants and boring for the spectators; hence efforts to insure a semblance of equality between opposing sides are a notable feature of sport. These efforts typically focus on the matters of size, skill, and experience. Examples of attempts to establish equality based on size are the formation of athletic leagues and conferences composed of social organizations of similar size and the designation of weight classes for boxers and wrestlers. Illustrations of efforts to insure quality among contestants on the basis of skill and experience are the establishment of handicaps for bowlers and golfers, the designation of various levels of competition within a given organization as evidenced by freshmen, junior varsity, and varsity teams in scholastic athletics, and the drafting of players from established teams when adding a new team to a league as done in professional football and basketball.

Unproductive. Playing does not in itself result in the creation of new material goods. It is true that in certain games such as poker there may occur an exchange of money or property among players. And it is a truism that in professional sports victory may result in substantial increases of wealth for given individuals. But the case can be made, nevertheless, that a game per se is non-utilitarian.[3] For what is produced during any sport competition is a game, and the production of the game is generally carried out in a prescribed setting and conducted according to specific rules.

Governed by Rules. All types of games have agreed-upon rules, be they formal or informal. It is suggested that sports can be distinguished from games in general by the fact that they usually have a greater variety of norms and a larger absolute number of formal norms (i.e., written prescribed and proscribed norms).[4] Similarly, there is a larger number of sanctions and more stringent ones in sports than in games. For example, a basketball player must leave the game after he has committed a fixed number of fouls; a hockey player must spend a certain amount of time in the penalty box after committing a foul; and a football player may be asked to leave the game if he shows unsportsmanlike conduct.

With respect to the normative order of games and sports, one explicit feature is that they usually have definite criteria for determining the winner. Although it is true that some end in a tie, most contests do not permit such an ambivalent termination by providing a means of breaking a deadlock and ascertaining the "final" victor. The various means of determining the winner in sportive endeavors are too numerous to enumerate. But it is relevant to observe that in many sport competitions where "stakes are high," a series of contests is held between opponents in an effort to rule out the element of chance and decide the winner on the basis of merit. A team may be called "lucky" if it beats an opponent once by a narrow margin; but if it does so repeatedly, then the appellations of "better" or "superior" are generally applied.

Make-Believe. By the term make-believe Huizinga and Caillois wish to signify that play stands outside "ordinary" or "real" life and is distinguished by an "only pretending quality." While some would deny this characteristic of play as being applicable to sport, it is interesting to note that Veblen at the [beginning of the twentieth] century stated:

> Sports share this characteristic of make-believe with the games and exploits to which children, especially boys, are habitually inclined. Make-believe does not enter in the same proportion into all sports, but it is present in a very appreciable degree in all. (Veblen, 1934, p. 256)

Huizinga observes that the "'only pretending' quality of play betrays a consciousness of the inferiority of play compared with 'seriousness'" (Huizinga, 1955, p. 8). We note here that occasionally one reads of a retiring professional athlete who remarks that he is "giving up the game to take a real job"[5] and that several writers have commented on the essential shallowness of sport.[6] Roger Kahn, for example, has written that:

> The most fascinating and least reported aspect of American sports is the silent and enduring search for a rationale. Stacked against the atomic bomb or even against a patrol in Algeria, the most exciting rally in history may not seem very important, and for the serious and semi-serious people who make their living through sports, triviality is a nagging, damnable thing. Their drive for self-justification has contributed much to the development of sports. (Kahn, 1957, p. 10)

On the other hand, Huizinga is careful to point out that "the consciousness of play being 'only pretend' does not by any means prevent it from proceeding with the utmost seriousness" (Huizinga, 1955, p. 8). As examples, need we mention the seriousness with which duffers treat their game of golf, the seriousness which fans accord discussions of their home team, or the seriousness that national governments give to Olympic Games and university alumni to collegiate football.[7,8]

Accepting the fact that the make-believe quality of play has some relevance to sport, it nevertheless remains difficult to empirically ground the "not-ordinary-or-real-life" characteristic of play. However, the "outside-of-real-life" dimension of a game is perhaps best seen in its "as-if" quality, its artificial obstacles, and its potential resources for actualization or production.

In a game the contestants act as if all were equal, and numerous aspects of "external reality" such as race, education, occupation, and financial status are excluded as relevant attributes for the duration of a given contest.[9]

The obstacles individuals encounter in their workaday lives are not usually predetermined by them and are "real" in the sense that they must be adequately coped with if certain inherent and socially conditioned needs are to be met; on the other hand, in games obstacles are artificially created to be overcome. Although these predetermined obstacles set up to be conquered can sometimes attain "life-and-death" significance, as in a difficult Alpine climb, they are not usually essentially related to an individual's daily toil for existence.[10]

Similarly, it is observed that in many "real" life situations the structures and processes needed to cope with a given obstacle are often not at hand; however, in a play or game situation all the structures and processes necessary to deal with any deliberately created obstacle and to realize any possible alternative in course of action are potentially available.[11]

In sum, then, games are playful in that they typically have one or more elements of play: freedom, separateness, uncertainty, unproductiveness, order, and make-believe. In addition to having elements of play, games have components of competition.

Competition

Competition is defined as a struggle for supremacy between two or more opposing sides. We interpret the phrase "between two or more opposing sides" rather broadly to encompass the competitive relationships between man and other objects of nature, both animate and inanimate. Thus competitive relationships include:

1. competition between one individual and another, e.g., a boxing match or a 100-yard dash;

2. competition between one team and another, e.g., a hockey game or a yacht race;

3. competition between an individual or a team and an animate object of nature, e.g., a bullfight or a deer-hunting party;

4. competition between an individual or a team and an inanimate object of nature, e.g., a canoeist running a set of rapids or a mountain climbing expedition; and finally,

5. competition between an individual or team and an "ideal" standard, e.g., an individual attempting to establish a world land-speed record on the Bonneville salt flats or a basketball team trying to set an all-time scoring record. Competition against an "ideal" standard might also be conceptualized as man against time or space, or as man against himself.[12]

The preceding classification has been set forth to illustrate what we understand by the phrase "two or more opposing sides" and is not intended to be a classification of competition per se. While the scheme may have some relevance for such a purpose, its value is limited by the fact that its categories are neither mutually exclusive nor inclusive. For instance, an athlete competing in a cross-country race may be competitively involved in all of the following ways: as an individual against another individual; as a team member against members of an opposing team; and as an individual or team member against an "ideal" standard (e.g., an attempt to set an individual and/or team record for the course).[13]

Physical Skill, Strategy, and Chance
Roberts and Sutton-Smith suggest that the various games of the world can be classified

> ... on the basis of outcome attributes: (1) games of *physical skill*, in which the outcome is determined by the players' motor activities; (2) games of *strategy*, in which the outcome is determined by rational choices among possible courses of action; and (3) games of *chance*, in which the outcome is determined by guesses or by some uncontrolled artifact such as a die or wheel. (Roberts and Sutton-Smith, 1962, p. 166)

Examples of relatively pure forms of competitive activities in each of these categories are weight-lifting contests, chess matches, and crap games, respectively. Many, if not most, games are, however, of a mixed nature. Card and board games, for instance, generally illustrate a combination of strategy and chance. Although chance is also associated with sport, its role in determining the outcome of a contest is generally held to a minimum in order that the winning side can attribute its victory to merit rather than to a fluke of nature. Rather interestingly it appears that a major role of chance in sport is to insure equality. For example, the official's flip of a coin before the start of a football game randomly determines what team will receive the kickoff and from what respective side of the field; and similarly the drawing of numbers by competitors in track and swimming is an attempt to assure them equal opportunity of getting assigned a given lane.

Physical Prowess

Having discussed the characteristics which sports share in common with games in general, let us turn to an account of the major attribute which distinguishes sports in particular from games in general. We observe that sports can be distinguished from games by the fact that they demand the demonstration of physical prowess. By the phrase "the demonstration of physical prowess" we mean the employment of developed physical skills and abilities within the context of gross physical activity to conquer an opposing object of nature. Although many games require a minimum of physical skill, they do not usually demand the degree of physical skill required by sports. The idea of "developed physical skills" implies much practice and learning and suggests the attainment of a high level of proficiency in one or more general physical abilities relevant to sport competition, e.g., strength, speed, endurance, or accuracy.

Although the concept of physical prowess permits sports to be generally differentiated from games, numerous borderline areas exist. For example, can a dart game among friends, a horseshoe pitching contest between husband and wife, or a fishing contest between father and son be considered sport? One way to arrive at an answer to these questions is to define a sport as any highly organized game requiring physical prowess. Thus a dart game with friends, a horseshoe pitching contest between spouses, or a fishing contest between a father and son would not be considered sport; but formally sponsored dart, horseshoe, or fishing tournaments would be legitimately labelled sport. An alternative approach to answering the aforementioned questions, however, is to define a sport as an institutionalized game demanding the demonstration of physical prowess. If one accepts the latter approach, then he will arrive at a different set of answers to the above questions. For this approach views a game as a unique event and sport as an institutional pattern. As Weiss has rather nicely put it:

A game is an occurrence; a sport is a pattern. The one is in the present, the other primarily past, but instantiated in the present. A sport defines the conditions to which the participants must submit if there is to be a game; a game gives rootage to a set of rules and thereby enables a sport to be exhibited. (1967, p. 82)

Sport as an Institutionalized Game

To treat sport as an institutionalized game is to consider sport as an abstract entity. For example, the organization of a football team as described in a rule book can be discussed without reference to the members of any particular team; and the relationship among team members can be characterized without reference to unique personalities or to particular times and places. In treating sport as an institutionalized game we conceive of it as distinctive, enduring patterns of culture and social structure combined into a single complex, the elements of which include values, norms, sanctions, knowledge, and social positions (i.e., roles and statuses).[14] A firm grasp of the meaning of "institutionalization" is necessary for understanding the idea of sport as an institutional pattern, or blueprint if you will, guiding the organization and conduct of given games and sportive endeavors.

The formulation of a set of rules for a game or even their enactment on a particular occasion does not constitute a sport as we have conceptualized it here. The institutionalization of a game implies that it has a tradition of past exemplifications and definite guidelines for future realizations. Moreover, in a concrete game situation the form of a particular sport need not reflect all the characteristics represented in its institutional pattern. The more organized a sport contest in a concrete setting, however, the more likely it will illustrate the institutionalized nature of a given sport. A professional baseball game, for example, is a better illustration of the institutionalized nature of a baseball than is a sandlot baseball game; but both games are based on the same institutional pattern and thus may both be considered forms of sport. In brief, a sport may be treated analytically in terms of its degree of institutionalization and dealt with empirically in terms of its degree of organization. The latter is an empirical instance of the former.

In order to illustrate the institutionalized nature of sport more adequately, we contrast the organizational, technological, symbolic, and educational spheres of sports with those of games. In doing so we consider both games and sports in their most formalized and organized state. We are aware that there are institutionalized games other than sports which possess characteristics similar to the ones we ascribe to sports, as for example chess and bridge; but we contend that such games are in the minority and in any case are excluded as sports because they do not demand the demonstration of physical prowess.

Organizational Sphere

For present purposes we rather arbitrarily discuss the organizational aspects of sports in terms of teams, sponsorship, and government.

Teams. Competing sides for most games are usually selected rather spontaneously and typically disband following a given contest. In sports, however, competing groups are generally selected with care and, once membership is established, maintain a stable social organization. Although individual persons may withdraw from such organizations after they are developed, their social positions are taken up by others, and the group endures.[15]

Another differentiating feature is that as a rule sports show a greater degree of role differentiation than games do. Although games often involve several contestants (e.g., poker), the contestants often perform identical activities and thus may be considered to have the same roles and statuses. By contrast, in sports involving a similar number of participants (e.g., basketball), each individual or combination of just a few individuals performs specialized activities within the group and may be said to possess a distinct role. Moreover, to the extent that such specialized and differentiated activities can be ranked in terms of some criteria, they also possess different statuses.

Sponsorship. In addition to there being permanent social groups established for purposes of sport competition, there is usually found in the sport realm social groups which act as sponsoring bodies for sport teams. These sponsoring bodies may be characterized as being direct or indirect. Direct sponsoring groups include municipalities which sponsor Little League baseball teams, universities which support collegiate teams, and business corporations which sponsor AAU teams. Indirect sponsoring groups include sporting goods manufacturers, booster clubs, and sport magazines.

Government. While all types of games have at least a modicum of norms and sanctions associated with them, the various forms of sport are set apart from many games by the fact that they have more—and more formal and more institutionalized—sets of these cultural elements. In games rules are often passed down by oral tradition or spontaneously established for a given contest and forgotten afterwards; or, even where codified, they are often simple and few. In sports rules are usually many, and they are formally codified and typically enforced by a regulatory body. There are international organizations governing most sports, and in America there are relatively large social organizations governing both amateur and professional sports. For example, amateur sports in America are controlled by such groups as the NCAA, AAU, and NAIA; and the major professional sports have national commissioners with enforcing officials to police competition.

Technological Sphere

In a sport, technology denotes the material equipment, physical skills, and body of knowledge which are necessary for the conduct of competition and potentially available for technical improvements in competition. While all types of games require a minimum of knowledge and often a minimum of physical skill and material equipment, the various sports are set apart from many games by the fact that they typically require greater knowledge and involve higher levels of physical skill and necessitate more material equipment. The technological aspects of a sport may be dichotomized into those which are intrinsic and those which are extrinsic. Intrinsic technological aspects of a sport consist of the physical skills, knowledge, and equipment which are required for the conduct of a given contest per se. For example, the intrinsic technology of football includes: (a) the equipment necessary for the game—field, ball, uniform, etc.; (b) the repertoire of physical skills necessary for the game—running, passing, kicking, blocking, tackling, etc.; and (c) the knowledge necessary for the game—rules, strategy, etc. Examples of extrinsic technological elements associated with football include: (a) physical equipment such as stadium, press facilities, dressing rooms, etc.; (b) physical skills such as possessed by coaches, cheerleaders, and ground crews; and (c) knowledge such as possessed by coaches, team physicians, and spectators.

Symbolic Sphere

The symbolic dimension of a sport includes elements of secrecy, display, and ritual. Huizinga contends that play "promotes the formation of social groupings which tend to surround themselves with secrecy and to stress their difference from the common world by disguise or other means" (1955, p. 13). Caillois criticizes his contention and states to the contrary that "play tends to remove the very nature of the mysterious." He further observes that "when the secret, the mask or the costume fulfills a sacramental function one can be sure that not play, but an institution is involved" (1961, p. 4).

Somewhat ambivalently we agree with both writers. On the one hand, to the extent that Huizinga means by "secrecy" the act of making distinctions between "play life" and "ordinary life," we accept his proposition that groups engaged in playful competition surround themselves with secrecy. On the other hand, to the extent that he means by "secrecy" something hidden from others, we accept Caillois's edict that an institution and not play is involved.

The latter type of secrecy might well be called "sanctioned secrecy" in sports, for there are associated with many forms of sport competition rather clear norms regarding approved clandestine behavior. For example, football teams are permitted to set up enclosed practice fields, send out scouts to spy on opposing teams, and exchange a limited number of game films revealing the strategies of future opponents. Other kinds of clandestine action such as slush funds established for coaches and gambling on games by players are not always looked upon with such favor.[16]

A thorough reading of Huizinga leads one to conclude that what he means by secrecy is best discussed in terms of display and ritual. He points out, for example, "the 'differentness' and secrecy of play and most vividly expressed in 'dressing up'" and states that the higher forms of play are "a contest *for* something or a representation *of* something"—adding that "representation means display" (1955, p. 13). The "dressing-up" element of play noted by Huizinga is certainly characteristic of most sports. Perhaps it is carried to its greatest height in bullfighting, but it is not absent in some of the less overt forms of sport. Veblen writes:

> It is noticeable, for instance, that even very mild-mannered and matter-of-fact men who go out shooting are apt to carry an excess of arms and accoutrements in order to impress upon their own imagination the seriousness of their undertaking. These huntsmen are also prone to a histrionic, prancing gait and to an elaborate exaggeration of the motions, whether of stealth or of onslaught, involved in their deeds of exploit. (1934, p. 256)

A more recent account of "dressing-up" and display in sports has been given by Stone (1955), who treats display as spectacle and as a counterforce to play. Stone asserts that the tension between the forces of play and display constitute an essential component of sport. The following quotation gives the essence of his account:

> Play and dis-play are precariously balanced in sport, and, once that balance is upset, the whole character of sport in society may be affected. Furthermore, the spectacular element of sport, may, as in the case of American professional wrestling, destroy the game. The rules cease to apply, and the "cheat" and the "spoilsport" replace the players.
>
> The point may be made in another way. The spectacle is predictable and certain; the game, unpredictable and uncertain. Thus spectacular display may be reckoned from the outset of the performance. It is announced by the appearance of the performers—their physiques, costumes, and gestures. On the other hand, the spectacular play is solely a function of the uncertainty of the game. (p. 98)

In a somewhat different manner another sociologist, Erving Goffman, has analyzed the factors of the uncertainty of a game and display. Concerning the basis of "fun in games" he states that "mere uncertainty of outcome is not enough to engross the players" (1961, p. 68) and suggests that a successful game must combine "sanctioned display" with problematic outcome. By display Goffman means that "games give the players an opportunity to exhibit attributes valued in the wide social world, such as dexterity, strength, knowledge, intelligence, courage, and self-control" (ibid.). Thus for Goffman display represents spectacular play involving externally relevant attributes, while for Stone display signifies spectacular exhibition involving externally non-relevant attributes with respect to the game situation.

Another concept related to display and spectacle and relevant to sports is that of ritual. According to Leach, "ritual denotes those aspects of prescribed formal behavior which have no direct technological consequences" (1964, p. 607). Ritual may be distinguished from spectacle by the fact that it generally has a greater element of drama and is less ostentatious and more serious. "Ritual actions are 'symbolic' in that they assert something about the state of affairs, but they are not necessarily purposive: i.e., the performer of ritual does not necessarily seek to alter the state of affairs" (ibid.). Empirically ritual can be distinguished from spectacle by the fact that those engaged in ritual express an attitude of solemnity toward it, an attitude which they do not direct toward spectacle.

Examples of rituals in sport are the shaking of hands between team captains before a game, the shaking of hands between team coaches after a game, the singing of the national anthem before a game, and the singing of the school song at the conclusion of a game.[17]

Educational Sphere

The educational sphere focuses on those activities related to the transmission of skills and knowledge to those who lack them. Many if not most people learn to play the majority of socially preferred games in an informal manner. That is, they acquire the required skills and knowledge associated with a given game through the casual instruction of friends or associates. On the other hand, in sports, skills and knowledge are often obtained by means of formal instruction. In short, the educational sphere of sports is institutionalized, whereas in most games it is not. One reason for this situation is the fact that sports require highly developed physical skills as games often do not; to achieve proficiency requires long hours of practice and qualified instruction, i.e., systematized training. Finally, it should be pointed out that associated with the instructional personnel of sport programs are a number of auxiliary personnel such as managers, physicians, and trainers—a situation not commonly found in games.

Sport as a Social Institution

Extending our notion of sport as an institutional pattern still further, we note that in its broadest sense, the term sport supposes a social institution. Schneider writes that the term institution

> ... denotes an aspect of social life in which distinctive value-orientations and interests, centering upon large and important social concern... generate or are accompanied by distinctive modes of social interaction. Its use emphasizes "important" social phenomena; relationships of "strategic structural signifi-cance." (1964, p. 338)

We argue that the magnitude of sport in the Western world justifies its considera-tion as a social institution. As Boyle succinctly states:

> Sport permeates any number of levels of contemporary society, and it touches upon and deeply influences such disparate elements as status, race relations, business life, automotive design, clothing styles, the concept of the hero, lan-guage, and ethical values. For better or worse it gives form and substance to much in American life. (1963, pp. 3-4)

When speaking of sport as a social institution, we refer to the sport order. The sport order is composed of all organizations in society which organize, facilitate, and regulate human action in sport situations. Hence, such organizations as sport-ing goods manufacturers, sport clubs, athletic teams, national governing bodies for amateur and professional sports, publishers of sport magazines, etc., are part of the sport order. For analytical purposes four levels of social organization within the sport order may be distinguished: namely, the primary, technical, managerial, and corporate levels.[18] Organizations at the primary level permit face-to-face rela-tionships among all members and are characterized by the fact that administra-tive leadership is not formally delegated to one or more persons or positions. An example of a social organization associated with sport at the primary level is an informally organized team in a sandlot baseball game.

Organizations at the technical level are too large to permit simultaneous face-to-face relationships among their members but small enough so that every member knows of every other member. Moreover, unlike organizations at the primary level, organizations at the technical level officially designate administrative leadership positions and allocate individuals to them. Most scholastic and collegiate athletic teams, for example, would be classified as technical organizations with coaches and athletic directors functioning as administrative leaders.

At the managerial level organizations are too large for every member to know every other member but small enough so that all members know one or more of the administrative leaders of the organization. Some of the large professional ball clubs represent social organizations related to sport at the managerial level.

Organizations at the corporate level are characterized by bureaucracy: they have centralized authority, a hierarchy of personnel, and protocol and procedural emphases; and they stress the rationalization of operations and impersonal relationships. A number of the major governing bodies of amateur and professional sport at the national and international levels illustrate sport organizations of the corporate type.

In summary, the sport order is composed of the congeries of primary, technical, managerial, and corporate social organizations which arrange, facilitate, and regulate human action in sport situations. The value of the concept lies in its use in macro-analyses of the social significance of sport. We can make reference to the sport order in a historical and/or comparative perspective. For example, we can speak of the sport order of nineteenth-century America or contrast the sport order of Russia with that of England.

Sport as a Social Situation

As was just noted, the sport order is composed of all social organizations which organize, facilitate, and regulate human action in sport situations. Human "action consists of the structures and processes by which human beings form meaningful intentions and, more or less successfully, implement them in concrete situations" (Parsons, 1966, p. 5). A sport situation consists of any social context wherein individuals are involved with sport. And the term situation denotes "the total set of objects, whether persons, collectivities, culture objects, or himself to which an actor responds" (Friedsam, 1964, p. 667). The set of objects related to a specific sport situation may be quite diverse, ranging from the elements of the social and physical environments of a football game to those associated with two sportniks[19] in a neighborhood bar arguing the pros and cons of the manager of their local baseball team.

Although there are many kinds of sport situations, most if not all may be conceptualized as social systems. A social system may be simply defined as "a set of persons with an identifying characteristic plus a set of relationships established among these persons by interaction" (Caplow, 1964, p. 1). Thus the situation represented by two teams contesting within the confines of a football field, the situation presented by father and son fishing from a boat, and the situation created by a golf pro giving a lesson to a novice each constitutes a social system.

Social systems of prime concern to the sport sociologist are those which directly or indirectly relate to a game occurrence. That is to say, a sport sociologist is often concerned with why man gets involved in sport and what effect his involvement has on other aspects of his social environment. Involvement in a social system related to a game occurrence can be analyzed in terms of degree and kind of involvement.

Degree of involvement can be assessed in terms of frequency, duration, and intensity of involvement. The combination of frequency and duration of involvement may be taken as an index of an individual's "investment" in a sport situation, while intensity of involvement may be considered an index of an individual's "personal commitment" to a given sport situation.[20]

Kind of involvement can be assessed in terms of an individual's relationship to the "means of production" of a game. Those having direct or indirect access to the means of production are considered "actually involved" and are categorized as "producers." Those lacking access to the means of production are considered "vicariously involved" and are categorized as "consumers." We have tentatively identified three categories of producers and three classes of consumers.

Producers may be characterized as being primary, secondary, or tertiary with respect to the production of a game. (1) "Primary producers" are the contestants who play the primary roles in the production of a game, not unlike the roles of actors in the production of a play. (2) "Secondary producers" consist of those individuals, who while not actually competing in a sport contest, perform tasks which have direct technological consequences for the outcome of a game. Secondary producers include club owners, coaches, officials, trainers, and the like. It may be possible to categorize secondary producers as entrepreneurs, managers, and technicians. (3) "Tertiary producers" consist of those who are actively involved in a sport situation but whose activities have no direct technological consequences for the outcome of a game. Examples of tertiary producers are cheerleaders, band members, and concession workers. Tertiary producers may be classified as service personnel.

Consumers, like producers, are designated as being primary, secondary, or tertiary. (1) "Primary consumers" are those individuals who become vicariously involved in a sport through "live" attendance at a sport competition. Primary consumers may be thought of as "active spectators." (2) "Secondary consumers" consist of those who vicariously involve themselves in a sport as spectators via some form of the mass media, such as radio or television. Secondary consumers may be thought of as "passive spectators." (3) "Tertiary consumers" are those who become vicariously involved with sport other than as spectators. Thus an individual who engages in conversation related to sport or a person who reads the sport section of the newspaper would be classified as a tertiary consumer.

In concluding our discussion of the nature of sport we note that a special type of consumer is the fan. A fan is defined as an individual who has both a high personal investment in and a high personal commitment to a given sport.

NOTES

1. This definition is based largely on the work of Caillois (1961) and Roberts and others (1959). Other definitions and classifications of games having social import are given in Berne (1964) and Piaget (1951).

2. As have done Huizinga (1955), Stone (1955), and Caillois (1961).

3. Cf. Goffman's discussion of "rules of irrelevance" as applied to games and social encounters in general (1961, pp. 19-26).

4. E.g., compare the rules given for games in any edition of Hoyle's *Book of Games* with the NCAA rule book for various collegiate sports.

5. There is, of course, the amateur who gives up the "game" to become a professional.

6. For an early discussion of the problem of legitimation in sport, see Veblen (1934, pp. 268-70).

7. An excellent philosophical account of play and seriousness is given by Kurt Riezler (1941, pp. 505-17).

8. A sociological treatment of how an individual engaged in an activity can become "caught up" in it is given by Goffman in his analysis of the concept of "spontaneous involvement" (1961, pp. 37-45).

9. For a discussion of how certain aspects of "reality" are excluded from a game situation, see Goffman's treatment of "rules of irrelevance." Contrawise see his treatment of "rules of transformation" for a discussion of how certain aspects of "reality" are permitted to enter a game situation (1961, pp. 29-34).

10. Professional sports provide an exception, of course, especially such a sport as professional bullfighting.

11. Our use of the term "structures and processes" at this point is similar to Goffman's concept of "realized resources" (1961, pp. 16-19).

12. Other possible categories of competition are, of course, animals against animals as seen in horse racing or animals against an artificial animal as seen in dog racing. As noted by Weiss: "When animals or machines race, the speed offers indirect testimony to men's excellence as trainers, coaches, riders, drivers and the like—and thus primarily to an excellence in human leadership, judgment, strategy, and tactics" (1967, p. 22).

13. The interested reader can find examples of sport classifications in Hesseltine (1964), McIntosh (1963), and Sapora and Mitchell (1961).

14. This definition is patterned after one given by Smelser (1963, p. 28).

15. Huizinga states that the existence of permanent teams is, in fact, the starting point of modern sport (1955, p. 196).

16. Our discussion of "sanctioned secrecy" closely parallels Johnson's discussion of "official secrecy" in bureaucracies (1960, pp. 295-96).

17. For an early sociological treatment of sport, spectacle, exhibition, and drama, see Sumner (1960, pp. 467-501). We note in passing that some writers consider the totality of sport as a ritual; see especially Fromm (1955, p. 132) and Beisser (1967, pp. 148-51 and pp. 214-25).

18. Our discussion of these four levels is similar to Caplow's treatment of small, medium, large, and giant organizations (Caplow, 1964, pp. 26-27).

19. The term sportnik refers to an avid fan or sport addict.

20. Cf. McCall and Simmons (1966, pp. 171-72).

REFERENCES

1. Beisser, Arnold R. *The Madness in Sports*. New York: Appleton-Century-Crofts, 1967.

2. Berne, Eric. *Games People Play*. New York: Grove P, 1964.

3. Boyle, Robert H. *Sport—Mirror of American Life*. Boston: Little, Brown, 1963.

4. Caillois, Roger. *Man, Play and Games*. Trans. Meyer Barash. New York: Free, 1961.

5. Caplow, Theodore. *Principles of Organization*. New York: Harcourt, Brace and World, 1964.

6. Friedsam, H.J. "Social Situations," in *A Dictionary of the Social Sciences*, ed. Julius Gould and William L. Kolb. New York: Free, 1964.

7. Fromm, Erich. *The Sane Society*. New York: Fawcett, 1955.

8. Goffman, Erving. *Encounters*. Indianapolis: Bobbs-Merrills, 1961.

9. Hesseltine, William B. "Sports," *Collier's Encyclopedia*, 1964.

10. Huizinga, Johan. *Homo Ludens—A Study of the Play-Element in Culture*. Boston: Beacon, 1955.

11. Johnson, Harry M. *Sociology: A Systematic Introduction*. New York: Harcourt, Brace, 1960.

12. Kahn, Roger, "Money, Muscles—and Myths," *Nation*, CLXXXV (July 6, 1957): 9-11.

13. Leach, E.R. "Ritual," in *A Dictionary of the Social Sciences*, ed. Julius Gould and William L. Kolb. New York: Free, 1964.

14. Luschen, Gunther. "The Interdependence of Sport and Culture." Paper presented at the National Convention of the American Association for Health, Physical Education, and Recreation, Las Vegas, 1967.

15. McCall, George J., and J.L. Simmons. *Identities and Interactions*. New York: Free, 1966.

16. McIntosh, Peter C. *Sport in Society*. London: C.A. Watts, 1963.

17. Parsons, Talcott. *Societies: Evolutionary and Comparative Perspectives*. Englewood Cliffs, NJ: Prentice Hall, 1966.

18. Piaget, Jean. *Play, Dreams, and Imitation in Childhood*. Trans. C. Gattegno and F.M. Hodgson. New York: W.W. Norton, 1951.

19. Riezler, Kurt. "Play and Seriousness," *The Journal of Philosophy*, XXXVIII (1941): 505-17.

20. Roberts, John M., and others. "Games in Culture," *American Anthropologist*, LXI (1959): 597-605.

21. ——, and Brian Sutton-Smith. "Child Training and Game Involvement," *Ethnology* I (1962): 166-85.

22. Sapora, Allen V., and Elmer D. Mitchell. *The Theory of Play and Recreation*. New York: Ronald, 1961.

23. Schneider, Louis. "Institution," in *A Dictionary of the Social Sciences*, ed. Julius Gould and William L. Kolb. New York: Free, 1964.

24. Smelser, Neil J. *The Sociology of Economic Life*. Englewood Cliffs, NJ: Prentice-Hall, 1963.

25. Stone, Gregory P. "American Sports: Play and Display," *Chicago Review*, IX (Fall 1955): 83-100.

26. Sumner, William Graham. *Folkways*. New York: Mentor, 1960.

27. Torkildsen, George E. "Sport and Culture." M.S. Thesis, University of Wisconsin, 1957.

28. Veblen, Thorstein. *The Theory of the Leisure Class*. New York: Modern Library, 1934.

29. Weiss, Paul. "Sport: A Philosophic Study." Unpublished manuscript, 1967.

4. Triad Trickery: Playing With Sport and Games*

Klaus V. Meier

At the [beginning of the twentieth] century, Graves (2: p. 6) observed that "there are few words in the English language which have such a multiplicity of divergent meanings as the word sport." Almost 100 years later the assertion is most certainly still relevant; that is, contemporary usage of the term demonstrates extensive variability and diversity of both applicability and utilization. Indeed, the specified problem extends beyond 'sport' to reflect similar circumstances also encompassing the terms 'games' and 'play.'

Further, even a rudimentary, and certainly a detailed, scrutiny of the literature developed within the last two or three decades in the field of the philosophy of sport and play demonstrates rather clearly that the problems of definition and classification are some of the most basic, contentious, and extensive issues to be found in the entire area. Indeed, it is possible to identify, with only moderate diligence, more than 80 North American, European, and Japanese published articles or chapters that dedicate themselves predominantly or exclusively to this specific task.[1]

The importance of this type of inquiry is readily apparent. To analyze, to clarify, and to understand the diverse nature and structures of games, sport, and play, as well as their significance for an individual or functions within various societies—and to develop substantiated philosophical theories concerned with the interrelationships present among these three forms of human activity—it is necessary, as a prerequisite, to define vigorously and to limit operationally the appropriate range of terminological applicability. Such efforts not only provide

---

* Klaus V. Meier, "Triad Trickery: Playing With Sport and Games," *Journal of the Philosophy of Sport* 15 (1988), pp. 11-30.

illumination but also facilitate legitimate discourse and, thereby, further pertinent philosophical research.

Despite the importance of the problem, however, consensus is conspicuous by its absence and the putative results may be generally characterized as inadequate. Be that as it may, the philosophical labors of Bernard Suits certainly may not be so labeled. In fact, Suits has contributed a remarkably long, successful, and seminal body of writings concerned with pertinent definitional matters. Indeed, his current "Tricky Triad" (21) paper is only the latest effort in, and in one sense perhaps the culmination of, four decades of rigorous reflection about one or more of the relevant three concepts, going back to his own graduate thesis work at the University of Chicago (14). Undoubtedly, his most profound extended work, originally published in 1978 and now generally recognized as one of the most substantive monographs in the field, is *The Grasshopper: Games, Life and Utopia* (16). In this work, Suits carefully defends a definition of games and game playing from a plethora of possible objections. His current work builds upon that strong foundation.[2]

I

I wish to commence my philosophical critique of Suits' latest position, as well as several components of his previously published writings, by registering, once again, my agreement with his definition of 'game' and 'game playing,' which I find to be both acceptable and eminently productive. It will surely be remembered that Suits (16: p. 34) provides the following basic description: "to play a game is to engage in an activity directed towards bringing about a specific state of affairs, using only means permitted by rules, where the rules prohibit more efficient in favour of less efficient means, and where such rules are accepted just because they make possible such activity."

The most salient feature of the previous definition, of course, is the deliberate introduction of less efficient, or more limited means, for the accomplishment of a specified task or the attainment of a goal. In this manner, a game may be distinguished readily from a nongame or 'technical' activity. Indeed, "in anything but a game the gratuitous introduction of unnecessary obstacles to the achievement of an end is regarded as a decidedly irrational thing to do, whereas in games it appears to be an absolutely essential thing to do" (17: p. 42).

As previously mentioned, I find this definition to be most acceptable. Since Suits' (15) first formulation, and subsequent refinements and adumbrations (17), several commentators have challenged his positions (e.g., see 1; 5; 13). In my opinion, Suits' (18) own response is sufficient to neutralize most if not all of the pertinent criticisms to be found in these sources. In addition, Morgan's (10) recent thoughtful and detailed reconsideration of a formalistic account of games provides additional, very substantive support. As a consequence, Suits' definition of a game is herein employed as a philosophically defendable starting point.

II

With this important foundation in hand, attention may now be directed to the other two members of the triad, namely, 'sport' and 'play.' I would like to begin with the former. Whereas the concept of 'game' now poses no remaining substantial problems of definition, that of 'sport,' as will become evident shortly, presents more serious difficulties. Prior to an extended critical discussion of Suits' thoughts on this matter, which comprises Section III of this paper, I wish to present a brief contextual note.

The extant philosophy of sport literature presents a manifold and diffuse range of specific activities, descriptions, and purposes claimed to be representative of sport. In addition, a multitude of individual characteristics and factors are often deemed to be essential components of the concept by various writers. A representative, but by no means exhaustive, delineation of selected postulated aspects forwarded as necessary features of sport includes the following: (a) it involves challenge, competition, and conflict; (b) its resolution is dependent upon the adroit utilization of strategy and tactics; (c) rules govern its structure by means of spatial, temporal, and additional restrictions; (d) it is free, unnecessary, and 'unreal'; (e) it may be serious or trivial; (f) it entails physical exertion, prowess, or 'locatedness,' all aimed at the manifestation of physical excellence; (g) participant motives are important to its essence, that is, it is pursued for extrinsic, instrumental reasons or, conversely, solely for intrinsic rewards; (h) it inevitably possesses social as well as moral dimensions; (i) it demands more than one person, or alternatively, it may be performed in solitude; (j) it involves ranking, stratification, organization, and other trappings of institutionalization; and finally (k) it is identical with games or play, it possesses only some of the essential attributes of both, or it is to be located at one end of a 'play-game-sport' continuum.

Most assuredly, the postulated attributes and depictions in the previous listing demonstrate the numerous difficulties with which the pertinent philosophy literature is fraught, namely, bland assumptions, spurious distinctions, unsupported generalizations, limited applications and, finally, simple contradictions and logical errors. Despite this regrettable state of affairs, and the continuing presence of diverse if not antinomical* views, I wish to contend herein that the task of successfully presenting adequate definitions of sport is by no means precluded. In other words, I think that it is indeed possible to locate the precise boundaries of this activity.

In contrast to the plethora of items previously listed, I wish to claim that all sports possess the same four essential characteristics of games previously delineated and, in addition, one significant, distinguishing feature, namely, sport requires the demonstration of physical skill and, as a consequence, the outcome is dependent, to a certain degree at least, upon the physical prowess exhibited by the participants. Therefore, whereas physical actions or particular motor movements are insignificant to the resolution of many games, the explicit and varied manifestation of these components is essential to the performance of sport ventures. That is, while the terms and manner of any physical movements conducted in some games are incidental to the position or state moved from or to (12: p. 13), this is certainly not the case in sport. For example, in chess, bridge, and numerous other games, manual dexterity or physical skill has no influence whatsoever on the outcome. Indeed, these games can be played without *any* pertinent motor movements demanded of the participants. Assistants or even machines can move the pieces or display the cards; verbal instructions or commands may suffice and, in fact, chess can be played by mail.

At this point, a qualifying note must be introduced. Although it may be granted readily that increased proficiency of execution is an important differential variable, usually culminating in greater levels of performance and success in the sport occurrence, this does not warrant the conclusion that significant or even moderate skill must be demonstrated by all or even any other participants in a particular sport contest. That is, the sport of racquetball remains a sport even if the participants are novices limited to one hour's previous experience or if they are very unevenly matched against highly skilled opposition. All that may be asserted legitimately is that the required skills demanded of players at an elite level are different from those required for participation at a lower level. Consequently, I wish to assert that the degree of physical skill exhibited in a sport is simply not a defining characteristic or an essential component of the concept of sport.

---

* = contradictory.

III

What is Suits' position on all of this? Unfortunately, despite the auspicious achievement attained in his delineation of the concept of game, when he turns his attention to sport problems arise rather quickly. For example, in a paper originally published in 1973, Suits (17: p. 43) asserts, "I believe that sports are essentially games. What I mean by this is that the difference between sports and other games is much smaller than the difference between humans and other vertebrates." His employment of the phrase "sport and other games" certainly implies at least some form of substantial identity between the two concepts. This is confirmed only one page later when he states that "all sports appear to be games of skill rather than games of chance" (17: p. 44).[3] However, Suits (17: p. 43) also contends, curiously, that "sport is not a species within the genus *game*. The distinguishing characteristics of sport are more peripheral, more arbitrary, and more contingent than are the differences required to define a species."

The aforementioned minor confusion notwithstanding, it is apparent that, at this stage at least, Suits did in fact wish to support the contention that all sports were forms of games. This may readily be seen to be the case in two later recantations, which by the very act of negation tend to affirm the opinion expressed here. First, in a paper published 8 years after his "Elements of Sport" article, Suits (18: p. 61) asserts, "I here repudiate the view I once expressed—though not in *The Grasshopper*—that all sports are simply athletic *games* institutionalized in certain ways." Second, of course, in the current article under discussion, he presents a similar claim: "In an article of mine recently reprinted in an anthology on the philosophy of sport, I maintained that sports of the kind we are now considering [that is, the kinds of activities exemplified in the Olympic Games] *were* the same as athletic games. Well, I was wrong" (21: p. 2).[4]

It is clear that in both of the previously mentioned instances Suits recants the position that he expressed earlier concerning sport as a species of game. However, since it is my intention to repudiate his repudiation, and to contend that his earlier position—albeit abbreviated in a very significant manner yet to be specified—is stronger than his current position, it is now necessary for me to scrutinize this former stance, to salvage at least one important characteristic therefrom, and to discard the rest.

Suits presents his earlier reflections on the nature of sport in the following manner:

> I would like to submit for consideration four requirements which, if they are met by any given game, are sufficient to denominate that game a sport. They

are: (1) that the game be a game of skill, (2) that the skill be physical, (3) that the game have a wide following, and (4) that the following achieve a certain level of stability.... the features are more or less arbitrary, since they are simply facts about sport (17: p. 43)

I can accept now, as I did for that matter in a paper originally presented in 1978 (6), the first two postulated additional requirements for a game also to be correctly labeled a 'sport.' It seems to me, however, that economy permits us to collapse the two into one more compact rendition, namely, that the outcome of the game is influenced by, and dependent upon, the demonstration of physical skills, ability, or prowess. This statement still, immediately and correctly, eliminates such activities as chess or bridge from consideration for inclusion.

The third and fourth characteristics, however, are far more problematic; in fact, I wish to argue that they are simply erroneous claims.[5] If taken together, these two components, as Suits (18: p. 61) admits in a passage quoted earlier, mandate that sports be viewed simply as institutionalized games. In forwarding such a claim, of course, Suits is certainly not alone. Despite substantial differences concerning numerous other characteristics, the literature readily attests that many philosophers, and for that matter sociologists and historians, consider sport to be, of necessity, an institutionalized activity. This condition refers to the establishment of norms and codified rules, as well as to the development of formal associations and specific administrative bodies that impose external organizational and regulatory patterns and programs upon previously more informally controlled sports activities. Although it may be readily acknowledged that the current modes of conduct of *certain* sports reflect these components—indeed there are numerous philosophical critiques to be found that stridently criticize the perceived extensive formalization, regulation, rationalization, professionalization, and bureaucratization of many contemporary sports—there is considerable difficulty in claiming that institutionalization is an integral component of the essence of all sport in general.

Is *all* sport institutionalized? I think not. Much has been made—erroneously I wish to contend—of the customs, traditions, regulatory features, external perspectives, and other trappings that surround many sports. However, these components appear to be modes of conducting and regulating the sport occurrence which add color and significance, and enhance particular sports. That is, in a very basic sense these are *peripheral* concerns, ancillary or accidental to the basic nature of the enterprise, not part of the essential constitutive form of sport, and certainly not part of its ontological status. It appears to be more sensible to view sport as extending along an organizational continuum from the relative absence of such aspects to that of extreme regulation.

Another somewhat similar problem concerned with the question of sport as an institutionalized activity arises when matters of degree and duration are considered. Precise identification *of the points of temporal and quantitative sufficiency* becomes a difficult undertaking at best; that is, how long must an activity or a game exist before it becomes eligible for the category of sport, and how many participants, groups, organizing bodies, and nations must engage in the activity? The adjudication of these and similar queries appears largely to be both arbitrary and unsatisfactory.

Perhaps comments on one study available in the philosophical literature will support these admittedly serious allegations. Osterhoudt (12: p. 13), in accepting the alleged necessity of institutional characteristics, lists some physical activities which he asserts fail to meet the full requirements of sport. He claims that such activities as hurling, jai alai, and hula-hooping, among similar others, have an insufficiently wide basis in our historicocultural experience to be included in this category. They have not affected the human circumstances in sufficient measure to have gained anything more than a geographically limited or a historically located practice.

Difficulties arise from this assertion. Osterhoudt suggests that perhaps the best criterion available for determining whether an activity has a sufficiently wide basis is the standard used by the International Olympic Committee (IOC) in its deliberations concerning the inclusion of specific sports in the quadrennial Olympic Games program. However, utilizing such factors as the number of national governing organizations in existence for a particular activity seems to be rather capricious. Also, the IOC must use a different criterion to determine the activities to be placed on the discussion table for consideration for inclusion in the Games. In addition, it would appear to follow that all those activities not included in the Olympics would not be considered sports, an assertion which is, at the very least, highly contentious. For example, any suggestion that rugby, curling, cricket, mountain climbing, and Grand Prix automobile racing are not sports because of failure to meet standards of sufficient measure for or inclusion in the Olympics would be greeted with significant debate and incredulity in not a few quarters. Finally, at times, the country hosting the Olympics is permitted to include an activity that is not a component of the permanent program; does this mean that the chosen enterprise is not a sport because it fails to demonstrate sufficient numerical allegiances elsewhere?

At this point it will be instructive to examine the two examples forwarded by Suits to pursue a similar point. He also dismisses the activity of hula-hooping by asserting that, "it would be proper to call Hula-Hoop a craze rather than a sport.... Even if Hula-Hoop had lasted for fifty years, it would still be a craze, only a very tiresome craze" (17: p. 45).

I find this comment to be curious indeed, since most dictionary definitions of the term 'craze' stipulate that it is "a short-lived popular fashion, a rage, or a limited fad." Thus a craze, by definition, simply cannot extend for half a century. In fact, if hula-hooping had lasted 50 years, would not this longevity in and of itself demonstrate a certain level of stability, if not a wide following? Indeed, very few recreational or sport activities have lasted this long without achieving a modicum of codification or stabilization, if not institutionalization.

The second example Suits (17: p. 45) utilizes in an attempt to buttress his case is the curious enterprise that he terms 'Sweat Bead.' This activity, although fascinating for Suits, and for that matter the reader, rightly should be dismissed from consideration as a sport. This exclusion, however, is not the direct consequence, as Suits suggests, of the fact that it is a highly idiosyncratic venture lacking a wide following; rather, it should in all probability not even have been forwarded as an appropriate exemplar in the first place, since it is difficult to ascertain, at least from the very sketchy description he provides, what physical skill, if any, is directly involved in sufficiently angering the high-ranking university official to produce the desired results during the pertinent meeting.

Further, to turn in a slightly different direction, it is perhaps worthy of note to state that even if it is accepted that many sports have metamorphized from a folk diversion, or even an elite recreational activity, to a highly visible and institutionalized component of the present social world, this state of affairs is simply a comment on the changing social conditions surrounding *some forms* of the enterprise; it is not a reflection of the essential nature of all sport in general, or support for institutionalization as a necessary characteristic. Unfortunately, spatial limitations preclude further discussion of this point and other aspects directly related to it.[6]

Be that as it may, in conclusion, it appears to be legitimate to contend that although many forms of contemporary sport have indeed become highly institutionalized, and further that institutionalized sport is very much a proper and productive area of concern for philosophers and sociologists interested in investigating the social structure, function, and processes of sport, it has not been satisfactorily demonstrated that institutionalization—even to the relatively minor extent indicated by Suits' last two postulated characteristics—is a necessary component of the essence of sport. Thus, I wish to assert that any recourse to institutionalization, as an integral, necessary component of the essential nature of sport, is arbitrary, as well as erroneous and counterproductive; consequently, it should be actively rejected.

IV

Some of the hesitancies that Suits expressed in several of the earlier quoted works are given full voice in the opening paragraphs of the current paper when he states, "I have changed my views in some important ways about play and sport (though not about games)." In the previous section, I have attempted to demonstrate that a change, or at least a partial deletion, is indeed warranted in the early conception of sport that Suits presented. It is now necessary to address specifically the new conceptions of sport and play that are forwarded in "Tricky Triad."

It will be remembered that Suits himself characterizes the first half of his paper as mere prelude. In fact, he labels most of the work undertaken in this portion of the article as an "abortive effort," disavows the tidy resolutions presented therein, and frankly admits that the conclusion arrived at there simply "isn't true" (21: pp. 5, 4). Although I do not intend to discuss most of the contentions or distinctions presented in this preliminary section that Suits eventually discards, it will of course be necessary to analyze the major point championed there and amplified in the second half of the article. I will be forced to conclude that it simply isn't true either.

Utilizing the kinds of activities to be found in the Olympic Games as a guide, Suits (21: p. 2) claims there are two distinct types of sports, namely, 'competitive athletic events' and 'athletic games.' Later he calls these two types of activities 'judged performances' and 'refereed games.' The two are not the same; the latter are asserted to be not performances per se, but rather "a rule-governed interplay of participants" which require "not judges but law-enforcement officers, that is, referees" (21: p. 2).

One of the postulated differences that Suits (21: p. 3) forwards to support his claim is that in football games, for example, "victory is not determined by the artistry" of the called plays or ensuring moves, but rather by "their effectiveness in winning games."[7] In contrast, such enterprises as "diving and gymnastics competitions are no more games than are judged competitive events, such as beauty contests and pie-baking competitions." This is a claim that I am unable to support.

For Suits (21: p. 5) the crux of the distinction is that games are essentially refereed events in which "referees see to it that the rules are followed, and impose penalties when they are not." On the other hand, Suits claims that performances are not rule-governed in that way at all:

> There are rules, to be sure, but not only are they *not* the crux of performances, they usually take the form of applying to the participants *outside* the arena of contention. I dislike mentioning steroids at this time, but the rule against their use would be the kind of rule typically at issue in the case of performances, what might be called perhaps a pre-event rule. But once a performance is under way, there are no rules, or scarcely any, that need enforcing. (21: p. 5)

I find much about the previous statement to be contentious, if not incorrect. However, there are certain aspects with which I am able to concur. The distinction alluded to in the previous quotation is between 'constitutive rules' and those that Suits terms 'pre-event rules.' I wish to address the latter category first. Elsewhere (7: p. 70), I have labeled edicts of this form 'auxiliary rules'; these rules specify and regulate "eligibility, admission, training, and other pre-contest requirements." I offer three examples of this particular type of regulation:

> first, rules pertaining to the participants' safety or exposure to physical stress, such as "all football players must wear a helmet with a fixed face-guard" or "no player may pitch more than three innings in any one age-group baseball game"; second, specific empirical restrictions placed upon participants concerning such attributes as age, sex, or weight; and third, an entire grouping of arbitrary regulations selectively imposed for a variety of social or political reasons. (7: p. 71)

The third category includes such things as the deliberate exclusion of professional athletes, representatives of the Republic of South Africa, or a limitation of no more than three athletes from any one country in a particular sports meet.[8]

Thus, it may be seen that I concur with a part of Suits' assertion in that I have claimed that a rule of this type "is of a different color or nature entirely than constitutive rules and, as such, *has nothing whatsoever to do with the essence of sport*" (7: pp. 70-71). However, I most assuredly *do not concur* with Suits' assertion that these are the only types of rules at work in performative sports, or that "once a performance is under way, there are no rules, or scarcely any, that need enforcing" (21: p. 5).

Let us presume, for the sake of argument, that Suits' assertion is correct—it is *not*, but I shall return to this aspect shortly—and that once a performance is under way, there are indeed no rules, or scarcely any, that need enforcing. Let us even be generous enough to ignore the waffling qualification contained in the phrase "or scarcely any," and agree that a particular event, once started, contains no restraining rules. Would this, on Suits' own definition of a game, disqualify it from being considered a game? No, it would not.

I would like to utilize one of Suits' own noteworthy examples to illustrate the contention forwarded here. Long-time devotees of Suits' writings—of which I am most assuredly one—will have little difficulty recalling the story of Ivan and Abdul, so wittily presented in *The Grasshopper* (16). It will be remembered that, after having explored all other opportunities for diversion during their retirement in the backwater capital of Rien-à-faire, the two generals agree to participate in a game without rules, namely, a no-holds-barred fight-to-the-finish. Suits (16: p. 66), in the persona of the Grasshopper, is "quite willing to accept that their fight to the finish *is* a game." Why? Because Ivan did not attempt to destroy Abdul immediately upon committing himself to a fight to the finish with him; that is, he voluntarily accepted the restriction (or rule) that forbade him from making a move in the game before a certain agreed-upon time of commencement. Suits (16: p. 64) acknowledges that a time restriction or limit "is in fact the same as a rule." Thus, the existence of this one rule, obviously one that is applicable to the performance itself, since it specifies the beginning of the event, is sufficient to classify the activity as a competitive *game* even if there are no additional rules in place during the contest or performance itself.

As a result of these deliberations, it would appear as if competitive gymnastics and diving performances—since they are guided, minimally, by rules that dictate such restrictive items as place of competition, starting time, internal diving rotations, each diver's permitted time interval before attempting the next specified dive, and so forth—surely satisfy at least the minimal qualifications for being accurately considered as competitive games. Although this state of affairs is sufficient in and of itself to support the claim being forwarded, there is more to be said.

V

Attention must now be directed toward the specific acts performed within the confines of the competition itself. It will be remembered that Suits asserts that during the types of competitive performances he addresses, there are no rules, or scarcely any, that need enforcing. Suits raises and responds to a potential argument against his own position in the following manner:

> Now, it may be objected that, contrary to what I have said, there clearly *are* rules that must be followed while actually engaged in performative sports. For example, the gymnast must not falter or stumble after dismounting from the parallel bars. It is perfectly permissible to call such a requirement a rule, but is quite clear, I should think, that such "rules" are entirely different from, say, the offside rules in football and hockey. The offside rule is what has come to be called, by me and by many others, a constitutive rule, while the standard of a clean dismount from the parallel bars is a rule of skill, or a tactical rule, or a rule of practice. (21: pp. 5-6)

This supposed contrast leads Suits (21: p. 6) to contend that "the rules to which the judges of performances address themselves are, I submit, rules of skill rather than constitutive rules."

In my opinion, there are several intriguing aspects to be found in the previous examples forwarded by Suits that warrant at least some comment. First, it is not at all clear that the offside rule in football, for example, is a constitutive rule. In fact, I have suggested elsewhere (7: p. 69) that rules such as these, which specify the penalties to be applied when particular constitutive rules have been violated, may be more appropriately called 'regulative.' These rules presuppose and regulate antecedently or independently existing forms of behavior, as specified by a set of constitutive rules. However, an absolute dichotomy is by no means championed here; rather, it is suggested that regulative rules are extensions of constitutive rules.

The previous point is of some importance when it is recognized that if the offside rule were solely a constitutive rule, then breaking it would qualify, on Suits' (17: p. 41) conception of a constitutive rule, as an instance of cheating, that is, as a failure to play the game at all, such as being discovered hand-carrying a golf ball across the green and dropping it into the cup. However, the defensive tackle who inadvertently lines up offside is still playing the game, but in a manner that requires, if detected of course, a 5-yard penalty to be assessed against his team.

To return to Suits' 'performative sports,' it is necessary to note that the gymnast who perceptibly falters or even stumbles after dismounting from the parallel bars is not simply breaking a desirable rule of skill, strategy, or practice. Rather, her failure to "stick the landing," if it is noticed by the judges who are charged with the task of watching for just such occurrences, inevitably results in a specific deduction of the points to be awarded. Indeed, in many of the performance sports (e.g., gymnastics, figure skating, diving) a specific predetermined point or percentage thereof is mandatorily deducted from the optimal score for each specified failure. Thus it may be contended that athletic performances have event rules of a regulative variety. This suggests, in turn, given their status as extensions of— and Suits (17: p. 41) also clearly considers them to be such—or perhaps even as subsets of constitutive rules, the presence of other underlying constitutive rules that specifically delineate appropriate and permitted actions.

To summarize partially at this point, it seems as if both the presence of pertinent rules prior to, and specifying the actual point of commencement of, athletic performances, as well as the demands imposed by the regulative if not indeed the constitutive rules necessarily applicable during a performance, cast doubt upon Suits' claim that such activities are not games. Be that as it may, there is a far stronger third claim to be made which, in my opinion, undermines his contention entirely, namely, that gymnastics and diving competitions seem to fulfill all of the essential characteristics originally posited by Suits to be integral to the nature of a game. The next section addresses this point in considerable detail.

VI

It will be remembered that Suits (16: p. 41; 21: p. 6) characterizes playing a game as "the voluntary attempt to overcome unnecessary obstacles"; in other words, games erect "barriers to be overcome." The essential component of Suits' definition, of course, is that in games "the rules prohibit use of more efficient in favor of less efficient means" to achieve the specified goal. It seems to me that both gymnastics and diving competitions readily fulfill these requirements.

To begin with the balance beam competition in gymnastics, for example, it may be asserted that the specified goal of the activity is to perform an interrelated series of stipulated compulsory moves a certain specific number of times, as smoothly and rhythmically as possible. It is readily apparent that achieving the goal of demonstrating the required physical actions would be made considerably easier if the gymnast were to be permitted to perform on the floor, or even if the beam itself were anchored directly to the floor. At the very least, the fear of sustaining potential injury through falling would be greatly minimized, thus facilitating the athlete's greater concentration solely on the execution of the prescribed actions. However, the essential defining characteristic of this particular competitive event is that the requisite actions must be performed while balancing on a wooden beam merely 4 inches wide, elevated a specific, mandatory vertical distance from the floor mats. Surely this restriction meets the requirement of being an unnecessary obstacle or a deliberate introduction of inefficient means. Further, all other apparatus events, such as the flying rings, the high bar, the uneven bars, also seem to demonstrate this same important limiting characteristic. In fact, even gymnastics events that utilize no piece of apparatus, such as the floor exercise event, have restraints incorporated; the exercise routine must contain a certain mandatory series of maneuvers performed within a rigidly prescribed floor area as well as time limitations and, in the women's events at least, must be coordinated to music.[9]

The previous contention requires further elaboration. The precise limitation of permissible floor space, for example, certainly makes it more difficult for the athlete to generate sufficient momentum or propulsion (that is, to build up enough 'steam') to execute successfully an extended and intricate series of flips or somersaults. In addition, stepping beyond the event boundary line elicits mandatory score reductions, which certainly handicaps the pursuit of high scores and may even result, if repeated a sufficient number of times, in disqualification. It is interesting to note that stepping out of bounds while in possession of the ball in such readily acknowledged games as basketball, for example, produces somewhat similar results; that is, the requisite penalty of forfeiture of the ball to the opposing team also handicaps the offending teams' efforts to obtain the highest possible score in the contest.

To turn our attention now to the sport of competitive diving, let us presuppose, for the sake of the current argument at least, that Suits (21: p. 4) is correct in contending that a major goal of the activity is to enter the water "in as nearly a vertical posture as possible" and with as little splash as possible. Be that as it may, there is more to diving competitions that this; otherwise jumping in, or even stepping, from the side of the pool would qualify as admissible acts. This of course is not the case. Instead, unnecessary difficulties or obstacles are deliberately added. For example, the rules of competitive diving dictate that the diver must perform certain prescribed acts from a 1- or 3-meter diving board, a 5-, 7-, or 10-meter platform, and so forth. Thus, the object is not just to enter the water in a vertical position but to do so only after having climbed up stairs to the specified height, walked or run out to the end of the apparatus, and then voluntarily departed to let gravity partially do its work.

However, this is not the only restriction in place. The diver must perform an elongated series of compulsory dives; further, these dives must be distributed over the various mandatory position categories of inward, layout, tuck, and pike. Finally, the number of body twists and/or somersaults required, as well as whether the entry shall be feet or head first, are also clearly specified and regulated (for example, a front dive, tuck position, with 2-1/2 somersaults). These are constitutive rules that define, and thereby make possible, the competition; they are not pre-event rules. If the internal requirements delineating each separate dive are not met (i.e., the diver executes an insufficient number of twists or utilizes the pike rather than the previously declared tuck position), the head diving referee may declare a 'no dive,' which means that the dive counts as an attempt for that compulsory group but no points are awarded to the diver.

In addition, it is rather apparent that the execution of the specific dive described in the previous paragraph could be facilitated greatly by moving from the 1- or even the 3-meter board to the 5- or 7-meter platform, thereby providing substantial additional time for the successful completion of the requisite intricate moves before hitting the water. Yet the diver accepts the limitation in height above the water as just one of the "barriers to be overcome" (21: p. 6). Surely it may be seen that these difficulties or performance obstacles are deliberate artificial constraints, imposed predominantly to increase the inefficiency of attaining the desired prelusory goal. They are, in sum, constitutive rules that are accepted by all concerned "just so the act made possible by such acceptance can occur"; in other words, they are clear examples of what Suits (17: p. 43) terms the "lusory attitude."

Thus it may be asserted that in the sport of diving—even if it is acknowledged, for example, that one of the purposes of the activity is to approximate and display performance ideals, as determined and evaluated by the judgments of the panel of expert judges—this experience is still to be found within, and regulated by, the specific confines of a game. In other words, there is still a deliberate choice of inefficient means to accomplish the task at hand.

To provide support for his postulated distinction between game rules and performance ideals, Suits forwards an example drawn from the sport of boxing. I do not find it to be convincing, however. He contends that boxing judges do not make their assessments against "an ideal of boxing, if there is such a thing, but of one competitor directly against another" (21: p. 6). But surely this also occurs in diving and gymnastics competitions. This state of affairs may be readily ascertained, for example, from the importance of the draw in both of these activities. Thus, judges readily admit that they "leave room" in their scoring to be able to grade the later performers higher in comparison to the earlier performers. That is, the standard of comparison is not only a supposed ideal but also an evaluation that the later competitor, perhaps in spite of a very slight stumble during an apparatus dismount, performed better, in sum, than an earlier competitor who had previously been awarded a score of 9.90 or 9.95 (witness the 'imperfect 10s' awarded to athletes late in the gymnastics rotation in the 1988 Seoul Olympic Games despite perceptible performance breaks).

At this point, I wish to offer one final observation concerning the major issue under consideration in this section. It may be helpful to state that elsewhere Suits (22: in press)* asserts that "it is perfectly obvious that the 100-yard dash, for example, is a game"; in fact, he goes so far as to claim that this activity is a "virtual paradigm of a game." It seems to me that if an event of this type, which is obviously exceedingly simple in terms of applicable performance rules, is to be termed a game, it is very difficult to ascertain how either gymnastics or diving competitions, each comprised of a complex series of imposed rules specifically limiting the means acceptable to attain the required goals, could fail to meet at least the minimal entrance requirements for inclusion in the category of games. The arbitrary restrictions imposed in running straight down a cinder track surely are far less than those exemplified in either gymnastics or diving competitions.

Finally, please note that simply because gymnastics and diving may not generally be called games, or even that they may not at first glance appear to be eligible for inclusion in this genre, is irrelevant by Suits' own admission:

> I submit that when some activity or enterprise not initially included in the hard core group (e.g., because it is not called a game) is seen, upon examination, to conform to the group's definition, then there exists a good prima facie reason for granting that the activity or enterprise *is* a game, despite the fact that it is not called one. (22: in press)†

In conclusion, I do not think that the arguments Suits presents are either sufficiently grounded or persuasive to establish clearly the proposed distinction between sports that are games and those that are performances. Consequently, I cannot support the distinction; rather, I wish to claim that both forms of activity do indeed satisfy Suits' own definition of games.

---

*   See editor's note to note 2.
†   See editor's note to note 2.

VII

In response to some criticism contained within a review of *The Grasshopper* written by Frank McBride, Suits (18: p. 61) offered the following conclusion: "If my definition is accepted, more sports are games than McBride would have thought, and that in general there are more games in heaven and earth than McBride has dreamt of in his philosophy." It would appear justified at this point to extend this criticism to Suits himself, and to assert that, if the previously presented argument is persuasive, there are far more sports that are games than are dreamt of in Suits' philosophy.

VIII

In the first sentence of the penultimate section of his paper, Suits (21: p. 7) forwards the "bald assertion" that not all sports are play. I have no quarrel with this statement; unfortunately however, I disagree with much of the remainder of the section. It will be remembered that Suits displays his suggested interrelationships among the concepts of sport, game, and play by means of three overlapping circles, subdivided into seven specific sections (see Figure 4.1).

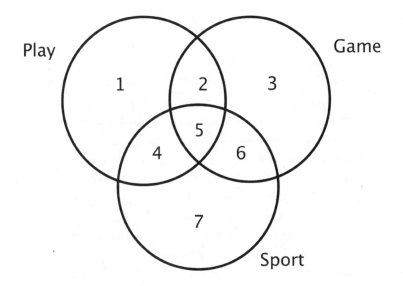

Figure 4.1 From Suits (21: p. 7)

It is necessary to commence my appraisal of this diagram by stating that although I find this specific graphic technique (i.e., the employment of Venn diagrams) to be an effective way of demonstrating the interrelationships among the three activities, I cannot agree with the particular model produced by Suits. More specifically, I find both Sections 4 and 7 to be untenable.

The crux of the matter, of course, is whether there are any sports that are not games. As I have attempted to delineate in the previous sections of this paper, I do not think Suits has demonstrated adequately that sport performances of the type he has chosen to utilize do not fulfill his own requirements for admission to the genus of 'game.' To reiterate a previously expressed opinion, I find portions of Suits' (17) earlier position on this matter to be more persuasive than his current revised stance.

It is now time for me to present the parameters of a model delineating the interrelationships among sport, games, and play that I think is more accurate than the one forwarded by Suits. I wish to contend that although not all games are sports, all sports are indeed games. That is, a game may also correctly be termed a sport if it possesses the additional characteristic of requiring physical skill or prowess to be demonstrated by the participants in the pursuit of its goal. Thus sport is neither an outgrowth nor an extension of game; rather, it is a game at the same time as it is a sport. Consequently, any form of postulated continuum extending from game to sport is rejected; instead, at least a partial conceptual identity is hereby championed.

IX

It is now necessary to turn to the third and last component of the triad, namely 'play.' There is, within the pertinent philosophical literature of course, considerable debate to be found about the nature and essence of play. Often it is described in terms of what it is not; that is, play is variously perceived as being "not serious, not real, disconnected, non-productive, unnecessary, and so forth" (4: p. 116). Despite this situation, I wish to provide a definition based upon the orientation, demeanor, or stance of the participant. It is my opinion that play may be viewed, simply and profitably, as an autotelic activity; in other words, an activity voluntarily pursued for predominantly intrinsic reasons.

If this position is accepted,[10] it is possible to limit the focus appropriately by asserting that depending upon the prevailing circumstances and factors, in other words the context at hand, sports and games may or may not be play. Thus, for present purposes, *context* is more important than *content*. Consequently, if games or sports are pursued voluntarily and for intrinsic reasons, they are also play forms; if they are pursued involuntarily or engaged in predominantly for extrinsic rewards, they are not play forms.

It is helpful to note two things about Suits' (21: pp. 8-9) position on this matter. First, his own distinction between undertakings that are autotelic ("an event or activity valued for itself") and instrumental ("an event or activity valued not only or even primarily for itself but for some further payoff that the event or activity is expected to provide") is very similar to the differentiation I wish to make between 'play' and 'non-play.'

Second, in an earlier paper, Suits (19: p. 19) also assumes that "*all* instances of play *are* instances of autotelic activity." In fact he regards autotelicity as a necessary, if not sufficient, condition of play. Unfortunately, space does not permit me to review and analyze this particular position at length. Nonetheless, for my current purpose—which is *not* to describe play exhaustively but rather is limited in scope to determining *when it is that games and sports are also play phenomena*—I wish to contend that autotelicity is both a necessary and sufficient trait for that aim.

Therefore, to return to the main thrust of the argument here presented, it may be seen that play and sport, for example, are not necessarily exclusive entities. Indeed, it can be maintained that "the competitive fullness of sport and the play gesture are, in a most fundamental sense, wholly compatible but not co-extensive. One can play sport without compromising elements essential to this highly polarized activity" (4: p. 113). Conversely, no trace of play whatsoever need be present in a particular sport venture. In other words, play is not, logically speaking, a necessary or sufficient condition or attribute of either sport or games; however, it may well be an element that enriches either or both endeavors.

The position forwarded here demonstrates the inadequacies of numerous assertions in the applicable literature which claim that play and sport are on opposite ends of a continuum and, thereby, have nothing at all in common. On the contrary, sports and games may be distinguished simply as play or non-play occurrences depending upon the contingencies surrounding or motivating participation. Thus, whereas National League baseball may indeed be viewed most often as a non-play activity, a sandlot game of baseball, incorporating many or even all of the same playing rules, may most definitely be a play occurrence. Despite perhaps radically different orientations in these two events, the sport of baseball is held in common. In other words, particular attitudes or stances manifested by the participants, including motives and inducements for engagement as well as the setting for the action, do not dictate whether a specific activity may legitimately be termed a sport. The essence of sport is independent of these concerns. However, such factors most certainly determine whether or not the sport activity at hand is also a form of play. These characteristics and relationships are summarized in Figure 4.2.

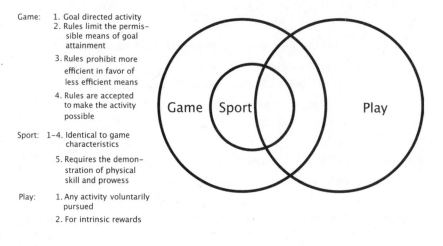

Game:
1. Goal directed activity
2. Rules limit the permis‐ sible means of goal attainment
3. Rules prohibit more efficient in favor of less efficient means
4. Rules are accepted to make the activity possible

Sport:
1–4. Identical to game characteristics
5. Requires the demon‐ stration of physical skill and prowess

Play:
1. Any activity voluntarily pursued
2. For intrinsic rewards

Figure 4.2 The Interrelationships among sport, game, and play.

Several points of information may be emphasized as a means of providing a further explanation of the preceding diagram: (a) all sports are games; (b) not all games are sports; (c) sport and games may or may not be play; (d) sports and games are play if voluntarily pursued for intrinsic rewards; (e) sports and games are non-play if involuntarily pursued or participated in for extrinsic rewards; and finally, (f) play may take forms other than sport or games.

X

How does all of this relate to the scheme outlined by Suits in Figure 4.1? First, it will be remembered that I wholeheartedly accept and adopt his definition of 'game,' as delineated, virtually unchanged, in many of his works; therefore we are in agreement here. Second, our conceptions of 'play' are sufficiently similar— at least for the herein deliberately limited purpose of ascertaining whether par‐ ticular instances of sports or games are play or non-play occurrences—not to present major difficulties. Third, the concept of 'sport,' of course, is the source of our greatest differences. I have attempted to demonstrate that Suits' distinction between athletic performances and athletic games is not as unproblematic as he suggests. In my opinion both are, at heart, forms of games. Therefore I wish to champion the claim, in contrast to Suits, that *all sports are indeed games.* Con‐ sequently, rather than accepting Suits' depiction of overlapping game and sport circles, as presented in Figure 4.1, I find the structure delineated in Figure 4.2, in which sport is wholly incorporated within the confines of the genus of games, to be more accurate. Be that as it may, I am prepared to accept the claim that there may be two workable species of sport, namely judged and refereed performances. Nonetheless, they both are forms of games.

In summary then, it should be clear that I have herein employed several useful facets of Suits' previous efforts, built upon this strong base, argued against what I perceived to be an erroneous distinction in his current work, and produced a scheme of the interrelationships among sport, game, and play which, in my opinion at least, is more appropriate than the one forwarded by Suits in "Tricky Triad."

XI

It may now be contended that if the definitional characteristics and structure delineated in the preceding analysis are deemed to be worthy of support, the basis and operational limits have thereby been provided to guide further research in the area of the philosophy of sport, play, and games.

Some indication of the direction such analytic endeavor might profitably pursue is given in the following three examples of this scheme's potential applicability: First, it is now possible to determine the proper role of competition in various sport ventures and educational programs by ascertaining what the intended purpose and outcome of the specific contests are. Second, the results of the inquiry described in the previous sentence contribute toward the determination of the proper place of 'winning' and victory in sport, and may indeed provide a substantial defense of a major emphasis on these outcomes. Third, and finally, it is now possible to reflect more rigorously on such cultural comments and critiques, for instance, as those who lament the absence or even the so-termed 'death of play' in contemporary sport. Contrary to Huizinga (3), who is perhaps most identified with formulating this particular last perspective, I see no inherent or inexorable play aspect in sport. Regrets may be appropriate, however, for the apparently continuing demise of play in the currently increasing commercialization of much of contemporary sport—as well as of many other facets of our social world, including the areas of art, literature, and architecture—but this state of affairs has nothing necessarily to do with sport and games.

Obviously there is much more to be said on many of the preceding matters that simply cannot be addressed here. However, it is clear that Suits' current work provides a major stimulus for continued reflection and analysis.[11] For this happy occurrence, all those who work in the sphere of the philosophy of sport, games, and play, once again, must be grateful.

NOTES

1. It must be acknowledged at the outset that, due to their specific applicability to the task at hand, selected portions of some sections of the current paper are restatements or direct usage of materials contained in two previously published articles (6; 8). When deemed helpful, the reader will be directed to specific additional explanatory or supportive passages contained therein.

2. I am pleased to report that Suits has just recently compiled a new collection of his writings, intended to serve, in part at least, as a sequel to *The Grasshopper*. The new volume, entitled *Grasshopper Soup: Philosophical Essays on Games* (22), is expected to be published within the next year or so.*

3. If we were to limit and to read this sentence very charitably to mean "of those sports which are games, they are games of skill rather than of chance," we would move closer to a position that is not incompatible with the stance Suits later forwards in "Tricky Triad."

4. The article to which Suits here refers is, of course, once again "The Elements of Sport" (17).

5. Much of the remainder of this particular section, admittedly, is somewhat of a digression from the main thrust of the essay. However, I think that the discussion provided therein is helpful to understand more fully such notions as the postulated transition of certain activities from "primitive" to "sophisticated," or even institutionalized status. This in turn, hopefully, will contribute some useful insight into the essential nature of sport and play.

6. For a much fuller treatment, albeit now somewhat dated, of this particular area of concern from both a philosophical and a sociological perspective, see Meier (6: pp. 85-90).

7. Here Suits appropriates for his own use a distinction more visibly, and certainly more frequently, employed in the aesthetics of sport literature. For a representative selection of papers addressing this particular issue, see Morgan and Meier's anthology (11: pp. 455-540).

8. For a further delineation of the nature and function of auxiliary rules, as well as additional pertinent examples, see Meier (7).

---

* This note predicts a book that seems not to have been published. The quotations from (22) in Section VI may be found in Appendix 1 of the revised edition of *The Grasshopper* (Broadview, 2005), pp. 162 and 166, respectively. The appendices to this edition provide concise responses to many of the more central criticisms of Suits's account, and so serve at least one of the roles presumably intended for the sequel.

9. These demands and restrictions, by the way, are also elements that provide figure skating with legitimate claims to being considered a game.

10. Clearly it is not possible to present an adequate explanation and supporting structure for the definition here. However, a previously published essay entitled "An Affair of Flutes: An Appreciation of Play" (9) does provide an extended argument dedicated largely to this specific task.

11. There are of course numerous other intriguing items and claims to be found in Suits' paper beyond those treated in the body of the present text: for example, the differentiation between primitive and sophisticated play, the restructuring of the amateur versus non-amateur distinction, and the notion that the compulsion to win somehow turns a game from play to non-play. Unfortunately, spatial limitations preclude a discussion of any of these intriguing issues here.

REFERENCES

1. D'Agostino, Fred. "The Ethos of Games." *Journal of the Philosophy of Sport*, VIII (1981), 7-19. Also in *Philosophic Inquiry in Sport*, Edited by William J. Morgan and Klaus V. Meier. Champaign, IL: Human Kinetics, 1988.

2. Graves, H. "A Philosophy of Sport." *Contemporary Review*, 77 (Dec. 1900), 877-93.

3. Huizinga, Johan. *Homo Ludens*. London: Routledge & Kegan Paul, 1950.

4. Kretchmar, R. Scott. "Ontological Possibilities: Sports as Play." *Philosophic Exchange*, 1 (1972), 113-22.

5. McBride, Frank. "A Critique of Mr. Suits' Definition of Game Playing." *Journal of the Philosophy of Sport*, VI (1979), 59-66. Also in *Philosophic Inquiry in Sport*. Edited by William J. Morgan and Klaus V. Meier. Champaign, IL: Human Kinetics, 1988.

6. Meier, Klaus, V. "On the Inadequacies of Sociological Definitions of Sport." *International Review of Sport Sociology* 16(2) (1981), 79-102.

7. Meier, Klaus V. "Restless Sport." *Journal of the Philosophy of Sport*, XII (1985), 64-77.

8. Meier, Klaus V. "Games, Sport, Play." *Proceedings of the PSSS Conference on the Philosophy of Sport Held in Tsukuba, 1986*. Tsukuba, Japan: University of Tsukuba, 1987, 83-89.

9. Meier, Klaus V. "An Affair of Flutes: An Appreciation of Play." *Journal of the Philosophy of Sport*, VII (1980), 24-45. Also in *Philosophic Inquiry in Sport*. Edited by William J. Morgan and Klaus V. Meier. Champaign, IL: Human Kinetics, 1988.

10. Morgan, William J. "The Logical Incompatibility Thesis and Rules: A Reconsideration of Formalism as an Account of Games." *Journal of the Philosophy of Sport*, XIV (1987), 1-20.

11. Morgan, William J., and Meier, Klaus V. (Editors). *Philosophic Inquiry in Sport.* Champaign, IL: Human Kinetics, 1988.

12. Osterhoudt, Robert G. "The Term Sport—Some Thoughts on a Proper Name." *International Journal of Physical Education,* 14 (Summer 1977), 11-16.

13. Paddick, Robert J. "Review of Bernard Suits' *The Grasshopper: Games, Life and Utopia.*" *Journal of the Philosophy of Sport,* VI (1979), 73-78.

14. Suits, Bernard. "Play and Value in the Philosophies of Aristotle, Schiller, and Kierkegaard." Unpublished master's thesis, University of Chicago, 1950.

15. Suits, Bernard. "What Is a Game?" *Philosophy of Science,* 34 (1967), 148-56.

16. Suits, Bernard. *The Grasshopper: Games, Life and Utopia.* Toronto: U of Toronto P, 1978.

17. Suits, Bernard. "The Elements of Sport." *Philosophic Inquiry in Sport.* Edited by William J. Morgan and Klaus V. Meier. Champaign, IL: Human Kinetics, 1988.

18. Suits, Bernard. "On McBride on the Definition of Games." *Philosophic Inquiry in Sport.* Edited by William J. Morgan and Klaus V. Meier. Champaign, IL: Human Kinetics, 1988.

19. Suits, Bernard. "Words on Play." *Journal of the Philosophy of Sport,* IV (1977), 117-31. Also in *Philosophic Inquiry in Sport.* Edited by William J. Morgan and Klaus V. Meier. Champaign, IL: Human Kinetics, 1988.

20. Suits, Bernard. "Defending Defining Games." Paper presented at the World Congress of Philosophy conducted in Brighton, England, August 25, 1988. Forthcoming in *Grasshopper Soup.*

21. Suits, Bernard. "Tricky Triad: Games, Play, and Sport." *Journal of the Philosophy of Sport,* XV (1988), 1-9.

22. Suits, Bernard. *Grasshopper Soup: Philosophical Essays on Games.* (At press). U of Toronto P.

QUESTIONS

1. How convincing is Loy's view that a certain degree of organization is necessary for an activity to count as sport?

2. What are the similarities and differences between Loy's definition of sport and Suits's? How about Suits's later definition?

3. Is Meier right to reject institutional definitions of sport? If so, in what non-institutional terms should sport be defined?

4. Should the offside rule be interpreted as regulative rather than constitutive? What rides on this interpretive dispute?

5. Does Meier adequately defend (the early) Suits from (the later) Suits on the question of whether all sports are games?

6. Is Meier committed to a particular definition of sport? If so, is that definition in need of further refinement?

FURTHER READING

Chisholm, Roderick (1999): "The Problem of the Criterion," in *The Theory of Knowledge: Classical and Contemporary Readings* (2nd edition), ed. Louis P. Pojman (Belmont, CA: Wadsworth), pp. 26–34.

MacIntyre, Alasdair (2007): *After Virtue: A Study in Moral Theory* (3rd edition) (Notre Dame, IN: U of Notre Dame P), especially chapter 14.

McFee, Graham (2004): *Sport, Rules and Values: Philosophical Investigations into the Nature of Sport* (London: Routledge), especially chapter 1.

Meier, Klaus V. (1981): "On the Inadequacies of Sociological Definitions of Sport," *International Review of Sport Sociology* 16 (2), pp. 79-102.

Suits, Bernard (1988): "Tricky Triad: Games, Play, and Sport," *Journal of the Philosophy of Sport* 15, pp. 1-9.

Wertz, S.K. (1995): "Is Sport Unique? A Question of Definability," *Journal of the Philosophy of Sport* 22 (1), pp. 83-93.

FURTHER INQUIRY

Loy's emphasis on sport requiring gross motor skill (as a part of physical prowess) has been marginalized by ensuing discussion and merits revival and exploration: Do sports require the exercise of gross motor skill, and if so how should such skills be characterized?—There are different ways. Debates between advocates and opponents of institutional theories continue to rage in other domains (e.g., aesthetics), and it might be useful to examine the issue further in those domains also, or in more general terms: for instance, MacIntyre's influential distinction between institutions and practices. Perhaps the concept of sport we seek is flexible enough to include both types of theory. If some sports are not games, should we follow Suits in defining them as activities that require judgment of physical superiority? Or perhaps we should be anti-essentialists about sport. Consider the plausibility of being an anti-essentialist about games but an essentialist about sport (even assuming that sports are a subset of games).

Section C

Sport Epistemology

'Epistemology' is the philosopher's term for the theory of knowledge, which began with Plato, who defined knowledge as justified true belief. Specifically, a subject knows something if and only if they *believe* that the world is that way, the world actually *is* as they believe, and they are *justified* in having that belief. More precisely, where S is a subject variable, and P a proposition variable (propositions being expressed by statements, e.g., 'It is raining'),

$$S \text{ knows that } P \longleftrightarrow (1) \ S \text{ believes that } P;$$
$$(2) \ 'P' \text{ is true};$$
$$(3) \ S \text{ is justified in believing that } P.$$

Justification was traditionally thought to be a matter of S being in a position to provide a good argument for P, to be aware of and able to articulate those reasons. More recent epistemology has challenged this traditional model on a number of fronts, including, for instance, whether justification requires full awareness or articulability. A related challenge concerns whether all knowledge really is propositional in nature, whether in addition to knowing *that*, there is also a genuine knowledge type describable as knowing *how*.

Physical skills are plausibly, for the philosophy of sport, the ideal example of knowing how: an athlete performing a highly skilled manoeuver (who knows how to perform it) almost invariably lacks the explicit theoretical knowledge that the kinesiologist seeks, in studying that very movement, (specifically, what precisely the athlete's body is doing). The physical skills under study likewise will often elude possession by, if not the understanding of, those who are investigating. In the first reading in this section, Steel focuses on physical skills as one among several types of knowledge that a person needs to learn so as to participate in sports and many games. Where Steel focuses on know-how from the first-person (subject's) perspective, in the second reading Holt and Holt approach skill from the third-person (investigator's) perspective, offering a preliminary exploration of what might be called the philosophy of kinesiology.

5. What We Know When We Know a Game*

Margaret Steel

Paul Ziff points out in "A Fine Forehand" (7) that there are significant epistemological problems in connection with sports. It is to some of these that I will address myself in this paper. I am asking the basic question: "What kind of knowledge is required to engage in a game or sport?" It is a question that deserves to be answered for itself, and we will find that the answers have implications for other areas of knowledge.

In "The Nature of Sport: A Definitional Effort" (4: pp. 48, 49), John W. Loy, Jr. classified knowledge as one of the technological aspects of games. What he has in mind is our knowledge of the rules and strategies and so on involved in playing the game, or participating in the sport. This is related to the statement that "What we know about a game is how to play it," and "how to play it" is characterized in terms of the rules and strategies. In fact, as I shall show, this is a much too simple view of the matter. A good deal more is involved in knowing a game.

I will begin by characterizing two kinds of learning, both of which are involved in learning how to play a game. This is a good place to begin, as knowledge is what we have learned. This first kind of learning is inductive, which is best described as forming expectations about future experience on the basis of past instances. It is the method by which we acquire many habits. It is also the method by which we make generalizations about the world in our every-day lives, and in science. Clearly, it is an important mode of learning. Much of what we call "factual" or "propositional" knowledge is acquired in this way. The simplest version of this is stimulus-response, but inductive learning can obviously be a good deal more complex than the simple level.

---

*   Margaret Steel, "What We Know When We Know a Game," *Journal of the Philosophy of Sport* 4 (1977), pp. 96-103.

The second mode is one I will call "learning by exemplars." This is most clearly characterized in T.S. Kuhn's (1, 2, 3) writings on the philosophy of science, so I will first give a brief summary of his views. Kuhn's view of science is developed in relation to the notion of a paradigm. He distinguishes two major senses of this term. The first is the paradigm as "disciplinary matrix." The second is the paradigm as "exemplar." A disciplinary matrix is a whole world view. It determines what kinds of things there are, what counts as a problem and as a solution, what the values are, what kinds of action and experimentation are acceptable and which are not. That is, it tells us what the world is like, what our relationship with it is and what our attitude to it should be. This notion was intended to explain both the ongoing enterprise of science, "normal science," and to account for scientific revolutions. Normal science is the practice of science within the framework of the accepted disciplinary matrix. When the latter begins to break down and become unsatisfactory, a revolution may occur, and the old disciplinary matrix be replaced by a new one. When the revolution is completed, normal science goes on with a new world view and new problems.

This account of science as a world view is supported and strengthened by Kuhn's account of the paradigm as exemplar. An exemplar, or shared example, is a standard scientific experiment or problem that the student has to work through. The theories of science are merely formal theories until they are given content in experimental situations. By performing the classic experiments, the student begins to see how the theory is realized in the world, in terms of what there is, and what we can do with it. He learns what counts as an entity, and what counts as a legitimate problem, by learning how problems are like each other. This likeness is not in terms of specific criteria, but rather in terms of what Kuhn calls "similarity classes." Kuhn claims that the student acquires a "learned ability to group objects and situations into similarity classes which are primitive in the sense that the grouping is done without an answer to the question 'similar with respect to what'" (2: p. 275). By acquiring this skill, the student can solve new problems in ways analogous to the ways he solved old ones. He can recognize new entities by seeing analogies between them and others. Science thus becomes something that can be extended, rather than a rigid body of fact and procedure.

Kuhn suggests that when we acquire a scientific education, we acquire a disciplinary matrix, and in doing so we enter into a new world and acquire a new language, the language of science, at the same time. A particular way of seeing nature is embedded in the language. The new world and the new language are acquired largely through the exemplars. Now the point is that the student in learning science is learning how to *do* something. In becoming a scientist, he acquires specific skills, and specific ways of perceiving. He learns to see the world in a new way, and this in itself is a skill, acquired by doing. We cannot learn to see the world the way the scientist sees it without trying and practising seeing it in this way. This trying and practising is embodied in the exemplars. In learning science we *do* science by working through the exemplars, the problems and classical experiments. Once the science is learned we can go on to new discoveries.

Note also that in learning science we learn something we cannot say. If we could explain, if we could say exactly what is to be learned, there would be no need for exemplars. As is clear from the quote from Kuhn above, we cannot answer the questions "similar with respect to what?", when we recognize that problems are analogous. We do not know how it is that we recognize similarities and dissimilarities because we do not do it in terms of specific criteria. We learn to perceive and to judge in a particular way, yet we do not know precisely how we do it. For some time we are learners, trying to assimilate the unfamiliar. Then at some point the unfamiliar becomes our own world, within which we move easily.

I will now go on to show that this account of the learning of science can be extended to account for the learning of all skills, from simple bodily skills such as an infant's hand-waving, to games such as tennis, and to sophisticated philosophical argumentation. These skills are not equally creative, nor are they equally sophisticated, but I think it will be clear that they are all learned in the same way.

In turning to the learning of games and sports, the first thing to be noticed is that there are two levels of learning involved. There is the level of the game as a whole, involving the rules and the strategies, the moves and the tactics. The other level is that of the particular physical skills that must be acquired; some examples would be such skills as dribbling or heading the ball in soccer, or serving or volleying in tennis. It is clear that if you are unable to dribble or head the ball in soccer, or serve or volley in tennis you will not be able to play these games properly. Even if the word "play" is stretched as far as possible, you will only be, at best, a marginal player. The particular physical skills, therefore, are necessary in order to play the game. It is with this level of learning that I will deal first.

To begin with, learning a physical skill is not an inductive process. We do not learn to play tennis by generalization from past instances. Once the player has "caught on," he knows how it feels to do it right, he knows from past experience that he *is* doing it right, but this is not how he learned. A player may serve incorrectly twenty times, then do it correctly. Those twenty incorrect performances do not teach him how to do it right, nor do they even teach him how to avoid doing it incorrectly. He is not learning a belief or forming an expectation about the future (although I do not deny that these play a part, for instance in estimating the angle and velocity of a tennis return). Rather he is learning how to do something. It is in this sense that what the tennis player knows can be said to be "knowing how" rather than "knowing that."

How *do* we learn a physical skill? First of all we have to know what it is we want to be able to do. We have to be shown the skill by another person, or a picture or diagram. In other words we have to have an exemplar. In order to learn a physical skill we have to try to do it, and practise doing it. To do this we have to know what we want to do, and to want to be able to do it. The instructor demonstrates a serve to a beginner, who attempts to copy him. He tries, by imitating the actions of the instructor, to duplicate the whole physical act, the whole *gestalt* of serving. He must throw the ball up a certain distance, must bring down the racket on it, and direct it to a certain specified area. All this requires a complex and sophisticated muscular control. The beginner can be helped by verbal instructions, such as "Throw the ball higher" or "Bring down the racket at an angle," but these will not tell him what to do. They merely function as clues in his search for the correct performance.

The beginner practises until the instructor says "Now you have it." At this point he has learned something. This is what it *feels like* to perform the serve correctly. He knows how to move his body in order to serve the ball into the opposite side. He knows how much effort to put into his movements, and how to swing and follow through. Of course, he must still practise, and even with practise will not always be successful, but this is because tennis serving is a very complex skill, requiring more muscular control than many others. But the learner now knows how to serve. He can show someone else how to do it. As with science, he has been led through a series of models, and the movements, from being strange and unfamiliar, have become natural and familiar.

Here it is important to consider what the learner does *not* know. He does not as a rule know how his muscles make his body move in the required way. He *does* know what it *feels* like for the muscles to move correctly, but he is not directing this movement, nor is he aware of it. This will be true even when the learner knows physiology, and can give an account of the muscle movements that take place in a tennis serve. Knowing the muscular movements, that is, knowing how the action takes place on the level of anatomy, is not the same as knowing how to perform the action in person. Teaching someone how the muscles move does not teach him how to serve. In fact, thinking about the muscle movements when trying to serve would inhibit, even paralyze action. We are not learning a series of muscle movements, but a whole flowing action. We do not see the forest when we look only at the trees. We do not see the action when we look only at the muscle movements.

There are several important things to notice here. The first is that the student is trying to learn a whole integrated movement. As he cannot "see" himself or what he is doing, he must learn what it *feels* like to do it right. This feeling is in fact a whole bodily *gestalt*. It comprises a new perception of the body's interaction with the world, in terms of balance, sight and so on. There is a particular set of perceptions and sensations that go along with a correct performance, and the student must learn to recognize these. This is learning what it feels like to do it right. This is particularly important, because feelings cannot be described, nor can they be taught. We must learn how to achieve a particular feeling, with our particular body, without knowing in advance what this feeling is. This is why the action must be learned by trial and error, following a model, and why knowledge of anatomy will not substitute.

Note also, that while the learning must be conscious, that is, we must be aware of what we are trying to do in order to attempt it, what we learn is also, in a certain sense, unconscious. We know how to serve, but we do not know how we do it. Our bodies must learn how to perform the actions, without our minds being aware of the movements on more than a surface level. It is on this point that Polanyi has some important points to make. He says that in the performance of a skill "we are attending *from* these elementary movements *to* the achievement of their joint purpose, and hence are usually unable to specify these elementary acts" (5: p. 10). In "The Logic of Tacit Inference" he says:

> If I know how to ride a bicycle or how to swim, this does not mean that I can tell how I manage to keep my balance on a bicycle, or keep afloat when swimming. I may not have the slightest idea of how I do this, or even an entirely wrong or grossly imperfect idea of it, and yet go on cycling or swimming merrily. Nor can it be said that I know how to bicycle or swim and yet do *not* know how to coordinate the complex pattern of muscular acts by which I do my cycling or swimming. I both know how to carry out these performances as a whole and also know how to carry out the elementary acts which constitute them though I cannot tell what these acts are. (6: p. 223)

It is the whole integrated action that we are aware of in the performance of these physical skills. The individual muscle movements are below the level of awareness. It is for this reason that Polanyi calls the knowledge we have when we know a physical skill "tacit knowing." This of course is not the only kind of tacit knowing, but it is an elementary and indeed important kind. There are a great many things we know how to do with our bodies (walking and talking are two of them) and in all of these the knowing is tacit.

Let us turn now to the other level of learning that is involved in games. The tennis player must not only know how to serve, and how to volley, but must know when and where to perform these actions. He must know when and where he is allowed or forbidden to do them. This involves knowledge of the rules and procedures of the game. Knowledge of this kind is at least initially explicit. We have to memorize the rules, and keep them in mind while playing. However, it is interesting to note that this is the kind of learning that can be "internalized" as moral rules are "internalized." That is, in Polanyi's terms, our knowledge of them becomes tacit rather than explicit, and we follow them in a natural and familiar way, without having to think much about them, rather than in a conscious and forced way. Playing tennis is, however, more than following rules and procedures. The aim of the game is to score points over one's opponent, and this involves strategy and tactics, movements and intelligence.

How does the player learn these? He does not learn every possible strategy in learning the game. He may learn some from his coach, and from watching the play of others. However, the good player develops his own strategies and moves, within the parameters of the rules. The rules do not specify every possible move. The player may invent his own. In this way games are to some extent creative endeavours. The player becomes creative by performing new moves and strategies by analogy to the ones he has seen performed by others. The new moves are similar in unspecifiable ways to the old moves. This skill also cannot be taught. The player must learn by himself to extend his repertoire of moves in terms of similarity criteria. This is clearly analogous to the way in which a scientist extends the field covered by a theory, and discovers new entities to be like old ones.

We should also notice that when playing the game, the player's mind is less on his strokes, but rather on the ball and on his opponent. Here we have another instance of Polanyi's "attending away from something towards something else." The player attends away from his service to the trajectory of the ball. He attends away from his own movements to the attempt to force movements on his opponent. Just as in practising service, the player knows only tacitly his own muscle movements, so in playing the game, he knows tacitly the strokes that he makes. This is perhaps less true of serving than of the other strokes, but even here, the mind is on the effect of the service, rather than on the service itself. The strokes are subsidiary to the game as a whole. One could perfectly execute strokes technically, yet be a poor player, if they are not used to further the game. The player must have in mind the game as a whole as he executes strokes, just as he must have in mind the total action as he performs muscle movements. Clearly, he is more conscious of his strokes than he is of his muscle movements, but the principle is the same.

What I have been claiming is that sports and games are acquired by demonstration, and not by teaching in the sense of being told. But there seems to be a problem with this. What is the role of the coach? Surely he teaches players. And often the best coaches are not good players. For instance some swimming coaches do not even swim. They therefore cannot function as exemplars or models for their students. They surely must be *telling* their students what to do, how to perform better, which would seem to contradict my thesis. This contradiction is only apparent, however, as I shall show.

Let us take two kinds of cases. The first is the one in which the player or athlete already knows how to perform, but he is not proficient, or there is room for improvement. Here the athlete does not need any demonstration. He has had that at an earlier level, and already knows what it feels like to perform reasonably successfully. What he needs is more proficiency. The role of the coach in this case is to tell the student when he is closer to a perfect action and when he is further from it. He then acts as a feedback, or mirror, so that the student knows what and how he is doing. The coach can also give hints. He can make suggestions such as "Raise your elbow higher" or "Follow through with your body." These do not tell the student "how to do it," rather they are ways in which he can adjust his body so that he can discover the most proficient *gestalt*. The student, in fact, is being helped to adjust his model, and to come closer to it. This does not mean that he will always be able to attain perfection in the future, but that he has a better idea of how to attain it, and thus a higher chance of succeeding.

The other kind of case is that in which one learns to do something without being shown by the teacher. For instance, I went to swimming lessons where I learned to swim, but the teacher never entered the water. But I knew that what I wanted to do was to float. I had seen objects and other people floating. I had models, exemplars, for what I wanted to do. What the instructor did was to give me clues. She demonstrated and suggested leg and arm movements, and told me when I was performing incorrectly. In this way she acted both as a partial model and as a feedback. But the actual learning to swim, to float on the surface of the water, was something I had to do myself with only demonstrations of floating to help me. Once learned, I could not say how I did it, but could do it any time I wanted to. The instructor could provide a great deal of helpful information, and act as a mirror to record my achievement, but I had to learn the crucial muscle movements myself.

Does this mean that physical instructors and coaches are unnecessary? By no means. But they are not teaching a set of facts. Rather they are leading their students through a series of movements in order to facilitate the student's learning something for himself. The student is not being spoon fed with information. He is being helped to discover for himself. And this discovery is one of how it feels to do certain things, and one of similarities, and how to extend them by analogy to other situations. The coach, by telling the student how he is doing, helps him to see how close he is coming to a perfect execution of the movement, and by making suggestions, helps him to come closer to his idea, or, one might say, to his model. This is why it is easier to improve with a coach than without one. On the level of the game as a whole, the coach helps the student to develop an ability to see how new strategies and moves are permissible, and are likely to be successful. By studying old moves, the student learns to recognize new ones as similar. Coaches thus function as facilitators in the student's own process of discovery.

What I have been claiming is that sports and games are acquired by demonstration, and by the player being "led through" the movements at both levels of the game. He learns what it is like to execute certain physical movements by copying the demonstration, and by being monitored and given feedback by his instructor. He learns strategies and tactics by watching other games, and develops new ones by analogy to those he has observed. This parallels Kuhn's account of learning in science. As we have seen, Kuhn claims that we learn science by being led through a series of classic experiments and problems, and by learning to extend what we have learned to new situations by means of recognizing similarities. Clearly, the kind of learning is the same.

Does this mean that physical educators are doing something different in their teaching from the teachers of other subjects? As I have been arguing, they are at least not doing something so very different from that done by teachers of science. I believe that much of what is called academic learning is in fact of this kind. The so-called "learning of facts" is of relatively minor importance. As a philosophy teacher, I am aware that I teach philosophy as a skill, rather than as a body of propositions to be memorized by the student. I lead my students through the work of a philosopher, explaining and criticizing. I show them how the philosophy is developed and integrated. I show them good arguments and bad arguments. Gradually, by reading, they learn how to read philosophy, and how to recognize important points. By observing, and by trying to argue themselves, they learn how to distinguish good arguments from bad ones. I do not *tell* them how to do these things. I show them, and hope that they will follow, and begin to internalize what they begin to see. This is the same general method as is followed in physical education. In fact, the more advanced the level of the student, the more like a coach a philosophy teacher becomes. This has always been the way in philosophy. A beautiful example is seen in Socrates, who taught philosophy by doing it, and in fact is still teaching philosophers by his example.

I began this paper with the question "What knowledge is required to play a game?" The answer has taken us beyond physical activities to science and philosophy. This is a significant discovery. Knowledge of physical activities is of the same kind as knowledge of those more intellectual areas. This is something we might expect. However, what is interesting is that the kind of knowledge and learning is seen more clearly in connection with physical activities. It may be that a study of learning in this area may be illuminating for the areas of science and philosophy, and many others.

REFERENCES

1. Kuhn, T.S. *The Structure of Scientific Revolutions*, Second Edition. Chicago: U of Chicago P, 1970.

2. Kuhn, T.S. "Reflections on My Critics," *Criticism and the Growth of Knowledge.* Edited by I. Lakatos and A. Musgrave. Cambridge: Cambridge UP, 1970.

3. Kuhn, T.S. "Second Thoughts on Paradigms," *The Structure of Scientific Theories.* Edited by F. Suppe. Urbana: U of Illinois P, 1974.

4. Loy, J.W., Jr. "The Nature of Sport: A Definitional Effort," *Sport and the Body: A Philosophical Symposium.* Edited by Ellen W. Gerber. Philadelphia: Lea and Febiger, 1972.

5. Polanyi, M. *The Tacit Dimension.* Garden City, New York: Doubleday & Company, 1967.

6. Polanyi, M. "The Logic of Tacit Inference," *Human and Artificial Intelligence.* Ed. Frederick J. Crosson. New York: Appleton-Century-Crofts, 1970.

7. Ziff, Paul. "A Fine Forehand," *Journal of the Philosophy of Sport*, 1 (1974) 92-109.

6. The "Ideal" Swing, the "Ideal" Body: Myths of Optimization*

Jason Holt and Laurence E. Holt

Movement is fascinating, especially when it is highly skilled, and most particularly in domains in which excellence in skilled performance is highly prized and even glorified. Golf, for better or worse, is one such domain. For the unfortunate masses—most of us—the golf swing is one of the most frustratingly complex and difficult maneuvers to master in all of sport. Wanting to improve one's golf swing, while hardly a desire common to all members of our species, is ubiquitous among those who play. The pursuit of optimal performance, making your good better and your better best, in such a game as golf is a natural and, within certain limits at least, laudable one.

So how do you begin the quest? You play, yes, and you practice, lots. Beyond that, you seek advice: lessons, books, magazines, those with best "links cred." Their credibility aside, these sources rely, often implicitly, on a theory of skilled movement, a vision of what the ideal is and how best to bring your play as close to it as possible—in a phrase, how to optimize your swing. Ironically, optimization models currently in vogue in golf culture tend not to improve performance but to hamstring it, setting objectives that are irrelevant, or even detrimental, to golf performance and its enhancement. The ideal is a false one, and it derives from a naive theory of physical skills generally and the golf swing in particular. To uncover this false ideal and correct for it, we must engage in what may be called the *philosophy of kinesiology*, where kinesiology is the study of movement, and philosophy informs, as is the case with any discipline, its conceptual foundations.

---

* From Wible (ed.), *Golf and Philosophy* (Lexington, KY: UP of Kentucky, 2010), pp. 209-20.

Here we will focus on two not only incorrect but self-defeating applications of the concept of optimization to golf performance: the averaging model of the golf swing and the athlete model of the golfer, both of which are prevalent in golf culture despite a lack of sound support for either and a wealth of evidence against them. The averaging model presupposes, roughly, that the optimum swing to strive for can be found by taking a mean score of mathematical models of the swing characteristics among elite golfers, along with the corresponding goal of shaping all golfers' swings to that supposed ideal. The athlete model presupposes that, all else being equal, the better the athlete is, the better the golfer will be, and so prescribes various kinds of cross-training and general fitness conditioning intended to maximize the athleticism of the golfer. Underlying the simplicity of teaching and analyzing the golf swing in terms of a single ideal, not to mention the presumed need to legitimize golf as a real sport by athleticizing its competitors, is what appears to be an aesthetic bias against quirky swings and unathletic players, regardless of how successful either is even at the most elite levels of competition.

Against the averaging model we will argue for a multiple realizability view: that there is no such thing as *the* perfect swing for everyone, and different techniques will be suitable for different people largely on the basis of particular body characteristics (including neuromusculature). Against the athlete model we will argue that the moderate physical demands of golf make a general athleticism in golf of negligible if any benefit, whereas certain cross-training regimens can interfere with much more important factors and so detract from, rather than enhance, golf performance. We will diagnose the problem as arising from certain aesthetic biases, and then show how our perspective applies more broadly by examining the question of whether golf is really a sport.

Homogenized Technique

We all have some understanding of what a great golf swing is or at any rate what it looks like. We know it when we see it, however difficult if not impossible it might seem for us to achieve, and however unaware we are of the very complex physiological mechanisms involved. We know that the majority of professionals approximate this ideal swing to varying degrees, and the presumption is that those who are the better players, those who have better swings, are the ones who most closely approximate if not outright instantiate the elusive ideal: the fixed head position, the slightly inside-the-line backswing that stops parallel to the ground at the top and in line with the target, the inside-out path of the clubhead during acceleration, the path of the clubhead in direct line with the target toward the end of the downswing, the smooth follow-through dissipating all unused kinetic energy, all in perfect tempo. We think we know, and observations of excellent players seem to confirm this. But beyond conveniently unschooled and, in both senses, partial observation, which tends to help us ignore or explain away recalcitrant evidence, what is the justification for this alleged knowledge of this alleged ideal?

Biomechanics is the subdiscipline of kinesiology that uses physics to analyze and explain human movement. One of the key objectives of this and all branches of science is to formulate general principles that apply universally. This type of thinking continues to be the objective of many biomechanists when it comes to human physical expression in the panoply of many and varied sports. From this perspective there should be an optimal model for accomplishing the objective of each type of movement. A simple way to start the process is to observe and measure one or two examples of golfers who are agreed to have the best swing (the classic swing of, say, Ben Hogan or Trevor Immelman). Another way is to scientifically analyze a large number of top performers, and then average their scores on selected movements, angles, positions, speeds, and so on, and create an optimization model for everyone to follow.

As persuasive as many find such an averaging model to be when applied to golf, the unquestioned assumption of a single ideal swing, the perfect swing, is unwarranted. First of all, it is easy to underestimate the extent to which elite players depart, and with successful results, from the ideal, and these departures are not always easy to spot, and sometimes they cannot be spotted with the unaided eye or even with an unschooled eye with all the advantages of the latest slow-motion digital video technology. Elite players often depart significantly from the ideal, and their success level does not correlate with the extent that such departures are minimized. Take the following artificial and abstract but illustrative example. Suppose that in performing some component of the golf swing, tour players achieve some angle of body parts between ten and twenty degrees. This does not mean that there is an ideal angle of fifteen degrees that players should aim for. Reasoning that such a statistical average, even among the best players, is the ideal for everyone, is simply fallacious. In this case, perhaps two very different but equally viable techniques are involved, perhaps warranted by two very different types of bodies. Given the varieties of elite players' swings and all-too-apparent variations in their body characteristics (unlike those in many other sports, in which elite play often mandates specific body types), we should expect to find greater variety than a single ideal would comfortably admit.

And we do. It turns out that the essential elements of a great golf swing are in fact rather minimal, though by no means easy to achieve reliably. Variations among swings are due not only to huge variances in body tissues, but also to the fact that many different types of actual ball contacts can result in the ball arriving at the desired target. Straight shots, fades, and draws of different paths from the same lie can all result in an excellent shot. The requirements are that all must be struck solidly, near the sweet spot, with the appropriate clubhead speed and contact angle of the face necessary for each type of shot. Slight variations in club path and clubface angle can, when applied correctly, be part of a repeatable and successful golf swing.

It is inescapable that so many of the world's greatest players on the professional tours do not have ideal golf swings. The great Bobby Jones had a sweeping backswing that at its top crossed far beyond parallel and past the intended line of aim. Most experts characterize this swing as old-fashioned, useful only because of the era of play and the equipment then available. But there is every reason to believe that modern clubs and balls would only enhance the effectiveness of Jones's swing, which would be helpful in any case to those with limited thoracic flexibility or lower back pain, for it minimizes torque of the thoracic-pelvic interaction. Walter Hagen was similarly successful with a wide stance coupled with a short, fast swing, a completely different approach from Jones's, and yet a very effective one. Ben Hogan's classic swing can be contrasted with Byron Nelson's shorter, more abbreviated swing with the noticeable downward-forward initiation of the striking movement. Both differ greatly from the Miller Barber swing, an upright, unusual series of movements and positions. The list of "deviant" swings would also have to include Doug Sanders, Lee Trevino, Craig Stadler, Jim Furyk, Jim Thorpe, Kenny Perry, Tom Lehman, Duffy Waldorf, and many others. The same type of thing has occurred on the women's tour, where many variations in rhythm, positions, and patterns can be observed. Of particular interest is the fact that these swings are unique to each golfer, and many who have tried to adopt the "ideal" swing have had difficulties. Successful golfers have learned or fallen into a pattern of movement that works for their anatomies, kinesiological predispositions, and neuromuscular systems.[1] There are very few cases of elite golfers completely altering their already successful swings and equaling or surpassing their previous achievements. The hoopla surrounding Tiger Woods's allegedly new swing is particularly overblown. The alterations might feel like major changes to Woods himself, but analysis reveals that his full swing is basically the same as it was a decade ago.

The notion that there is more than one way to perform a certain type of action (more than one way to skin a cat) is a familiar one. The philosophical term for this, one that originated in cognitive science and the philosophy of mind, is *multiple realizability.*[2] To say that the optimal golf swing is multiply realizable means that there is no one physical manifestation, no single type of swing, that constitutes the optimum across the board. A Hogan-style swing might be optimal for Hogan himself but be an inferior option for Jones, who lacked Hogan's trunk flexibility, and for whom a Jones-style swing is far more suitable. The optimum, if it makes sense to speak of one at all, is non-transferable. The quirky, even bizarre variations among elite swings, as we mentioned, and the appreciable success of these players, given how far they stray from the alleged ideal, are perhaps all the evidence we need to discard the ideal as false. Of course, most swings are ineffective, so it is not the case that anything goes; but all swings that meet the speed, path, and clubface requirements for a given shot can be counted as being on equal footing, regardless of the movement patterns producing them. The important thing for golfers is to discover a swing that works for them given their particular body characteristics.

The Athleticized Golfer

Golf is no different from many sports that have seen a strikingly radical and potentially disturbing increase, almost to the point of fanaticism at professional and other elite levels, of extreme cross-training and general fitness conditioning that have little if anything to do with performance enhancement in the specific sport and sometimes actually compromise performance. In the best-case scenario one's performance is relatively unaffected, whereas in other cases one might well enhance some capacities at the expense of others that are crucial, if not more so, to excellent performance in the sport. At worst, such conditioning, either inappropriate in itself or untowardly extreme, can directly cause or predispose body tissues to unnecessary injuries, whether unfortunate and temporary or distressingly chronic.

A number of fallacious inferences, betraying a sometimes merely superficial and sometimes hopelessly flawed understanding of the body and how to improve its skilled performance, are lurking in the background. One such fallacious inference is to reason that a certain outcome (say, driving distance) will be improved by increasing a certain basic physical capacity (say, strength), even though the athlete may already have an optimal level for that particular skill, that is, a level beyond which performance will not be further enhanced by increasing the capacity. Another fallacy is reasoning that other desirable capacities (say, flexibility) or outcomes (say, accuracy) will remain unaffected if not enhanced by increasing other capacities in certain ways (say, strength by lifting heavy weights). Yet another fallacy is to reason that an increase in one's general fitness will yield better performance in an activity like golf. One more fallacy can be captured by the slogan "More is better": if some conditioning is good, then more frequent, longer, and more demanding conditioning is presumably better, and the more demanding the better, even though there is clearly a point of diminishing returns beyond which tissues, worked harder and harder still, eventually break down.

The physical requirements necessary to play golf at a very high level are modest indeed. A player has to be able to walk a few miles at a slow to moderate pace, stop to strike the ball, and wait for others to do the same. The most vigorous part of any round is ball striking (propulsive phase, the downswing), which takes about half a second each time. For elite players this means about thirty-six strokes and eighteen seconds of dynamic movement per round. Strokes like putting and chipping require precision and very little energy. Each round is also played without the burden of carrying one's clubs, since this is not mandated by the rules. Elite players and wealthy amateurs have caddies who not only carry the clubs, bag, umbrellas, and other paraphernalia, but also keep the players covered when it rains and clean the equipment as needed. The rank and file often uses either golf carts, which carry both the players and their equipment, or power or push caddies, which eliminate the need to carry the clubs and continually pick up the bag and put it down for each shot.

To function effectively, golfers need to maintain a walking regimen, preferably on mixed terrain to mimic most traditional courses, and swing golf clubs enough to maintain the dynamic flexibility of their musculoskeletal systems. Running, cycling, or other forms of aerobic training are not necessary, and excessive amounts might be detrimental, as they can result in diminished flexibility, particularly in the hip and knee joints, which can alter the full golf swing by placing tension on the shortened muscles earlier in the movement pattern, thereby altering the swing mechanics. Another problem associated with running (though not cycling) is the possibility of injuring the lower limbs as a result of excessive accumulative forces being absorbed during each landing. An interesting interaction can occur when one puts together a heavy weight-training program with a running program, in that the added upper-body muscle bulk compounds the loading problem at foot contact and may lead to ankle, knee, or hip joint injuries or, in the case of Tiger Woods, stress fractures in the tibia.

The world's most famous athlete, who has taken the "cult of conditioning" to extremes, might be the best example of why concentrating on this aspect of preparation for golf is unnecessary.[3] Tiger Woods was a superb golfer at age twenty, capable of taking on and beating the best players in the world. At six-foot-two and 160 pounds, he could generate 120-mile-per-hour clubhead speeds and hit drives of great length, and he had the other subtle golf skills that make for great play. He won his first Masters title by twelve strokes, and he did it with a basically lean (ectomorphic) and relatively unconditioned body. He continued to win at an astounding rate, even as he experimented with stroke adjustments, changed caddies, and then embarked on his extensive nonspecific exercise program. The reason for his successes lies in his nervous system; he has the right neuromuscular circuitry to run great golf programs, and he can call them up when needed. But over the past few years, although Tiger's fitness scores have been high, he has not produced his "A" game as often as he did in the past; his wins are often accomplished by struggling against various opponents, and his margins of victory have been narrow. Arguably, rather than improving Tiger's game, excessive concentration on fitness and conditioning has actually detracted from it, even though he has continued to win.[4] Woods missed half the 2008 season owing to injuries suffered preparing for and exacerbated during the U.S. Open, as he had to recover from anterior cruciate ligament (ACL) surgery on his knee and heal his stress fractures. There is no plausible way to attribute these injuries to playing golf.

The further benefits that are touted to accrue from adding a vigorous fitness and conditioning program to one's preparation did not seem to be realized when Woods met Darren Clarke for the finals in match play a few years ago (before any fitness efforts by Clarke). Instead of the unconditioned Clarke's gradually becoming less effective as the thirty-six-hole match progressed, and Woods's finely tuned athletic body keeping up the pace and wearing down his opponent, Clarke went on to win the match rather easily. Of course, the reason is that Clarke hit better shots on that day, and that is what counts. On any given day, heavyset tour players like John Daly, Tim Herron, Jason Gore, and Rocco Mediate, or lighter, thinner players like Charles Howell, Jeff Sluman, and Sean O'Hair, can outplay Woods and the rest of the field. Even that player whom Woods is chasing, Jack Nicklaus, won most of his titles with what may be labeled by fitness gurus as a less-than-athletic physique. No matter: his skills, physical and mental, were unmatched during his competitive period. Nicklaus winning the Masters at age forty-six and Tom Watson missing winning the Open in his *sixtieth* year by *one putt* illustrate this point to a tee. The capacity to play top-level golf thus seems to be related more to having the high level of skills needed to stroke the ball effectively, a capacity to execute these skills under pressure, and the ability to deal with interferences (bad weather, play stoppages, and the like) that are par for the course in the beautiful game of golf.

Aesthetic Biases

There is nothing wrong with aesthetic preferences, in liking some things more than others because they are more beautiful, elegant, graceful, and so on. Indeed, it is hard to imagine how we could even begin to go about uprooting aesthetic preferences from our thinking, so interwoven are they with our choices, motives, judgments, and values. There is nothing wrong with making aesthetic judgments about a wide variety of things. In matters of purely personal taste, for instance, it seems that anything goes; you find something lovely and I do not: *chacun à son goût*, to each his own. In other domains, however, there seem to be more objective standards for what counts as exhibiting some aesthetic property. In such aesthetic sports as figure skating, diving, and gymnastics there are judicable facts of the matter about, for example, whether athletes maintain or break form and so achieve or fail to achieve the requisite aesthetic standard. In fact, the meeting of such standards is an integral part of the scoring of such events.

Even in purposive sports, where the scoring is in no way based on or affected by aesthetic achievements, praising graceful or stylish performance is often appropriate and perhaps even unavoidable. How else did Ernie Els earn the nickname "The Big Easy" but with a swing that few would hesitate to call beautiful? Generally speaking, great players in purposive sports often exhibit aesthetic properties like grace, elegance, and style, and nothing is amiss in our praising them for it. Something is amiss, however, when we blame a successful player in a sport like golf, even subtly by innuendo or lightheartedly by joke, for failing to perform with the sort of grace or style exhibited by other players, and this is not just because such performative beauty is supererogatory, above and beyond the call of duty. Such criticism is also amiss because it smuggles in the questionable concept of the ideal swing. Put the other way round, part of the implicit justification for and lingering appeal of the false ideal of the perfect swing appears to be a latent, unnecessary, potentially misleading, and decidedly aesthetic bias. Without question, the averaging model provides an attractive simplicity when it comes to commentary, criticism, and teaching of the golf swing. But this does not warrant negative judgments about the quirky or "ugly" swings of a Trevino or Furyk. We should at least bracket our traditionally minded aesthetic judgments about such departures from the norm of the alleged ideal so that these judgments do not infect truly germane discussion. (Sometimes aesthetic discussions are relevant, sometimes not.) Or better still, we should guide our aesthetic sensibilities toward a more pragmatic, pluralistic outlook, so as to be able to recognize the functional beauty in the quirky and the classic swings alike.

There seems to be a similar though differently motivated aesthetic bias underlying the athlete model of the golfer, and here the bias's aesthetic nature might be more readily apparent. Athletic-looking bodies are attractive, aesthetically pleasing. Most of us want such bodies, and many of us feel a need to see athletes not only *be* athletic but also *look* athletic. We tend, *à la* the ancient Greeks, to associate the physical excellence we admire in athletes with the physical beauty we want them to have, a sort of virtue by association. From this viewpoint, the phenomenon of a Babe Ruth in baseball or a John Daly in golf is difficult to take. The motivation for this aesthetic bias in golf is plausibly and in part a perceived need, from the perspective of players who want to be regarded as genuine athletes or fans or others who want them to be so regarded, to cement the status of the game as a legitimate, bona fide, fully fledged sport. The odd presumption seems to be that the more closely golfers resemble athletes in other sports (the classically athletic bodies prevalent in decathlon and gymnastics, defensive backs in football, and the lighter weight classes in boxing), the more we will be drawn toward admitting golf as a real sport.

Other Sports

Tendencies toward homogenized technique, undue athleticization, and aesthetic biases are often also found in other sports. Wide application of our multiple-realizability and activity-specific perspective on physical skill is more significant than its narrower if still important application to the domain of golf alone. Thus, to move from what we have said about golf and generalize to other sporting domains, it will be useful to examine briefly the essential nature of sport.

By drawing on and modifying various definitions of sport that already exist in the philosophy of sport literature, we may define sports, provisionally, as *competitive games of inclusively gross physical skill*.[5] Qualifying sports as competitive games distinguishes them from activities, even vigorous physical activities, that intuitively do not count as sport by virtue of being non-competitive; outdoor team-building activities, for instance, and so-called cooperative games are not sports. Sports are games in that they consist in what Bernard Suits describes as "the voluntary attempt to overcome unnecessary obstacles," these obstacles, like the games themselves, being defined by the rules.[6] We include the requirement that sports must involve not only physical skill but, crucially, gross physical skill to distinguish them from contests that require merely fine motor skills, that is, those that do not involve the movement or control of the entire body. Games of pickup sticks and guitar duels are not sports, because although they do require physical skills, they involve not gross motor skills but fine motor skills. Sports, by contrast, necessarily involve skilled movement or control of the entire body.[7]

Although it differs from many other sports in important ways, golf meets such a definition of sport, since it is a competitive game of inclusively gross physical skill, the skill required involving the movement and control of the entire body to participate in the activity. Those who would resist classifying golf as a sport no doubt at least implicitly think that all sports require, as many indeed do, great degrees of bodily strength, speed, or endurance. Though such basic physical capacities, in isolation or in combination, are required for many sports, this frequency should not mislead one into thinking that it is a necessary condition for sport that a game place extreme physical demands on those who play it. Counterexamples abound, including bowling, billiards, croquet, darts, shooting competitions of all types, archery—and golf. With the exception of a few moments of sprinting, baseball and softball players also have few physical demands placed on them (pitchers and catchers excepted); the same is true of cricket. Despite the selective importance of strength, speed, and endurance in many sports, what counts most of all in classifying a game like golf as a sport is the presence or absence of gross physical skill.

Because golf and certain other activities count as low-demand sports, we cannot generalize from the mild physical demands of golf to the physical requirements of high-demand sports. We can, however, generalize from the multiple realizability of the golf swing to the nature of skills in other sports, especially those that involve very complex movements like the golf swing. We can also make the reasonably confident claim that sport-specific conditioning should always take priority over general conditioning or cross-training when the goal is improved performance in that particular sport and not, among other possible goals, overall fitness or athleticism. Even in the latter case, it should be noted, extreme training is rarely if ever warranted—and excessive training, never.

As the physical demands in a sporting activity diminish, the potential for variations in bodies increases, as does the opportunity for different patterns of movement. Interestingly, more variations of movement patterns exist when striking or throwing light objects, and less when throwing heavier objects. The idea of multiple realizability, of the possibility for success in a sport resulting from diverse approaches to technique, is based on obvious differences that have evolved in the form and function of individuals within our species. Where a sport both involves the performance of a required set of skills and is judged on its aesthetic qualities, multiple realizability is possible, although judging attitudes often place constraints on the diversity of patterns that will be acceptable, as is true in figure skating, gymnastics, diving, and dance.

A philosophy of skilled human movement must be sensitive to the various ways in which skills can be performed, what the performance of those skills actually requires, and variations among the bodies performing those skills. Pursuing optimal performance must not gloss over these varieties, from body characteristics to skills types and means of execution. At the same time, attempts to optimize performance should not be infected by overtraining or inappropriate cross-training or general fitness conditioning, which will at best leave performance unaffected and at worst be extremely counterproductive. False theories of skilled movement, together with the fallacies that subtend them, must be abandoned on pain of undermining the very goal at which they aim. Achieving the optimum, in golf as in life, requires an awareness of what really matters, hand in glove with a sensitivity to differences among people and ways of getting things done.

NOTES

Special thanks to Andy Wible for patient encouragement and helpful suggestions. Thanks also to two anonymous reviewers for useful questions.

1. An anonymous reviewer has suggested the possibility that elite players with unorthodox swings have managed to develop compensatory skills for departing from fundamentals, whereas this would not be practical for golf instructors teaching players who lack the time required to develop such mechanisms. We, however, are offering an alternative account of what the fundamentals are. And as for practicality, approximately 80 percent of the population lacks sufficient thoracic flexibility for anything like the ideal backswing.

2. For an earlier application of the concept of multiple realizability to golf, see Laurence E. Holt, *An Experimenter's Guide to the Full Golf Swing* (Lantz, NS: Aljalar, 2004), 9-11.

3. Lorne Rubenstein, "Are Tiger's Injuries Self-Inflicted?" *Globe and Mail*, July 12, 2008, S5.

4. Note the irony of the apparent decrease in clubhead velocity generated by tour players, including Tiger Woods, despite recent significant strength gains. For discussion of Dick Rugge's study, see Thomas Maier, "Golf Players Stronger, but Swing Speeds Down?" *Newsday*, June 20, 2009.

5. Elements of this formula may be found in John W. Loy, Jr., "The Nature of Sport: A Definitional Effort"; Bernard Suits, "Tricky Triad: Games, Play, and Sport"; and Klaus V. Meier, "Triad Trickery: Playing With Sports and Games," all in *Philosophy of Sport: Critical Readings, Crucial Issues*, ed. M. Andrew Holowchak (Upper Saddle River, NJ: Prentice-Hall, 2002), 20, 30, and 40, respectively.

6. Bernard Suits, *The Grasshopper: Games, Life and Utopia* (1978; rept., Peterborough, ON: Broadview, 2005), 55.

7. An anonymous reviewer has suggested that the game Twister might be a counterexample to our definition of sport, since intuitively Twister is not a sport, and yet it seems to meet our conditions for sport (as a game involving gross physical skill). Twister involves positioning of the body and requires some flexibility, but gross physical skill implies dynamic motion to achieve a specific outcome, not merely holding a contorted position. Likewise, in Twister chance figures too largely in the determination of outcomes—it is more a game of chance involving skill than a game of skill per se. Sports, by contrast, are games *of* gross physical skill, in which chance may figure not too prominently. The *inclusively* in our definition is meant to allow other outcome determiners, such as strategy and fine motor skills, so long as these do not unseat gross physical skill from its privileged position.

QUESTIONS

1. Do you agree with Steel that learning physical skills is very much like learning scientific skills or philosophical reasoning? What disanalogies suggest themselves?

2. How important is proprioception (the internal perception of one's own body position) to Steel's account?

3. How, if at all, does Steel's notion of a movement exemplar relate to what Holt and Holt call an optimization model? What are the implications?

4. Do certain inferences Holt and Holt identify as fallacious seem compelling to you? What implicit assumptions are being made?

5. Are there examples of undue athleticization in other sports? Is there an aesthetic bias also at work, or is aesthetic preference less problematic in such cases?

6. If golf is not a sport, what other alleged sports should we dismiss on similar grounds? Are there hard cases that cannot be decided either way?

FURTHER READING

Fodor, Jerry A. (1974): "Special Sciences (Or: The Disunity of Science as a Working Hypothesis)," *Synthese* 28, pp. 97-115.

Kuhn, Thomas S. (1970): *The Structure of Scientific Revolutions* (2nd edition) (Chicago: U of Chicago P).

Polanyi, Michael (1967): *The Tacit Dimension* (Garden City, NY: Doubleday).

Ross, Saul (1998): "Epistemology, Intentional Action, and Physical Education," in *Philosophy of Sport and Physical Activity*, ed. Pasquale J. Galasso (Toronto: Canadian Scholars' P), pp. 131-40.

Twietmeyer, Gregg (2012): "What is Kinesiology? Historical and Philosophical Insights," *Quest* 64 (1), pp. 4-23.

Yeadon, M.R. (2005): "What Are the Limitations of Experimental and Theoretical Approaches in Sports Biomechanics?" in *Philosophy and the Sciences of Exercise, Health and Sport: Critical Perspectives on Research Methods*, ed. Mike McNamee (New York: Routledge), pp. 133-43.

FURTHER INQUIRY

One of the challenges for epistemology is how to fit knowing how into the overall scheme of things, which would involve specifying the relationship between it and knowing that. The two seem to overlap in the cases of procedures and recipes, in that knowing a procedure or recipe implies both an ability to do something and awareness, on some level, of the steps involved. Perhaps one of the two types is more basic, and may be used in providing a reductive theory of the other type: perhaps knowing how involves the *system* knowing that even if the *subject* fails to. The task of developing a more robust philosophy of kinesiology also seems potentially fruitful, whether on a modest scale, for instance discovering the scope of the multiple realizability model across various domains (novel skill techniques), or on the grander scale of specifying what exactly kinesiology is. With such a wide swath of subdisciplines, from the natural and applied sciences to the arts and humanities—from physiology to philosophy, really—kinesiology provides the ultimate testing ground for any theory of interdisciplinarity.

Exploring Physicality

If sports are athletic games and, as such, require the demonstration of physical prowess in the determination of outcomes (i.e., who wins), and if such physical skill is to be understood as a kind of know-how, a species of knowledge, several questions arise. What, for instance, are the boundaries of those skills which, when sufficiently physical in the right way, make a contest a sport? What does it mean for an intelligence, a mind, a person, to be, at least in some respects, *embodied*—and what are the implications of that embodiment? Each of these questions will be addressed in some form in this section.

At the outer limits of the domains of physical skill we might consider including in the domain of sports, certain kinds of computer games may seem plausible. For Dennis Hemphill these include those computer games requiring not only physical skill, which most do, but also those involving sport or sport-like skill and intelligence: sport simulations in particular. Debate about this particular topic cannot help but be divisive, a clash of subcultures. Still, if sports are games of physical skill, it is not clear how, if we are so motivated, to deny certain videogames sport status unless there lurk as-yet unspecified refinements in our concept of sport.

Modern philosophy of mind began with Descartes's long-since dominant view of mind and body as distinct substances: spiritual substance, essentially mental, and material substance, essentially spatial. These interact in sense perception (matter affecting mind) and intentional action (mind affecting matter). Despite the intuitive appeal and cultural saturation of this dichotomy, many philosophers have proposed alternative views, most attempting to unify mind and body somehow. Some thinkers would identify the mind with certain states or functions of the brain, whereas others would emphasize the character of a subject's embodied experience and the various factors shaping it. In the latter vein, Iris Marion Young, using the concept of "throwing like a girl" to illustrate, explores how gender influences one's experience and underlying attitudes of oneself and one's body as situated in space among various skilled movement possibilities.

7. CYBERSPORT[*]

DENNIS HEMPHILL

Computers are a prominent feature of the (post)modern landscape. Whether for commercial, educational, or entertainment purposes, cybernetic technologies are being designed to augment human capacities and reproduce biological, mechanical, social, and other environments in electronic form. Computer-generated models or simulations are increasingly finding their way into areas such as building design and safety, air-flight training and controlling, medical training and surgery, transport systems, and ergonomics, as well as tourism and education. Under the label of "entertainment," video arcades and home computers now offer up a range of electronically generated simulations of activities such as auto racing, golf, football, skiing, boxing, and basketball. This article explores the possibility that computer-game simulations of this type can be considered sport.[1]

Against Computer Games

There are several reasons, philosophical, sociological, and conventional, to be skeptical about the possibility of regarding computer games as sport. Many descriptions of cybernetic activities suggest that simulated activities are "virtual," not "real." The word "virtual" has connotations of something being real in effect, or real for all practical purposes, but not real in substance. Being virtual suggests something artificial or contrived. Stone refers to the body in cyberspace as "something close to a metaphor" (28: p. 104),[2] and Gibson refers to communities in cyberspace as a "consensual hallucination" (cited in 28: p. 94). For all the fascinating possibilities of virtual reality, Heim claims that it also has a dark side:

---

[*]   Dennis Hemphill, "Cybersport," *Journal of the Philosophy of Sport* 32 (2005), pp. 195-207.

At the computer interface, the spirit migrates from the body to a world of total representation. Information and images float through the Platonic mind without a grounding in bodily experience. You can lose your humanity at the throw of the dice. (11: p. 101)

Heim equates virtual reality with the world of imagination, but cautions that we still need to have some type of bodily groundedness, some reality check occasionally so that the imaginary doesn't become the real (11: pp. 136-137).

Creators or denizens of these virtual worlds are often represented in films and novels as social misfits, voyeurs, and nerds or as criminal hackers, fringe dwellers, outriders, and the like. Adults might be uncomfortable with children and adolescents running free in these "imaginary," "fantasy," and sometimes dystopian worlds, especially when they seem so adept at negotiating their way in and around them. This, combined with the apparent link to the rise in childhood obesity, often lead to computer gaming and television viewing being discouraged. Although the presence of a link to social and physical fitness is not essential for understanding the nature of computer games, its absence, I suspect, adds to their dubious reputation.

There are other social factors at work shaping what is thought to be "real" sport. For example, athletes distinguish themselves from others, including other athletes, in terms of their particular sporting vocabularies and training regimens. It is no secret that sport is heavily coded as a masculine activity, and English (6) argues that the most popular and lucrative sports (e.g., football) feature height, weight, strength, and speed, giving most men, statistically speaking, certain advantages over most women. Masculinity of this type can operate to define "real" sport as sport that involves the most face-to-face aggression, power, and body contact. This could be cause to bully women and nonathletic males, devalue women's (version of "male") sports, or overlook the athleticism of fine-motor-skill sports (e.g., archery) or those coded "aesthetic" (e.g., synchronized swimming).[3]

When it comes to day-to-day descriptions of computer games, there often occurs a demarcation between virtual activity and sport. Many of the simpler arcade or home-computer football, basketball, and auto-racing programs are referred to as "games," not sports. An advertisement for Smart Golf simulators refers to the system as as "close to the real thing as possible" (25). Bale refers to another golf simulator called Caddy Shack as a "simulacrum of the world of sport" (2: p. 172). In a chapter titled "Trash Sport," Bale refers disparagingly to these electrosports, which in his words are characterized by the "continued artificialization and immurement of human movement culture" (2: pp. 180-81).[4]

Descriptions such as these suggest that there is still something about simulated golf or other such activities that discount them from the realm of sport.

Games, per se, can be thought of as less than the real thing in several other ways. For example, when the claim is made that, say, football is "more than a game," it is thought that the stakes are higher, as is the case when sport is considered a "big business," a "civic religion," or a collective expression of national identity. Alternatively, when the exhortation "it's only a game" is made during a sporting activity, it is often used as a form of consolation for someone who might be overly disappointed with a loss or as a reprimand to someone who is perhaps taking the game "too seriously." In both cases, however, "game" has the status that it does in contrast to something that is presumably more serious.

The effect of labeling "game" in this manner is not inexplicable. Sport and especially games are very often linked to play, and some of the language in play theory, for example, by Huizinga (13) and Schmitz (24), associates play with "unreality," "nonseriousness," or "suspension of reality." Although these authors go some way to discuss play as a separate reality or new order and fervently defend its "extraordinary" seriousness and value, the need to defend play at all betrays its subordinate social status. Moreover, games and play are often associated with childhood, a relatively protected stage (at least in well-off Western capitalist states) before full-fledged adulthood. Linked to this view are sociological accounts that place play, game, and sport on a continuum, where the playful freedom of childhood gradually becomes restrained, structured, and codified as games and, when fully institutionalized, becomes sport.

From these philosophical, sociological, and conventional accounts, computer games appear to come up short as instances of sport. That is, tagging computer games as "virtual" (i.e., unreal, artificial), disembodied, unhealthy, and even "unmanly" may feed skepticism about their status as sport and fuel any condemnation we might want to level against them. As pervasive and convincing as these accounts may be, however, they need not go unchallenged. It may be the case that certain philosophical and sociological accounts are limited and, as such, simply prop up pernicious social stereotypes that can limit our ability to consider computer games otherwise.

Games and Sport

A philosophical case can be mounted to support the claim that certain forms of computer games can be considered sport. The first step requires a consideration of physicality and the nature of sport. When compared with the virtual, the real is often thought of as something more concrete, substantial, or tangible. This usually means what is experienced in a more bodily, immediate, and face-to-face way.[5] The priority accorded to the bodily and the physical in distinguishing sport from games and other activities is prominent in the sport-philosophy literature. Osterhoudt (20) has done some of my work here when he cites the number of philosophers who subscribe to the idea that sport's physicality distinguishes it from games. Santayana, Slusher, Suits, Fogelin, Weiss, Vanderzwaag, Roochnik, and Meier, to name a few, are cited as proponents of the view that physical prowess is an essential characteristic of sport.

The emphasis on physicality is certainly not to suggest that mental or intellectual components are lacking. Based on Paddick's view (cited in 20) that the physical and the intellectual are everywhere admixed in human experience, that the degree of each in any human activity is indeterminate, and that notions of "inherent" physicality depreciate the rich intellectual content of sport, Osterhoudt (20) claims that "physicality" is one of the internal goods of sport. However, what distinguishes sport from games or other activities on the Paddick/Osterhoudt account is not inherent physicality but the rather peculiar way that bodily movements are valued. That is, in contrast to activities where the means selected are often the most expedient in achieving the given ends, bodily movements in sport have intrinsic value because sports employ other than the most expedient means to achieve their given ends.

This prominent view about the nature of sport finds its most formal expression in Suits's (26; 27) and Meier's (17; 18) discussions of games and sport. For Suits, to play a game is the attempt to

> achieve a specific state of affairs (*pre-lusory goal*), using only means permitted by the rules (*lusory means*), where the rules prohibit use of more efficient in favor of less efficient means (*constitutive rules*), and where such rules are accepted just because they make possible such activity (*lusory attitude*). (27: p. 11)

The pithy version of this definition is as follows: Games are the voluntary attempt to overcome unnecessary or gratuitous obstacles.

On this account, all sports are games but not all games are sport. There are certain other features that distinguish sports from games. For Suits (27: p. 12), "all sports appear to be games of skill rather than games of chance," and, further, the skill is physical. Despite their other disagreements, including the partial recantation by Suits (27) that some sports may not be games and Meier's (18) repudiation of his recantation, both Suits and Meier still maintain that physical skill or prowess is an essential criterion for distinguishing sport from games. If we take chess as an example, Suits argues that

It is not difficult to draw a line between games which require physical skill and games which do not. It is not necessary first to decide very grave metaphysical issues, such as the relation between mind and body. It is a plain fact that how chess pieces are moved has nothing whatever to do with manual dexterity or any other bodily skill. (27: p. 12)

On this account, chess is clearly a game but not a sport.

As Suits, Meier, and others have argued, manual dexterity or physical skill is incidental to determining the outcome of chess. To quote Meier's summary of this view,

In chess, bridge, and numerous other games, manual dexterity or physical skill has no influence whatsoever on the outcome. Indeed these games can be played without any pertinent motor movements demanded of the participants. Assistants or even machines can move the pieces or display the cards; verbal instructions or commands may suffice and, in fact, chess can be played by mail. (18: p. 25)

In other words, although the movement of chess pieces is circumscribed by the rules, the physical dexterity of that movement is neither relevant to understanding the nature of the game nor valued as a game-relevant skill.

Meier wants to be clear about this physical-prowess dimension. That is, it is part of a project to "locate the precise boundaries of sport, to ferret out its central structure and essential core, and to close accurately the conceptual limits of the term" (17: p. 82). This he does on one occasion by pointing out the inadequacies of many sociological definitions of sport. Many standard sociological accounts (e.g., the play-game-sport continuum), wherein sport is considered an institutionalized game, identify gross motor activity and proficiency, as well as codification and professionalism, as essential properties of sport. Nonetheless, although notions about gross motor skills, proficiency, and institutionalization can give us some insight into the nature of some sports, how well (or poorly) they can be played, and their degree of social organization, they certainly do not reveal the common core of sport as such (17; 18). To sum up Meier's analysis,

It may be asserted that all sports are games ... the outcome of which is necessarily and significantly determined by the demonstration and exercising of physical skills or prowess. Further, it is argued that a high level of athletic skill or excellence, despite importance to the level of performance achieved, is not necessary for participants to engage in sport. Finally, any postulated distinction between gross and fine motor activities, as a criterion for distinguishing sports from games, is rejected as arbitrary, unnecessary, and counter-productive. (17: p. 85)

In other words, if we try to distinguish sport from games on the basis suggested by the prominent sociological accounts of play, game, and sport, there is the problem of "temporal and quantitative sufficiency" (18: p. 26). That is, the mind boggles when considering where you draw the line between a gross and fine motor skill or how much institutionalization (including longevity) is enough that play becomes game and game becomes sport.[6]

On the basis of the philosophically standard account of how physical prowess is the key feature distinguishing sport from games, there are some compelling reasons to consider certain types of computer games (e.g., sport simulations) sport. What will need to be demonstrated is how the skill involved in these computer games can be thought of as sufficiently physical to have them qualify as instances of sport. In other words, a case will need to be made that computer games of this type are not virtual or simply imaginary but embodied, skilled sport practices.

Computer Games as Sport

As I have shown, computer games as virtual reality tend to be regarded as something less than sport for a variety of reasons. It might be more useful and interesting, however, to describe virtual reality as alternative reality[7] and cybernetic simulations of sports as different but nonetheless real. "Cybersport" is the term I will use to refer to these alternative sport realities, that is, to electronically extended athletes in digitally represented sporting worlds.

In order to understand electronically extended action, it is first necessary to examine the technological interface to these computer-generated worlds. An interface in this case means the type and quality of interaction between a human user and a computer. Important to the understanding of the human-computer interface, and how it might be understood in a sporting sense, are the notions of "immersion" and "interactivity." Different computer-gaming systems offer varying degrees of one or both features.

One important distinction needs to be made, and that is between augmented- and virtual-reality computer programs. On the spectrum between virtual reality and the so-called real world, augmented reality is thought to be closer to the latter

(3). The basic idea of augmented reality is "to superimpose graphics, audio and other sense enhancements over a real-world environment in real-time" (3). This it does in order to supplement or enhance conventional (i.e., so-called real-time and real-space) activities and decision-making processes. For example, computers can generate and project useful images and information as a "head-up display" in a conventional forward field of vision. It is used in military aircraft to superimpose flight, navigational, or targeting data on the pilot's visor (10) or onto automobile windshields to provide drivers with information on fuel levels, traffic flow, hazards, and alternative routes to their destination (9).

In sport, head-up displays can be used as a means of improving performance. For example, in a laboratory setting, golfers can have a video image of their golf swing (from front, behind, or side) superimposed on a transparent visor while they are executing a golf swing. Simultaneous feedback is thought to provide information for the golfer to detect and correct anomalies that might be producing injury or less than optimal swing mechanics. Head-up displays are also used in professional-automobile-racing helmets to help pit crews communicate better with drivers, alerting them to engine performance and track conditions (8).[8]

Virtual reality, though, is thought to be more than augmentation. Rather, it is a computer-simulated world within which one is immersed and is interactive with virtual objects and persons. Immersion generally refers to the technology that facilitates entry into, and the experience of engagement in, the virtual world. Depending on the nature and sophistication of the technology, the experience may feel more or less believable, natural, and seamless in relation to so-called real-time movements, sounds, and shapes. In other words, immersion is the extent to which one forgets about the (human-machine) interface, or incorporates the machine as one would the body in a "lived body" experience.

Immersion in most of the traditional computer games is facilitated with the use of three-dimensional, high-definition optic displays and stereo or surround-sound headphones. More recently, game realism has been promoted by the development of tactile or haptic* user interfaces. For example, the installation of motors into conventional input devices (e.g., joystick, steering wheel, game pad) produces rumbling vibrations that mimic, for example, the pull on the wheel during a sharp turn or a jolt on collision (14). New-generation games attempt to promote a more "natural" user interface by freeing the participant from the keyboard, involving them in more than simply hand or foot movements (30).

---

* = relating to the sense of touch.

Immersion can also depend on what participant position is portrayed or occupied in the computer-game action. At certain times, players are positioned much like onlookers who can survey the unfolding game action from a distance. That is, a player controls a game character but observes the actions of this character from a third-person perspective. The problem here for realistic immersion is, for Low (16), how game players can be "inside" the game when they see "themselves" from a detached point of view. Alternatively, and increasingly, players can be positioned as first-person agents—seeing, hearing, and responding to the unfolding game actions and landscapes as one would from the perspective of, for example, a pilot or Formula 1 driver.

In addition to visual, auditory, and tactile realism, immersion is also about "things making sense" (16). According to Poole (cited in 16) the virtual game world breaks down if there is logical incoherence of causality, function, and space. "Incoherence of causality" occurs when the same game action produces conflicting results under different conditions, as when a rocket launcher can blow up a human being but not a door. "Incoherence of function" occurs when a game tool can only be used for one purpose or only in specified places. "Incoherence of space" occurs when a game character is prevented from performing actions, for example, being permitted to crawl through one opening but not another when it would seem the logical thing to do.

It goes beyond the scope of this article to discuss this point in detail, but it is worth noting that one of the promises of virtual reality is not simply to replicate conventional worlds but its ability to create fantastically possible and captivating ones. For example, the ability of a game character to leap what would be humanly impossible heights and distances and land without injury may not collapse the virtual reality. Rather than being seen as "incoherency" that shatters the virtual game world, game players can suspend their disbelief and enter into creative possible worlds. Vertical and horizontal jumping capabilities may be extended but are still the game "givens" or limited means that, when mastered through the game controller, permit a range of game-specific and -relevant actions.

Interactivity refers to the degree of control the user has in the virtual world. In many conventional computer games, the ability to negotiate one's way in these environments depends on manipulating a mouse, keyboard, or game pad or joystick, steering wheel, and foot pedals. The more exotic types of game controllers make use of head-tracking devices and data gloves. Some types of controllers permit body movements other than simply those of the hands and feet. These include hydraulically controlled motion platforms and bicycle ergometers that involve larger muscle groups of the upper and lower body. Still others make use of motion-sensor flooring, infrared sensors, and cameras to track whole-body movements and register them through an electronic game character or object.

Immersion and interactivity are facilitated in computer games and simulated sports in several ways. In a standard auto-racing computer game, for example, the landscapes of racing action are represented three-dimensionally on a computer screen, often with accompanying sound effects. As the racing action unfolds on the screen, effective action to overcome obstacles or deal with opponents is made possible by manipulation of a joystick or game pad—moving the joystick and/or depressing certain keys or buttons controls direction and speed. In some computer-game systems, control is exercised by a steering wheel and foot pedals.

In another example, computerized downhill ski racing, immersion is similar, but interactivity is somewhat different. The portrayed downhill ski action, with its alpine scenery, steep slopes, and high-velocity turns and jumps, unfolds on a large-screen monitor. The player faces the screen while standing on and manipulating ski-like foot pedals, which act as force platforms that compute and translate shifts in weight into changes in direction of the virtual skier. In addition to a visual and auditory interface with the projected sporting action, these two examples show that there is also a mechanical interface, one that allows a motor action in one plane to be translated into an electronic sporting movement in a corresponding one.

There are examples of computer games in which the interactivity involves more conventional sporting movements. In a version of simulated golf called Smart Golf (25), players stand in an 18- by 10- by 12-ft cubicle facing a 10- by 12-ft video screen that can display three-dimensional computer-generated versions of golf courses. The screen graphics also include waving flags, aircraft, birds, animals, other players, water reflections, and the like. Players, using their own clubs, hit a ball from a tee, rough grass, or sand mat into the three-dimensional fairway or green screen image. The "real" ball hits the screen and drops to the ground, but during its flight infrared sensors track ball trajectory and a computer calculates velocity and plots vector curve and spin rate. The flight characteristics, from the "slightest draw of the golf ball to the biggest slice right down to the subtleties of a putting stroke" are then reproduced on the screen (25). With each stroke, the virtual golfing landscape adjusts to match the ball's position and the player's first-person perspective on the golf course.

Another interactive computer game of this type is GameBike, a computerized bicycle ergometer and video-game controller, one that translates movements on a stationary bicycle to a character or object on a video screen. GameBike can be connected to video-game consoles (e.g., PlayStation, Xbox, Game Cube) to play racing or other types of video games. While one pedals and watches a video game (e.g., *Simpsons Hit and Run*), handlebars control the steering, pedal revolutions per minute (rpm) control the speed, and the player controls the strategy of the on-screen game character or vehicle (4). In other words, the cycling movements the player makes on GameBike are translated into virtual cycling, running, or driving outcomes, depending on the selected game system.

Other computer games are being designed to allow even greater range of movement to control the action. The Lumetila project, for example, explores how people can use their own bodies as an interface and how they can interact with other players by moving around in a room. In a game called LumePong, a player stands on a stage facing a three-dimensional image of a rectangular room and a moving ball image. EMFi (Electro Mechanical Film) sensors underneath the 4- by 4-m floor area track bodily movements, and a computer translates them into the movement of a virtual racquet that propels the ball toward and off a virtual back wall. While the running movements are translated into virtual racquet strokes in a court-like setting, the researchers claim that "the technology of the game space worked and players felt that the spatial user interface was a natural playing environment" (30).

As I have described, conventional motor skills such as golf swings have consequences in a computer-generated golf course. Similarly, shifts of weight on a mechanical skiing device correlate with virtual skiing movements on an electronically represented downhill course. In other cases, motor actions in the virtual sports plane are executed as extensions of keyboard, mouse, and game pad or joystick control. Depending on the sophistication of the technology, there can be a visual, auditory, and tactile connectedness to the electronically replicated, albeit compressed, sporting world and what happens in it. In all these cases, bodily or "manual" dexterity in one medium has a bearing on the actions of an electronic correlate in another.

Skillful Play

Although games of chance have their own attraction, it has been shown that the term "sport" is reserved for games that feature and value physical prowess. The use of fine or gross motor actions, whether similar to conventional sporting movements or not, to control computer-generated game characters or objects can be considered sufficiently "physical" to qualify computer-simulated gaming as sport in its own right. To avoid the possible conclusion, however, that prowess is reducible to simply a physical or motor skill, a more rounded notion of prowess can be added to this account.[9]

"Dad, I just did my first speccie!" In Australian Rules Football (AFL*), the lauda-tory term 'speccie'[†] is reserved for a spectacular highflying mark (i.e., catch). It is a maneuver that requires daring and power, not to mention precise timing. While tracking the ball's flight path and judging its descent, the athlete executes a running vertical jump, often propelling him- or herself off the back or shoulders of an oppon-ent high into the air to achieve "hang-time" at the point of reception. In the case of my 11-year old son, this occurred from behind an analog game controller in a PlayStation 2 computer game called *AFL Live: Premiership Edition*. Subtract the "real" gross motor component, and the virtual "speccie" requires tactical daring (to attempt a maneuver with such a low probability of success) and nimble, fine motor (game-controller) skills to produce an equally well-timed and effective highflying mark.

The extension of the player through a game character or object is achieved in *AFL Live: Premiership Edition* through a game controller. It is a handheld device with several types of navigation buttons that control virtual-player movements, including direction (forward, back, sideways) and speed, as well as kicking (tor-pedo, drop punt, stab, chip, off ground), marking, bumping/pushing, hand ball (passing), tackling, shrugging a tackle, evading a tackle, punching the ball away, and so on. Any particular game action will involve the sequential tapping or hold-ing of a button and, in many cases, tapping and holding two buttons simultan-eously to execute more advanced game skills.

The navigation sequence of a "speccie," for example, could be as follows: The game player detects a kicked ball (on screen), estimates velocity and trajectory, and judges that the ball will land in the midst of a pack of players 30 meters in front of his game character. The right analog button is pushed to move the virtual player toward the pack, and the circle-marked button, to evade an oncoming opponent. The right analog button is depressed to move the virtual game character toward the pack, and the left-shoulder button (L1) simultaneously depressed to accelerate. As the virtual player approaches the pack, the square-marked button is tapped at the same time the right-shoulder button (R1) is depressed in order to execute a high-jumping motion, with timing precise enough to successfully complete the highflying mark.

This anecdote is telling for at least two reasons. The first goes to the issue

---

*   = Australian Football League.

†   pronounced (and sometimes spelled) speckie; short for 'spectacular.'

of immersion and embodiment in this computer game. My son triumphantly claimed, "I just did my first speccie!" not "Dad, I just mastered the game controller in such a way that my game character just achieved its first speccie." In spite of the fact that the game player occupies a third-person perspective in this particular game, the distinction between the game player and the game character seems to disappear, or at least merge, in the lived experience. In phenomenological terms, the game controller, as an extension of the body, recedes into the background, so to speak, as the player becomes immersed in the action.

The second, related point has to do with skillful and effective interaction. The acquisition of the game-controller skills necessary to negotiate one's way in and around the virtual football landscape is by no means an easy feat, judging by my son's persistent trial-and-error attempts to master them, not to mention my feeble attempts to keep a game character moving toward the ball let alone attempt a "speccie." Just like any other sport, there are certain bodily movements, including various motor skills, that must become in a sense "automatic" in order for an athlete to execute tactics and strategies.

It is important to note, though, that skillful play in this and other computer-simulation games can be understood as more than simply technical skill, that is, as game pad, keyboard, or joystick dexterity. Along the lines suggested by Tamboer (29), physical prowess or motor skills are not discrete things in themselves. Rather, their meaning is context dependent and is intelligible in terms of the game in which they figure. Whereas, in computer games, the game character's movements are an extension of keyboard or game-pad functions (or other game controllers such as those in GameBike, Smart Golf and LumePong), they are circumscribed by, and meaningful in relation to, the rules of the particular cybersport.

It may be more fruitful to consider skillful play or prowess as form of sporting intelligence. In order to make this move, "intelligence" needs to be pictured as something more than detached, abstract, or theoretical thinking, more than something often considered the prerogative of a coach. As an athletic or sporting skill, prowess can be considered synonymous with effective knowledge and skills, that is, with game sense and (tactical and strategic) judgment to act effectively to settle the issue at hand (1) or help the athlete solve the game problem (15). For Kretchmar, sport intelligence can be considered an embodied intelligence that allows the participant to understand and express meaning, as well as solve problems and perform creatively (15: pp. 74-76). Accordingly, cybersport-intelligent action can be considered the acquisition of practical game sense and a movement vocabulary that links actions in one plane to the game problems and challenges represented in another.

Conclusion

Contrary to the view that computer games are virtual (i.e., unreal, artificial) and disembodied practices, this article has gone to some lengths to demonstrate that the prowess involved in certain computer games is sufficiently "physical" and "skillful" to qualify them as sport in their own right. The computer games highlighted were shown to facilitate immersion and permit a range of visual, auditory, and haptic interactions within electronically generated sporting worlds. It is by virtue of the haptic or tactile connectedness and interactivity, whether through keyboard, game pad, foot pedal, cycling ergometer, or whole-body game controllers, that cybersport can be said to be consistent with the widely accepted (Suits/Meier) formalistic definition of sport.

I do not claim, however, that cybersport, based as it is on this formalistic notion of sport, settles the issue. I am mindful of Deleuze and Guattari's notion of philosophy as "the discipline that involves *creating* concepts," that concepts are processual* and reflect the creator's ongoing conversation with the past and the current context or problematic[†] (5: pp. 5, 17). The cybersport conversation in this article, dealing as it does with the status of sport and the new lived experiences and ways of knowing it makes possible, forces us to confront old, supposedly stable conceptual boundaries of sport.[10]

Although much more can be said about the phenomenology of computer gaming, or the status of cybersport as a form of practice intelligence, I hope that enough has been said about the consistency of certain computer games with sport to be convincing. Many might not be able to put their fingers on just what may still be disturbing about cybersport. It may be that cybersport seems like remote-control sport. It may be that computer-game dexterity is difficult to reconcile with athleticism, or athleticism with intelligence, for that matter. Committed sport practitioners, including athletes, coaches, and journalists, who have had their identities forged and refined in conventional, especially "manly," contact sports, may reject cybersport on grounds similar to those used to dismiss certain noncontact, fine-motor, and aesthetic sports. Put another way, the barbarians are yet again at the gate and threatening to wreck the place.[11] In this case, it may be the children and

---

*   = related to a process.
†   = a problem in the particular field.

adolescents, among them the so-called technoheads and computer nerds, whose computer dexterity threatens to undermine the status of "real" athletes.

I suspect that it will take more than cybersport's consistency with a formalistic definition of sport to sway the skeptics, but it may be a start. Although the concept of cybersport can expose certain pernicious stereotypes about computer gaming, it can also expand what it means to be an athlete and play sport. Philosophers can then turn their attention to the identities and practice communities created and sustained by cybersports, as well as other so-called alternative sport activities. It may involve, as Roberts suggests, paying closer attention to "the movements and noises of the cheats, the children, the eccentrics, and the excluded" (21: p. 7) to gain some clue as to how sport might be more inclusive and interesting.

NOTES

1. I am grateful for the helpful comments of the two anonymous reviewers on a previous version of this paper. I would also like to acknowledge the School of Communication, Arts and Critical Enquiry at La Trobe University in Melbourne, Australia, for supporting my sabbatical, during which time I wrote this article.

2. Rorty notes how the Western philosophical tradition has treated metaphor as alluring, seductive, and dangerous and a temptation to escape from reality (23: p. 125).

3. See M. Burton Nelson (19), who discusses how men, when their social position is threatened, tend to renew their interest in playing or watching heavy-contact sports, where they tend to have the upper hand.

4. It is interesting that in the same section of the book in which Bale discusses "Alternative Alternatives" and clandestine sports, there is no mention of any subversive potential of electrosport (2). Rather, sport's potential for subversion or anarchy is reserved for more playful, noneconomic alternatives to high-tech sport.

5. Yet we should not assume that face-to-face communications are somehow more realistic or authentic. Although it goes beyond the scope of this article, it can be argued that interests and expectations based on features such as occupation, gender, skin color, age, and physical attractiveness mediate every face-to-face encounter. These encounters often require some degree of interpretation and perhaps negotiation in order to respond appropriately.

6. This criticism applies equally well to Suits's early formulation of sport, wherein he states that in addition to skill (not luck) and physical prowess, sports are distinguished from games on the basis of a wide following and stability. For an extended version of this criticism, see Meier (18).

7. Elsewhere (12) I have suggested that virtual reality is closer to experience than what we might expect. There are a number of ways that our face-to-face interactions with others are mediated by a textual, visual, or auditory device and remain "real" and acceptable. When reading a hand-written letter or listening to a phone call, we typically suspend our belief that we are only relating to letters on a page or sound waves and become present to the message sender. In other words, face-to-face viewing or listening is mediated in such a way that the body, located in one place, is passed over as the so-called I enters into the imagined space with another person. For the purposes of the present article, I have restricted my discussion to the type of electronic mediations offered by computer technologies.

8. For a brief description how head-up displays are being used to augment performance for swimmers, runners, hang gliders, and hikers, see Gromer (7).

9. Tamboer (29) acknowledges that although the physical-prowess basis of defining sport is the received view in the philosophy-of-sport literature, he contends that there is a dubious mind-body dualism at the heart of it. Tamboer suggests that an alternative view about the nature of sport can be generated from a different premise, in this case, a relational perspective. I have borrowed slightly from Tamboer, but there is much more that could be explored and applied to the cybersport issue.

10. Special thanks go to Scott Kretchmar for his thoughtful suggestion here and elsewhere in the article.

11. See Roberts's Rorty-inspired discussion of accommodating change in sporting practices (22: pp. 253-54).

REFERENCES

1. Algozin, K. "Man and Sport." In *Philosophic Inquiry in Sport*, W.J. Morgan and K.V. Meier (Eds.). Champaign, IL: Human Kinetics, 1988, 183-87.

2. Bale, J. *Landscapes of Modern Sport*. London: Leicester UP, 1994.

3. Bonsor, Kevin. "How Augmented Reality Will Work." Available at http://computer. howstuffworks.com/augmented-reality1.htm

4. "Cateyefitness." Available at www.cateyefitness.com/GameBike.html

5. Deleuze, G., and F. Guattari. *What Is Philosophy?* Trans. H. Tomlinson and G. Burchell. New York: Columbia UP, 1994.

6. English, J. "Sex Equality in Sport." In *Philosophic Inquiry in Sport*, W.J. Morgan and K.V. Meier (Eds.). 2nd ed. Champaign, IL: Human Kinetics, 1995, 284-88.

7. Gromer, C. "Better Strokes: Revolutionary New Head-Up Display Gives Swimmers a

Wealth of Instant Feedback." *Popular Mechanics*. September 2000. Available at http://www.popularmechanics.com/outdoors/outdoors/1277556.html

8. "Head-Up Display." Available at www.bmwworld.com/racing/f1/head-up_display.thm

9. "Head-Up Display." Available at www.bmw.com/au/script/technology/technology.asp?id=63

10. "Heads-Up Display." The American Heritage® Dictionary of the English Language. 4th ed. 2004, Available at http://www.answers.com/topic/head-up-display

11. Heim, M. *The Metaphysics of Virtual Reality*. New York: Oxford UP, 1993.

12. Hemphill, D. "Revisioning Sport Spectatorism." *Journal of the Philosophy of Sport*, 1995, XXII, 48-60.

13. Huizinga, J. "The Nature of Play." In *Philosophic Inquiry in Sport*, W.J. Morgan and K.V. Meier (Eds.). 2nd ed. Champaign, IL: Human Kinetics, 1995, 5-7.

14. "Joysticks/Gamepads." Available at http://geek.pricegrabber.com/search_attrib.php/page_id=52

15. Kretchmar, R.S. *Practical Philosophy of Sport and Physical Activity*. Champaign, IL: Human Kinetics, 1994.

16. Low, G. "Understanding Realism in Computer Games Through Phenomenology." Available at http://xenon.stanford.edu/~geksiong/papers/cs378/cs378paper.htm

17. Meier, K. "On the Inadequacies of Sociological Definitions of Sport." *International Review of Sport Sociology*, 2(16), 1981, 79-100.

18. Meier, K. "Triad Trickery: Playing With Sport and Games." In *Philosophic Inquiry in Sport*, W.J. Morgan and K.V. Meier (Eds.). 2nd ed. Champaign, IL: Human Kinetics, 1995, 16-35.

19. Nelson, M. *The Stronger Women Get, the More Men Love Football: Sexism and the American Culture of Sports*. New York: Harcourt Brace, 1994.

20. Osterhoudt, R. "'Physicality': One Among the Internal Goods of Sport." *Journal of the Philosophy of Sport*, 1996, XXIII, 91-103.

21. Roberts, T. "It's Just Not Cricket! Rorty and Unfamiliar Movements: History of Metaphors in a Sporting Practice." *Journal of the Philosophy of Sport*. 1997, XXIV, 67-78.

22. Roberts, T. "Private Autonomy and Public Morality in Sporting Practices." In *Ethics and Sport*, M.J. McNamee and S.J. Parry (Eds.). London: E & F Spon, 1998, 240-55.

23. Rorty, R. "Non-Reductive Physicalism." In *Objectivity, Relativism and Truth: Philosophical Papers*, R. Rorty (Ed.). Vol. I. Cambridge, MA: Cambridge UP, 1991, 113-25.

24. Schmitz, K. "Sport and Play: Suspension of the Ordinary." In *Sport and the Body: A Philosophical Symposium*, Ellen W. Gerber (Ed.). Philadelphia: Lea & Febiger, 1972, 25-32.

25. "Smart Golf." Available at http://www.smartgolf.com/index.html

26. Suits, B. "The Elements of Sport." In *Philosophic Inquiry in Sport*, W.J. Morgan and K.V. Meier (Eds.). 2nd ed. Champaign, IL: Human Kinetics, 1995, 8-15.

27. Suits, B. "Tricky Triad: Games, Play and Sport." In *Philosophic Inquiry in Sport*, W.J. Morgan and K.V. Meier (Eds.). 2nd ed. Champaign, IL: Human Kinetics, 1995, 16-22.

28. Stone, A. "Will the Real Body Please Stand Up? Boundary Stories About Virtual Cultures." In *Cyberspace: First Steps*, M. Benedikt (Ed.). Cambridge, MA: MIT, 1992, 81-118.

29. Tamboer, J. "Sport and Motor Actions." *Journal of the Philosophy of Sport*, 1992, XIX, 31-45.

30. VTT Information Technology. "Virtual Space–User Interfaces of the Future." Available at http://www.vtt.fi/tte/projects/lumetila

8. Throwing Like a Girl: A Phenomenology of Feminine Body Comportment, Motility, and Spatiality*

Iris Marion Young

In discussing the fundamental significance of lateral space, which is one of the unique spatial dimensions generated by the human upright posture, Erwin Straus pauses at "the remarkable difference in the manner of throwing of the two sexes" (157).[1] Citing a study and photographs of young boys and girls, he describes the difference as follows:

> The girl of five does not make any use of lateral space. She does not stretch her arm sideward; she does not twist her trunk; she does not move her legs, which remain side by side. All she does in preparation for throwing is to lift her right arm forward to the horizontal and to bend the forearm backward in a pronate position.... The ball is released without force, speed, or accurate aim.... A boy of the same age, when preparing to throw, stretches his right arm sideward and backward; supinates the forearm; twists, turns and bends his trunk; and moves his right foot backward. From this stance, he can support his throwing almost with the full strength of his total motorium[†] ... The ball leaves the hand with considerable acceleration; it moves toward its goal in a long flat curve (157-60).[2]

Though he does not stop to trouble himself with the problem for long, Straus makes a few remarks in the attempt to explain this "remarkable difference." Since

---

*   Iris Marion Young, "Throwing Like a Girl: A Phenomenology of Feminine Body Comportment, Motility, and Spatiality," *Human Studies* 3.1 (1980), pp. 137-56.

†   The part of the nervous system involved in movement.

the difference is observed at such an early age, he says, it seems to be "the manifestation of a biological, not an acquired, difference" (157). He is somewhat at a loss, however, to specify the source of the difference. Since the feminine style of throwing is observed in young children, it cannot result from the development of the breast. Straus provides further evidence against the breast by pointing out that "it seems certain" that the Amazons, who cut off their right breasts, "threw a ball just like our Betty's, Mary's and Susan's" (158). Having thus dismissed the breast, Straus considers the weaker muscle power of the girl as an explanation to compensate for such relative weakness with the added preparation of reaching around and back. Straus explains the difference in style of throwing by referring to a "feminine attitude" in relation to the world and to space. The difference for him is biologically based, but he denies that it is specifically anatomical. Girls throw in a way different from boys because girls are "feminine."

What is even more amazing than this "explanation" is the fact that a perspective that takes body comportment and movement as definitive for the structure and meaning of human lived experience devotes no more than an incidental page to such a "remarkable difference" between masculine and feminine body comportment and style of movement, for throwing is by no means the only activity in which such a difference can be observed. If there are indeed typically "feminine" styles of body comportment and movement, this should generate for the existential phenomenologist* a concern to specify such a differentiation of the modalities of the lived body. Yet Straus is by no means alone in his failure to describe the modalities, meaning, and implications of the difference between "masculine" and "feminine" body comportment and movement.

A virtue of Straus's account of the typical difference of the sexes in throwing is that he does not explain this difference on the basis of physical attributes. Straus is convinced, however, that the early age at which the difference appears shows that it is not an acquired difference, and thus he is forced back onto a mysterious "feminine essence" in order to explain it. The feminist denial that the real differences in behavior and psychology between men and women can be attributed to some natural and eternal feminine essence is perhaps most thoroughly and systematically expressed by Beauvoir. Every human existence is defined by its *situation*; the particular existence of the female person is no less defined by the historical, cultural, social, and economic limits of her situation. We reduce women's condition simply

---

* Phenomenology is the philosophical study of consciousness as experienced, that is, from a first-person point of view. Existential phenomenology concentrates in particular on our experiences of free choice and action, in concrete situations.

to unintelligibility if we "explain" it by appeal to some natural and ahistorical feminine essence. In denying such a feminine essence, however, we should not fall into that "nominalism"* that denies the real differences in the behavior and experiences of men and women. Even though there is no eternal feminine essence, there is "a common basis which underlies every individual female existence in the present state of education and custom."[3] The situation of women within a given sociohistorical set of circumstances, despite the individual variation in each woman's experience, opportunities, and possibilities, has a unity that can be described and made intelligible. It should be emphasized, however, that this unity is specific to a particular social formation during a particular epoch.

Beauvoir proceeds to give such an account of the situation of women with remarkable depth, clarity, and ingenuity. Yet she also, to a large extent, fails to give a place to the status and orientation of the woman's body as relating to its surroundings in living action. When Beauvoir does talk about the woman's bodily being and her physical relation to her surroundings, she tends to focus on the more evident facts of a woman's physiology. She discussed how women experience the body as a burden, how the hormonal and physiological changes the body undergoes at puberty, during menstruation and pregnancy, are felt to be fearful and mysterious, and she claims that these phenomena weigh down the woman's existence by tying her to nature, immanence, and the requirements of the species at the expense of her own individuality.[4] By largely ignoring the situatedness of the woman's actual bodily movement and orientation to its surroundings and its world, Beauvoir tends to create the impression that it is woman's anatomy and physiology *as such* that at least in part determine her unfree status.[5]

This essay seeks to begin to fill a gap that thus exists in both existential phenomenology and feminist theory. It traces in a provisional way some of the basic modalities of feminine body comportment, manner of moving, and relation in space. It brings intelligibility and significance to certain observable and rather ordinary ways in which women in our society typically comport themselves and move differently from the ways that men do. In accordance with the existentialist concern with the situatedness of human experience, I make no claim to the universality of this typicality of the bodily comportment of women and the phenomenological description based on it. The account developed here claims only to describe the modalities of feminine bodily existence for women situated

---

* The position that some distinction is only a matter of words, and does not represent a real difference in the world.

in contemporary advanced industrial, urban, and commercial society. Elements of the account developed here may or may not apply to the situation of woman in other societies and other epochs, but it is not the concern of this essay to determine to which, if any, other social circumstances this account applies.

The scope of bodily existence and movement with which I am concerned here is also limited. I concentrate primarily on those sorts of bodily activities that relate to the comportment or orientation of the body as a whole, that entail gross movement, or that require the enlistment of strength and the confrontation of the body's capacities and possibilities with the resistance and malleability of things. The kind of movement I am primarily concerned with is movement in which the body aims to accomplish a definite purpose or task. There are thus many aspects of feminine bodily existence that I leave out of this account. Most notable of these is the body in its sexual being. Another aspect of bodily existence, among others, that I leave unconsidered is structured body movement that does not have a particular aim—for example, dancing. Besides reasons of space, this limitation of subject is based on the conviction, derived primarily from Merleau-Ponty, that it is the ordinary purposive orientation of the body as a whole toward things and its environment that initially defines the relation of a subject to its world. Thus a focus upon ways in which the feminine body frequently or typically conducts itself in such comportment or movement may be particularly revelatory of the structures of feminine existence.[6]

Before entering the analysis, I should clarify what I mean here by "feminine" existence. In accordance with Beauvoir's understanding, I take "femininity" to designate not a mysterious quality or essence that all women have by virtue of their being biologically female. It is, rather, a set of structures and conditions that delimit the typical *situation* of being a woman in a particular society, as well as the typical way in which this situation is lived by the women themselves. Defined as such, it is not necessary that *any* women be "feminine"—that is, it is not necessary that there be distinctive structures and behavior typical of the situation of women.[7] This understanding of "feminine" existence makes it possible to say that some women escape or transcend the typical situation and definition of women in various degrees and respects. I mention this primarily to indicate that the account offered here of the modalities of feminine bodily existence is not to be falsified by referring to some individual women to whom aspects of the account do not apply, or even to some individual men to whom they do.

The account developed here combines the insights of the theory of the lived body as expressed by Merleau-Ponty and the theory of the situation of women as developed by Beauvoir. I assume that at the most basic descriptive level, Merleau-

Ponty's account of the relation of the lived body to its world, as developed in *The Phenomenology of Perception*, applies to any human existence in a general way. At a more specific level, however, there is a particular style of bodily comportment that is typical of feminine existence, and this style consists of particular *modalities* of the structures and conditions of the body's existence in the world.[8]

As a framework for developing these modalities, I rely on Beauvoir's account of woman's existence in patriarchal society as defined by a basic tension between immanence and transcendence.*[9] The culture and society in which the female person dwells defines woman as Other, as the inessential correlate to man, as mere object and immanence. Woman is thereby both culturally and socially denied the subjectivity, autonomy, and creativity that are definitive of being human and that in patriarchal society are accorded the man. At the same time, however, because she is a human existence, the female person necessarily is a subjectivity and transcendence, and she knows herself to be. The female person who enacts the existence of women in patriarchal society must therefore live a contradiction: as human she is a free subject who participates in transcendence, but her situation as a woman denies her that subjectivity and transcendence. My suggestion is that the modalities of feminine bodily comportment, motility,† and spatiality exhibit this same tension between transcendence and immanence, between subjectivity and being a mere object.

Section I offers some specific observations about bodily comportment, physical engagement with things, ways of using the body in performing tasks, and bodily self-image, which I find typical of feminine existence. Section II gives a general phenomenological account of the modalities of feminine bodily comportment and motility. Section III develops these modalities further in terms of the spatiality generated by them. Finally, in Section IV, I draw out some of the implications of this account for an understanding of the oppression of women as well as raise some further questions about feminine being-in-the-world that require further investigation.

I

The basic difference that Straus observes between the way boys and girls throw is that girls do not bring their whole bodies into the motion as much as the boys do.

---

*   Immanence is existence within (especially physical) worldly things. By contrast, transcendence lies beyond or outside the (physical) world, and thus is not subject to this world's limits. Existentialists like de Beauvoir view transcendence in terms of possibilities for action freely chosen by a conscious subject.

†   Comportment is the way one behaves; motility is the capacity for movement.

They do not reach back, twist, move backward, step, and lean forward. Rather, the girls tend to remain relatively immobile except for their arms, and even the arms are not extended as far as they could be. Throwing is not the only movement in which there is a typical difference in the way men and women use their bodies. Reflection on feminine comportment and body movement in other physical activities reveals that these also are frequently characterized, much as in the throwing case, by a failure to make full use of the body's spatial and lateral potentialities.

Even in the most simple body orientations of men and women as they sit, stand, and walk, one can observe a typical difference in body style and extension. Women generally are not as open with their bodies as are men in their gait and stride. Typically, the masculine stride is longer proportional to a man's body than is the feminine stride to a woman's. The man typically swings his arms in a more open and loose fashion than does a woman and typically has more up and down rhythm in his step. Though we now wear pants more than we used to and consequently do not have to restrict our sitting postures because of dress, women still tend to sit with their legs relatively close together and their arms across their bodies. When simply standing or leaning, men tend to keep their feet farther apart than do women, and we also tend more to keep our hands and arms touching or shielding our bodies. A final indicative difference is the way each carries books or parcels; girls and women most often carry books embraced to their chests, while boys and men swing them along their sides.

The approach that people of each sex take to the performance of physical tasks that require force, strength, and muscular coordination is frequently different. There are indeed real physical differences between men and women in the kind and limit of their physical strength. Many of the observed differences between men and women in the performance of tasks requiring coordinated strength, however, are due not so much to brute muscular strength as to the way each sex *uses* the body in approaching tasks. Women often do not perceive themselves as capable of lifting and carrying heavy things, pushing and shoving with significant force, pulling, squeezing, grasping, or twisting with force. When we attempt such tasks, we frequently fail to summon the full possibilities of our muscular coordination, position, poise, and bearing. Women tend not to put their whole bodies into engagement in a physical task with the same ease and naturalness as men. For example, in attempting to lift something, women more often than men fail to plant themselves firmly and make their thighs bear the greatest proportion of the weight. Instead, we tend to concentrate our effort on those parts of the body most immediately connected to the task—the arms and shoulders—rarely bringing the power of the legs to the task at all. When turning or twisting something, to take another example, we frequently concentrate effort in the hand and wrist, not bringing to the task the power of the shoulder, which is necessary for its efficient performance.[10]

The previously cited throwing example can be extended to a great deal of athletic activity. Now, most men are by no means superior athletes, and their sporting efforts display bravado more often than genuine skill and coordination. The relatively untrained man nevertheless engages in sport generally with more free motion and open reach than does his female counterpart. Not only is there a typical style of throwing like a girl, but there is a more or less typical style of running like a girl, climbing like a girl, swinging like a girl, hitting like a girl. They have in common first that the whole body is not put into fluid and directed motion, but rather, in swinging and hitting, for example, the motion is concentrated in one body part; and second that the woman's motion tends not to reach, extend, lean, stretch, and follow through in the direction of her intention.

For many women as they move in sport, a space surrounds us in imagination that we are not free to move beyond; the space available to our movement is a constricted space. Thus, for example, in softball or volleyball women tend to remain in one place more often than men do, neither jumping to reach nor running to approach the ball. Men more often move out toward a ball in flight and confront it with their own countermotion. Women tend to wait for and then *react* to its approach, rather than going forth to meet it. We frequently respond to the motion of a ball coming toward us as though it were coming *at* us, and our immediate bodily impulse is to flee, duck, or otherwise protect ourselves from its flight. Less often than men, moreover, do women give self-conscious direction and placement to their motion in sport. Rather than aiming at a certain place where we wish to hit a ball, for example, we tend to hit it in a "general" direction.

Women often approach a physical engagement with things with timidity, uncertainty, and hesitancy. Typically, we lack an entire trust in our bodies to carry us to our aims. There is, I suggest, a double hesitation here. On the one hand, we often lack confidence that we have the capacity to do what must be done. Many times I have slowed a hiking party in which the men bounded across a harmless stream while I stood on the other side warily testing my footing on various stones, holding on to overhanging branches. Though the others crossed with ease, I do not believe it is easy for *me*, even though once I take a committed step I am across in a flash. The other side of this tentativeness is, I suggest, a fear of getting hurt, which is greater in women than in men. Our attention is often divided between the aim to be realized in motion and the body that must accomplish it, while at the same time saving itself from harm. We often experience our bodies as a fragile encumbrance, rather than the medium for the enactment of our aims. We feel as though we must have our attention directed upon our bodies to make sure they are doing what we wish them to do, rather than paying attention to what we want to do *through* our bodies.

All the above factors operate to produce in many women a greater or lesser feeling of incapacity, frustration, and self-consciousness. We have more of a tendency than men do to greatly underestimate our bodily capacity.[11] We decide beforehand—usually mistakenly—that the task is beyond us and thus give it less than our full effort. At such a half-hearted level, of course, we cannot perform the tasks, become frustrated, and fulfill our own prophecy. In entering a task we frequently are self-conscious about appearing awkward and at the same time do not wish to appear too strong. Both worries contribute to our awkwardness and frustration. If we should finally release ourselves from this spiral and really give a physical task our best effort, we are greatly surprised indeed at what our bodies can accomplish. It has been found that women more often than men underestimate the level of achievement they have reached.[12]

None of the observations that have been made thus far about the way women typically move and comport their bodies applies to all women all of the time. Nor do these women who manifest some aspect of this typicality do so in the same degree. There is no inherent, mysterious connection between these sorts of typical comportments and being a female person. Many of them result, as will be developed later, from lack of practice in using the body and performing tasks. Even given these qualifications, one can nevertheless sensibly speak of a general feminine style of body comportment and movement. The next section will develop a specific categorical description of the modalities of the comportment and movement.

II

The three modalities of feminine motility are that feminine movement exhibits an *ambiguous transcendence*, an *inhibited intentionality*, and a *discontinuous unity* with its surroundings. A source of these contradictory modalities is the bodily self-reference of feminine comportment, which derives from the woman's experience of her body as a *thing* at the same time that she experiences it as a capacity.

1. In his *Phenomenology of Perception*,[13] Merleau-Ponty takes as his task the

articulation of the primordial structures of existence, which are prior to and the ground of all reflective relation to the world. In asking how there can be a world for a subject, Merleau-Ponty reorients the entire tradition of that questioning by locating subjectivity not in mind or consciousness but in the *body*. Merleau-Ponty gives to the lived body the ontological status that Sartre, as well as "intellectualist" thinkers before him, attribute to consciousness alone: the status of transcendence as being for itself. It is the body in its orientation toward and action upon and within its surroundings that constitutes the initial meaning-giving act (121, 146-47). The body is the first locus of intentionality, as pure presence to the world and openness upon its possibilities. The most primordial intentional act is the motion of the body orienting itself with respect to and moving within its surroundings. There is a world for a subject just insofar as the body has capacities by which it can approach, grasp, and appropriate its surroundings in the direction of its intentions.

While feminine bodily existence is a transcendence and openness to the world, it is an *ambiguous transcendence*, a transcendence that is at the same time laden with immanence. Now, once we take the locus of subjectivity and transcendence to be the lived body rather than pure consciousness, all transcendence is ambiguous because the body as natural and material is immanence. But it is not the ever-present possibility of any lived body to be passive, to be touched as well as touching, to be grasped as well as grasping, which I am referring to here as the ambiguity of the transcendence of the feminine lived body. The transcendence of the lived body that Merleau-Ponty describes is a transcendence that moves out from the body in its immanence in an open and unbroken directedness upon the world in action. The lived body as transcendence is pure fluid action, the continuous calling-forth of capacities that are applied to the world. Rather than simply beginning in immanence, feminine bodily existence remains in immanence or, better, is *overlaid* with immanence, even as it moves out toward the world in motions of grasping, manipulating, and so on.

In the previous section, I observed that a woman typically refrains from throwing her whole body into a motion and rather concentrates motion in one part of the body alone, while the rest of the body remains relatively immobile. Only part of the body, that is, moves out toward a task, while the rest remains rooted in immanence. I also observed earlier that a woman frequently does not trust the capacity of her body to engage itself in physical relation to things. Consequently, she often lives her body as a burden, which must be dragged and prodded along and at the same time protected.

2. Merleau-Ponty locates intentionality in motility (110-12); the possibilities that are opened up in the world depend on the mode and limits of the bodily "I can" (137, 148). Feminine existence, however, often does not enter bodily relation to possibilities by its own comportment toward its surroundings in an unambiguous and confident "I can." For example, as noted earlier, women frequently tend to posit a task that would be accomplished relatively easily once attempted as beyond their capacities before they begin it. Typically, the feminine body underuses its real capacity, both as the potentiality of its physical size and strength and as the real skills and coordination that are available to it. Feminine bodily existence is an *inhibited intentionality*, which simultaneously reaches toward a projected end with an "I can" and withholds its full bodily commitment to that end in a self-imposed "I cannot."[14]

An uninhibited intentionality projects the aim to be accomplished and connects the body's motion toward that end in an unbroken directedness that organizes and unifies the body's activity. The body's capacity and motion structure its surroundings and project meaningful possibilities of movement and action, which in turn call the body's motion forth to enact them. "To understand is to experience the harmony between what we aim at and what is given, between the intention and the performance" (144; see also 101, 131, and 132). Feminine motion often severs this mutually conditioning relation between aim and enactment. In those motions that when properly performed require the coordination and directedness of the whole body upon some definite end, women frequently move in a contradictory way. Their bodies project an aim to be enacted but at the same time stiffen against the performance of the task. In performing a physical task the woman's body does carry her toward the intended aim, often not easily and directly, but rather circuitously, with the wasted motion resulting from the effort of testing and reorientation, which is a frequent consequence of feminine hesitancy.

For any lived body, the world appears as the system of possibilities that are correlative to its intentions (131). For any lived body, moreover, the world also appears to be populated with opacities and resistances correlative to its own limits and frustrations. For any bodily existence, that is, an "I cannot" may appear to set limits to the "I can." To the extent that feminine bodily existence is an inhibited intentionality, however, the same set of possibilities that appears to be correlative to its intentions also appears to be a system of frustrations correlative to its hesitancies. By repressing or withholding its own motile energy, feminine bodily existence frequently projects an "I can" and an "I cannot" with respect to the very same end. When the woman enters a task with inhibited intentionality, she projects the possibilities of that task—thus projects an "I *can*"—but projects them merely as the possibilities of "someone," and not truly *her* possibilities—and thus projects an "*I* cannot."

3. Merleau-Ponty gives to the body the unifying and synthesizing function that Kant locates in transcendental subjectivity. By projecting an aim toward which it moves, the body brings unity to and unites itself with its surroundings; through the vectors of its projected possibilities it sets things in relation to one another and to itself. The body's movement and orientation organize the surrounding space as a continuous extension of its own being (143). Within the same act in which the body synthesizes its surroundings, moreover, it synthesizes itself. The body synthesis is immediate and primordial. "I do not bring together one by one the parts of my body; this translation and this unification are performed once and for all within me; they are my body itself" (150).

The third modality of feminine bodily existence is that it stands in *discontinuous unity* with both itself and its surroundings. I remarked earlier that in many motions that require the active engagement and coordination of the body as a whole in order to be performed properly, women tend to locate their motion in part of the body only, leaving the rest of the body relatively immobile. Motion such as this is discontinuous with itself. The part of the body that is transcending toward an aim is in relative disunity from those that remain immobile. The undirected and wasted motion that is often an aspect of feminine engagement in a task also manifests this lack of body unity. The character of the inhibited intentionality whereby feminine motion severs the connection between aim and enactment, between possibility in the world and capacity in the body, itself produces this discontinuous unity.

According to Merleau-Ponty, for the body to exist as a transcendent presence in the world and the immediate enactment of intentions, it cannot exist as an *object* (123). As subject, the body is referred not onto itself, but onto the world's possibilities. "In order that we may be able to move our body towards an object, the object must first exist for it, our body must not belong to the realm of the 'in-itself,'" (139). The three contradictory modalities of feminine bodily existence—ambiguous transcendence, inhibited intentionality, and discontinuous unity—have their root, however, in the fact that for feminine existence the body frequently is both subject and object for itself at the same time and in reference to the same act. Feminine bodily existence is frequently not a pure presence to the world because it is referred onto *itself* as well as onto possibilities in the world.[15]

Several of the observations of the previous section illustrate this self-reference. It was observed, for example, that women have a tendency to take up the motion of an object coming *toward* them as coming *at* them. I also observed that women tend to have a latent and sometimes conscious fear of getting hurt, which we bring to a motion. That is, feminine bodily existence is self-referred in that the woman takes herself to be the *object* of the motion rather than its originator. Feminine bodily existence is also self-referred to the extent that a woman is uncertain of her body's capacities and does not feel that its motions are entirely under her control. She must divide her attention between the task to be performed and the body that must be coaxed and manipulated into performing it. Finally, feminine bodily existence is self-referred to the extent that the feminine subject posits her motion as the motion that is *looked at*. In section IV, we will explore the implications of the basic fact of the woman's social existence as the object of the gaze of another, which is a major source of her bodily self-reference.

In summary, the modalities of feminine bodily existence have their root in the fact that feminine existence experiences the body as a mere thing—a fragile thing, which must be picked up and coaxed into movement, a thing that exists as *looked at and acted upon*. To be sure, any lived body exists as a material thing as well as a transcending subject. For feminine bodily existence, however, the body is often lived as a thing that is other than it, a thing like other things in the world. To the extent that a woman lives her body as a thing, she remains rooted in immanence, is inhibited, and retains a distance from her body as transcending movement and from engagement in the world's possibilities.

III

For Merleau-Ponty there is a distinction between lived space, or phenomenal space, and objective space, the uniform space of geometry and science in which all positions are external to one another and interchangeable. Phenomenal space arises out of motility, and lived relations of space are generated by the capacities of the body's motion and the intentional relations that that motion constitutes. "It is clearly in action that the spatiality of our body is brought into being and an analysis of one's own movement should enable us to arrive at a better understanding" (102; cf. 148, 149, 249). In this account, if there are particular modalities of feminine bodily comportment and motility, it must follow that there are also particular modalities of feminine spatiality. Feminine existence lives spaces as *enclosed* or confining, as having a *dual* structure, and the woman experiences herself as *positioned* in space.

1. There is a famous study that Erik Erikson performed several years ago in which he asked several male and female preadolescents to construct a scene for an imagined movie out of some toys. He found that girls typically depicted indoor settings, with high walls and enclosures, while boys typically constructed outdoor scenes. He concluded that females tend to emphasize what he calls "inner space," or enclosed space, while males tend to emphasize what he calls "outer space," or a spatial orientation that is open and outwardly directed. Erikson's interpretation of these observations is psychoanalytical: girls depict "inner space" as the projection of the enclosed space of their wombs and vaginas; boys depict "outer space" as a projection of the phallus.[16] I find such an explanation wholly unconvincing. If girls do tend to project an enclosed space and boys to project an open and outwardly directed space, it is far more plausible to regard this as a reflection of the way members of each sex live and move their bodies in space.

In the first section, I observed that women tend not to open their bodies in their everyday movements, but tend to sit, stand, and walk with their limbs close to or closed around them. I also observed that women tend not to reach, stretch, bend, lean, or stride to the full limits of their physical capacities, even when doing so would better accomplish a task or motion. The space, that is, that is *physically* available to the feminine body is frequently of greater radius than the space that she uses and inhabits. Feminine existence appears to posit an existential enclosure between herself and the space surrounding her, in such a way that the space that belongs to her and is available to her grasp and manipulation is constricted and the space beyond is not available to her movement.[17] A further illustration of this confinement of feminine lived space is the observation already noted that in sport, for example, women tend not to move out and meet the motion of a ball, but rather tend to stay in one place and react to the ball's motion only when it has arrived within the space where she is. The timidity, immobility, and uncertainty that frequently characterize feminine movement project a limited space for the feminine "I can."

2. In Merleau-Ponty's account, the body unity of transcending performance creates an immediate link between the body and the outlying space. "Each instant of the movement embraces its whole space, and particularly the first which, by being active and initiative, institutes the link between a here and a yonder" (140).

In feminine existence, however, the projection of an enclosed space severs the continuity between a "here" and a "yonder." In feminine existence there is a *double spatiality*, as the space of the "here" is distinct from the space of the "yonder." A distinction between space that is "yonder" and not linked with my own body possibilities and the enclosed space that is "here," which I inhabit with my bodily possibilities, is an expression of the discontinuity between aim and capacity to realize the aim that I have articulated as the meaning of the tentativeness and uncertainty characterizing the inhibited intentionality of feminine motility. The space of the "yonder" is a space in which feminine existence projects possibilities in the sense of understanding that "someone" could move within it, but not I. Thus the space of the "yonder" exists for feminine existence, but only as that which she is looking into, rather than moving in.

3. The third modality of feminine spatiality is that feminine existence experiences itself as *positioned in* space. For Merleau-Ponty, the body is the original subject that constitutes space; there would be no space without the body (102, 142). As the origin and subject of spatial relations, the body does not occupy a position coequal and interchangeable with the positions occupied by other things (143, 247-49). Because the body as lived is not an *object*, it cannot be said to exist *in* space as water is *in* the glass (139-40). "The word 'here' applied to my body does not refer to a determinate position in relation to other positions or to external coordinates, but the laying down of the first coordinates, the anchoring of the active body in an object, the situation of the body in the face of its tasks" (100).

Feminine spatiality is contradictory insofar as feminine bodily existence is both spatially constituted and a constituting spatial subject. Insofar as feminine existence lives the body as transcendence and intentionality, the feminine body actively constitutes space and is the original coordinate that unifies the spatial field and projects spatial relations and positions in accord with its intentions. But to the extent that feminine motility is laden with immanence and inhibited, the body's space is lived as constituted. To the extent, that is, that feminine bodily existence is self-referred and thus lives itself as an *object*, the feminine body does exist *in* space. In section I, I observed that women frequently react to motions, even our own motions, as though we are the object of a motion that issues from an alien intention, rather than taking ourselves as the subject of motion. In its immanence and inhibition, feminine spatial existence is *positioned* by a system of coordinates that does not have its origin in a woman's own intentional capacities. The tendency for the feminine body to remain partly immobile in the performance of a task that requires the movement of the whole body illustrates this characteristic of feminine bodily existence as rooted *in place*. Likewise does the tendency of women to wait for an object to come within their immediate bodily field, rather than move out toward it.

Merleau-Ponty devotes a great deal of attention to arguing that the diverse senses and activities of the lived body are synthetically related in such a way that each stands in a mutually conditioning relation with all the others. In particular, visual perception and motility stand in a relation of reversibility; an impairment in the functioning of one, for example, leads to an impairment in the functioning of the other (133-37). If we assume that reversibility of visual perception and motility, the previous account of the modalities of feminine motility and the spatiality that arises from them suggests that visual space will have its own modalities as well.

Numerous psychological studies have reported differences between the sexes in the character of spatial perception. One of the most frequently discussed of these conclusions is that females are more often "field-dependent." That is, it has been claimed that males have a greater capacity for lifting a figure out of its spatial surroundings and viewing relations in space as fluid and interchangeable, whereas females have a greater tendency to regard figures as embedded within and fixed by their surroundings.[18] The above account of feminine motility and spatiality gives some theoretical intelligibility to these findings. If feminine body spatiality is such that the woman experiences herself as rooted and enclosed, on the reversibility assumption it would follow that visual space for feminine existence also has its closures of immobility and fixity. The objects in visual space do not stand in a fluid system of potentially alterable and interchangeable relations correlative to the body's various intentions and projected capacities. Rather, they too have their own *places* and are anchored in their immanence.

IV

The modalities of feminine bodily comportment, motility, and spatiality that I have described here are, I claim, common to the existence of women in contemporary society to one degree or another. They have their source, however, in neither anatomy nor physiology, and certainly not in a mysterious feminine essence. Rather, they have their source in the particular *situation* of women as conditioned by their sexist oppression in contemporary society.

Women in sexist society are physically handicapped. Insofar as we learn to live out our existence in accordance with the definition that patriarchal culture assigns to us, we are physically inhibited, confined, positioned, and objectified. As lived bodies we are not open and unambiguous transcendences that move out to master a world that belongs to us, a world constituted by our own intentions and projections. To be sure, there are actual women in contemporary society to whom all or part of the above description does not apply. Where these modalities are not manifest in or determinative of the existence of a particular woman, however, they are definitive in a negative mode—as that which she has escaped, through accident or good fortune, or, more often, as that which she has had to overcome.

One of the sources of the modalities of feminine bodily existence is too obvious to dwell upon at length. For the most part, girls and women are not given the opportunity to use their full bodily capacities in free and open engagement with the world, nor are they encouraged as much as boys are to develop specific bodily skills.[19] Girls' play is often more sedentary and enclosing than the play of boys. In school and after-school activities girls are not encouraged to engage in sport, in the controlled use of their bodies in achieving well-defined goals. Girls, moreover, get little practice at "tinkering" with things and thus at developing spatial skill. Finally, girls are not often asked to perform tasks demanding physical effort and strength, while as the boys grow older they are asked to do so more and more.[20]

The modalities of feminine bodily existence are not merely privative, how-ever, and thus their source is not merely in lack of practice, though this is cer-tainly an important element. There is a specific positive style of feminine body comportment and movement, which is learned as the girl comes to understand that she is a girl. The young girl acquires many subtle habits of feminine body comportment—walking like a girl, tilting her head like a girl, standing and sitting like a girl, gesturing like a girl, and so on. The girl learns actively to hamper her movements. She is told that she must be careful not to get hurt, not to get dirty, not to tear her clothes, that the things she desires to do are dangerous for her. Thus she develops a bodily timidity that increases with age. In assuming herself to be a girl, she takes herself to be fragile. Studies have found that young children of both sexes categorically assert that girls are more likely to get hurt than boys are,[21] and that girls ought to remain close to home, while boys can roam and explore.[22] The more a girl assumes her status as feminine, the more she takes herself to be fragile and immobile and the more she actively enacts her own bodily inhibition. When I was about thirteen, I spent hours practicing a "feminine" walk, which was stiff and closed, and rotated from side to side.

Studies that record observations of sex differences in spatial perception, spatial problem-solving, and motor skills have also found that these differences tend to increase with age. While very young children show virtually no differences in motor skills, movement, spatial perception, etc., differences seem to appear in elementary school and increase with adolescence. If these findings are accurate, they would seem to support the conclusion that it is in the process of growing up as a girl that the modalities of feminine bodily comportment, motility, and spatiality make their appearance.[23]

There is, however, a further source of the modalities of feminine bodily existence that is perhaps even more profound than these. At the root of those modalities, I have stated in the previous section, is the fact that the woman lives her body as *object* as well as subject. The source of this is that patriarchal society defines woman as object, as a mere body, and that in sexist society women are in fact frequently regarded by others as objects and mere bodies. An essential part of the situation of being a woman is that of living the ever-present possibility that one will be gazed upon as a mere body, as shape and flesh that presents itself as the potential object of another subject's intentions and manipulations, rather than as a living manifestation of action and intention.[24] The source of this objectified bodily existence is in the attitude of others regarding her, but the woman herself often actively takes up her body as a mere thing. She gazes at it in the mirror, worries about how it looks to others, prunes it, shapes it, molds and decorates it.

This objectified bodily existence accounts for the self-consciousness of the feminine relation to her body and resulting distance she takes from her body. As human, she is a transcendence and subjectivity and cannot live herself as mere bodily object. Thus, to the degree that she does live herself as mere body, she cannot be in unity with herself but must take a distance from and exist in discontinuity with her body. The objectifying regard that "keeps her in her place" can also account for the spatial modality of being positioned and for why women frequently tend not to move openly, keeping their limbs closed around themselves. To open her body in free, active, open extension and bold outward-directedness is for a woman to invite objectification.

The threat of being seen is, however, not the only threat of objectification that the woman lives. She also lives the threat of invasion of her body space. The most extreme form of such spatial and bodily invasion is the threat of rape. But we daily are subject to the possibility of bodily invasion in many far more subtle ways as well. It is acceptable, for example, for women to be touched in ways and under circumstances that it is not acceptable for men to be touched, and by persons—i.e., men—whom it is not acceptable for them to touch.[25] I would suggest that the enclosed space that has been described as a modality of feminine spatiality is in part a defense against such invasion. Women tend to project an existential barrier closed around them and discontinuous with the "over there" in order to keep the other at a distance. The woman lives her space as confined and closed around her, at least in part as projecting some small area in which she can exist as a free subject.

This essay is a prolegomenon* to the study of aspects of women's experience and situation that have not received the treatment they warrant. I would like to close with some questions that require further thought and research. This essay has concentrated its attention upon the sorts of physical tasks and body orientation that involve the whole body in gross movement. Further investigation into woman's bodily existence would require looking at activities that do not involve the whole body and finer movement. If we are going to develop an account of the woman's body experience in situation, moreover, we must reflect on the modalities of a woman's experience of her body in its sexual being, as well as upon less task-oriented body activities, such as dancing. Another question that arises is whether the description given here would apply equally well to any sort of physical task. Might the kind of task, and specifically whether it is a task or movement that is sex-typed, have some effect on the modalities of feminine bodily existence? A further question is to what degree we can develop a theoretical account of the connection between the modalities of the bodily existence of women and other aspects of our existence and experience. For example, I have an intuition that the general lack of confidence that we frequently have about our cognitive or leadership abilities is traceable in part to an original doubt of our body's capacity. None of these questions can be dealt with properly, however, without first performing the kind of guided observation and data collection that my reading has concluded, to a large degree, is yet to be performed.

NOTES

This essay was first presented at a meeting of the Mid-West Division of the Society for Women in Philosophy (SWIP) in October 1977. Versions of the essay were subsequently presented at a session sponsored by SWIP at the Western Division meetings of the American Philosophical Association, April 1978, and at the third annual Merleau-Ponty Circle meeting, Duquesne University, September 1978. Many people in discussions at those meetings contributed gratifying and helpful responses. I am particularly grateful to Professors Sandra Bartky, Claudia Card, Margaret Simons, J. Davidson Alexander, and William McBride for their criticisms and suggestions. Final revisions of the essay were completed while I was a

* = preliminary discussion.

fellow in the National Endowment for the Humanities Fellowship in Residence for College Teachers program at the University of Chicago.

1. Erwin W. Straus, "The Upright Posture," *Phenomenological Psychology* (New York: Basic Books, 1966), 137-65. References to particular pages are indicated in the text.

2. Studies continue to be performed that arrive at similar observations. See, for example, Lolas E. Kalverson, Mary Ann Robertson, M. Joanne, and W. Roberts, "Effect of Guided Practice on Overhand Throw Ball Velocities of Kindergarten Children," *Research Quarterly* (American Alliance for Health, Physical Education, and Recreation) 48 (May 1977): 311-18. The study found that boys achieved significantly greater velocities than girls did. See also F.J.J. Buytendijk's remarks in *Woman: A Contemporary View* (New York: Newman, 1968), 144-45. In raising the example of throwing, Buytendijk is concerned to stress, as am I in this essay, that the important thing to investigate is not the strictly physical phenomenon, but rather the manner in which each sex projects her or his Being-in-the-world through movement.

3. Simone de Beauvoir, *The Second Sex* (New York: Vintage Books, 1974), xxxv. See also Buytendijk, 175-76.

4. See de Beauvoir, *The Second Sex*, chapter 1, "The Data of Biology."

5. Shulamith Firestone claims that de Beauvoir's account served as the basis of her own thesis that the oppression of women is rooted in nature and thus to be overcome requires the transcendence of nature itself. See *The Dialectic of Sex* (New York: Bantam Books, 1970). de Beauvoir would claim that Firestone is guilty of desituating woman's situation by pinning a source on nature as such. That Firestone would find inspiration for her thesis in Beauvoir, however, indicates that perhaps de Beauvoir has not steered away from causes in "nature" as much as is desirable.

6. In his discussion of the "dynamics of feminine existence," Buytendijk focuses precisely on those sorts of motions that are aimless. He claims that it is through these kinds of expressive movements—e.g., walking for the sake of walking—and not through action aimed at the accomplishment of particular purposes that the pure image of masculine or feminine existence is manifest (*Woman: A Contemporary View*, 278-79). Such an approach, however, contradicts the basic existentialist assumption that Being-in-the-world consists in projecting purposes and goals that structure one's situatedness. While there is certainly something to be learned from reflecting upon feminine movement in non-instrumental activ-

ity, given that accomplishing tasks is basic to the structure of human existence, it serves as a better starting point for investigation of feminine motility. As I point out at the end of this essay, a full phenomenology of feminine existence must take account of this non-instrumental movement.

7. It is not impossible, moreover, for men to be "feminine" in at least some respects, according to the above definition.

8. On this level of specificity there also exist particular modalities of masculine motility, inasmuch as there is a particular style of movement more or less typical of men. I will not, however, be concerned with those in this essay.

9. See Beauvoir, *The Second Sex*, chapter 21, "Woman's Situation and Character."

10. It should be noted that this is probably typical only of women in advanced industrial societies, where the model of the bourgeois woman has been extended to most women. It would not apply to those societies, for example, where most people, including women, do heavy physical work. Nor does this particular observation, of course, hold true in our own society of women who do heavy physical work.

11. See A.M. Gross, "Estimated versus Actual Physical Strength in Three Ethnic Groups," *Child Development* 39 (1968): 283-90. In a test of children at several different ages, at all but the youngest age level, girls rated themselves lower than boys rated themselves on self-estimates of strength, and as the girls grow older, their self-estimates of strength become even lower.

12. See Marguerite A. Clifton and Hope M. Smith, "Comparison of Expressed Self-Concept of Highly Skilled Males and Females Concerning Motor Performance," *Perceptual and Motor Skills* 16 (1963): 199-201. Women consistently underestimated their level of achievement in skills such as running and jumping far more often than men did.

13. Maurice Merleau-Ponty, *The Phenomenology of Perception*, trans. Colin Smith (New York: Humanities P, 1962). All references to this work are noted in parentheses in the text.

14. Much of the work of Seymour Fisher on various aspects of sex differences in body image correlates suggestively with the phenomenological description developed here. It is difficult to use his conclusions as confirmation of that description, however, because there is something of a speculative aspect to his reasoning. Nevertheless, I shall refer to some of these findings with that qualification in mind.

   One of Fisher's findings is that women have a greater anxiety about their legs than men do, and he cites earlier studies with the same results. Fisher interprets such leg anxiety as being anxiety about motility itself, because in body conception and body image the legs are the body parts most associated with motility. See Fisher, *Body Experience in Fantasy and Behaviour* (New York: Appleton-Century

Crofts, 1970), 537. If his findings and his interpretation are accurate, this tends to correlate with the sort of inhibition and timidity about movement that I am claiming is an aspect of feminine body comportment.

15. Fisher finds that the most striking difference between men and women in their general body image is that women have a significantly higher degree of what he calls "body prominence," awareness of and attention to the body. He cites a number of different studies that have the same results. The explanation Fisher gives for this finding is that women are socialized to pay attention to their bodies, to prune and dress them, and to worry about how they look to others. Fisher, *Body Experience in Fantasy and Behavior*, 524-25. See also Fisher, "Sex Differences in Body Perception," *Psychological Monographs* 78 (164), no. 14.

16. Erik H. Erikson, "Inner and Outer Space: Reflections on Womanhood," *Daedelus* 2 (1964): 582-606. Erikson's interpretation of his findings is also sexist. Having in his opinion discovered a particular significance that "inner space," which he takes to be space *within* the body, holds for girls, he goes on to discuss the womanly "nature" as womb and potential mother, which must be made compatible with anything else the woman does.

17. Another of Fisher's findings is that women experience themselves as having more clearly articulated body *boundaries* than men do. More clearly than men do, they distinguish themselves from their spatial surroundings and take a distance from them. See Fisher, *Body Experience in Fantasy and Behavior*, 528.

18. The number of studies with these results is enormous. See Eleanor E. Maccoby and Carol N. Jacklin, *The Psychology of Sex Differences* (Palo Alto, CA: Stanford UP, 1974), 91-98. For a number of years psychologists used the results from tests of spatial ability to generalize about field independence in general, and from that to general "analytic" ability. Thus it was concluded that women have less analytical ability than men do. More recently, however, such generalizations have been seriously called into question. See, for example, Julia A. Sherman, "Problems of Sex Differences in Space Perception and Aspects of Intellectual Functioning," *Psychological Review* 74 (1967): 290-99. She notes that while women are consistently found to be more field-dependent in spatial tasks than men are, on non-spatial tests measuring field independence, women generally perform as well as men do.

19. Nor are girls provided with examples of girls and women being physically active. See Mary E. Duquin, "Differential Sex Role Socialization toward Amplitude Appropriation," *Research Quarterly* (American Alliance for Health, Physical Education, and Recreation) 48 (1977): 188-92. A survey of textbooks for young children revealed that children are thirteen times more likely to see a vigorously

active man than a vigorously active woman and three times more likely to see a relatively active man than a relatively active woman.

20. Sherman, "Problems of Sex Differences," argues that it is the differential socialization of boys and girls in being encouraged to "tinker," explore, etc., that accounts for the difference between the two in spatial ability.

21. See L. Kolberg, "A Cognitive-Developmental Analysis of Children's Sex-Role Concepts and Attitudes," in *The Development of Sex Differences*, ed. E.E. Maccoby (Palo Alto, CA.: Stanford UP, 1966), 101.

22. Lenore J. Weitzman, "Sex Role Socialization," in *Woman: A Feminist Perspective*, ed. Jo Freeman (Palo Alto, CA.: Mayfield Publishing Co., 1975), 111-12.

23. Maccoby and Jacklin, *The Psychology of Sex Differences*, 93-94.

24. The manner in which women are objectified by the gaze of the Other is not the same phenomenon as the objectification by the Other that is a condition of self-consciousness in Sartre's account. See *Being and Nothingness*, trans. Hazel E. Barnes (New York: Philosophical Library, 1956), part 3. While the basic ontological category of being for others is objectified for itself, the objectification that women are subject to is being regarded as a mere in itself. On the particular dynamic of sexual objectification, see Sandra Bartky, "Psychological Oppression," in *Philosophy and Women*, ed. Sharon Bishop and Marjorie Weinzweig (Belmont, CA: Wadsworth Publishing Co., 1979), 33-41.

25. See Nancy Henley and Jo Freeman, "The Sexual Politics of Interpersonal Behavior," in Freeman, *Woman: A Feminist Perspective*, 391-401.

QUESTIONS

1. Despite Hemphill's argument to the contrary, should cybersport be called virtual rather than actual sport? What does this imply about the concept of sport?

2. Do videogame systems that involve gross motor skill, like Wii and Kinect, make cybersport more plausible?

3. Are cybersports Suitsian games, with prelusory goals and constitutive rules? How, or why not? Does this affect our concept of sport? Of games? Of videogames?

4. Is it appropriate to regard a person the way phenomenologists do: as an ambiguous kind of "subject/object"? Is there a better alternative? '

5. Do you agree with Young's take on the differences between feminine and masculine spatial orientation, movement, and bodily comportment?

6. What does Young's account suggest about the importance of sport for females? What other activities might foster such or similar benefits?

FURTHER READING

Boxill, J.M. (1984): "Beauty, Sport, and Gender," *Journal of the Philosophy of Sport* 11, pp. 36-47.

Meier, Klaus V. (1979): "Embodiment, Sport, and Meaning," in *Sport and the Body: A Philosophical Symposium*, ed. Ellen W. Gerber and William J. Morgan (Philadelphia: Lea and Febiger), pp. 192-98.

Moe, Vegard Fusche (2005): "A Philosophical Critique of Classical Cognitivism in Sport: From Information Processing to Bodily Background Knowledge," *Journal of the Philosophy of Sport* 32 (2), pp. 155-83.

Ross, Saul (1986): "Cartesian Dualism and Physical Education: Epistemological Incompatibility," in *Mind and Body: East Meets West*, ed. Seymour Kleinman (Champaign, IL: Human Kinetics), pp. 15-24.

Spelman, Elizabeth V. (1982): "Woman as Body: Ancient and Contemporary Views," *Feminist Studies* 8 (1), pp. 109-31.

Tamboer, Jan W.I. (1992): "Sport and Motor Actions," *Journal of the Philosophy of Sport* 19, pp. 31-45.

FURTHER INQUIRY

Videogames seem somehow disembodied, despite the obvious physicality of skills involved in playing them. This prompts the question of whether it is not just the *skills* themselves that count in determining whether an activity is sport, but also the domain of *application* of those skills and the results achieved: videogames require physical skill, but to what non-virtual end? If an athlete somehow transposed their movements into music—freeform jazz, say—and their purpose, even in a game situation, was to generate that music, would that make music a sport? Notice, too, the difficulty in specifying prelusory goals for videogames, although cheat codes seem like a nod to the Suitsian intuition that players must restrict themselves accordingly. In terms of embodiment broadly, it remains unclear what role philosophy of mind should play in philosophy of sport, as even the dualism of Descartes is strictly consistent with anything we might ever discover about skilled movement. Yet the importance of proprioception—the sense of position of one's body—in experience, and of skilled movement particularly, merits further inquiry. As sport may help people overcome restrictions that are not game-constitutive but manifestly *unjust*, our focus now shifts laterally from descriptive (matters of fact, of what sport *is*) to normative (matters of value, of what it *ought* to be).

Part II

Rules and Values

Sport Aesthetics

A esthetics is the branch of philosophy concerned with beauty in general and art in particular. Sport aesthetics is concerned in the first place with the aesthetic appeal of sport, the beauty of it as activity and as spectacle. Undoubtedly part of the value of sport, for players and spectators alike, is aesthetic, as suggested by aptly hackneyed phrases like "poetry in motion": think of what it's like to watch such beautiful movements in slow motion replays, or for the athlete to execute such skill under competitive pressure, or to appreciate, as participant or observer, the tension, the drama of an important competition. To appreciate sport for these qualities is to adopt an aesthetic attitude toward it, to be interested, among other things, in having an experience not unlike the kind one has when appreciating a work of art: a moving song, a great film, an inspired dance, and so on. No wonder sport lends itself to musical accompaniment, to filmic expression, and sometimes—from boxing to figure skating—appears as, and maybe is itself, a kind of dance.

Whether the analogy between sport and art can be drawn any closer than this, whether sport can be art, that is, has been hotly debated among sport aestheticians. Note, however, that when 'art' is taken to refer to a technique or skilled practice—as in "the art" of persuasion, "the art" of succeeding in business, "the art" of shopping on a budget—then *of course* sport is art, as it is undeniably a skilled practice. Likewise when we speak of the "artistry" of highly skilled or notably stylish, even creative athletes, that is clearly not the sense at issue, the sense in which a sport may be justifiably said to be a *fine* art, like certain forms of dance. The first step would be to distinguish purposive sports which do not rely on aesthetic criteria for scoring (like hockey), from aesthetic sports which do (like figure skating). Whether, in sport, pretty plays in dramatic games or graceful movements in flawless routines can *ever* constitute art is then the issue. This section divides between David Best, who argues that sport is never art, and Peter J. Arnold, who argues that sport is sometimes art. Along the way each discusses such issues as the nature of art and what makes something, whether athletic or artistic, a source of aesthetic pleasure.

9. The Aesthetic in Sport*

David Best

Introduction

There appears to be a considerable and increasing interest in looking at various sporting activities from the aesthetic point of view. In this chapter I shall examine a central characteristic of paradigm cases of objects of the aesthetic attitude, namely works of art, in order to see to what extent it is applicable to sport. Finally, I shall consider the question of whether sports in general, or at least those sports in which the aesthetic is ineliminable, can legitimately be regarded as forms of art. It will be shown that discussion of this topic is confused by a failure to recognise the significance of the distinction between the aesthetic and the artistic.

The Aesthetic Point of View

It might be asked whether all sports can be considered from the aesthetic point of view, when one takes account of the great and increasingly varied range of such activities. That question at least can be answered clearly in the affirmative, for any object or activity can be considered aesthetically—cars, mountains, even mathematical proofs and philosophical arguments.

This raises a point discussed in Chapter 5 [of *Philosophy and Human Movement*], that it is less conducive to error to regard the aesthetic as a way of perceiving an object or activity than as a constituent feature of it. I mention this because the term 'aesthetic content' is often used, and it carries the misleading implication that the aesthetic is some sort of element which can be added or subtracted. In order to clarify the point

---

* From David Best, *Philosophy and Human Movement* (London: Allen & Unwin, 1978), pp. 99-122. When granting permission to reprint this chapter, Best wished it known that his views on sport aesthetics have since changed. Some of these developments are discussed in the next chapter.

it may be worth considering a way in which the notion of aesthetic content was once defended. It was argued that the aesthetic cannot be merely a point of view since this fails to account for the fact that some objects and activities are more interesting aesthetically than others. Thus, it was said, there must be aesthetic content since, for instance, the appearance of a car could be affected by altering physical features of it, and in a similar way gracefulness could be added to or subtracted from a movement.

A factor which may well contribute to confusion on this issue is a failure to distinguish two ways in which 'aesthetic' is used. These can be broadly characterised as (1) evaluative, and (2) conceptual. An example of the former is: 'Borzov is an aesthetic athlete.' This is to use the term in a positive evaluative way, and is roughly equivalent to 'graceful,' or 'aesthetically pleasing.' But it is clearly the latter usage which is our concern, and this includes both the beautiful and the ugly; the graceful and the clumsy; the aesthetically interesting and the aesthetically uninteresting. Thus, whatever one's opinion of the appearance of the car, it has to be considered from the aesthetic point of view in order for any relevant judgement to be offered.

Now certainly it does not necessarily indicate a misapprehension to use the term 'aesthetic content.' It depends what is meant by it, and there are two possibilities:

(1) To assert that A is part of the content of B would normally imply that A is a constituent feature or component of B, and that therefore a close examination of B will reveal it. This naturally leads to the kind of error discussed in Chapters 5 and 6 [of *Philosophy and Human Movement*]. For, since statements about aesthetic content cannot be supported by empirical investigation, there will be a strong temptation to assume either that the aesthetic content is non-physical and some-how lying behind the physical object or activity, or that the aesthetic is a purely subjective content, not in the object itself but solely in the mind of the perceiver. And since in neither case can any sense be given to the notion of justification of aesthetic judgements, this is to reduce them to vacuity.

(2) However, if the term 'aesthetic content' is used to make the point that it is only by reference to objective features that aesthetic judgements can be justified, then the notion is unexceptionable. There is a complex issue here, which involves the distinction between physical movements and actions, which was explained in Chapter 5 [of *Philosophy and Human Movement*]. To make the point briefly, precisely the same physical movements may be aesthetically pleasing in one context yet displeasing in another. For example, one may regard a series of movements in a dance as poor aesthetically until it is pointed out that one has misinterpreted the performance. Under the different interpretation they can now be seen as superb. Although there is no physical difference in the movements, the revised judgement

is based upon the way in which the new interpretation has determined a different context. Nevertheless, the new interpretation and aesthetic judgement depend solely upon *objective* aspects of the movements. (I consider the nature of the objective reasons given in support of aesthetic judgements in another book, 1974.)

Thus aesthetic judgements are certainly answerable in this way to observable physical features, and if the point of using the term 'aesthetic content' is to emphasise the fact no confusion need arise. However, since it is so frequently used in, or with the misleading implications of, the former sense, it is, in my view, wiser to eschew the term.

The Aesthetic Concept

Although anything can be considered from the aesthetic aspect, some activities and objects are more centrally of aesthetic interest than others. Works of art, to take a paradigm case, are primarily of aesthetic interest, although even they can be considered from other points of view. For instance, paintings are commonly considered as an investment. Hence we need to ask what distinguishes the aesthetic from other ways of looking at objects. One important characteristic is that the aesthetic is a nonfunctional or non-purposive concept. To take a central example again, when we are considering a work of art from the aesthetic point of view we are not considering it in relation to some external function or purpose it serves. It cannot be evaluated aesthetically according to its degree of success in achieving some such extrinsic end. By contrast, when a painting is considered as an investment, then it is assessed in relation to an extrinsic end, namely that of maximum appreciation in financial value.

This characteristic of the aesthetic immediately raises an insuperable objection to theories which propose an over-simple relation between sport and the aesthetic by identifying them too closely. For example, it is sometimes claimed that sport just is an art form (for example, see Anthony, 1968), and it has been suggested that the aesthetic is the concept which unifies all the activities subsumed under the heading of physical education (see Carlisle, 1969). But there are many sports, indeed the great majority, which are like the painting considered as an investment in that there is an aim or purpose which can be identified independently of the way it is accomplished. That is, the *manner* of achievement of the primary purpose is of little or no significance as long as it comes within the rules. For example, it is normally far more important for a football or hockey team *that* a goal is scored than *how* it is scored. In very many sports of this kind the over-riding factor is the achievement of some such independently specifiable end, since that is the mark of success.

This non-purposive character of the aesthetic is often misunderstood. Such a misunderstanding is manifested in the commonly supposed consequence that therefore there can be no point in art. The presupposition underlying this misunderstanding is that an activity can intelligibly be said to be of point or value only in relation to some external purpose towards which it is directed. Now in cases where such an extrinsic end is the primary consideration, evaluation does depend on it. As we have seen, a painting considered solely as an investment would be evaluated entirely according to its degree of success in achieving maximum capital appreciation. Where the attainment of the end is the over-riding consideration, the means of attaining it obviously becomes relatively unimportant. It would not matter, for instance, what sort of painting it was as long as the end was realized. Similarly, if someone should wish to improve the petrol consumption of his car by changing the carburettor, the design of the new one and the materials from which it is made would be unimportant as long as it succeeded in giving maximum mileage per gallon.

However, the purpose of art cannot be specified in this way, although the misapprehension we are now considering stems from the mistaken assumption that the point of an activity *must* somehow be identifiable as an end or purpose distinct from the activity itself. Yet where art, or more generally the aesthetic, is concerned, the distinction between means and end is inapplicable. For instance, the question "What is the purpose of that novel?" can be answered comprehensively only in terms of the novel itself. It might be objected that this is not entirely true, since the purpose of some novels could be given as, for example, exposing certain deleterious social conditions. But this objection misses the point I am trying to make, for if the purpose is the external one of exposing those social conditions then in principle it could equally well, or perhaps better, be realised in other ways, such as the publication of a social survey or a political speech. The report of the social survey is evaluated solely by reference to its purpose of effectively conveying the information, whereas this would be quite inappropriate as a standard for the aesthetic evaluation of a novel. To put the same point another way, from the point of view of efficient conveying of information, the precise form and style of writing of the report is unimportant except insofar as it affects the achievement of that purpose. One report could be as good as another, although the style of writing or compilation was different from or even inferior to the other. There could not be a parallel situation in art in which, for example, one poem might be said to be as good as another although not so well written. This is an aspect of the complex problem of form and content in the arts. To put it briefly, there is a peculiarly intimate connection between the form of an object of aesthetic appreciation, i.e., the particular medium of expression, and its content, i.e., what is expressed in it. So that in art there cannot be a change of form of expression without a corresponding change in what is expressed. It is important to recognise that this is a logical point. For even if one way of writing the report were the clearest and most efficient, this is a mere contingent matter since it is always possible that a better method may be devised. But it is not a contingent matter that the best way of expressing the content of Solzhenitsyn's *One Day in the Life of Ivan Denisovich* is in the particular form of that novel, i.e., it would make no sense to suggest that its content could be more effectively conveyed in another way. So that the question becomes: "What is the purpose of this particular way of exposing the social conditions?" The end cannot be specified as "exposing such and such social conditions," but only as "exposing such and such social conditions in this particular way and no other." And to give a comprehensive account of what is meant by "in this particular way and no other" one would have to produce nothing less than the whole novel. The end cannot be identified apart from the manner of achieving it, and that is another way of saying that the presupposition encapsulated in the question, of explanation in terms of purposive action directed onto an external end, is unintelligible in the sphere of aesthetics. In short, in an important sense the answer to "What is the purpose of that novel?" will amount to a rejection of the question.

A further objection, which has important implications for the aesthetic in sport, might be that in that case how can we criticise a work of art if it can be justified only in terms of itself and there is nothing else with which it can be compared? There is a great deal to be said about the common misapprehension that to engage in critical reasoning is necessarily to generalise (see Bambrough, 1973). It is sufficient for my argument to recognise that critical appreciation of art consists largely in giving reasons why particular features contribute so effectively to or detract from *this particular* work of art. The important point for our purposes is to see again that the end is inseparable from the means of achieving it, for any suggested improvement is given in terms of the particular work of art in question. Another way of putting this point is to say that every feature of a work of art is relevant to the aesthetic assessment of it, whereas when we are judging something as a means to an end, there are irrelevant features of the means, or equally effective alternative means, of achieving the required end. To say that X is an irrelevant feature is always a criticism of a work of art, whereas this is not true of a functional object.

It is true that the aim in a sport cannot be considered in isolation from the rules or norms of that particular sport. Scoring a goal in hockey is not just a matter of getting the ball between the opponents' posts, but requires conformity to the laws of the game. Such requirements are implicit in the meaning of the term 'scoring a goal.' Nevertheless, in contrast to a work of art, within those limits there are many ways of achieving the end, i.e., of scoring a goal, in hockey.

The Gap: Purposive and Aesthetic Sports

At this point we need to direct our attention to the difference between types of sporting activities with respect to the relative importance of the aesthetic. On the one hand, there are those sports, which I shall call 'purposive' and which form the great majority, where the aesthetic is normally relatively unimportant. This category would include football, climbing, track and field events, orienteering and squash. In each of these sports the purpose can be specified independently of the manner of achieving it as long as it conforms to the limits set by the rules or norms—for example, scoring a goal and climbing the Eiger. Even in such sports as these, of course, certain moves or movements, indeed whole games or performances, can be considered from the aesthetic point of view, but it is not central to the activity. It should be recognised that this is a logical point. For example, an activity could obviously still count as football even if there were never a concern for the aesthetic. By contrast, it could not count as football if no one ever tried to score a goal. That is, in these sports it is the independently specifiable purpose which at least largely defines the character of the activity, and the aesthetic is incidental.

On the other hand, there is a category of sports in which the aim cannot be specified in isolation from the aesthetic, for example, synchronised swimming, trampolining, gymnastics, figure-skating and diving. I shall call these 'aesthetic' sports since they are similar to the arts in that their purpose cannot be considered apart from the manner of achieving it. There is an intrinsic end which cannot be identified apart from the means. Consider, for example, the notion of a vault in formal gymnastics. The end is not simply to get over the box somehow or other, even if one were to do so in a clumsy way and collapse afterwards in an uncontrolled manner. The way in which the appropriate movements are performed is not incidental but central to such a sport. That is, the aim cannot be specified simply as 'getting over the box,' but only in terms of the manner of achievement required. Indeed, aesthetic norms are implicit in the meaning of terms like 'vault' and 'dive,' in that to vault over a box is not the same as to jump over it, or to get over it somehow or other. Although such terms as 'vault' are not employed in Modern Educational Gymnastics, the same issue of principle applies. There may be greater flexibility in the possibilities of answering a particular task in Educational as compared with more formal gymnastics, yet it is still important to consider how, aesthetically, the task is answered. Clumsy, uncontrolled movements would not be regarded as contributing to an adequate way of answering the task, whichever of the indefinite number of ways may be chosen. Similarly, not any way of dropping into the water would count as a dive. One would have to satisfy at least to a minimal extent the aesthetic requirement built into the meaning of the term for a performance to count as even a bad dive.

The distinction, then, is clear. A purposive sport is one in which, within the rules or conventions, there is an indefinite variety of ways of achieving the end which at least largely defines the game. By contrast, an aesthetic sport is one in which the purpose cannot be specified independently of the manner of achieving it. For instance, it would make no sense to suggest to a figure-skater that it did not matter *how* he performed his movements, as long as he achieved the purpose of the sport, since that purpose inevitably *concerns* the manner of performance. It would make perfectly good sense to urge a football team to score goals without caring how they scored them. Perhaps the point can be made most clearly by reference to the example given above, of the aesthetic norms built into terms such as 'vault' and 'dive,' for whereas not *any* way of dropping into the water could count as even a bad dive, *any* way of getting the ball between the opponents' posts, as long as it is within the rules, would count as a goal, albeit a very clumsy or lucky one.

There is a common tendency to distinguish between these two types of sports in terms of competition. For example, in an interesting article on this topic, Reid (1970) distinguishes between what I have called purposive and aesthetic sports in the following way:

> Games come at the end of a kind of spectrum. In most games, competition against an opponent (individual or team) is assumed.... At the other end of the spectrum there are gymnastics, diving, skating ... in which grace, the manner in which the activity is carried out, seems to be of central importance.

Against this, I would point out that competition in Olympic gymnastics, skating and diving can be every bit as keen as it can be in rugby football. Reid is adopting the prevalent but mistaken practice of contrasting the competitive with the aesthetic. Yet, for instance, it is quite apparent that, on occasion, competition between dance companies, and between rival dancers within the same company, can be as intense and as nasty as it can in ice-hockey. Moreover, to take a paradigm case, there are competitive music festivals, in which a similar spirit may be engendered. The great Korean violinist, Kyung-Wha Chung, after winning first prize in one competition, remarked: "It was one of the worst experiences of my life, because competitions bring out the worst in people."

Closing the Gap

We can now return to the original question concerning the characterisation of the aesthetic way of looking at sport. By examining the paradigm cases of sports in which the aesthetic is logically inseparable from what the performer is trying to achieve, we might hope to discover aspects of this way of considering them which can be found to apply even to purposive sports, when they are looked at aesthetically.

In figure-skating, diving, synchronised swimming, trampolining and Olympic gymnastics it is of the first importance that there should be no wasted energy and no superfluous movements. Champion gymnasts, like Nadia Comaneci and Ludmilla Tourischeva, not only perform striking physical feats, but do so with such remarkable economy and efficiency of effort that it often looks effortless. There is an intensive concentration of the gymnast's effort so that it is all directed precisely and concisely onto that specific task. Any irrelevant movement or excessive expenditure of energy would detract from the quality of the performance as a whole, just as superfluous or exaggerated words, words which fail to contribute with maximum compression of meaning to the total effect, detract from the quality of a poem as a whole.

However, even in the case of the aesthetic sports there is still, although no doubt to a very limited extent, an externally identifiable aim; for example the requirements set by each particular movement, and by the particular group of movements, in gymnastics. Now it might be thought that it would be justifiable to regard such stringencies as analogous to, say, the form of a sonnet. That is, it may be thought more appropriate to regard them as setting a framework within which the performer has the opportunity to reveal his expertise in moving gracefully than as an externally identifiable aim. There is certainly something in this notion, but it is significant that there is no analogy in aesthetic sports with poetic licence. The poet may take liberties with the sonnet form without necessarily detracting from the quality of the sonnet, but if the gymnast deviates from the requirements of, for instance, a vault, however gracefully, then that inevitably does detract from the standard of the performance. Nevertheless, the main point for our purposes is that even if, in the aesthetic sports, the means never quite reaches the ultimate of complete identification with the end which is such an important distinguishing feature of the concept of art, it at least closely approximates to such an identification. The gap between means and end is almost, if not quite, completely closed.

Now I want to suggest that the same consideration applies to our aesthetic appreciation of sports of the purposive kind. However successful a sportsman may be in achieving the principal aim of his particular activity, our *aesthetic* acclaim is reserved for him who achieves it with maximum economy and efficiency of effort. We may admire the remarkable stamina and consistent success of an athlete such as Zátopek, but he was not an aesthetically attractive runner because so much of his movement seemed irrelevant to the ideal of most direct accomplishment of the task. The ungainliness of his style was constituted by the extraneous rolls or jerks which seemed wasteful in that they were not concisely aimed at achieving the most efficient use of his energy.

So to consider the purposive sports from the aesthetic point of view is to reduce the gap between means and end. It is, as nearly as possible, to telescope them into the ideal of unity. From a purely purposive point of view any way of winning, within the rules, will do, whereas not *any* way of winning will do as far as aesthetic considerations are concerned. There is a narrower range of possibilities available for the achievement of the end in an aesthetically pleasing way, since the end is no longer simply to win, but to win with the greatest economy and efficiency of effort. Nevertheless, the highest aesthetic satisfaction is experienced and given by the sportsman who not only performs with graceful economy, but who also achieves his purpose. The tennis player who serves a clean ace with impeccable style has, and gives to the spectator, far more aesthetic satisfaction than when he fractionally faults with an equally impeccable style. In the case of the purposive sports there is an independently specifiable framework, i.e., one which does not require the sort of judgement to assess achievement which is necessary in the aesthetic sports. Maximum aesthetic success still requires the attainment of the end, and the aesthetic in any degree requires direction onto that end, but the number of ways of achieving such success is reduced in comparison with the purely purposive interest of simply accomplishing the end in an independently specifiable sense.

This characteristic of the aesthetic in activities which are primarily functional also applies to the examples cited earlier of mathematical proofs and philosophical arguments. The proof of a theorem in Euclidean geometry or a philosophical argument is aesthetically pleasing to the extent that there is a clean and concisely directed focus of effort. Any over-elaborate, irrelevant, or repetitious section, in either case, would detract from the maximum economy in achieving the conclusion which gives greatest aesthetic satisfaction. Rhetorical flourishes, however aesthetically effective in other contexts, such as political speech, detract aesthetically from a philosophical argument by fussily blurring the ideal of a straight, direct line to the conclusion. The aesthetic satisfaction given by rhetoric in a political speech is related to the latter's different purpose of producing a convincing or winning argument rather than a valid one.

The aesthetic pleasure which we derive from sporting events of the purposive kind, such as hurdling and putting the shot, is, then, derived from looking at, or performing, actions which we take to be approaching the ideal of totally concise direction toward the required end of the particular activity. Skiing provides a good example. The stylish skier seems superbly economical, his body automatically accommodating itself, apparently without conscious effort on his part, to the most appropriate and efficient positions for the various types of conditions of terrain. By contrast, the skiing in a slalom race often appears ungainly because it looks forced and less concisely directed. The skier in such an event may achieve greater speed, but only by the expenditure of a disproportionate amount of additional effort. Similarly, athletes at the end of a distance race often abandon the smooth, graceful style with which they have run the greater part of the race. They achieve greater speed but at disproportionate cost, since ungainly, irrelevant movements appear—the head rolls, the body lurches, and so on. In rowing, too, some oarsmen can produce a faster speed with poor style but more, if less effectively produced, power. Even though it is wasteful, the net effective power may still be greater than that of the oarsman who directs his more limited gross power with far more efficiency and therefore with more pleasing aesthetic effect. It is often said that a good big 'un will beat a good little 'un. It is also true in many sports, unfortunately, that a poor big 'un may well beat a far better little 'un.

Perhaps these considerations do something to explain the heightened aesthetic awareness which is achieved by watching slow-motion films and television replays, since (1) we have more time to appreciate the manner of the performance, and (2) the object of the action, the purpose, in an extrinsic sense, becomes less important. That is, our attention is directed more to the character of the action than to its result. We can see whether and how every detail of every movement in the action as a whole contributes to making it the most efficient and economical way of accomplishing that particular purpose. A smooth, flowing style is more highly regarded aesthetically because it appears to require less effort for the same result than a jerky one. Nevertheless, as was mentioned above, achievement of the purpose is still important. However graceful and superbly directed the movements of a pole-vaulter, our aesthetic pleasure in his performance is marred if he knocks the bar off.

One additional and related factor is that some people naturally move gracefully whatever they may be doing, and this may contribute to the aesthetic effect of their actions in sport. If I may be pardoned for the outrageous pun, Muhammad Ali provides a striking example.

Several questions remain. For example, why are some sporting events regarded as less aesthetically pleasing than others, i.e., where we are not comparing actions within the same context of direction onto a common end, but comparing actions in different contexts? For instance, in my view the butterfly stroke in swimming, however well performed, seems less aesthetically pleasing than the crawl. Perhaps this is because it looks less efficient as a way of moving through the water, since there appears to be a disproportionate expenditure of effort in relation to the achievement. A similar example is race walking which, even at its best, never seems to me to be an aesthetically pleasing event. Perhaps, again, this is because one feels that the same effort would be more efficiently employed if the walker broke into a run. In each of these cases one is implicitly setting a wider context, seeing the action in terms of a wider purpose, of movement through water and movement over the ground respectively. But what of a sport such as weight-lifting, which many regard as providing little or no aesthetic pleasure, although it is hard to discover a wider context, a more economical direction on to a wider or similar end in another activity, with which we are implicitly comparing it? Perhaps the explanation lies simply in a general tendency to prefer, from an aesthetic point of view, sports which allow for smooth, flowing movements in the achievement of the primary purpose. Nevertheless, for the devotee, there are, no doubt, "beautiful" lifts, so called because they accomplish maximum direction of effort.

Now the objection has been made against my account that it fails to differentiate the aesthetic from the skilful. I think two points are sufficient to overcome this objection. First, as a careful reading of the chapter will reveal, my argument, if valid, shows that in sport the two concepts are certainly intimately related, but it also shows that they are not entirely co-extensive. I have marked some ways in which they diverge.

The second and more important point is this. Even if it were true that my argument had not revealed a distinction between the two concepts, that would not constitute an objection to it. For why should not those features of an action in virtue of which it is called skilful also be those in virtue of which it is called aesthetically pleasing? Wittgenstein once wrote: "Ethics and aesthetics are one." Whether or not one would want to accept that statement will depend on Wittgenstein's argument for it. One cannot simply dismiss it on the grounds that it *must* be self-defeating to offer a characterisation of the aesthetic which also characterises the ethical.

The supposed objection seems to incorporate the preconception that to have characterised the aesthetic is to have specified those essential features which can be shared by no other concept. This would be like denying that ginger can be an essential ingredient in ginger cakes on the ground that it is *also* an ingredient in ginger ale. The objector produced no argument, but simply assumed that an account which also fitted the skilful could not be adequate as an account of the aesthetic. So, in response to this supposed objection, I could simply reply: "You are right, I concede that my argument does not entirely distinguish the aesthetic from the skilful. But so far from constituting an objection to my argument, what you have provided amounts to a rough summary of it."

Context and Aesthetic Feeling

The foregoing argument raises two related considerations which have an important bearing upon the notion of aesthetic *experience* in sport. First, a movement cannot be considered aesthetically in isolation, but only in the context of a particular action in a particular sport. A graceful sweep of the left arm may be very effective in a dance, but the same movement may look ugly and absurd as part of a service action in tennis, or of a pitcher's action in baseball, since it detracts from the ideal of total concentration of effort to achieve the specific task. A specific movement is aesthetically satisfying only if, in the context of the action as a whole, it is seen as forming a unified structure which is regarded as the most economical and efficient method of achieving the required end.

Secondly, there is a danger of serious misconception arising from a mistaken dependence upon feelings as criteria of aesthetic quality, whether in sport or in any other activity, including dance and the other arts. This is part of the misconception to which we alluded in Chapter 6 [of *Philosophy and Human Movement*], and consists of taking the feeling of the performer or spectator as the ultimate arbiter. Yet, as we have seen, any feeling is intelligible only if it can be identified by its typical manifestation in behaviour. This is what Wittgenstein (1953) meant by saying that an inner process stands in need of outward criteria. Thus, in the present case, it is the observable physical movement which identifies the feeling and not, as is often believed, the inner feeling which suffuses the physical movement with aesthetic quality or meaning. The feeling could not even be identified if it were not normally experienced in certain objectively recognisable circumstances. One should resist the temptation, commonly encountered in discussion of dance and other forms of movement, to believe that it is how a movement feels which determines its character or effectiveness, whether aesthetic or purposive. That it feels right is no guarantee that it is right. Inexperienced oarsmen in an "eight" are often tempted to heave their bodies round violently in an attempt to propel the boat more quickly, because such an action gives a feeling of much greater power. Yet in fact it will upset the balance of the boat and thus reduce the effectiveness of the rowing of the crew as a whole. The most effective stroke action can best be judged by the coach who is watching the whole performance from the bank, not by the feeling of the individual oarsmen or even of all the crew. Similarly, in tennis and skiing, to take just two examples, the feeling of an action is often misleading as to its maximum efficiency. A common error in skiing is to lean into the slope and at a certain stage in his progress a learner starts to make turns for the first time which feel very good. Yet, however exhilarating the feeling, if he is leaning the wrong way he will be considerably hampered from making further progress, because in fact he is not directing his efforts in the most effective manner. There are innumerable other such examples one could cite, and this, of course, has important implications for education. If the arbiter of success in physical activities is what the students feel, rather than what they can be observed to do, it is hard to see how such activities can be learned and taught.

However, to refer to an objection which we considered in Chapter 6 [of *Philosophy and Human Movement*], it is important not to misunderstand this point by going to the opposite extreme, for I am not saying that we cannot be guided by such feelings, or that they are of no value. My point is that they are useful and reliable only to the extent that they are answerable to patterns of behaviour which can be *observed* to be most efficiently directed onto the particular task. This reveals the connection between this and the preceding point, for it is clear that the character and efficiency of a particular movement cannot be considered in isolation from the whole set of related movements of which it forms a part, and from the purpose towards which they are, as a whole, directed. Thus the context in which the movement occurs is a factor of an importance which it is impossible to exaggerate, since the feeling could not even be identified, let alone evaluated, if it were not normally experienced as part of an objectively recognisable action.

In this respect I should like to question what is often said about the aesthetic attitude, namely that it is essentially or predominantly contemplative. Reid (1970), for instance, says: "In an aesthetic situation we attend to what we perceive in what is sometimes called a 'contemplative' way." Now it may be that a concern with the arts and the aesthetic is largely contemplative, but I see no reason to deny, indeed I see good reason to insist, that one can have what are most appropriately called aesthetic *feelings* while actually performing an activity. There are numerous examples, such as a well-executed dive, a finely timed stroke in squash, a smoothly accomplished series of movements in gymnastics, an outing in an "eight" when the whole crew is pulling in unison, with unwavering balance, and a training run when one's body seems to be completely under one's control. For many, the feelings derived from such performances are part of the enjoyment of participation, and "aesthetic" seems the most appropriate way to characterise them. Reid says that "a dancer or actor in the full activity of dancing or acting is often, perhaps always, in some degree contemplating the product of his activity." Later, he says of games players: "There is no time while the operation is going on to dwell upon aesthetic qualities.... Afterwards, the participant may look back upon his experience contemplatively with perhaps some aesthetic satisfaction." Again, of the aesthetic in cricket, he remarks: "the batsman may enjoy it too, although at the moment of play he has no time to dwell upon it. But to produce exquisite strokes for contemplation is not part of his dominating motive as he is actually engaged in the game...." Yet the batsman's aesthetic experience is not necessarily dependent upon his having time at the moment of playing the stroke to "dwell upon it," nor is it limited to a retrospective contemplation of his performance. If he plays a perfectly timed cover drive with the ball flashing smoothly and apparently effortlessly from the face of his bat to the boundary, the aesthetic satisfaction of the batsman is intrinsic to what he is doing. The aesthetic is not a distinct but perhaps concurrent activity, and it need not depend upon detached or retrospective contemplation. His experience is logically inseparable from the stroke he is playing, in that it is identifiable only by his particular action in that context. And it is quite natural, unexceptionable, and perhaps unavoidable to call such an experience "aesthetic." "Kinaesthetic" or "tactile" would not tell the whole story by any means, since producing the same physical movement in a quite different context, for instance in a laboratory, could not count as producing the same feeling. Indeed, it is significant that we tend naturally to employ aesthetic terms to describe the feelings involved in such actions. We say that a stroke felt "beautiful," and it was so to the extent that it was efficiently executed in relation to the specific purpose of the action in the sport concerned. Many participants in physical activities have experienced the exquisite feeling, for instance, of performing a dance or gymnastic sequence, of sailing over the bar in a pole vault, or of accomplishing a fluent series of Christis with skis immaculately parallel. It is difficult to know how to describe these feelings other than as "aesthetic." It is certainly the way in which those of us who have taken part in such activities tend spontaneously to refer to them. So, although I do not wish to deny that contemplation is an important part of the aesthetic, I would contend that it is not exhaustive. It is by no means unusual to experience aesthetic feelings, properly so called, while actually engaged and fully involved in physical activities. Moreover, many of us who have derived considerable pleasure from a wide variety of sporting activities would want to insist that such aesthetic experience constitutes a large part of the enjoyment of participation.

The Aesthetic and the Artistic

In the case of the purposive sports, then, as the actions become more and more directly aimed, with maximum economy and efficiency, at the required end, they become more and more specific, and the gap between means and end is to that extent reduced. That is, increasingly it is less possible to specify the means apart from the end. In these sports the gap will, nevertheless, never be entirely closed in that there cannot be the complete identification of means and end, or more accurately perhaps, the inappropriateness of the distinction between means and end, which obtains in the case of art. For even if in fact there is a single most efficient and economical way of achieving a particular end, this is a contingent matter. The evolution of improved high-jumping methods is a good example. The scissor jump was once regarded as the most efficient method, but it has been overtaken by the straddle, the Western roll and the Fosbury flop.

There remains an interesting question. The aesthetic sports have been shown to be similar to the arts with respect to the impossibility of distinguishing means and ends. Does this mean that such sports can legitimately be regarded as art forms? I should want to insist that they cannot, for two reasons. First, as we have seen, there is good reason to doubt whether the means/end distinction ever quite becomes inappropriate, although it almost reaches that point, even in the aesthetic sports. That is, unlike dance, in these sports there is still an externally specifiable aim even though, for instance, it is impossible entirely to specify what the gymnast is trying to achieve apart from the way in which he is trying to achieve it. Perhaps this is what some physical educationists are getting at when they say, rather vaguely, that a distinction between gymnastics and dance is that the former is objective while the latter is subjective.

However, it is the second reason which is the more important one, and this concerns the distinction which is almost universally overlooked or oversimplified, and therefore misconceived, between the aesthetic and the artistic. The aesthetic applies, for instance, to sunsets, birdsong and mountain ranges, whereas the artistic tends to be limited, at least in its central uses, to artifacts or performances intentionally created by man—*objets trouvés*,* if regarded as art, would be so in an extended sense.

---

* = found objects, whether natural or discarded human artifacts, seen as aesthetically interesting and often displayed for that reason.

Throughout this chapter I have so far followed the common practice of taking 'aesthetic' to refer to the genus of which the artistic is a species. My reason for doing so is that any other difference between the two concepts is of no consequence to my main argument, since their logical character with respect to the possibility of distinguishing between means and end is the same. However, in order to consider the question of whether any sport can justifiably be regarded as an art form a more adequate distinction between the aesthetic and the artistic is required, and on examination it becomes clear that there is a much more important issue here than is commonly supposed. I can begin to bring out the issue to which I refer by considering Reid's answer to the question. He is prepared to allow that what I call the aesthetic sports may justifiably be called art, but in my view his conclusion is invalidated because his own formulation of the distinction overlooks a crucial characteristic of art. He writes (1970):

> When we are talking about the category of art, as distinct from the category of the aesthetic, we must be firm, I think, in insisting that in art there is someone who has made (or is making) purposefully an artifact, and that in his purpose there is contained as an essential part the idea of producing an object (not necessarily a "thing": it could be a movement or a piece of music) in some medium for aesthetic contemplation ... the movement (of a gymnast, skater, diver), carried out in accordance with the general formula, has aesthetic quality fused into it, transforming it into an art quality.... The question is whether the production of aesthetic value is intrinsically part of the purpose of these sports. (If so, on my assumptions, they will be in part, at least, art.)

This certainly has the merit of excluding natural phenomena such as sunsets and roses, but some people might regard his exclusion of *objets trouvés* as somewhat difficult to justify. What, in my view, is worse, this conception would include much which we should be strongly disinclined to call "art." For example, a wallpaper pattern is normally designed to give aesthetic pleasure, but it would not on that account, at least in the great majority of cases, be regarded as art. Many such counter-examples spring to mind; for instance the paint on the walls of my office, the shape of radiators and spectacles, and coloured toilet paper. In each case the intention is to give aesthetic pleasure, but none is art (which is not necessarily to deny that, in certain unusual circumstances, any of them could be considered as art, or as part of a work of art).

Reid has done sufficient in my view to show clearly that the great majority of sports cannot legitimately be regarded as art. For the *principal* aim in most sports is certainly not to produce performances for aesthetic pleasure. The aesthetic is incidental. And if it should be argued against me that nevertheless such purposive sports could be considered from the aesthetic point of view, my reply would be that so could everything else. Hence, if that were to be regarded as the distinguishing feature of art then *everything* would be art, and thus the term 'art' would no longer have any application.

Nevertheless, Reid's formulation fails, I think, because he overlooks the central aspect of the concept of art which underlies the fact that there are cases where one may appreciate a work of art aesthetically but not artistically. To understand the significance of this point, consider the following example. Some years ago I went to watch a performance by Ram Gopal, the great Indian classical dancer, and I was enthralled by the exhilarating quality of his movements. Yet I did not appreciate, because I could not have understood, his dance artistically, for there is an enormous number of precise meanings given to hand gestures in Indian classical dance, of which I knew none. So it seems clear that my appreciation was of the aesthetic not the artistic.

This example brings out the important characteristic of the concept of art which I particularly want to emphasise, since it is generally overlooked by those who conflate 'aesthetic' and 'artistic.' Moreover, the failure to recognise it is probably the main source of misconceived distinctions between the two terms. I shall first outline the point roughly, and go on to elucidate it more fully in relation to other claims made for sport as art.

It is distinctive of any art form that its conventions allow for the possibility of the expression of a conception of life situations. Thus the arts are characteristically concerned with contemporary moral, social, political and emotional issues. Yet this is not true of the aesthetic. I think it is because he does not recognise the significance of this point that Reid is prepared to allow that the aesthetic sports may legitimately be regarded as art forms. But it is this characteristic of art which is my reason for insisting that even those sports in which the aesthetic is intrinsic, and which are therefore performed to give aesthetic satisfaction, cannot justifiably be considered as art. For in synchronised swimming, figure-skating, diving, trampolining and gymnastics, the performer does not, as part of the convention of the activity, have the possibility of expressing through his particular medium his view of life situations. It is difficult to imagine a gymnast who included in his sequence movements which expressed his view of war, or of love in a competitive society, or of any other such issue. Certainly if he did so it would, unlike art, *detract* to that extent from his performance.

Of course there are cases, even in the accredited arts, such as abstract paintings and dances, where we are urged not to look for a meaning but simply to enjoy the line, colour, movement, etc., without trying to read anything into them. But it is intrinsic to the notion of an art form that it can at least allow for the possibility of considering issues of social concern, and this is not possible in the aesthetic sports. Incidentally, if I am right that the activities of art and sport are quite distinct, this poses problems for those who suggest that the aesthetic sports may provide one method of, perhaps an introduction to, education in the arts, although of course this is not in the least to cast doubt on their aesthetic value. At their best these sports are undoubtedly superb aesthetically, but they are not, in my view, art.

Sport and Art

Partly in order to bring out more fully the important characteristic of the concept of art which I have just outlined, and partly because of the widespread misconception on the issue, I should like further to elucidate my reasons for denying the common supposition that sport can legitimately be considered as art.

As we have seen, it is clear that there is a distinction between the aesthetic and the artistic, even though it may be difficult precisely to delineate it. Yet, in the literature on sport, one still very frequently encounters an illicit slide from such terms as 'beautiful' and 'graceful' to 'art.' An author will refer to a general interest in the beauty of the movement in various sporting activities, and will assume implicitly or explicitly that this entitles such activities to be considered as art. Anthony (1968) and Reid (1970) give several examples, and the same confusion runs through Carlisle (1969) who writes, for instance, that "various forms of dance are accepted as art forms and aesthetic criteria are also applied in other activities, e.g., ice-skating, diving, Olympic gymnastics and synchronised swimming." A more recent example is Lowe (1976) who writes: "By analysing dance, as one of the performing arts, with the object of deducing the aesthetic components ... a step will be taken closer to the clarification of the beauty of sport as a performing art." So far as I can understand this, Lowe seems to be guilty of the confusion to which I refer, since clearly 'beauty' and its cognates do not necessarily imply 'art.' To say that a young lady is beautiful is not to say that she is a work of art.

For the reasons already given, I submit that, despite the amount of literature on the topic, we should finally abandon this persistent but misguided attempt to characterise sport *in general* as art. Quite apart from what seems to me the obvious misconception involved, I just do not see why it should be thought that sport would somehow be endowed with greater respectability if it could be shown to be art.

There is, of course, a much more convincing case to be made for the credentials of the aesthetic sports as art, although even here I do not think it succeeds. My rejection of the case hinges on the way I have characterised the distinction between the aesthetic and the artistic. It would seem that any attempt to draw this distinction in terms of definition, or by reference to particular kinds of objects or performances, is almost certainly doomed to failure. Hence I distinguish the two concepts by drawing attention to a characteristic which is central to any legitimate art *form*, rather than to a work of art within that medium. Thus, to repeat the point, my own formulation is that any art form, properly so-called, must at least *allow for* the possibility of the expression of a conception of life issues, such as contemporary moral, social and political problems. Such a possibility is an *intrinsic* part of the concept of art, by which I mean that without it an activity could not count as a legitimate art form. It is certainly a crucial factor in the ways in which the arts have influenced society. Examples abound. For instance, it is reported that during the occupation of France in the war a German officer, indicating the painting *Guernica*, asked Picasso, "Did you do that?" To which Picasso replied, "No, you did."

By contrast, such a possibility is not intrinsic to any sport. However, this point has been misunderstood, as a result of which it has been argued against me that in sport, too, there can be comment on life issues. The commonest example cited was that of black American athletes on the rostrum at the Olympic Games, who gave the clenched-fist salute for Black Power during the playing of the national anthem. But this does not constitute a counter-example, since such a gesture is clearly *extrinsic* to, not made from within, the conventions of sport as such. The conventions of art are in this respect significantly different from those in sport, since it is certainly intrinsic to art that a view could be expressed, for instance on colour discrimination, as in Athol Fugard's plays about the issue in South Africa.

We have seen that since aesthetic terms such as 'beauty' are often applied to sport, it is sometimes erroneously supposed that therefore sport is art. A similar misconception occurs with respect to the terms 'dramatic,' 'tragic,' and their cognates. These terms are used in a notoriously slippery way, hence it certainly cannot be assumed that they are used in other contexts as they are in art. For instance, if I were to leap up during a meeting, shout abusive terms, and hurl a cup through a window, that would certainly be dramatic, but I am modest enough to assume that no one would regard it as artistic.

It is an understood part of the convention that tragedy in a play happens to the *fictional characters* being portrayed, and not to the actors, i.e., the living people taking part. By contrast, and ignoring for a moment the issue of whether it would be legitimately employed in such a context, "tragedy" in sport *does* happen to the participants, i.e., to the living people taking part. For example, let us imagine that I am playing the part of Gloucester, in the play *King Lear*. In the scene where his eyes are put out it is agonising for the character in the play, Gloucester; not for me, the actor. There is no comparable convention in sport such that it would make sense to say of a serious injury in rugby that it occurred to the full-back, and not to the man who was playing full-back. While in Canada recently I was given an interesting illustration of the point. A party of Eskimos, attending a performance of *Othello*, were appalled to see what they took to be the killing of people on the stage. They had to be reassured by being taken backstage after the performance to see the actors still alive. The Eskimos had assumed that different actors would be required for each performance.

To put the point roughly, it is a central convention of art, in contrast to sport, that the object of one's attention is an *imagined* object. Thus a term such as 'tragic,' used of art, has to be understood as deriving its meaning from that convention. Yet, although this is a central convention of art, it is overlooked or misconstrued by most of those who argue that sport is art, or drama. This omission vitiates a good deal of the literature on the topic. Reid (1970) gives several examples, including that of Maheu, who claims that "spectator sports are the true theatre of our day"; Carlisle (1969) who supports the contention that cricket is "an art form both dramatic and visual"; Kitchin, who in an article on "Sport as drama" writes of international soccer: "This is the authentic theatre in the round, from which Hungary's Manager made a thirty-yard running exit with both hands clenched over his eyes.... Soccer is drama without a script." Similarly, Keenan (1973) in an article entitled "The athletic contest as a 'tragic' form of art," writes: "There is no doubt that athletic contests, like other human endeavours, provide drama. No one would question whether Bannister's effort which produced the first sub-four-minute mile was dramatic." But I would seriously question whether, indeed I would deny that, 'dramatic' is being used here in the same sense as when it occurs in the context of discussion of a play, since the relevant convention is lacking. That there is no comparable convention in sport can be brought out most clearly by the lack of any analogue with a fictional character. What happens to Gloucester does not happen to the person playing the part of Gloucester. The analogue in sport would have to be something like: "What happened to Hungary's Manager did not happen to the man who held the position as manager," and "What happened to the athlete who completed the first sub-four-minute mile did not happen to Bannister, who took part in the race," both of which are palpably absurd.

There are two common uses of the term 'tragic' which are outside, and which therefore should not be confused with its use within, the conventions of drama:

(1) Where the term is used, for instance, of serious injury to a sportsman, the analogue in a play would be serious injury to an actor, for example in an accident during a duelling scene. 'Tragic' in this sense does not depend on conventions at

all, whether sporting or artistic, but is used to refer to a poignantly sad and distressing event in real life, such as a seriously crippling or fatal accident or illness.

(2) On the other hand, in the irritatingly prevalent but barbarously debased sense of the term where 'tragic' is used, for instance, of the failure of a sportsman to achieve a success on which he had set his heart, the analogue in drama would be not some tragic event in a play but, for instance, the failure of an actor in a crucial role, or his failure to obtain a role which he earnestly wanted. It is still quite different from the use of the term within the conventions of drama. Strangely enough, Keenan (1973) recognises this point to some extent, yet fails to realise that it undermines his whole case. He writes: "We can truly sympathise with classic efforts of athletic excellence that end in tragedy. They parallel the difficult episodes in life." As one example, he cites an Olympic marathon race:

> The amazing Pietri entered the stadium with an enormous lead on the field, needing only to negotiate the last 385 yards to win. His effort had left him in an obvious state of extreme physical fatigue.... The crowd cheered lustily for him to continue, to fight off the fatigue, to win. His final collapse came near the finish line as the eventual winner ... was just entering the stadium.

This example, so far from supporting Keenan's case reveals the fatal flaw in it, for 'tragedy' here is used in the latter sense adumbrated above and is totally different from the way the term is used within and as part of the conventions of drama. The point can be brought sharply into focus by recognising that a poignantly tragic moment in drama is a *triumph*, a mark of *success*, for an actor, whereas, by contrast a 'tragic' moment in sport is a *failure*, even if a noble and courageous failure, for the competitor.

The importance of the conventions of art can be brought out in another way, by reference to the use of the term 'illusion.' In the context of the arts 'illusion' is not employed as it would be of, for instance, a mirage. One actually, if mistakenly, believes that an oasis is there, whereas one does not actually believe that someone is being murdered on a stage. Or at least, if one should actually believe that someone is being murdered this significantly reveals a failure to grasp one of the most important conventions of drama. The term 'illusion' is used in a different, if related, sense in the context of art. I say that the sense is related because, for instance, the actors, theatre management and producer, by means of lighting, stage effects and a high standard of acting, try to induce the audience to suspend their disbelief, as it were. Nevertheless, as Scruton (1974) puts it, our experience of representation and expression in art "derives from imagination, not belief."

Of course this is not in the least to deny that it is possible to be imaginative in sport, although I have been rather surprisingly misunderstood in this respect. What it does deny is that there are analogous conventions in sport such that the participants have to be imagined, as one has to imagine the characters in a play or novel.

In short, the misconception of those writers who persist in what I firmly believe are misguided attempts to argue that sport is an art form, stems from their ignoring or misconstruing the crucial importance of the *art* aspect of a work of art. For instance, one commonly experiences emotional responses to both artistic and sporting performances, and as both spectator and performer. Now, emotional feelings can be identified only by criteria, of which the most important is what is called the "intensional object," i.e., the kind of object towards which the emotion is directed. In the case of art, the intensional object cannot be characterised in isolation from the relevant conventions. The point becomes particularly clear, perhaps, when we think how we can be moved by completely non-naturalistic works of art, such as surrealism, abstract expressionism, and an allegory such as *Le Petit Prince* by Saint-Exupéry.

Now of course with respect to sport, too, the intensional object cannot be characterised independently of the conventions of that particular kind of activity. The point was brought home vividly to me when for the first time I watched an American football match, which was a keenly contested local derby between two rival high schools. There was considerable partisan excitement, but I was unable to share in it because I did not understand the game. As an even clearer example, a friend in Jasper told me of his experience, while working in the North West Territories, of trying to teach the local Eskimos how to play soccer. He was frustrated, apparently, by their inability to understand, or at least refusal to accept, that the purpose of the game was to defeat the opposing team. The Eskimos were much too genial to adopt such an uncivilised, competitive ethos, hence if a team were winning, members of it would promptly score in their own goal in order to be generous to their opponents.

So one certainly needs to understand the conventions of sport, too, in order to become emotionally involved in the appropriate way. But the conventions of sport are in important respects very different from those of art, even in the case of aesthetic sports such as figure-skating. The champion skater John Curry has strongly expressed his conviction that figure-skating *should* be regarded as an art form, and the superb Canadian skater, Toller Cranston, is frequently quoted as a counter-example by Canadians. He, too, apparently, has often insisted that figure-skating is an art. However, this contention is based on a confusion, and in my opinion it would be clearer to conceive of them as two quite distinct kinds of activity. Then we should have on one hand the *sport* of figure-skating, and on the other hand the *art* of modern dance on ice, which these skaters want to create as a new art form. It is interesting that Toller Cranston is said to have expressed annoyance at the limitations imposed by the conventions and rules of the *sport*, and has made his point forcefully by *deliberately* performing his figure-skating in several competitions *as* an art form. For instance, in response to the music he had flouted the canons of the sport by performing movements which *did* express his view of life situations. But it is significant that, much to his further chagrin, he lost marks for doing so. In my view the judges were quite right. The context of sport, even an aesthetic sport, is not appropriate for art. It is significant, perhaps, and tacitly concedes my point, that John Curry has put his convictions into practice by creating "The John Curry Theatre of Skating."

Now it might be objected that in denying in this way that sport can legitimately be regarded as art I am simply being stipulative. That is, it might be said that this is arbitrarily to lay down how the term 'art' should be used. This objection is of the same kind as that which was discussed in Chapter 4 [of *Philosophy and Human Movement*] with respect to the use of 'intellectual,' and it can be met in a similar way. Certainly philosophers cannot legislate how words should be used, and what is to count as correct usage. 'Artistic' could be used as synonymous with 'aesthetic,' and there could be no *philosophical* objection to what I regard as barbarously degenerate uses such as 'the art of cooking.' The philosophical point is that, however the term may be used, this will not *remove*, even although it may blur, the relevant distinction. That is, if 'art' were to be used as broadly as this, there would still be a distinction between those forms of activity which have, and those which do not have, intrinsic to their conventions, the possibility of comment on life issues in the way described. And in such a case, it would be necessary to employ some other term to mark those which have this kind of convention. Hence it seems to me much less conducive to confusion to restrict 'art' to such activities.

To repeat the point, then, in my opinion it is high time we buried once for all the prolix attempts to show that sport is art. It may be of interest to point up illuminating similarities, but only confusion can accrue from the attempt to equate the two kinds of activity. In the case of an aesthetic sport such as figure-skating the suggestion is at least initially plausible because of the widespread failure to recognise the important distinction between the aesthetic and the artistic, and because figure-skating, unlike, for instance, football, can so easily become an art form. But in the case of the purposive sports, which constitute the great majority, there is not even a *prima facie* case, even though there may be many movements in such sports which are superb aesthetically.

Rather ironically, the fact that sporting activities and the movements of athletes have been the subject for art, for instance in painting and sculpture, is sometimes adduced, at least by implication, in support of the contention that sport is art. For example, Lowe (1976) writes:

> Among sculptors, R. Tait McKenzie has brought a fine sense of movement to his athletic studies cast in bronze. There is no question about the aesthetic qualities of these art works: hence they provide intrinsic clues to our grasp of the elusive nature of beauty in sport.

I say that it is ironic because examination reveals that this kind of argument achieves the very opposite of what its authors intend, since it makes the point which could also be regarded as a summary of my distinction between the aesthetic and the artistic. For whereas sport can be the subject of art, art could not be the subject of sport. Indeed, the very notion of a *subject* of sport makes no sense.

REFERENCES

1. Anthony, W.J., "Sport and physical education as a means of aesthetic education," *British Journal of Physical Education*, vol. 60, no. 179 (March 1968).

2. Bambrough, J.R., "To reason is to generalise," *The Listener*, vol. 89, no. 2285 (11 January 1973).

3. Best, D., *Expression in Movement and the Arts* (London: Lepus Books, Henry Kimpton Publishers, 1974).

4. Carlisle, R., "The concept of physical education," *Proceedings of the Philosophy of Education Society of Great Britain*, vol. 3 (January 1969).

5. Keenan, F., "The athletic contest as a 'tragic' form of art," in *The Philosophy of Sport*, ed. R.G. Osterhoudt (Springfield, Illinois: C.C. Thomas, 1973).

6. Lowe, B., "Towards scientific analysis of the beauty of sport," *British Journal of Physical Education*, vol. 7, no. 4 (July 1976).

7. Reid, L.A., "Sport, the aesthetic and art," *British Journal of Educational Studies*, vol. 18, no. 3 (1970).

8. Scruton, R., *Art and Imagination* (London: Methuen, 1974).

9. Wittgenstein, L., *Philosophical Investigations* (Oxford: Basil Blackwell, 1953).

10. SPORT, THE AESTHETIC AND ART: FURTHER THOUGHTS*

PETER J. ARNOLD

O ver the past few years the relationship of sport to art has been a matter of some considerable controversy. It centres not on whether sport can be a subject of art, which is clearly possible, but whether or not sport itself can be regarded as an art. Put more specifically the question is: Are there any sports that are so constituted that they may be regarded as a form of art? It is a further attempt to look at this question that is the main concern of this paper.

In recent years there have been broadly speaking two groups of writers: those who have argued that some sports can or should be considered as art, and those that have rejected such a view. It is because both groups have not, either individually or collectively, been wholly convincing that it is proposed to examine this topic once more, having taken note of the exchanges that have taken place and the clarifications and distinctions that have been made. In particular I aim:

(i) to show that the concept of the aesthetic is not to be confused with that of art;

(ii) to reaffirm that there are three logically distinct categories in relation to physical activities when looked at from the perspective of the aesthetic and art;

(iii) to critically examine previous attempts to establish sport as an art as well as Best's view that sport is not art;   ·

(iv) to look at certain of the aesthetic sports, particularly figure skating, to see whether or not they may or may not be considered as vignette art forms.

* Peter J. Arnold, "Sport, the Aesthetic and Art: Further Thoughts," *British Journal of Educational Studies* 38.2 (1990), pp. 160-79.

1. The Aesthetic and Art

It is normally recognised that the notion of the aesthetic is wider than that of art. Yet with many writers this distinction is often disregarded. The elision of one with the other can lead to considerable confusion. It is sometimes said, for example, by physical educationists who are seeking to find an acceptable educational argument for the inclusion of physical activities in the curriculum, that because physical activities can be seen in an aesthetic way that this in itself provides a justification for them having a place.[1] Alternatively, and perhaps somewhat more strangely, it is sometimes claimed that sport is a form of art and because art is considered educationally respectable then *ipso facto* so too should sport be.[2]

In view of these blanket and ill-considered claims it will be helpful to make some brief preliminary remarks about the aesthetic in relation to art in order to help clear the ground for what is to follow.

It can be said that an aesthetic situation develops whenever an *aesthetic attitude* is adopted, or evoked towards an object and is entered into for no other reason than the enjoyment it affords. It differs from that of the *practical attitude* where things tend to be seen in instrumental terms. Thus, if a diamond necklace, for example, is seen only in terms of its commercial viability or as a gift in order to pacify one's wife the attitude adopted would be practical rather than aesthetic. That is to say instead of the necklace being perceived in an aesthetic way it is seen rather as means towards some other end.

The aesthetic attitude is sometimes referred to as being a distinctive mode of consciousness; a particular way of perceiving something. Stolnitz[3] speaks of it as a form of:

> disinterested and sympathetic attention to and contemplation of any object of awareness whatever, for its own sake alone.

The aesthetic then is a concept which refers to the possibility of perceiving things from a particular point of view. Mass produced objects such as washing machines or stamps; hand made objects such as chairs or drinking mugs; natural objects such as sunsets or mountain peaks; and *objets trouvés* such as a stone or piece of drift wood, are all possible objects of aesthetic perception, as well as those objects which are normally considered art objects.

Aesthetic perception, it should be noted, always takes on an *object* (the aesthetic object) but it should be made clear that the aesthetic is not necessarily confined to the visual. It relates to all modes of perception—to taste, touch, sound, smell and not least the kinaesthetic. The taste of wine, the touch of silk, the sound of music, the smell of fresh cut hay, the feel of a tennis serve or the motion of scything, are all possible aesthetic "objects" and all are capable of yielding aesthetic satisfaction. It will be seen then that the aesthetic in life is open and almost boundless. It is not, as is sometimes implied, confined to a particular type of context or a particular kind of *recherché* sensibility.

Aesthetic experience is normally regarded as being related to and dependent upon the aesthetic attitude towards something. Stolnitz[4] for example, refers to it as "being the experience we have while the aesthetic attitude is sustained."

What characterises it is that our whole interest and attention is given to the object in question. We are absorbed by it and by what it has to offer. It is often said to be concerned with the "here and now" without regard to practical concerns or future consequences. In our looking at a painting, for example, our engrossment might be with the perceptual qualities it makes available to us. What should be understood as Schlesinger makes clear is that:

> A person lacking a grasp of what a given experience is like cannot be made to acquire it by any amount of talk alone. He has to be subjected to the experience in order to sense how it feels....[5]

What then has been said is that when objects are perceived aesthetically they are perceived in a *particular way for their own sake.* To put the point another way when an object is perceived aesthetically it carries its own intrinsic satisfaction or reward regardless of its function or utilitarian value.

What then of art? Art is important in the realm of the aesthetic in that its objects are often considered paradigm cases of the aesthetic. Art objects, it is sometimes said, are attempts to exemplify the aesthetic. The arts of painting, sculpture, dance and drama are distinctive in that they are imaginative creations of man that are *intended* to be objects of aesthetic delight and/or aesthetic appreciation. Beardsley,[6] for example, writes that an artwork can be defined "as an intentional arrangement of conditions for affording experiences with marked aesthetic character."

Tatarkiewicz, as quoted by Osborne,[7] in an attempt to take account of a number of art theories, suggests the following definition:

> Art is a conscious human activity of either reproducing things, or constructing forms, or expressing experiences: the product of this reproduction, construction or expression is capable of evolving delight, or emotion or shock.

Despite such attempts to get at the meaning of art it is now generally recognised that art is an open concept. That is to say no single theory has yet been formulated or set of necessary and sufficient conditions produced to accommodate the varied ways in which the term is used. Weitz,[8] in recognising the adventurous and ever-changing character of art, suggests that it is likely to remain impossible to explain its meaning by referring to any one set of defining properties. Nonetheless, it is helpful to point to the descriptive and evaluative senses in which it is used. Thus, it is not uncommon when "we *describe* something as work of art, we do so under conditions of there being present some sort of artifact, made by human skill, ingenuity, and imagination, which embodies in its sensuous public medium—stone, wood, sound, words, etc.—certain distinguishable elements and relations." On the other hand when an artifact is *evaluated* as an art object it is perceived and judged according to aesthetic criteria. The question then arises as to what counts as "aesthetic" criteria. The answer to this is often found to be dependent upon which particular theory of art is favoured. Thus, for formalists a painting may be appraised predominantly in terms of its organisation and interrelationship of its elements—its lines, colour, shapes and so on. For emotionalists it would be looked at predominantly from the point of view of its expressive power and its potential capacity to have an impact upon the percipient. What makes the various theories of art valuable is not that they have provided a universal agreement about what art means but rather that they have yielded important insights about its nature whether these are to do with "form," "emotional impact" or the unique presentation of a particular kind of truth. Reasons for excellence in art are not confined to any one theoretical construct of it.

Two specific aspects of the term *work of art* should be stressed. The first is that it is an artifact. It is not something that exists only in the mind but is a product that has been creatively and skilfully brought into the world most frequently in an intentional and purposeful way to be aesthetically appreciated. "It is not just an inner vision" as Croce[9] argued it could be. The second specific aspect of the work of art and one which reaffirms the point above is that it is characterised by the unique way in which "content" and "medium" are indivisibly fused so that it becomes one "organic unity." Whatever aesthetic merit or significance a particular painting, poem, sculpture, dance, play or piece of music has, arises from the fact that it embodies the fusion that has taken place. Every work of art, it is sometimes said, has its own meaning, and that this distinctively emanates from the work itself. This is what makes it *sui generis* or one of its kind. It is sometimes said that what a work of art expresses can only be expressed in that particular way.

What is necessary to realise about art in general is that it is not removed or detached from life but grows out of it and plays back into it. The emotions expressed in art, for example, could not be understood without understanding the emotions of people in everyday life. They could not be intelligibly evoked, in other words, unless they had something in common with the contexts of life from which they come. It is because of this that art is able sometimes to encapsulate societal issues which are of social, moral or political significance. One example of this last kind is found in Jooss's "Green Table" where the ineptitude and posturing of statesmen before the Second World War is parodied with delicious irony. As Best[10] puts it "in the arts, the notions of learning, understanding and experience cannot intelligibly be regarded as distinct from learning, understanding and experience of life situations generally." In certain forms of art particularly this is a point worth remembering.

Finally, it is perhaps necessary to emphasize that although what is designated art can be described, interpreted and evaluated it does not and cannot necessarily guarantee the provision of *aesthetic experience*. Conversely, it should be understood, that just because an object is found to be aesthetic, interesting or rewarding in some way it does not necessarily suggest that it is art. Both these points should be borne in mind in the sections that follow.

2. Three Categories of Activities in Relation to Sport and Dance

Bearing in mind what has so far been said about the aesthetic and its relationship to art, it is proposed now to look at sport in relation to each. In doing so I am going to suggest that physical activities in general can be divided up into three logically distinct categories: i) those that are non-aesthetic, ii) those that are partially aesthetic; and iii) those that can be considered art. It will be argued that those activities commonly called sport fall most readily into the first two categories and judgement will be reserved as to whether any fall into the third one.

a. Non-Aesthetic Sports

In an effort to clear up some of the confusions endemic in the literature to do with aesthetics and sports Best[11] made a distinction between "purposive" sport and "aesthetic" sports. *Purposive sports*, he maintains, are characterised by the fact that each of these sports can be specified independently of the manner of achieving it, as long as it conforms to the rules or norms which govern it. Included in the category of purposive sports are those like football, rugby, hockey, track and field, basketball, baseball and tennis. The point about them is that the aesthetic is not intrinsic to their purpose which is to win by scoring the most goals, tries, baskets, points, runs: or the recording of the best times and distances and so on. The point is a logical one. An activity like handball would still count as handball even if there was no reference to or concern for the aesthetic at all. This is not to deny that such sports can still be considered from the aesthetic point of view. It means rather that they are not inherently concerned with the aesthetic. They can and do provide from time to time, either by accident or design, aesthetic moments but these are not *necessarily* or logically a part of their purpose.

What occurs, it may be said, occurs fortuitously. In sports like tennis or soccer, for example, scintillating patterns of play may arise which both astonish and delight but the constituting rules of neither lay down that this is required or necessary. Rather they may be regarded as a bonus. The point is that their purpose can be fulfilled without reference to the aesthetic.[12]

b. Partially Aesthetic Sports

Aesthetic sports are so called because "the aim cannot intelligibly be specified independently of the means of achieving it."[13] Included in this smaller category are such activities as gymnastics, diving, skating, synchronised swimming, trampolining, ski jumping* and surfing. Inherent in all these sports is a concern for the way or manner in which they are performed. How they are done is part or purpose of the activity. It is not accidental or fortuitous but a necessary feature of what that activity is. It helps define the nature and character of what is being done. The Olympic gymnast, for example, whose *only* concern was to perform her routine on the horizontal bars without reference to the *manner* in which she performed would have misconceived the purpose of the activity. As one reference[14] on gymnastics states:

> A perfect exercise with a maximum rating is one that is presented with elegance, ease, precision and in a style and rhythm well adapted to the nature of the aesthetic performance with no faults in execution. The faults in execution or style are penalized by a deduction in points or fraction of points according to the following direction.
>
> Defects in elegance in general. An exercise, although executed without fault, but presented in a rhythm too quick or too slow, or with an ill-proportioned display of force, counts less than a perfect exercise as described....

---

* In ski jumping, points are awarded for style as well as distance.

An example of the way in which gymnastics can be both technically commented upon as well as aesthetically perceived by a knowledgeable onlooker[15] is conveyed by the following descriptions of Ludmilla Tourischeva's floor exercise sequence in the 1972 Munich Olympics, where she won a gold medal. *Technically* it was said:

> This sequence demonstrates a very high level of Olympic Gymnastic proficiency, combining difficult techniques with a high level of originality.
>
> Her sequence required only two superior difficulties in order to obtain the maximum marks of four points and for these she chose a double twisting back-somersault and a half-twisting back somersault; these she executed with mechanical perfection, with amplitude and with virtuoso integration of parts.
>
> In addition to the minimum requirements in superior difficult exercises, she elaborated her composition with a full twist and an aerial cartwheel as well as an aerial walk-over.
>
> The sequence as a whole has precision, continuity, climax and a total integration of elements, her movements skilfully matching the music.

But *qualitatively* it was possible to say of Tourischeva's performance that:

> She commanded the restricted and circumscribed floor space with illusory ease and elegance; her floor patterns, aerial designs and dynamics were integrated into a composition of contrasts, complexity and completeness.
>
> Of qualities of form, she displayed poise, controlled balance, cleanness of line, and each in turn—an arched, curled, twisted and extended torso; her long supple limbs described sinuous and circular movements and her shapely flexible fingers made florid gestures in space. Her footwork had a precision at times forceful and firm and yet again dainty with impeccably shaped and patterned placings.
>
> Of sensory qualities there were combined in this sequence a softness of movement, a sharp crispness, and again a great delicacy together with smoothness, flowing continuity, resilience and elasticity.
>
> Of intensity qualities there were evidenced: a disguised power, an ease and effortlessness in flight, a freedom to fly, float and soar and a seeming denial of natural inertia and gravity.
>
> Qualities of complexity drew forth the crowd's ecstatic applause—intricate revolutions with speed, deft and devious trunk rotations—and always landing with the same secure precision and control.

Her sequence was above all expressive with a medley of qualities from nonchalance, playful arrogance and pride to coyness, piquancy and at times cool dignity. Even dramatic qualities emerged with tension, climax and resolution; but perhaps dominantly characteristic were her rhythmical lyricism and closely integrated movements with the accelerandos, rubatos and rallentandos of the music.

Interesting though these two quotes are the point they help bring out is that with an "aesthetic sport" its purpose can only be specified in terms of the aesthetic manner of achieving it. Put the other way round *the aesthetic sport is one in which the purpose cannot be specified without reference to the aesthetic manner of achieving it.*

c. Artistic Activities

As was made clear earlier to speak of the aesthetic is not necessarily to speak of art yet, as has been shown, it is not unusual to think of art as a paradigm in case of the aesthetic. In speaking of some physical activities as art I am thinking in particular of the activities of dance and mime. Such activities are characterised by the fact that there is no separation between the nature of the activity and its mode of presentation. Artistic activities by their very make-up are intrinsically concerned with aesthetic considerations. This is their *raison d'être*. What gives a work of art its distinctive character, as has been previously suggested, is that there is an inseparable fusion of "content" and "medium." In music (e.g., in a Bach fugue) this inseparability perhaps becomes most strikingly evident. All art, it has been said, aspires to this condition of "oneness." To speak of ends and means in art is misconceived for, as in education, the means are in part the ends. Just as in education the *moral manner* in which things are taught is as important as *what* is done, so in art the *aesthetic form* is as important as the *content*. What marks out a work of art is that its meaning cannot be expressed in any way other than the way it is. It is this fact about a work of art that makes it *sui generis*. To put the matter another way, a work of art is a unique presentation of embodied meaning. It is of interest that Friessen[16] in writing of the perception of dance observes:

> The dancer must remain one with the dance to preserve the unity and continuity of aesthetic image. The technical competence of the dancer includes not only the physical skills required to perform the dance, but the ability to exist within the dynamic illusion of the dance.[17]

It will be seen that the difference between *partially aesthetic* physical activities, such as gymnastics, and those which *are artistic activities* such as dance is that whereas with some activities in the former group (e.g., ski jumping) the gap between their purpose and the aesthetic is never entirely closed (i.e., their purpose could still to some extent be fulfilled in the absence of the aesthetic), in the latter it would be logically misconceived to think in terms of a gap at all. Another way to put this is to say that the purpose of art lies in the aesthetic, i.e., it lies in the creation of a significant aesthetic object which is its purpose. Talk therefore between ends and means in art is singularly inappropriate for they cannot be independently specified: they are in an important sense one and the same. In artistic activities like dance and mime aesthetic qualities, whether formal or expressive, are not there merely by accident, nor are they just called upon to demonstrate a qualitative distinction between one type of performance and another. They are there because in an indispensably central way they help characterise and constitute the very nature of the activity. It is for this reason they are important activities in aesthetic education.

In common with other arts, dance has features that distinguish it as being an "art object." "Its fundamental office" in the words of Phenix,[18] "unlike most sports, is to create in the percipient a significant emotion, valuable in itself and not merely to serve as an instrument of some other purpose." Each dance, unlike most sports, is a unique composition, expressing its own immanent structure and as such is subject only to its own inherent demands. Each dance, unlike most sports, seeks an imaginative response that is not governed or unduly influenced by what has been done or witnessed before.

3. Sport and Art: A Critique of Previous Approaches

It has been argued so far that although all sports can be seen from an aesthetic point of view, only some sports are inherently concerned with the aesthetic as a part of their purpose. It has been left open as to whether or not some, if not all, of the latter group can be regarded as art. In the light of what has been said it will be appreciated that the somewhat blanket question: Is sport art? is perhaps better replaced by the question: Can some sports be considered art? Before coming back to this question, however, it will be instructive to examine why some writers who have looked for a positive relationship between sport and art have not been successful.

a. Unsuccessful Attempts to Establish Sport as Art

Roughly speaking unsuccessful attempts to establish sport as art can be seen as falling under four headings. I shall refer to them as the aesthetic approach, the analogous approach, the intentionalist approach, the institutionalist approach and propose looking briefly at each in turn.

The Aesthetic Approach: The aesthetic approach, as represented by writers like Boxill[19] and Kovich,[20] despite making a strong case for the recognition of the aesthetic in sport, unfortunately conflates the concept of the aesthetic with that of art. In short, as has been shown, it is not necessary for something to be considered art in order to demonstrate that it can be beautiful or a source of aesthetic experience.

The Analogous Approach: To their credit writers like Simpson[21] and Cordner[22] having explored a whole range of similarities and resemblances between sport and art in terms of skills, intrinsic satisfaction, aesthetic possibility as well as the fact that both can be creative and can be watched as well as participated in and so on, come to the conclusion that, despite these analogous features the question of whether sport can be art, cannot be settled in this way because of more fundamental axiological* issues concerned with the nature of art that need to be resolved. In other words it is necessary to be clear about what art is in its evaluative sense before claiming that sport is art. Many writers that claim sport is art fail to do this.

The Intentionalist† Approach: Another misconception about art which is occasionally encountered is the belief that having artistic intentions is sufficient for something to be called art. Thus as it is sometimes maintained of skaters like Cranston and Curry that what they produced was art because their intentions were artistic. Certainly as Wertz[23] has correctly pointed out the intention to produce a work of art is no less important than its context but this, of course, is not the same as saying, as Wertz[24] recognises, that the ascription of artistic intentionality to an activity necessarily makes it art, either in the descriptive (classificatory) or evaluative sense. What needs to be made clear here is that somebody's intention to create a work of art is not the work of art itself. Important though a person's intention may be in the creation of a work of art, it is what is produced that counts. Only then can it be publicly evaluated and accorded that status. A person may even actually realise what was aesthetically intended but not necessarily have it recognised by others as art. Conversely a person may not quite achieve in a work what was intended but nonetheless have it acclaimed as a masterpiece. The point is that, interesting though it may be to know to what extent a person's intentions have been fulfilled in what is produced, once a work has come into being it takes on an independent life of its

---

* = relating to the study of values (moral, aesthetic, etc.).

† = concerning intentions as playing a key theoretical role. Note the difference between 'intentional' in this sense and the term 'intensional (object).'

own and stands or falls on its own merit in the public forum of evaluation. To put the matter another way, the ascription of intentionality to an aesthetic activity is not sufficient to say that the object produced is an art object.[25]

The Institutional Approach: The institutional approach is essentially a sociological one. As formulated by Dickie[26] it maintains that objects, in the classificatory sense, can have the status of art conferred upon them by a person or persons acting on behalf of the art world. Thus, he[27] maintains, "The status in question may be acquired by a single person's treating an artifact as a candidate for appreciation." The fact that an art gallery director decides to exhibit a particular object, whether it is a urinal or tin cans,* tends to confer the status of art object to them, but as Dickie[28] admits, calling something an art object does not necessarily mean that it is a good one or is even of value. What is being emphasized is that art and what is called art is influenced as much by tradition, convention and promotion as it is by an appeal to a work's intrinsic worth.

Perhaps, in part, influenced by such a view as well as being impressed by the way others see sport, whether as participants or observers, writers like Saw[29] and Wertz[30] have argued that sport, or at least some sports, should be considered an art. Saw,[31] an aesthetician and impressed by the fact that "Sports commentators use the terms aesthetic appraisal as freely as do art critics" and the fact that "Star performers in ice hockey, cricket, football, and sports generally are valued as much for their elegance in motion as for their run-making and goal-getting ability," classifies sport as an art under the category[32] of "Performances carried on for some end other than contemplation, but nevertheless arouse it."

Wertz[33] too, in supporting the view of performers like Fleming, Cranston and Curry that ice dancing should be considered an art rather than a sport, argues not only that such activities have artistic merit, but that much depends upon the context and changing the attitudes of judges and audiences to get this recognized. In other words, he is maintaining that only when conventions and perceptions are altered and artistic status has been conferred upon such performers and that their products are seen as art, will they become art. There is of course, something in this view but whether or not the straightforward act of "conferring" is sufficient or even desirable in order to bring about change is doubtful.

---

* Marcel Duchamp (1887–1968) famously submitted an ordinary factory-made urinal (*Fountain*, 1917) to an art exhibit; the committee running the exhibit rejected it, as not being art. The original has been lost, but replicas are now on exhibit in a number of art museums. *Fountain* has since been hailed as perhaps the quintessential avant-garde work of the twentieth century, a challenge to ordinary views—and philosophies—of art. The other reference here is perhaps to the works (starting in the early 1960s) of David Wasserman, created from cut-up discarded tin cans.

What is clear then is that, in the institutional or classificatory sense, a sport can become art if an agent or a person's acting on behalf of the art world confers the status of candidate for appreciation upon it, even though it may turn out to be trivial or worthless when an attempt is made to evaluate it from the aesthetic point of view.

All in all the institutional theory of art is an empty one. It virtually abandons any sense of appraisal and depends upon the act of "conferring," regardless of whatever motives may be at work whether of profit or self interest. If somebody from the art world calls something art it becomes art. Dickie[34] himself admits that it is a bit like saying "I christen this object a work of art." Ultimately, however, the theory is a failure as Ward[35] observes "because it rides roughshod over the common sense distinction between art and non art." As Ward[36] comments "If everything were capable of becoming art it would no longer be possible to have a concept of art." One would not be able to differentiate it from anything else. From the philosophic point of view, therefore, just to confer the status of art on sport does not do much to establish whatever artistic merit it may have.

If the question of whether or not sport can ever be considered art is to be settled it must clearly be examined in a more evaluative way.

b. An Examination of Best's View That Sport Is Not Art

A number of writers[37] having explored the relationship between sport and art have come to the conclusion that although sport can sometimes be aesthetic it nonetheless should not be considered art. The reasons for this vary and are summarised by Boxill.[38] Since some of these are based upon points already raised and clarified it is not proposed to go over the same ground again. Rather it will be more productive if the work of Best[39] is taken as a basis of discussion for it is he, perhaps more clearly than anyone, who has expressed the view that sport is not art.

Best[40] argues that sport is not art on two grounds. Firstly, that art, unlike sport, allows for "the possibility of the expression of a conception of life issues such as contemporary moral, social and political problems." Such a possibility, he argues, "is an intrinsic part of the concept of art" by which he means "that without it an activity would not count as a legitimate art form." Secondly, he[41] argues that in art, unlike in sport, the object of one's attention is "an imagined object," that it is imaginatively constituted. When one goes to the theatre, for example, we respond not to John Smith, the actor playing the part, but to Othello, the character in the play.[42]

Two questions arise from these features which Best maintains are distinctive of art but not of sport. The first is that, although both features are obviously true of some forms of art are they necessarily characteristic of *all* art? The second is that even if they are only characteristic of some art forms are they invariably absent from all forms of sport? In other words is it possible to make such sweeping generalisations?

Cordner,[43] for one, is very sceptical of Best's claim that the possibility of "life issues" is characteristic of all forms of art. He writes: "It just seems mistaken, because too intellectualist, to hold that abstract paintings express a conception of life issues." Clearly, the paintings of Hogarth do make "comment" upon the social conditions of the eighteenth century, just as Picasso's *Guernica* in the twentieth century depicts something of the horror of warfare, but all art is by no means like this, nor does it have to be. How can it be said of Mondrian's *Composition VII*, for example, which comprises a picture of lines and colours, that it concerns such life issues as poverty, pestilence or famine or would even want to make them a possibility? The fact is that art comes in many forms and large sections of it are not concerned with life issues in any shape or form. Best,[44] to his credit, recognises that what he wants to regard as a "necessary condition"[45] of art is difficult to uphold. This is not only true of painting but of other art forms also, especially perhaps music and architecture. Concerning the former, he[46] is gracious enough to conclude "that there are... so many pieces of music which are unquestionably art but in which the suggestion that there may be some expression of conception of life seems intolerably forced and absurd."

The second criterion that Best[47] puts forward as separating the arts from sport, is that the subject of our attention is imaginatively constituted. What Best seems to mean by this is that whereas art employs certain well-known conventions to make an analogous response to a real life situation, sport has no such conventions because it is real. Everybody who goes to the theatre knows that when in *King Lear* Gloucester's eyes are gouged out that the eyes of the person playing Gloucester actually remain their sockets. Tragedy, as depicted on the stage, is *analogous* with situations that arise in real life but they are not in fact real. The conventions of drama permit something to be perceived *as if* it were the case, yet both players and onlookers know that is not the case. However convincingly an actor portrays a character and in a sense becomes the character, he remains a different person. He is playing a role. I take Best to mean here that sport has no comparable set of conventions. When Bobby Robson is hurt on the soccer pitch we know and understand that it is him that is injured and in pain.

Neither he nor the fans are under any illusion about this and perhaps, as Best would want me to add, they are not expected to be. In this way sport differs from art. It is real as opposed to imagined. Best, I think, is essentially correct on this point though not perhaps as decisively as he would wish. He writes[48] "the possibility of an imaginative portrayal (of a conception of life issues) ... applies only to the arts." But, as has been shown, although some arts—the theatre, the novel, figurative painting, and some forms of dance—may treat "life issues" in an imaginative way as objects of our attention, other forms of art are not dependent upon such "subject matter." Hence, to say that "art could not be the subject of sport"[49] is not as damaging as Best intends it to be. The fact is that the imaginative treatment of "life issues" as objects of our attention is no more pre-requisite of some arts—abstract art, architecture and music, for example—than it is of sport. Sport in other words is not necessarily discounted from being an art on account of the fact that it does not deal as a necessary part of its practice in an imaginative way with political, economic or religious issues. All this goes to show that although an art such as drama has certain expectations about role playing that are conventional to it and different from the types of role playing in such sports as rugby, soccer and cricket, it does not follow from this that sport cannot be art. What would seem to be true of each art and each sport is that imagination is required whether it relates to a "conception of life issues" or whether it relates to a conception of how best to play a particular game in terms of tactics and strategy and so on.[50]

In summary then, despite some important insights into the subject matter of some arts, Best has neither produced what amount to necessary conditions for what constitutes an art form in general, and neither has he, as a result, satisfactorily shown that some forms of sport cannot be art.[51]

4. Artistry and Art Within Sport

It was suggested earlier that sport can be divided into those activities which are not inherently concerned with the aesthetic as a part of their purpose (non-aesthetic) and those that are partially aesthetic. It was implied, though not actually said that no sporting activity, unlike the activities of dance and mime, qualified as an artistic activity on account of there always being a logical gap between the aesthetic element and the overall purpose to be fulfilled. Thus, in ski-jumping, for example, the aesthetic form of the jump is a separate consideration from the distance achieved. In most partially aesthetic sports, the opportunity to create a significant aesthetic object unencumbered by other considerations is not present. There is, however, within certain sports, figure skating and synchronised swimming, for example, the freedom within certain sections of them to imaginatively create in an artistic way aesthetic objects of interest that qualify as vignette art forms comparable to the sonnet, an etching or a short story. In figure skating, in addition to the requirement to skate three specific figures and the prescribed free skating element, there is a section which is devoted to a creative free style performance to a chosen piece of music.

Similarly, in synchronised swimming each competition has two sections. One is for certain prescribed "figures." The other is for original choreographed "routines" set to a piece of chosen music. As with the third section of figure skating the interpretation of the music and the manner of presentation count towards the marks awarded by the judges. My contention then is that, although in each of these aesthetic sports there are certain restrictions imposed upon what can be done, just as there is within the genre of a sonnet or an etching, there is nonetheless sufficient freedom and inventive scope for the artistic process to take place and an art work to emerge.

In looking at the relevant sections of figure skating and synchronised swimming as vignette art forms it will be seen that they have certain features in common. Both are performative in nature; both are concerned with a "calculated display" of aesthetic qualities. As in ballet there is a need for the performer to be physically attractive, well proportioned, have sound technique, a musical sense as well as expressive ability. An envisaged performance must take account of such factors as balance, shape, space, dynamics and form so that they are articulated and embodied in the performance in the way intended.[52]

In free style skating, which in effect is a form of dancing, the medium of ice permits an extensive range of aesthetically devised movements which, unlike ballet, can be held whilst the body flows over the ice. Probably, no other medium, unless it be water, allows the performer to produce such easy, sweeping, flowing movements, which can be sustained, if necessary, so that a particular shape can be enjoyed to the full. As with ballet or modern dance, the chosen music determines what can be meaningfully accomplished. The music can be thematic and concerned with "life issues" or it can be abstract and non-thematic in the sense of having no story to tell. Either way, the music, once chosen, has to be interpreted and choreographed. As with all creative endeavours there must be a plan, a will to work on it, and the artistic vision to make it come right. In this way the outcome could be comparable to such works in ballet as *Blood Wedding*,* a thematic dance, or *Symphonic Variations*,† an abstract one. Apart from the choreographed music to suit the particular performer(s) there is the question of costume. This must enhance and complement the other factors so that the whole becomes an aesthetic event that has poignancy and significance. In this respect although the arena is not the theatre, in effect it becomes one. The audience is not there simply to gasp and admire but to be aesthetically awakened and satisfied. What ultimately matters in the eyes of the judges and audience alike is not what was intended in the minds of the dancer(s) and choreographer but what is there for all to behold. Whether or not what is presented is a great artistic performance, rather than a mediocre or poor one, rests upon what is imaginatively and objectively expressed so that its features can, if necessary, be pointed to and discussed. As in musical competitions, the fact that in free style skating the official judges allocate marks in terms of "technical merit" and "artistic impression," and that one performance is judged to be better than another, does not in itself debar free style skating from being considered an art. What matters is not that there is an order of merit table but rather whether the aesthetic quality of a given performance and the meaning it is able to generate are sufficiently significant. It is more than possible to be placed third at the Olympics or a world championship and still be regarded as having artistic standards of the first order. The question of whether or not an activity counts as art is not settled by whether or not it is competitive but rather, as Dewey[53] suggested, by a "quality of doing and of what is done." In the solo performances of a skater like Katarina Witt, it is possible to see not only skill and the mastery of technique, but more importantly an ability to incorporate these into her skating in a creative and dynamically expressive way so that she embodies and articulates her aesthetic intent. Such a skater is not only able to hold our aesthetic attention but bring about in the onlooker an emotional response which seems to arise from the beauty and vitality of her movements. In her rendering of the music from Bizet's *Carmen* at the 1988 Olympics she was able to do this with perfection.

Similarly in the pair skating of Torvill and Dean it is the grace, style and harmony of their relationship as they express the spirit of the music that impresses the onlooker.

---

* Adapted as a flamenco-ballet by Alfredo Mañas (1974) from Federico García Lorca's play *Bodas de Sangre* (*Blood Wedding*, 1933). Themes of the play, according to the dust jacket of Ted Hughes's translation (1997), include "desire, repression, ritual, and the constraints and commitments of the rural Spanish community in which the play is rooted."

† This ballet choreographed by Frederick Ashton (1946) uses César Franck's music (*Variations Symphoniques*, 1885).

In skating to the music of Ravel's *Bolero* they do not so much interpret it as embody its essence as they sweep back and forth across the ice as if spellbound by its rhythmic content and compelling force. Any mistake or misplaced gesture would spoil the unity or oneness of the presentation. When the music stopped it was as if the world stopped with it. The dancers, seemingly released from its hold, gradually became themselves once more. The peculiarly kineasthetic experience which had surged through the bodies of the audience took a little longer to subside. Everybody present had been caught up and transported by the poignancy and aesthetic syncopations of the occasion. New possibilities of awareness had been aroused, heightened and consummated.

It has been argued that the free style section of the sport of figure skating is a minor art form. It is in fact a sport-art. Like ballet or modern dance it is intrinsically concerned with such aesthetic considerations as form, expression, line, symbol and illusion, and its choreography can be thematic or remain abstract. It is quintessentially concerned with the use of the body as an instrument of expression in such a way that it relates to the chosen music and is aided in its effects by costume design and the effects of lighting. The arena becomes a form of theatre. As with all arts the imagination must be employed in such a way that what is presented is both coherent and novel. Its constituent parts must be relevant and create an articulate unity which can be enjoyed and appreciated for what it is. The free style dance vignette is a distinctive type of artistic activity and, like the choreographed setting of synchronised swimming, should be recognised as such. It must be judged, as all arts must be judged, by its power to embody and express something that touches upon the human condition and be capable of evoking an aesthetic response.

Summary and Conclusions

It has been suggested:

(a) that there is abundant evidence to show that sport can be and often is a subject of art;

(b) that in discussing the relation of sport to art the concept of the aesthetic should not be confused with that of art;

(c) that a number of attempts have been made to show that sport is or could be considered art, and conversely that sport is not art. None of these has been entirely successful;

(d) that, from what has been argued sports can be categorised into three main groups: those that are non-aesthetic; those that are partially aesthetic; and those that can be considered as art.

NOTES

1. Carlisle's argument is based upon this premise. See R. Carlisle: "The Concept of Physical Education," *Proceedings of the Philosophy of Education & Society*, I (1969), pp. 5-22.

2. R. Maheu: "Sport and Culture," *International Journal of Adult and Youth Education*, 14 No. 4 (1962), pp. 6-12.

3. J. Stolnitz: *Aesthetics and the Philosophy of Art Criticism*, (Boston: Houghton Mifflin, 1960), p. 35.

4. J. Stolnitz: ibid, p. 65.

5. G. Schlesinger: "Aesthetic Experience and the Definition of Art," *British Journal of Aesthetics*, 19 No. 2 (1979), p. 172.

6. M.C. Beardsley: "In Defence of Aesthetic Value," Presidential Address at the American Philosophical Association, *Proceedings*, 52 No. 6 (1979), p. 729.

7. H. Osborne: "What is a Work of Art?" *British Journal of Aesthetics*, 21 No. 1 (1981), pp. 3-11.

8. M. Weitz: "The Role of Theory in Aesthetics," in *Problems in Aesthetics*, Edited by M. Weitz (Toronto: Macmillan, 1970), pp. 177-78.

9. B. Croce: *The Essence of Aesthetic*, translated by Ainslie, (London: Heinemann, 1921).

10. D. Best: *Reason and Feeling in the Arts*, (London: George Allen and Unwin, 1985), pp. 163-64.

11. D. Best: "Sport is Not Art," *Journal of the Philosophy of Sport*, XII (1985), pp. 25-40.

12. There are numerous examples of how the aesthetic can fortuitously arise from all forms of sport without them being required or intended. For some interesting instances of these see the following references:

    P.J. Arnold: *Education, Movement and the Curriculum*, (London: Falmer, 1988).

    P.J. Arnold: *Meaning in Movement, Sport & Physical Education*, (London: Heinemann, 1979).

    D. Aspin: "Sport and the Concept of the Aesthetic," in *Readings in the Aesthetics of Sport*, Edited by H.T.A. Whiting and D.W. Masterson, (London: Lepus Books, 1974).

    R.K. Elliot: "Aesthetics and Sport," in H.T.A. Whiting & D.W. Masterson, op. cit.

    B. Lowe: *The Beauty of Sport*, (New Jersey: Prentice Hall, 1977).

    P. Ziff: "A Fine Forehand," *Journal of the Philosophy of Sport*, I (1974), pp. 49-64.

    For an account of the aesthetic aspects of being in sport from the performer's point of view, rather than that of the spectator, see P.J. Arnold: "Aesthetic Aspects of Being in Sport: The Performer's Perspective in Contrast to that of the Spectator," *Journal of the Philosophy of Sport*, XII (1985), pp. 1-7.

13. D. Best: *Philosophy and Human Movement*, (London: George Allen and Unwin, 1978), p. 105.

14. J.R. White (ed.): "Gymnastics," in *Sports Rules Encyclopaedia*, (Palo Alto: National P, 1966), p. 61.

15. G.F. Curl: Commentary given at a lecture at Dunfermline College, Edinburgh, Scotland, 1980.

16. J. Friessen: "Perceiving Dance," *Journal of Aesthetic Education*, 9 No. 4 (1975), p. 101.

17. Arnold has looked at the particular role the dancer has in relation to the dance as an agent, a guardian of aesthetic standards, as a creator, and as the embodiment of expressive form. See P.J. Arnold: "The Dancer as Artist and Agent," *Journal of the Philosophy of Sport*, XV (1988), pp. 49-55.

18. P.H. Phenix: "Relationship in Dance to Other Art Forms," in *Dance: An Art in Academe*, Edited by M. Haberman and T.G. Meisel, (New York: Teachers College, 1970), p. 10.

19. J.M. Boxill: "Beauty, Sport, and Gender," in *Philosophic Inquiry in Sport*, Edited by William J. Morgan and Klaus V. Meier (Champaign, IL: Human Kinetics, 1988).

20. M. Kovich: "Sports as an Art Form," *Journal of Health, Physical Education and Recreation*, 42 (October 1971), p. 42.

21. A. Simpson: "Art and Games," *British Journal of Aesthetics*, 26 No. 3 (1986), pp. 270-76.

22. Cordner: "Differences between Sport and Art," *Journal of the Philosophy of Sport*, XV (1988), pp. 31-47.

23. S.K. Wertz: "Context and Intention in Sport and Art," in *Philosophic Inquiry in Sport*, Edited by William J. Morgan and Klaus V. Meier (Champaign, IL: Human Kinetics, 1988), p. 524.

24. S.K. Wertz: "Artistic Creativity in Sport," *Sport Inside Out: Readings in Literature and Philosophy*, Edited by D. Vander Werken and S.K. Wertz (Fort Worth: Texas Christian U, 1986), p. 10.

25. Blocker in clarification of this point writes: "Once the artist (or performer) has embodied her intentions in a publicly communicable form of expression, the intention becomes a part of the art object which is now a part of the public domain." See G. Blocker: *Philosophy of Art*, (New York: Charles Scribner, 1979), p. 249.

26. G. Dickie: *Aesthetics: An Introduction*, (Bobbs Merrill, 1971), p. 108.

27. Ibid, p. 103.

28. Ibid.

29. R.L. Saw: *Aesthetics: An Introduction*, (London: Macmillan, 1972).

30. Op. cit. Ref. 24 above, p. 20.

31. Op. cit. Ref. 29 above, p. 48.

32. Op. cit. Ref. 29 above, p. 42.

33. Op. cit. Ref. 23 above, p. 525.

34. Op. cit. Ref. 26 above, p. 107.

35. P.M. Ward: "Sport and the Institutional Theory of Art," *Journal of Human Movement Studies*, (1977), pp. 73-81.

36. Op. cit. Ref. 35 above, p. 80.

37. Op. cit. Ref. 11 and 12 above, and L.A. Reid: "Sport, the Aesthetic and Art," *British Journal of Educational Studies*, 18 (1970), pp. 245-58.

38. Op. cit. Ref. 19 above.

39. Op. cit. Refs. 10, 11 and 13 above, and D. Best: "Art and Sport," *Journal of Aesthetic Education*, 14 (1980), pp. 67-80.

40. Op. cit. Ref. 13 above, p. 117.

41. Op. cit. Ref. 11 above, p. 31.

42. Op. cit. Ref. 11 above, p. 31.

43. Op. cit. Ref. 22 above, p. 37.

44. Op. cit. Ref. 10 above, p. 165.

45. Op. cit. Ref. 10 above, p. 160.

46. Op. cit. Ref. 10 above, p. 167.

47. Op. cit. Ref. 11 above, p. 32.

48. Op. cit. Ref. 11 above, p. 32.

49. Op. cit. Ref. 11 above, p. 32.

50. For further comments on this point see Cordner: Op. cit. Ref. 22 above.

51. A third criticism of Best's view about how art differs from sport concerns the question of particularity, whereas Best maintains that art is characterised by its "particularity" of expression or feeling sport is not. Roberts however, questions this and maintains that just as in painting sadness can be expressed in many ways so in soccer, for example, can a goal be scored in many ways. Just as in a painting sadness is expressed in a particular way so in a game a goal is scored in a particular way. See: T.J. Roberts: "Sport, Art, and Particularity: The Best Equivocation," *Journal of the Philosophy of Sport*, XIII (1986), pp. 49-63; 58-59.

52. It is of interest that Arnheim writes of these same qualities as being applicable to the way in which art objects are or should be perceived, if they are to be appreciated for what they are. See: R. Arnheim: *Art and Visual Perception*, (Los Angeles, CA: U of California P, 1974).

53. J. Dewey: *Art as Experience*, (New York: G.P. Pitman, 1980).

QUESTIONS

1. Do aesthetic scoring criteria undermine objectivity in judging? Are there aesthetic biases or commitments sometimes in the coaching or fandom of purposive sports?

2. Is Best's "life situations" requirement for art forms justified? Do certain sports seem to meet this requirement? How?

3. If, as Best argues, the sport of figure skating cannot count as art, are there art forms (such as dance) that, in certain cases, could count as sport?

4. Arnold rejects a number of approaches aimed at establishing that some sport can be art. Are some of these approaches more viable than he admits?

5. Does Arnold make a convincing case that figure skating should be considered both sport and art? Would other aesthetic sports be less plausible?

6. What is at stake in the debate about whether sport can be art? Does the answer to whether it can depend on having a solid theory of either or both?

FURTHER READING

Arnold, Peter J. (1985): "Aesthetic Aspects of Being in Sport: The Performer's Perspective in Contrast to That of the Spectator," *Journal of the Philosophy of Sport* 12, pp. 1-7.

Boxill, J.M. (1984): "Beauty, Sport, and Gender," *Journal of the Philosophy of Sport* 11, pp. 36-47.

Cordner, C.D. (1984): "Grace and Functionality," *British Journal of Aesthetics* 24 (4), pp. 301-13.

Kaelin, E.F. (1968): "The Well-Played Game: Notes Toward an Aesthetics of Sport," *Quest* 10 (1), pp. 16-28.

Roberts, Terence J. (1986): "Sport, Art, and Particularity: The Best Equivocation," *Journal of the Philosophy of Sport* 13, pp. 49-63.

Wertz, Spencer K. (1984): "Context and Intention in Sport and Art," *Southwest Philosophical Studies* 8 (2), pp. 144-47.

FURTHER INQUIRY

Further research on specific aesthetic properties—graceful movements in different sports, the dramatic quality of competition, and so on—seems potentially fruitful, as would exploring the interrelationships among such properties (pretty plays, for example, fuse stylish execution with dramatic situation). Note how certain moves in purposive sports, like dekes, seem essentially to involve aesthetic means to achieve the desired end. Commonalities and differences between on the one hand the aesthetics of art and sport, and on the other the aesthetics of different domains (ordinary life, extraordinary situations like war), also warrant attention. Perhaps a link between athletes' and spectators' aesthetic experience can be established by appeal to the mirror neurons of the human brain, which are activated by certain movements whether *performed or perceived* by the subject. This might be extended to explain the power of fan involvement in games or the compelling character of great sport films. A complete sport aesthetics would also address sport as a peculiarly effective subject of artwork broadly. And as to whether sport can *be* art, perhaps focus should shift from activities' *forms* to their *instances*, in which case the sportworld and the artworld could more plausibly be seen to overlap in, if not institutions, convergent descriptions where the requisites for both sport and art ("spart"?) are met.

Section F

Banning Drugs

Many sports ban performance-enhancing drugs such as anabolic steroids. Rules incorporating these bans are *auxiliary* rules—governing eligibility; similarly, certain sports restrict eligibility according to weight, age, sex, competitive standing, and so on. This sort of rule contrasts with *constitutive* rules—formally defining a sport, and *regulative* rules—governing legal play. Eligibility rules govern who is allowed to play, not what counts as playing, or how players must play. For philosophers of sport the chief concern here is not empirical, about the effects and side effects of steroids, for instance, or about the legal or psychiatric status of users (though note discussion of the prisoner's dilemma in the next section). Philosophers rather raise a moral question, but not about the morality of using such drugs given the bans—that is a form of cheating, and thus straightforwardly morally wrong. One assumption here is that rules against steroid and other drug use in sport are not obviously immoral restrictions; if they were, then violation of these rules would be morally permissible (as in the case of unjust laws).

At issue then is not whether to break the rule, but whether to have the rule at all, and the two readings in this section offer opposing viewpoints on this issue, based in part on competing plausible notions of the nature of sport. In the first reading, Robert L. Simon offers criteria for performance-enhancing drugs, then argues that, whatever risks might be incurred by users, whatever the consequent harms to others, including coercive pressure to follow suit, the decisive reason that we should maintain such bans is that they foster the central aim of sport (in part a "mutual quest for excellence"). By contrast, W.M. Brown argues that bans on steroids are often excessively paternalistic. The nature of sport, he argues, is compatible with steroid use; the imposition of restrictions denies athletes those very values—achievement, self-reliance, autonomy—that are realized and symbolized so strikingly in sport.

11. Good Competition and Drug-Enhanced Performance*

Robert L. Simon

Competition in sport frequently has been defended in terms of the search for excellence in performance.[1] Top athletes, whether their motivation arises from adherence to the internal values of competition or desire for external reward, are willing to pay a heavy price in time and effort in order to achieve competitive success. When this price consists of time spent in hard practice, we are prepared to praise the athlete as a worker and true competitor. But when athletes attempt to achieve excellence through the use of performance-enhancing drugs, there is widespread condemnation. Is such condemnation justified? What is wrong with the use of drugs to achieve excellence in sport? Is prohibiting the use of perform-ance-enhancing drugs in athletic competition justified?

The relatively widespread use of such drugs as anabolic steroids to enhance performance dates back at least to the Olympics of the 1960s, although broad public awareness of such drug use seems relatively recent. Anabolic steroids are drugs, synthetic derivatives of the male hormone testosterone, which are claimed to stimulate muscle growth and tissue repair. While claims about possible bad consequences of steroid use are controversial, the American College of Sports Medicine warns against serious side effects. These are believed to include liver damage, atherosclerosis, hypertension, personality changes, a lowered sperm count in males, and masculinization in females. Particularly frightening is that world-class athletes are reportedly taking steroids at many times the recom-mended medical dosage—at levels so high that, as Thomas Murray (4: p. 26) has pointed out, under "current federal regulations governing human subjects ... no

---

*   Robert L. Simon, "Good Competition and Drug-Enhanced Performance," *Journal of the Philosophy of Sport* 11 (1984), pp. 6-13.

institutional review board would approve a research design that entailed giving subjects anywhere near the levels ... used by the athletes."

The use of such high levels of a drug raises complex empirical as well as ethical issues. For example, even if steroid use at a low level does not actually enhance athletic performance, as some authorities claim, it is far from clear whether heavy use produces any positive effects on performance. At the very least, athletes who believe in the positive effects of heavy doses of steroids are not likely to be convinced by data based on more moderate intake.

As interesting as these issues are, it will be assumed in what follows that the use of certain drugs does enhance athletic performance and does carry with it some significant risk to the athlete. Although each of these assumptions may be controversial, by granting them, the discussion can concentrate on the ethical issues raised by use of performance-enhancing drugs.

I. What Is a Performance-Enhancing Drug?

If we are to discuss the ethics of using drugs to enhance athletic performance, we should begin with a clear account of what counts as such a drug. Unfortunately, a formal definition is exceedingly hard to come by, precisely because it is unclear to what substances such a definition ought to apply.

If it is held to be impermissible to take steroids or amphetamines to enhance performance, what about special diets, the use of coffee to promote alertness, or the bizarre practice of "blood doping," by which runners store their own blood in a frozen state and then return it to their body before a major meet in order to increase the oxygen sent to the muscles?

It is clear that the concept of an "unnatural" or "artificial" substance will not take us very far here since testosterone hardly is unnatural. Similarly, it is difficult to see how one's own blood can be considered artificial. In addition, we should not include on any list of forbidden substances the use of medication for legitimate reasons of health.

Moreover, what counts as a performance-enhancing drug will vary from sport to sport. For example, drinking alcohol normally will hurt performance. However, in some sports, such as riflery, it can help. This is because as a depressant, alcohol will slow down one's heart rate and allow for a steadier stance and aim.

Rather than spend considerable time and effort in what is likely to be a fruitless search for necessary conditions, we would do better to ignore borderline cases and focus on such clear drugs of concern as amphetamines and steroids. If we can understand the ethical issues that apply to use of such drugs, we might then be in a better position to handle borderline cases as well. However, it does seem that paradigm cases of the drugs that are of concern satisfy at least some of the following criteria.

1. If the user did not believe that use of substance in the amount ingested would increase the chances of enhanced athletic performance, that substance would not be taken.
2. The substance, in the amount ingested, is believed to carry significant risk to the user.
3. The substance, in the amount ingested, is not prescribed medication taken to relieve an illness or injury.

These criteria raise no concern about the normal ingestion of such drugs as caffeine in coffee or tea, or about medication since drugs used for medicinal purposes would not fall under them (1). The use of amphetamines and steroids, on the other hand, do fall under the criteria. Blood doping seems to be a borderline case and perhaps this is as it should be. It is employed only to enhance performance, is not medication, is not part of any normal training routine, yet seems to pose no significant risk to the user.[2]

However, the important issue for our purposes is not the adequacy of the three criteria as a definition for, as I have suggested, any search for a definition in the absence of the correct normative perspective will likely turn out to be a fruitless hunt for the nonexistent snark.* Rather, the major concern is not with defining performance-enhancing drugs but with evaluating their use. In particular, it is one thing to claim that the three criteria (or any other proposed set) are satisfied to a particular degree. It is quite another to make the normative claim that use of the substance in question is morally questionable or impermissible.

Why should the use of possibly harmful drugs solely for the purpose of enhancing athletic performance be regarded as impermissible? In particular, why shouldn't individual athletes be left at liberty to pursue excellence by any means they freely choose?

---

* = fictional animal invented by Lewis Carroll in his poem "The Hunting of the Snark" (1876).

II. Performance-Enhancing Drugs, Coercion, and the Harm Principle

One argument frequently advanced against the use of such performance-enhancing drugs as steroids is based on our second criterion of harm to the user. Since use of such drugs is harmful to the user, it ought to be prohibited.

However, if we accept the "harm principle," which is defended by such writers as J.S. Mill,* paternalistic interference with the freedom of others is ruled out. According to the harm principle, we are entitled to interfere with the behavior of competent, consenting adults only to prevent harm to others. After all, if athletes prefer the gains that the use of drugs provides along with possible side effects to the alternative of less risk but worse performance, external interference with their freedom of choice seems unwarranted.

However, at least two possible justifications of paternalistic interference are compatible with the harm principle. First, we can argue that athletes do not give informed consent to the use of performance-enhancing drugs. Second, we can argue that the use of drugs by some athletes does harm other competitors. Let us consider each response in turn.

Informed Consent

Do athletes freely choose to use such performance-enhancing drugs as anabolic steroids? Consider, for example, professional athletes whose livelihood may depend on the quality of their performance. Athletes whose performance does not remain at peak levels may not be employed for very long. As Carolyn Thomas (6: p. 198) maintains, "the onus is on the athlete to ... consent to things that he or she would not otherwise consent to.... Coercion, however, makes the athlete vulnerable. It also takes away the athlete's ability to act and choose freely with regard to informed consent." Since pressures on top amateur athletes in national and world-class competition may be at least as great as pressures on professionals, a comparable argument can be extended to cover them as well.

However, while this point is not without some force, we need to be careful about applying the notion of coercion too loosely. After all, no one is forced to try to become a top athlete. The reason for saying top athletes are "coerced" is that if they don't use performance-enhancing drugs, they may not get what they want. But they still have the choice of settling for less. Indeed, to take another position is to virtually deny the competence of top athletes to give consent in a variety of sports related areas including adoption of training regimens and

---

* *On Liberty*, Chapter 1.

scheduling. Are we to say, for example, that coaches coerce athletes into training and professors coerce students into doing work for their courses? Just as students can choose not to take a college degree, so too can athletes revise their goals. It is also to suggest that *any* individual who strives for great reward is not competent to give consent, since the fear of losing such a reward amounts to a coercive pressure.

While the issue of coercion and the distinction between threats and offers is highly complex, I would suggest that talk of coercion is problematic as long as the athlete has an acceptable alternative to continued participation in highly competitive sport. While coercion may indeed be a real problem in special cases, the burden of proof would seem to be on those who deny that top athletes *generally* are in a position to consent to practices affecting performance.

Harm to Others

This rejoinder might be satisfactory, critics will object, if athletes made their choices in total isolation. The competitive realities are different, however. If some athletes use drugs, others—who on their own might refrain from becoming users—are "forced" to indulge just to remain competitive. As Manhattan track coach Fred Dwyer (3: p. 25) points out, "The result is that athletes—none of whom understandingly, are willing to settle for second place—feel that 'if my opponent is going to get for himself that little extra, then I'm a fool not to.'" Athletes may feel trapped into using drugs in order to stay competitive. According to this argument, then, the user of performance-enhancing drugs is harming others by coercing them into becoming users as well.

While the competitive pressures to use performance-enhancing drugs undoubtedly are real, it is far from clear that they are unfair or improperly imposed. Suppose, for example, that some athletes embark on an especially heavy program of weight training. Are they coercing other athletes into training just as hard in order to compete? If not, why are those athletes who use steroids "coercing" others into going along?[3] Thus, if performance-enhancing drugs were available to all, no one would cheat by using them; for all would have the same opportunity and, so it would be argued, no one would be forced into drug use any more than top athletes are forced to embark on rigorous training programs.

Perhaps what bothers us about the use of drugs is that the user may be endangering his or her health. But why isn't the choice about whether the risk is worth the gain left to the individual athlete to make? After all, we don't always prohibit new training techniques just because they carry along with them some risk to health.

Perhaps the stress generated by a particularly arduous training routine is more dangerous to some athletes than the possible side effects of drugs are to others?

Arguably, the charge that drug users create unfair pressures on other competitors begs the very question at issue. That is, it presupposes that such pressures are morally suspect in ways that other competitive pressures are not, when the very point at issue is whether that is the case. What is needed is some principled basis for asserting that certain competitive pressures—those generated by the use of performance-enhancing drugs—are illegitimately imposed while other competitive pressures—such as those generated by hard training—are legitimate and proper. It will not do to point out that the former pressures are generated by drug use. What is needed is an explanation of why the use of performance-enhancing drugs should be prohibited in the first place.

While such arguments, which describe a position we might call a libertarianism of sports, raise important issues, they may seem to be open to clear counter-example when applied in nonathletic contexts. Suppose for example that your co-workers choose to put in many extra hours on the job. That may put pressure on you to work overtime as well, if only to show your employer that you are just as dedicated as your colleagues. But now, suppose your fellow workers start taking dangerous stimulants to enable them to put even more hours into their jobs. Your employer then asks why you are working less than they are. You reply that you can keep up the pace only by taking dangerous drugs. Is the employer's reply, "Well, no one is forcing you to stay on the job, but if you do you had better put in as many hours as the others" really acceptable?

However, even here, intuitions are not a particularly reliable guide to principle. Suppose you have other less stressful alternatives for employment and that the extra hours the others originally work without aid of drugs generate far more harmful stress than the risk generated by the use of stimulant? Perhaps in that case your employer is not speaking impermissibly in telling you to work harder. If not, just why does the situation change when the harmful effects are generated by drugs rather than stress? Alternatively, if we think there should be limits both on the stress generated by pressures from overtime *and* the risks created by drug use, why not treat similar risks alike, regardless of source? Similarly, in the context of sport, if our goal is to lower risk, it is far from clear that the risks imposed by performance-enhancing drugs are so great as to warrant total prohibition, while the sometimes equal risks imposed by severe training regimens are left untouched.

Harm and the Protection of the Young

Even if athletes at top levels of competition can give informed consent to the use of performance-enhancing drugs, and even if users do not place unfair or coercive competitive pressures on others, the harm principle may still support prohibition.

Consider, for example, the influence of the behavior of star athletes on youngsters. Might not impressionable boys and girls below the age of consent be driven to use performance-enhancing drugs in an effort to emulate top stars? Might not high school athletes turn to performance-enhancing drugs to please coaches, parents, and fans?

Unfortunately, consideration of such remote effects of drug use is far from conclusive. After all, other training techniques such as strict weight programs also may be dangerous if adopted by young athletes who are too physically immature to take the stress such programs generate. Again, what is needed is not simply a statement that a practice imposes some risk on others. Also needed is a justification for saying the risk is improperly imposed. Why restrict the freedom of top athletes rather than increase the responsibility for supervision of youngsters assigned to coaches, teachers, and parents? After all, we don't restrict the freedom of adults in numerous other areas where they may set bad examples for the young.

III. Drugs and the Ideal of Competitive Sport

Our discussion so far suggests that although the charges that use of performance-enhancing drugs by some athletes harms others do warrant further examination, they amount to less than a determinative case against such drug use. However, they may have additional force when supported by an account of competitive sport which implies a distinction between appropriate and inappropriate competitive pressures. What we need, then, is an account of when risk is improperly imposed on others in sport. While I am unable to provide a full theory here, I do want to suggest a principled basis, grounded on an ethic of athletic competition, for prohibition of paradigm performance-enhancing drugs.

My suggestion, which I can only outline here, is that competition in athletics is best thought of as a mutual quest for excellence through challenge (2: pp. 133-39). Competitors are obliged to do their best so as to bring out the best in their opponents. Competitors are to present challenges to one another within the constitutive rules of the sport being played. Such an account may avoid the charges, often directed against competitive sports, that they are zero-sum games which encourage the selfish and egotistical desire to promote oneself by imposing losses on others.

In addition, the ideal of sport as a *mutual* quest for excellence brings out the crucial point that a sports contest is a competition between *persons*. Within the competitive framework, each participant must respond to the choices, acts, and abilities of others—which in turn manifest past decisions about what one's priorities should be and how one's skills are to be developed. The good competitor, then, does not see opponents as things to be overcome and beaten down but rather sees them as persons whose acts call for appropriate, mutually acceptable responses. On this view, athletic competition, rather than being incompatible with respect for our opponents as persons, actually presupposes it.

However, when use of drugs leads to improved play, it is natural to say that it is not athletic ability that determines outcome but rather the efficiency with which the athlete's body reacts to the performance enhancer. But the whole point of athletic competition is to test the athletic ability of persons, not the way bodies react to drugs. In the latter case, it is not the athlete who is responsible for the gain. Enhanced performance does not result from the qualities of the athlete *qua* person, such as dedication, motivation, or courage. It does not result from innate or developed ability, of which it is the point of competition to test. Rather, it results from an external factor, the ability of one's body to efficiently utilize a drug, a factor which has only a contingent and fortuitous relationship to athletic ability.[4]

Critics may react to this approach in at least two different ways. First, they may deny that drug use radically changes the point of athletic competition, which presumably is to test the physical and mental qualities of athletes in their sport. Second, they may assert that by allowing the use of performance-enhancing drugs, we expand the point of athletic competition in desirable ways. That is, they may question whether the paradigm of athletic competition to which I have appealed has any privileged moral standing. It may well be an accepted paradigm, but what makes it acceptable?

Drugs and Tests of Ability

Clearly, drugs such as steroids are not magic pills that guarantee success regardless of the qualities of the users. Athletes using steroids must practice just as hard as others to attain what may be only marginal benefits from use. If performance enhancers were available to all competitors, it would still be the qualities of athletes that determined the results.

While this point is not without force, neither is it decisive. Even if all athletes used drugs, they might not react to them equally. The difference in reaction might determine the difference between competitive success and failure. Hence, outcomes would be determined not by the relevant qualities of the athletes themselves but rather by the natural capacity of their bodies to react to the drug of choice.

Is this any different, the critic may reply, from other innate differences in athletes which might enable them to benefit more than others from weight training or to run faster or swing harder than others? Isn't it inconsistent to allow some kinds of innate differences to affect outcomes but not the others?

Such an objection, however, seems to ignore the point of athletic competition. The point of such competition is to select those who do run the fastest, swing the hardest, or jump the farthest. The idea is not for all to come out equally, but for differences in outcome to correlate with differences in ability and motivation. Likewise, while some athletes may be predisposed to benefit more from a given amount of weight training than others, this trait seems relevant to selection of the best athlete. Capacity to benefit from training techniques seems part of what makes one a superior athlete in a way that capacity to benefit from a drug does not.

Competition and Respect for Persons

At this point, a proponent of the use of performance-enhancing drugs might acknowledge that use of such drugs falls outside the prevailing paradigm of athletic competition. However, such a proponent might ask, "What is the *moral* force of such a conclusion?" Unless we assume that the accepted paradigm not only is acceptable, but in addition that deviance from it should be prohibited, nothing follows about the ethics of the use of performance-enhancing drugs.

Indeed, some writers seem to suggest that we consider new paradigms compatible with greater freedom for athletes, including freedom to experiment with performance-enhancing drugs. W.M. Brown seems to advocate such a view when he writes,

> Won't it [drug use] change the nature of our sports and ourselves? Yes.... But then people can choose, as they always have, to compete with those similar to themselves or those different.... I can still make my actions an "adventure in freedom" and "explore the limits of my strength" however I choose to develop it. (1: p. 22)

I believe Brown has raised a point of fundamental significance here. I wish I had a fully satisfactory response to it. Since I don't, perhaps the best I can do is indicate the lines of a reply I think are worth considering, in the hope that it will stimulate further discussion and evaluation.

Where athletic competition is concerned, if all we are interested in is better and better performance, we could design robots to "run" the hundred yards in 3 seconds or hit a golf ball 500 yards when necessary. But it isn't just enhanced performance that we are after. In addition, we want athletic competition to be a test of *persons*. It is not only raw ability we are testing for; it is what people do with their ability that counts at least as much. In competition itself, each competitor is reacting to the choices, strategies, and valued abilities of the other, which in turn are affected by past decisions and commitments. Arguably, athletic competition is a paradigm example of an area in which each individual competitor respects the other competitors as persons. That is, each reacts to the intelligent choices and valued characteristics of the other. These characteristics include motivation, courage, intelligence, and what might be called the metachoice* of which talents and capacities are to assume priority over others for a given stage of the individual's life.

However, if outcomes are significantly affected not by such features but instead by the capacity of the body to benefit physiologically from drugs, athletes are no longer reacting to each other as persons but rather become more like competing bodies. It becomes more and more appropriate to see the opposition as things to be overcome—as mere means to be overcome in the name of victory—rather than as persons posing valuable challenges. So, insofar as the requirement that we respect each other as persons is ethically fundamental, the prevailing paradigm does enjoy a privileged perspective from the moral point of view.

It is of course true that the choice to develop one's capacity through drugs is a choice a person might make. Doesn't respect for persons require that we respect the choice to use performance enhancers as much as any other? The difficulty, I suggest, is the effect that such a choice has on the process of athletic competition itself. The use of performance-enhancing drugs in sports restricts the area in which we can be respected as persons. Although individual athletes certainly can make such a choice, there is a justification inherent in the nature of good competition for prohibiting participation by those who make such a decision. Accordingly, the use of performance-enhancing drugs should be prohibited in the name of the value of respect for persons itself.

NOTES

1. This paper was presented at the Olympic Scientific Congress in Eugene, Oregon (July, 1984) as part of a symposium, sponsored by the Philosophic Society for the Study of Sport, on the use of performance-enhancing drugs in sport. Some

---

* = a choice about choices.

of the material in this paper is included in Robert L. Simon, *Sports and Social Values* (Englewood Cliffs, NJ: Prentice-Hall, 1985), and published by permission of Prentice-Hall.

2. The ethical issues raised by blood doping are discussed by Perry (5).

3. The charge of coercion does seem more plausible if the athlete has no acceptable alternative but to participate. Thus, professional athletes with no other career prospects may fit the model of coercion better than, say, a young amateur weight lifter who has been accepted at law school.

4. Does this approach have the unintuitive consequence that the dietary practice of carbohydrate loading, utilized by runners, also is ethically dubious? Perhaps so, but perhaps a distinction can be made between steroid use, which changes an athlete's capabilities for athletically irrelevant reasons, and dietary practices, which enable athletes to get the most out of the ability they have.

REFERENCES

1. Brown, W.M. (1980). "Ethics, Drugs, and Sport." *Journal of the Philosophy of Sport*, VII, 15-23.

2. Delattre, Edward. (1975). "Some Reflections on Success and Failure in Competitive Athletics." *Journal of the Philosophy of Sport*, I, 133-39.

3. Dwyer, Fred. (1982). "The Real Problem: Using Drugs to Win." *The New York Times*, July 4, 2S.

4. Murray, Thomas H. (1983). "The Coercive Power of Drugs in Sports." *The Hastings Center Report*, 13, 24-30.

5. Perry, Clifton. (1983). "Blood Doping and Athletic Competition." *International Journal of Applied Philosophy*, 1, 39-45.

6. Thomas, Carolyn E. (1983). *Sport in a Philosophic Context*. Philadelphia: Lea & Febiger.

12. PATERNALISM, DRUGS, AND THE NATURE OF SPORTS*

W.M. BROWN

During the marathon run at the 1972 Munich Olympics, Frank Shorter is said to have sipped decarbonated Coca-Cola provided along the route by his assistants as he headed for a gold medal. Clearly, for Shorter, caffeine was the drug of choice for that most demanding of running events. Since that time, caffeine has become one of an increasingly long list of banned drugs no longer permitted by the International Olympic Committee for competing athletes.[1] The list includes both a variety of chemically synthesized drugs as well as naturally occurring substances that are artificially prepared for human use.[2] The central issue of the use of such substances is not their so-called recreational use, the most prominent example of which is probably the widely publicized use of cocaine by some professional athletes. (Alcohol is apparently not currently a prohibited drug for Olympic athletes.) Rather, the issue is the use of drugs to enhance the benefits of training and to improve peak performance in competition.

Controversy on this issue centers on several factors which have both an empirical aspect and a moral one. The empirical questions concern both the effectiveness of drug use for training and competition and the possible harm such use can have for users.[3] The moral questions concern the appropriateness of the use of drugs in sports, especially when their use is seen as a kind of cheating, a breach of principles of fair play. It is sometimes claimed, too, that the use of drugs in sports is somehow unnatural or incompatible with the very nature of sports. I intend to discuss these matters, but from the perspective of the moral principle of paternalism that I believe motivates many people who are concerned with this issue. First

---

* W.M. Brown, "Paternalism, Drugs, and the Nature of Sports," *Journal of the Philosophy of Sport* II (1984), pp. 14-22.

I want to look closely at the issue of drug use in sports by children and young people—cases which may appear to justify paternalistic choices—and then turn to the harder case of the paternalistic control of drug use by adults in sports.

Even John Stuart Mill (7), in his sustained attack on paternalistic restrictions on individual liberty, limited the application of his principles to mature individuals, adults in the full possession of their cognitive and emotional capacities. In the case of children, and perhaps others whose mature development of these capacities and a wider experience of life's possibilities has yet to be achieved, restrictions on individual liberty may be justified as preventing significant harm that might not otherwise be recognized and avoided. In such cases it seems clear that paternalistic interference is not only permissible but may indeed be obligatory to prevent harm and allow for a full flourishing of the child's potential development. Of course, judgment must be balanced: An important part of growing up is making mistakes and learning from them. All parents know the anguish of allowing failure to help guide the maturation of their children. Following Joel Feinberg and Gerald Dworkin, we can distinguish between "soft" and "hard" paternalism (2; 3; 4).[4]

Soft paternalism is defined by Dworkin (3: p. 107) as "the view that (1) paternalism is sometimes justified, and (2) it is a necessary condition for such justification that the person for whom we are acting paternalistically is in some way not competent." The key element here is clearly the determination that the person for whom we are acting is in fact not acting voluntarily, perhaps due to various circumstances including immaturity, ignorance, incapacity, or coercion. It may be that the non-voluntary character of the behavior is evident or justifiably assumed on other grounds. This is typically the case with young children; but it is sometimes also true of adults whose situation makes clear that their actions are not fully voluntary. The more problematic cases are those of adult behavior that is not obviously non-voluntary, but whose consequences are potentially dangerous or serious enough to call for careful deliberation. In these cases, as Feinberg (4: p. 8) suggests, we may be justified in intervening at least temporarily to determine whether the conduct is voluntary or not.

If soft paternalism is most clearly relevant to intervention in the lives of children and incompetent persons, hard paternalism must deal with cases of fully voluntary action and show nevertheless that paternalism is justified. Here we may have every reason to suppose that the action in question is voluntarily undertaken by someone who has carefully appraised the consequences, weighed all available information, is emotionally responsive to the circumstances, but still opts to act in ways that involve the probability of serious harm, degradation, or impairment of opportunity or liberty. The most frequently cited cases are of those who seek to sell themselves into slavery, or persist in ignoring basic safety precautions such as wearing helmets while riding motorcycles. I shall return to the hard paternalistic thesis and its application to the case of adult sports after considering first the view of the soft paternalist and its application to the case of children and young people and their participation in sports. I shall not be directly concerned with the soft paternalist attitude toward adult sports except as an extension of its application to the case of children.

The soft paternalist argues that limitation of one's liberty is justified when one's behavior or actions are not fully voluntary because they are not fully informed, or because one is not fully competent or is in some relevant way coerced. All of these factors may plausibly be seen as present in the case of children's sports. By virtue of their youth, limited education, and inexperience, young people may frequently act in imprudent and potentially harmful ways, ways that may have unforeseen but long-term or irreversible consequences. Before considering the case of drugs, let me review several other cases in which the soft paternalist has what seems to be a strong argument for intervention or control of the young athlete's participation in sports.

The first kind of situation can best be called "safety cases."[5] These involve efforts by coaches, trainers, parents, and others to ensure that young players are provided with proper safety equipment and that they use it while engaged in playing the sport. Especially in contact sports such as football or hockey, such equipment as helmets and padded uniforms may be essential to protect the players against serious injury. Other sports may require other kinds of precautions. For example, swimmers may be prohibited from training alone in a pool, runners may be required to wear proper shoes, contact lenses may be forbidden, and so on. Some of these precautions may simply be prescribed by thoughtful parents or coaches, but others may be written into the rules of the sports by athletic associations, schools, or boards of education, thereby restricting participation to those who are properly equipped, or prohibiting certain kinds of play as too dangerous.

Indeed, most of the rules governing contact between players are formulated with the intention of ensuring the safety of enthusiastic and energetic players. The reasons for these requirements and rules are evident. Young athletes are frequently marvelously competent and talented in performing the intricate or arduous or swift feats called for in their sports. But they are typically equally unaware of their own limitations, their susceptibility to injury, and the long-term consequences of injuries to their development or effective participation. What justifies intervention in these cases, of restrictions on what young athletes may do, is precisely the belief that they are thus being prevented from harming themselves and that on mature reflection they themselves will come to see the reasonableness of the restrictions now placed on them. As their own experience broadens, and as their knowledge of themselves and their actions deepens and their values mature, they are, we anticipate, likely to join in accepting the restrictions they may have seen before as irksome and unnecessary.

A second set of cases I propose to refer to as "health cases." Insofar as injuries are closely connected with our views of health, there is clearly a considerable overlap between these two types of cases. Nevertheless, I believe there are some significant differences that warrant a separate category. Even in the absence of injuries and of circumstances likely to promote them, other matters of health rightly should concern the parent or coach of young athletes. I have in mind here matters that concern training, medical examinations and corresponding medical treatment or therapy, and nutrition and rest. They may involve the need for periodic medical examinations, the proper treatment of injuries, insistence on adequate nutrition and rest, and thoughtful organizing of training schedules that carefully consider the age, preparation, and health of the athlete.

In these cases, the young person typically lacks information to make adequate judgments—information that may be the purview of specially trained persons with long experience working with athletes and others. Furthermore, the young person is not generally expected even to be aware of his or her own ignorance or of the importance of acquiring medical or other information at an age when health may be taken for granted. Moreover, even when information is available, its significance may not be readily appreciated, habits of restraint and caution may be ill-formed, and self-discipline in maintaining therapeutic or training regimens may be minimal. The opposite may also occur. Youthful determination may manifest itself in excessive restraint, debilitating training, or stubborn persistence. Here ancient wisdom of balance, moderation, measure or variation may be the needed antidote, provided by more experienced people who insist on more wholesome approaches to sports preparation.

Of course, other factors than ignorance and inexperience may need to be overcome in paternalistic control of youthful sports. Peer and perhaps especially adult pressures are often a critical factor that adult advisors must deal with firmly and sensitively. One other important distinction should be mentioned here. So far, I have ignored the difference between health as the absence of disease or injury and health as a positive feature of growth and development. If it is clear that adults are justified in controlling the sports activities of young people in the interest of preventing injuries or speeding recuperation, and in maintaining the health of their children and students in the sense of keeping them injury-free and minimally healthy, it is also plausible that they are justified in seeking a greater degree of health or fitness for them. This seems to involve more centrally an educational function, though this feature is clearly present in the other two kinds of cases I have discussed, and I now turn to consider what might be called "educational cases."

Sports in our schools and universities, even when they involve intercollegiate competition, are almost invariably associated with departments of physical education. I mention this because it seems that a neglected but focal role for parents and coaches is educational, and the educational function goes far beyond the training of skills to include the inculcation of attitudes and values, the dissemination of information, and the formation of habits of mind as well as of body. It is difficult to illustrate cases in which paternalistic issues arise here, because the guidance of parents and coaches is often so subtle and pervasive as to be unnoticed by those it influences. Its character as interfering with or controlling the behavior of unwilling charges is more difficult to discern. Nevertheless, I think there are some fairly clear cases.

One type of case brings us back to efforts to prevent injury and to foster wholesome development by prescribing training schedules and nutritional standards designed to maximize training effectiveness. The effort here should never be merely to prescribe, but also to educate by explaining the rationale for the requirements, presenting the evidence available to substantiate the judgments, and requiring that the student understand as much as possible how the decisions were made. What can be expected here will vary with the age and educational level of the student, but resistance can often be expected, not only to following the requirements but to making efforts to understand them. I offer no formula for success in these efforts. As in all educational contexts many options are available to gifted teachers' cajolery, punishment, rewards, example, the inducements of affection, friendship, and respect, and lessons of failure and success. But I do wish to stress that these efforts are made because we believe the lessons should be learned, willingly or not, in the gym and playing field as well as the classroom. In doing so we counter the thoughtless or irrational or emotionally immature behavior of our students with paternalistic measures we believe are acceptable to fully rational and emotionally mature individuals.

A second type of educational case involves values. I have in mind instances of cheating or foul play in which adults may intervene to correct unfair, dishonest, or unsportsmanlike actions. Here again the goal is not merely to remedy or referee but is fundamentally educational. We should seek to instill values of fairness and honesty, countering whatever tendencies to the contrary we observe on the grounds that such action is not in the best interest of the players, whatever they may think about it. The development of values like the acquisition of knowledge in general is but one aspect of the central aim of education, which is the discovery of self-knowledge. Since, especially in young people, this is inextricably bound up with what they will become as well as with what they now are, the paternalistic guidance by adults must both inform and shape in light of what the adults believe to be the characteristics of persons in the fullness of their cognitive and emotional powers.

We are now ready to discuss control of the use of drugs by children and young people as an aspect of their participation in sports. Although I think a good general case can be made for proscribing drug use by young people, and even that a recreational use of drugs has some negative relevance to participation in sports, I plan to limit my remarks to a consideration of the use of drugs to influence athletic training and performance. I have not hesitated to offer here what I consider to be defensible moral judgments on the topics and issues I have raised. My point is not to insist that these judgments are unavoidable, but to suggest that they correspond with widely held intuitions relating to the acceptability of paternalism in regard to children and their sports activities.

Two aspects of drug use can be distinguished in advance, one being the use of drugs as medication. When medical treatment does not prevent sports participation entirely, it may significantly curtail that involvement. And when injury or illness requires medication which nevertheless will allow some sports activity, the decisive criterion will be improvement of the participant's health, not athletic achievement. There may also be times when use of medication is unrelated to sports and seems in no way to affect participation except perhaps to allow it where otherwise it might not be possible. (An example might be drugs used to control mild epilepsy.) Here, too, the primary concern is the health and safety of the child. Such use may enhance participation in the limiting sense of making it possible, but where the purpose and effect of such usage is limited to medically justifiable ones, we may reasonably disregard this trivial enhancement. In the event that a medication did significantly improve performance over what would otherwise be expected, we could consider it in the next category.

This category involves cases in which drugs are used by otherwise healthy people for the express purpose of enhancing training or competition. There are a number of reasons why such usage should be prohibited. Foremost, of course, are the clear threats to the health and safety of the persons taking them. Among the many drugs available to athletes are some that have a powerful effect on the balance of the hormonal system, such as testosterone and other steroids, or human growth hormone, or L-dopa and ß-blockers which can stimulate such hormones. Psychomotor or central nervous system stimulants can have a variety of powerful effects on the human body. Young people are especially vulnerable not only to the primary effects of such drugs but also to many deleterious side effects and to possible long-range effects that in many cases are only now beginning to be determined.[6] Damaging effects on growth patterns, and on psychosocial development, are probably high risks of such drugs for children and young people—risks far outweighing any possible benefits of temporary superior athletic prowess.

I should mention that in this respect, drugs are not different in kind, though perhaps in degree, from other features of sports which conflict with our values of health for young people. Arduous and extreme training methods, excessively rough contact between players, and insufficient recuperation or recovery from illness or injury, for example, may all violate our reasonable standards of wholesome athletics. Indeed a paramount concern for any tendency to overemphasize achievements in young people's sports is that it encourages a disregard for the health and balanced development of the young players.

I suspect that these judgments are relatively uncontroversial. But I now want to renew our discussion of the relation of such possible drug use and the development of attitudes and values by young players which I have already defended as among the legitimate paternalistic concerns of guardians and athletic supervisors. Drug use of the kind we are discussing (and of course many other features of training and competition) is clearly associated with winning, indeed with winning at virtually all costs. The chief consideration will always be how use of drugs will enable a young athlete to develop more quickly and effectively the strength, speed, or endurance needed to win, and how subsequent use will provide an improved competitive performance. This attitude is one that we can fairly consider to be nearly a defining characteristic of professionalism as it has come to be understood.

This use of drugs therefore carries with it, or encourages the development of, attitudes and values that conflict with those we hope to instill in children and young people through their very early participation in athletics. Among these latter values are sportsmanship, honesty, fairness, self-reliance as well as cooperation, grace under pressure, and health. Others could also be mentioned. But a central value is that of experiencing achievement through personal effort, of responding willfully to challenge, and thereby of coming to realize, that is, both to create and to understand, one's self, the complex bundle of skills, dispositions, beliefs, values, and capacities which constitute a personality.

Merit in a young athlete should reflect factors that are fully within his or her control. Ability and achievement should be a reflection of the amount of effort and self-motivation that are consonant with a normal life not characterized by fanaticism (an unreasonable purposiveness). We seek to stress a history of training and competitive effort that may to some extent cancel the uncontrollable differences among people so that superior skill is the result of a growing strength or personal resolve. In our paternalistic limiting of the freedom of young athletes, we are not emphasizing freedom to do anything or to have anything done to one, but rather the freedom of self-determination which accords with ideals of a reasoned, autonomous, well-balanced life, led in relation to a sensible ranking of values. It is because success due to some special technique or technology is only marginally reflective of athletic skill or training or motivation that we discount it or forbid it in the repertoire of young athletes.[7]

I want to emphasize that sports are not the only context in which these values are developed; indeed, they may not even be the best one. But they are a place, and for many people a very important one, where this learning process does occur. The conflict raised by drug usage of the kind we are discussing is that, by emphasizing one value over all others, it skews the context of learning and growth so as to deny sufficient credibility to other values. Moreover, it may conflict directly with efforts to encourage the young athlete to grasp the relation between personal effort and achievement so closely tied to both the experience of joy, excitement, and satisfaction of the athletes themselves, and to a similar appreciation by spectators.

It should be clear that we can extend the claims of soft paternalism, which I have so far discussed in regard to children, to various cases of adult behavior which presume incapacity of some sort, for example, ignorance, lack of opportunity or resources, or immaturity. But these are the easy cases for the soft paternalist and I shall not dispute them here. The difficult cases are surely those that give us every reason to believe that the actors are rational, informed, emotionally mature adults. The soft paternalist in turn must dispute such presumptions. We could of course hold that adult athletes who take drugs to enhance training or performance are in some way irrational, that they do not fully appreciate the dangers of such actions or the seriousness of side effects, or cannot adequately weigh the evidence that drug usage is not beneficial to performance. Moreover, we could claim that such athletes, in addition to ignoring relevant information, are unable to resist the pressures of others to succeed at all costs, that their weakness of will warrants paternalistic interference.

But such a reply is unconvincing, at least in many readily imaginable cases.

It cannot be the very use of drugs which is the sole evidence for irrationality or self-destructiveness or weakness of will, on pain of begging the central question. And the evidence, once in, is very unlikely to support the claim that all cases of drug use are non-voluntary in the requisite way. Rather, the truth seems to be that in these cases other values come into play. Adult values and motivations are not always the same as those we may encourage for young people. Adult life *is* more complicated, and though we intend the training in values and skills of childhood and youth to carry over to maturity, we are well aware that they will inevitably compete with other values that are often at odds with those we can reasonably insist on earlier. Often for adults winning *is* more important, and the circumstances of life may encourage a new range of motives: fame, wealth, power, social mobility, patriotism, pride of class, or race or ideology.

We may not accept such values or wish to encourage such motivations but, in a free society, they are permissible; we may not deny them, to those who choose them, on grounds of paternalism. Where such values predominate, the risks of drugs may be outweighed by the benefits they may bring. Perhaps we come here to one of the sources of the distinction between "amateur" and "professional." If so, the distinction does not match the one I am suggesting between the values of youth and adulthood. Some professional skills and the knowledge of professional experience are clearly applicable to youth sports, and, conversely, professional values need not conflict with other values. It is always a matter of emphasis, role, age, commitments, and goals that determine which values dominate.

Indeed, even in our approach to sports for children, and especially of youths, we will at some point begin to anticipate some of the competing values that will increasingly vie for their attention and commitment as they grow older. As always, there are important questions of timing, emphasis, role, and age. But teachers and parents must at some point help facilitate the transition to full autonomy at which earlier limits to freedom can no longer be tolerated.

The soft paternalist could of course insist that where drug use or sports activities carry with them high risk, even risk of death or permanent injury, we are justified in intervening to prevent serious costs to the rest of us even when the athletes are willing to take the risks.[8] But society does not typically support the costs of such injury, and we could in any case require proper insurance for the athletes. Moreover, the psychic cost to others is surely minimal and, even in cases such as boxing, it is normally outweighed by the psychic gains of the spectator: the vicarious thrill and excitement, the shared pride, the satisfaction of knowledgeable viewing. In any case the balance of risks and benefits concerning drug usage is not likely to be clear. Efforts are no doubt being made to control for undesirable side effects, and the benefits may often need to be measured only in fractions of seconds. And why should we single out one class of risk when others, perhaps equally great, are already tolerated for the sake of excellence? Finally though it involves interference in the lives of others, such a response does not seem paternalistically motivated.

At this point, we may resort to something like a principle of "hard" paternalism if we are to persist in our efforts to control the choices and options of athletes. We are in effect seeking to impose on those who resist it an alternative set of values. But what would justify such an imposition? There seems no reason to suppose that taking risk in sports, even great risk, is inevitably irrational, self-destructive, or immature, as we have seen. Nor is it plausible to suggest that we forbid all of the sports which involve such risk, such as mountain climbing, sky-diving, or even boxing. As Mill argued, such intervention in people's lives would itself be a greater wrong than the possible injury of activities voluntarily chosen.

It may nevertheless be argued that the use of drugs is somehow inconsistent with the nature of sports, and that sports in turn are linked with a broader set of values—a conception of the good life—which is betrayed by the use of drugs, so that interference in the choices of athletes in this respect is done to preserve a greater good, one they may have lost sight of in their preoccupation with the more narrow concerns of training and competition. Such an argument a priori,* as I have argued elsewhere, is not cogent (1). There is, I believe, no single conception of sports on which we need agree. In competitive sports we stress fairness and balanced competition; but in more solitary pursuits these values seem irrelevant. In the case of drugs, fairness may dictate equal access and widely available information. But even this is not clear: athletes and coaches seem justified in keeping secret their training regimens, and even, when permitted by the rules, equipment modifications.

Often, too, we stress human factors such as determination, fortitude, and cooperativeness over risk taking and technology. But in other cases—luge, skiing, mountain climbing, hang-gliding—risk and technology dominate. We believe in the capacity of sports to promote health and fitness, but many originated in the practice of war and routinely involve stress and injury, sometimes death. We fashion rules and continually modify them to reduce hazards and minimize serious injury, but few would seek to do so entirely. Perhaps we are tempted to require in athletes only what is normal. But our sports have evolved with our technology and our best

---

*   = an argument based on the essence of something, its central necessary nature, the
      definition of that kind of thing, or the concept we have of it.

athletes are often unnaturally, statistically, endowed with abilities and other characteristics far beyond the norm. It seems artificial indeed to draw the line at drugs when so much of today's training techniques, equipment, food, medical care, even the origin of the sports themselves, are the product of our technological culture.

Nevertheless, something more may be said for the claim that sports reflect a broader set of values. In discussing the justification of paternalism in coaching the young, I have stressed the formation of the values of honesty, fairness, and autonomy, values central to my conception of personhood. But they are not the only ones that might be stressed. Obedience, regimentation, service to others, or sacrifice might have been proposed. These, too, in the proper context, might also be developed together with the skills of athletics. The values, perhaps even a conception of what is good for human life, are associated with sports, not because of their nature, but due to the way we choose to play them. We can indeed forbid the use of drugs in athletics in general, just as we do in the case of children. But ironically, in adopting such a paternalistic stance of insisting that we know better than the athletes themselves how to achieve some more general good which they myopically ignore, we must deny in them the very attributes we claim to value: self-reliance, personal achievement, and autonomy.

NOTES

1. The current ban on caffeine is defined in terms of a maximum level in urine of 15 μg/mL. For athletes this certainly means no direct ingestion of caffeine tablets, but also a need to avoid combinations of coffee, soft drinks, and over-the-counter medications like Anacin or Empirin* which could lead to excessive accumulations of the drug.

2. A good example of such substances is the hormone testosterone. Since it occurs naturally in the body, it has been difficult to detect exogenous † testosterone. A new test, however, now measures the ratio of testosterone to a metabolite, epitestosterone, which normally occur in a one-to-one ratio. Since exogenous testosterone isn't converted as readily to epitestosterone, it changes the ratio. The IOC requires the ratio of testosterone to its epimer in urine to be less than six to one. See Zurer (10).

3. Much of the evidence available to athletes in this regard is anecdotal, based on the personal experience of coaches, trainers, a few sports physicians, and the

---

* Empirin is a brand name for ASA (Aspirin). Anacin is ASA plus caffeine.
† = coming from outside the body—i.e., not produced by the normal processes of the body.

athletes themselves. The research literature is skimpy and the results conflicting. See Zurer (10) for a brief discussion of the conflicting views on the evidence. See also Williams (9).

4. These articles are conveniently reprinted in (8). Dworkin makes the distinction between "soft" and "hard" paternalism in (3). A slightly broader definition of paternalism is defended by Gert and Culver (5). (A version of this article appears in 6: Ch. 7.)

5. Dworkin (3: p. 108) uses this rubric, but for a different type of case.

6. Among the side effects of anabolic steroids are acne and liver tumors. For children and adolescents who are still growing, premature bone fusing and precocious puberty are likely results. See Zurer (10: pp. 73-75).

7. I'm grateful to Bill Puka for discussing this point with me, though in a somewhat different context.

8. Dworkin (3: p. 109) briefly discusses this argument for a different kind of case.

REFERENCES

1. Brown, W.M. (1980). "Drugs, Ethics, and Sport." *The Journal of the Philosophy of Sport*, VII, 15-23.

2. Dworkin, Gerald. (1972). "Paternalism." *The Monist*, 56, 64-84.

3. Dworkin, Gerald. (1983). "Paternalism: Some Second Thoughts." *Paternalism*. Edited by Rolf Sartorius. Minneapolis: U of Minnesota P.

4. Feinberg, Joel. (1971). "Legal Paternalism." *Canadian Journal of Philosophy*, 1, 106-24.

5. Gert, Bernard, and Charles Culver. (1976). "Paternalistic Behavior." *Philosophy and Public Affairs*, 6, 45-57.

6. Gert, Bernard, and Charles Culver. (1982). *Philosophy in Medicine: Conceptual and Ethical Issues in Medicine and Psychiatry*. New York: Oxford UP.

7. Mill, J.S. (1978). *On Liberty*. Indianapolis: Hackett Publ.

8. Sartorius, Rolf. (1983). *Paternalism*. Minneapolis: U of Minnesota P.

9. Williams, Melvin H. (1974). *Drugs and Athletic Performance*. Springfield, IL: Thomas.

10. Zurer, Pamela S. (1984). "Drugs in Sports." *Chemical and Engineering News*, April 30, pp. 69-79.

QUESTIONS

1. Are Simon's criteria for performance-enhancing drugs plausible? Is he too quick to dismiss defining such drugs as artificial?

2. Does sport imply, as Simon says, a "mutual quest for excellence"? Does this require that we uphold bans on certain performance-enhancers?

3. In cases of taking steroids recreationally, that is, outside competitive contexts, on what moral grounds, if any, should we prohibit such use? Is it different in competitive contexts?

4. Are there practical difficulties in lifting bans on performance-enhancing drugs (emulation by youth, for instance)? Are alcohol and tobacco consumption useful analogies here?

5. Do bans on steroids in adult sport amount to treating adults as children, as Brown suggests? When, in terms of steroid use, might this be appropriate?

6. To what extent do bans on steroids reflect the general concern that athletic achievement is already being replaced by technological (here, pharmacological) achievement?

FURTHER READING

Gardner, Roger (1989): "On Performance-Enhancing Substances and the Unfair Advantage Argument," *Journal of the Philosophy of Sport* 16, pp. 59-73.

Hoberman, John M. (1988): "Sport and the Technological Image of Man," in *Philosophic Inquiry in Sport*, ed. William J. Morgan and Klaus V. Meier (Champaign, IL: Human Kinetics), pp. 319-27.

Holowchak, M. Andrew (2000): "'Aretism' and Pharmacological Ergogenic Aids in Sport: Taking a Shot at the Use of Steroids," *Journal of the Philosophy of Sport* 27, pp. 35-50.

Lavin, Michael (1987): "Sports and Drugs: Are the Current Bans Justified?" *Journal of the Philosophy of Sport* 14, pp. 34-43.

Tamburrini, Claudio M. (2000): "What's Wrong with Doping?" in *Values in Sport: Elitism, Nationalism, Gender Equality and the Scientific Manufacture of Winners*, ed. Claudio Tamburrini and Torbjörn Tännsjö (London: E & FN Spon), pp. 200-16.

Thompson, Paul B. (1982): "Privacy and the Urinalysis Testing of Athletes," *Journal of the Philosophy of Sport* 9, pp. 60-65.

FURTHER INQUIRY

Further refinement in the criteria for performance-enhancing drugs seems desirable if we want bans on them to be principled rather than arbitrary. The concept of artificiality might be useful here after all insofar as blood doping involves a natural substance but surely an unnatural mode of delivery. The major misgiving about (post)modern sport, that *athletic* achievement is being replaced by *scientific* achievement (technological, pharmacological), deserves further study, as does the issue of performance enhancers in other areas, such as so-called "cognitive enhancers," from mild (caffeine), through medium (Adderall, Ritalin), to extreme (amphetamines). Whether athletics and academics are in step here, whether there should be bans on alleged performance-enhancing drugs in academe, or none in either domain, is a live and significant question beyond legal and general moral concerns. The arbitrariness of constitutive and regulative rules (besides considerations of good game-design) suggests a comparable leeway in upholding or eliminating steroid bans. The elasticity of 'good' here is telling, as what is good for the spectator and for the athlete might well conflict. Should the fate of the bans be decided by vote? It perhaps would not help to have steroid leagues alongside clean ones, yet the analogy between driving the autobahn and speed-limit highways seems provocative. The temptation to cheat in the clean league would be offset by the opportunity in the "dirty" league to maximize performance without hypocrisy.

Breaking Rules

"Breaking the rules" often conjures images in one's mind of rebellious types, the innovators and outlaws, who refuse, for noble or bad reasons, to follow conventions and the dictates of others. Usually, though, breaking rules is something else, something more mundane. In sport, breaking rules divides into two types: deliberate cases, like cheating and so-called professional fouls (as when one trips an opponent on a breakaway), and accidental cases owing to either inexperience or accident. The deliberate cases are central here, particularly, though not exclusively, cheating: rule-breaking aimed at covert competitive advantage.

"Cheaters never win" is, even for an adage, clichéd. It is usually interpreted as implying that a victorious cheat suffers, for having cheated, an even greater loss—a loss in the moral game of life. Hence a losing effort, if clean, may be a moral victory. The logical-incompatibility thesis, discussed by Craig K. Lehman, however, takes the slogan literally, asserting that it is impossible for someone to win when they have cheated. The thesis is implied by Suitsian formalism: games are defined by their rules, and since winning a game implies playing the game, and since playing a game implies following its rules, winning a game implies following its rules (and therefore, no cheating); so, likewise, cheating implies not winning. In challenging the logical-incompatibility thesis, Lehman argues that certain rule violations may be, and often are, tolerated by convention without any doubt cast on whether a game has occurred or a victor decided.

The opposition of morality and rationality, specifically rational self-interest, is a familiar one. Morality constrains our self-interest in various ways. Different kinds of rules, from the law to those governing games, limit what we may permissibly do in pursuit of whatever ordinary or prelusory goals we have. Against the background of this apparent conflict between morality and rationality, Simon Eassom—in a useful if technical reading—looks at cheating through a game-theoretic lens, the focus being the prisoners' dilemma, which has enormous implications for how morality and rationality not only *di*verge but also appreciably *con*verge, elsewhere and in sport.

13. CAN CHEATERS PLAY THE GAME?*

CRAIG K. LEHMAN

A number of recent philosophers of sport have endorsed the thesis that it is
logically impossible to win, or even compete, in a game while at the same
time breaking one of its rules (intentionally, at least). For instance, Suits argues:

> The end in poker is not to gain money, nor in golf simply to get a ball into a
> hole, but to do these things in prescribed (or, perhaps more accurately, not to
> do them in proscribed) ways: that is, to do them only in accordance with rules.
> Rules in games thus seem to be in some sense inseparable from ends.... If the
> rules are broken, the original end becomes impossible of attainment, since one
> cannot (really) win the game unless he plays it, and one cannot (really) play the
> game unless he obeys the rules of the game. (5: pp. 149-50)

The thesis that cheating in a game is logically incompatible with winning that game
may sound initially plausible. I imagine everyone has a vague feeling of having heard
it somewhere before—perhaps in high school physical education—but I am going
to argue that it is false. Undoubtedly, following some "framework" rules is essential
to playing any particular game as we know it, and even violation of rules covering
"finer points" may in some cases lead us to say that no game worthy of the name has
taken place, no real winner been determined. But counterexamples to the unqualified
incompatibility thesis advocated by Suits and others (1, 4) are not hard to come by.

I

Consider, first, what people ordinarily say about certain sporting events in which
deliberate violations of the rules are known (or at least thought) to take place. (I

---

* Craig K. Lehman, "Can Cheaters Play the Game?" *Journal of the Philosophy of Sport* 8,
(1981), pp. 41-46.

take it for granted that the issue here is the conventional meaning of such phrases as "compete in a game," "win a game," "deliberately violate the rules of a game," etc. Of course someone can stipulate a sense in which it is impossible for cheaters to "really" win, but the nontrivial question is whether this conclusion is implicit in the ordinary meanings of the words.)

For instance, many baseball fans believe that Atlantic Braves' pitcher Gaylord Perry throws a spitball. Throwing a spitball is a violation of the rules of baseball. Suppose these fans are right about Perry. Does anyone seriously want to say that no baseball game is ever played when Perry pitches? Should Perry be ineligible for the Hall of Fame on the grounds that he has never won a game, let alone competed, in baseball? Yet this seems to follow if we accept the unqualified thesis that cheating and competing are incompatible. And, of course, cases like Perry's—many of them more elaborate, some of them legendary—can be multiplied indefinitely.

A second point is as follows: Why, if Suits's argument is sound, should only *intentional* violation of rules be relevant to the question of whether genuine participation in a certain game (and hence victory) has taken place? (In the first sentence of this essay, I tried to be charitable by adding intention as a parenthetical condition of the logical-incompatibility thesis, but it will be noted that Suits himself does not say this.) The major premise of Suits's argument, after all, is just that one cannot play a game without following the rules of that game; or in the words of another proponent (4: p. 117) of the incompatibility thesis, "the rules of a game are the definition of that game." But the failure of something to conform to an established definition or set of rules is not abolished by the absence of an intention to nonconformity on the part of its creator. If I draw a four-sided figure with sides of unequal lengths, then I have failed to draw a square, even if I intended to make the sides equal. Thus, it seems that even unintentional violations of the rules of a game should lead us to say that no game (and hence no victory) has occurred, if the usual argument for the logical-incompatibility thesis is correct.

This points the way to more counterexamples. Amateurs almost certainly commit unwitting violations of some rule or other in any game they play, especially while learning. Even in major professional sports, sharp-eyed commentators (and instant replays) often expose accidental violations of the rules, but no one is tempted to say that no game has therefore occurred. Indeed, in team sports, the presence of just one secret cheater on a squad whose members otherwise intend to follow the rules religiously would render the whole team logically incapable of winning.

Let me approach the matter from a different direction. In "Some Reflections on Success and Failure in Competitive Athletics," Delattre, another defender of the logical-incompatibility thesis, remarks:

> Both morally and logically, then, there is only one way to play a game. [That is, by the rules.] Grantland Rice makes clear his appreciation of this point in his autobiography, *The Tumult and the Shouting*. For emphasis, he employs the example of a rookie professional lineman. The athlete responds to Rice's praise for his play during his rookie year by observing that he will be better when he becomes more adept at holding illegally without being caught. Of course, to Rice this confused vision of successful competition is heartbreaking. (1: p. 137)

Now, admittedly, I cannot quite work up a broken heart over this incident, but that is not the main point. My question is rather, what kind of confusion did Rice think his lineman had fallen prey to—conceptual confusion, of the sort which fails to notice the impossibility of round squares and married bachelors, or (alleged) moral confusion of the sort which places winning (or, more precisely, "winning") ahead of playing strictly by the rules? The thesis that cheating and competing are logically incompatible would require the former interpretation (and then, perhaps, we should think of the lineman as heartbreakingly stupid), but I strongly suspect that Rice was disappointed in his lineman's alleged moral confusion. I also suspect that the logical-incompatibility thesis draws part of its appeal from being conflated with the moral thesis; Delattre, for instance, speaks of Rice as appreciating "this point," when there are really two points involved.

II

When one cannot see a pattern to them, counterexamples often seem like trivial nit-picking. In this case, however, I think there is a clear pattern, though perhaps not a particularly profound one. The counterexamples all seem to stem from social custom or convenience (i.e., utility). Games are played within a framework of social practices and priorities, and violations of rules must be assessed within this framework to determine whether competition and victory, in the normal sense of the words, have occurred.

Hence, the spitball and offensive holding are a part of the game of baseball and football, respectively, and are techniques sometimes practiced by winners in those sports. Custom seems the primary reason why a game in which the spitball rule is violated is still baseball: The folklore of the game abounds with gleefully told stories of doctored pitches, bats, playing fields, etc., and booing the umpire (i.e., the embodiment of the rules) is a hallowed tradition. On the other hand, the fact that offensive holding can occur in a game of football seems to be mainly a concession to utility: There is simply no practical way for the officials to see everything that occurs in the interior of the line, and the game would probably be much less enjoyable to watch if all the infractions were punished (i.e., the offense would be continually frustrated by penalties, if not by the defensive line).

Of course, as I conceded at the outset, a game cannot be played if too many of its rules are violated. There would be no point in calling an activity a game of baseball if none of the rules of baseball were followed, and it is certainly hard to imagine the point when only a few of the rules are followed. Admittedly, too, one can imagine a society of sanctimonious sports purists who allow that a certain game is played only if every rule of that game is strictly followed. But perfect adherence to every rule is not usually essential to the occurrence of a given game, with a genuine winner.

Between the two extremes of angelic obedience to rules and destruction of a game by wholesale violation of its rules is an interesting set of borderline cases, as in professional wrestling: Here, rules against punching, kicking, strangling, etc., are routinely violated, so that even if the outcome were not fixed, there would be considerable question about whether the resulting show was wrestling. In the social context of certain ultra-violent science-fiction movies, the objective of sport usually seems to be the provision of spectacles of mayhem; perhaps in those societies, "illegal" biting and choking would seem as innocuous as the spitball does in American baseball. But in the actual context of our society, I am not sure what to say about professional wrestling.

So, although I concede that at some (probably hard-to-define) point, excessive rule violations become incompatible with playing a given game, and that there also may be certain ideal cases in which exacting conformity to rules is essential, I maintain that (due to social custom and convenience) it is not in general necessary to the playing or winning of games that every rule of those games be obeyed. Pearson (4: p. 116), however, yet another defender of the logical-incompatibility thesis, remarks that "a particular game is no more (in terms of its careful definition) than its rules." She then goes on, in best Lockean* fashion,[1] to state the corollary that "problems of identity and diversity of games are decided by the rules for

---

* = in the manner of John Locke, seventeenth-century English philosopher. See author's note 1 for a place in Locke's work where he makes an analogous point (not about games, however).

each game. Identical games have identical rules and diverse games have differing rules." But if I am correct, it should be possible to imagine different games with identical rules (because they are played in the context of different social customs and utilities), and identical games with different rules (because social customs and utilities negate the difference of rules "in practice"). For example, it seems conceivable (although I do not know this to be the case) that Japanese baseball players are much more earnest about following the rules of the game than American players are. If the spitball were more widely used than it is in American baseball, and if its effect were greater than I think it is, I can easily imagine a Japanese player saying that, because of the spitball, Americans play a different game. In my view, this would be the literal truth rather than just a manner of speech. Also, of course, it is simple to imagine the cases of differential enforcement of rules canceling out differences in rules.

III

So far I have been concentrating on the thesis that cheating and competing are logically incompatible. But the logical-incompatibility thesis often serves as a premise (or at least a background assumption) in moral arguments designed to show that cheating is, without qualification, unethical and/or unsportsmanlike. I therefore want to conclude this essay with a brief examination of one such argument.

The most explicitly worked-out version of this argument that I know of is advanced by Pearson:[2]

> I have argued earlier that a particular game is defined by its rules—that the rules of a game are the definition of that game. If this is the case, a player who deliberately breaks the rules of that game is deliberately no longer playing that game.... These acts [i.e., deliberate violations of rules] are designed to interfere with the purpose of the game. If the arguments presented here are correct thus far [and it has been asserted earlier that (1) "the purpose of these games is to test the skill of one individual, or group of individuals, against another ..." and (2) "If an act is designed by a willing participant in an activity to interfere with the purpose of that activity, then that act can properly be labeled unethical"] we can conclude that the intentional commission of a foul ["an act that is not in compliance with the rules"] in athletics is an unethical act. Ordinarily, when we refer to unethical acts on the part of athletes, we call these acts unsportsmanlike. (4: pp. 116-17)

The major premise of this argument [i.e., item (2) in the brackets] is reminiscent of Kant's second illustration of the first form of the categorical imperative;* Pearson also speaks elsewhere of players entering into a contract with their opposition. Obviously, however, discussion of such fundamental principles is beyond the scope of this essay. I grant them for the sake of argument. But consider the other premises.

Understood narrowly enough, I would have no quibble with the assertion that the rules of a game "define" that game; my point has only been that in certain contexts, breaking the rules that "define" a game will not entail that one is not playing that game. Suppose, however, that I am wrong, and the logical-incompatibility thesis is correct. It will still not follow that a player who deliberately breaks the rules of a game is deliberately no longer playing that game. For "deliberately" introduces an intentional context, and validity is not preserved in intentional contexts. (The man behind the arras was Polonius, but it does not follow that in deliberately killing the man behind the arras, Hamlet was deliberately killing Polonius.) Similarly, if someone is too "confused" to appreciate the logical-incompatibility thesis, he or she may deliberately violate a rule without deliberately opting out of the game.

Still, someone might reply, this is irrelevant to Pearson's main point. If her ethical major premise is correct, and if the purpose of games is to test the skill of the participants, then if we just add the premise that someone who deliberately violates the rules of a game is deliberately interfering with a test of the skill of the participants, without trying to deduce it from the logical-incompatibility thesis, the conclusion can still be secured. To be sure, some qualifications might be needed to take care of cases in which rules are deliberately broken for some unusual reason, but the idea would be that in deliberately throwing a spitball (or so we suppose), Perry is deliberately interfering with a test of the batter's skill at hitting a (legal) pitch. In general, cheaters know very well that they are trying to minimize an opponent's chances in a test of skill.

Nevertheless, even if these emendations are allowed, I think the argument is still infected with the same disease I was trying to cure in the last section. For how does one establish that the purpose of a game is a test of its participants' skill? So

---

* The "categorical imperative" is what Kant argues is the central principle of morality. Its first formulation is "Act only on the basis of a rule you could logically will to be a universal law for humanity." His second illustration of this is the immorality of promising to pay back a loan while intending not to keep that promise. Kant argues that this cannot consistently be willed to be a universal law, since it involves (something like) a self-contradiction: the very idea of a promise involves keeping it.

far as I can see, only by supposing a certain romanticized social context in which custom and convenience dictate that games are played solely to test the players' skill within a certain framework of rules. But that, I would argue, is not the social context of most sports as we know them. Indeed, to the extent that it is intelligible to talk of sports having purposes at all (an assumption which apparently goes undefended), sports seem to be multipurpose. Baseball, for example, serves the purposes of providing an income for owners and players, an afternoon's diversion for the casual fan, another installment in a unique kind of larger-than-life drama for a passionate devotee of "the national pastime." Of course, competing in or observing an event in which there are tests of skill basically within the framework of a set of (very complicated) rules is a main purpose of almost everyone concerned with baseball, but a pure test of skill featuring saintly observance of every rule is *the* purpose of baseball only to a few purists.

Thus, I think that Pearson's attempt to derive unsportsmanlike conduct from some kind of frustration of the purpose or goal of a game implicitly falls victim to the same oversight as the thesis that cheating and competing are logically incompatible: It assumes that one can read off what a game (or the purpose of a game) is just by examining the rule book. Admittedly, rule books for games do not contain statements of purposes for those games. But they do set down conditions for winning, and they do proceed on the assumption that the rules are rigorously followed; this makes the hypothesis that the purpose of a game is to determine a winner according to its rules by far the most obvious hypothesis.

I suspect, then, that no argument that makes deliberate violation of rules a sufficient condition for unsportsmanlike conduct is likely to apply to many of the sports we know. And this seems to me as it should be: I have no reason to believe that Perry, if he throws a spitball, or offensive linemen, if they hold, are generally regarded as poor sports by their peers or the fans. On the contrary, it seems likely that many of them are regarded as displaying all the essentials of good sportsmanship. Sportsmanship seems to transcend the rulebook, not only in the sense of sometimes requiring more than adherence to the rules, but also in the sense of sometimes permitting less.

NOTES

1. See (3), esp. Bk. II, Ch. 27, sec. 8. "Idea of Identity Suited to the Idea it is Applied to."
2. For similar views, see (1, 2). Keating does not defend the logical-incompatibility thesis, but he does tie unsportsmanlike conduct to frustration of the goal of sport.

REFERENCES

1. Delattre, Edwin J. "Some Reflections on Success and Failure in Competitive Athletics." *Journal of the Philosophy of Sport* 2 (1975), 133-39.

2. Keating, James W. "Sportsmanship as a Moral Category." *Ethics* 75 (October 1964), 25-35.

3. Locke, John. *Essay Concerning Human Understanding.* Many editions.

4. Pearson, Kathleen. "Deception, Sportsmanship, and Ethics." *Quest* 19 (January 1973), 115-18.

5. Suits, Bernard. "What is a Game?" *Philosophy of Science* 34 (June 1967), 148-56.

14. Playing Games With Prisoners' Dilemmas*

Simon Eassom

In recent years several authors have used the problem of the prisoners' dilemma[1] as a model representing the decision making processes involved in an athlete's motivation to cheat or not to cheat, particularly with the example of illegal use of performance-enhancing substances (3, 4, 22, 23). Breivik offers the most thorough game-theoretical analysis in his examination of the "doping problem" as a decision dilemma (4). Some of his ideas were taken up by Schneider and Butcher in the previous issue of this journal and were used to inform their rationale for a way forward in seeking both the avoidance of drug use by athletes and elimination of performance-enhancing substances from the Olympic Games (22).

Given the long and prominent history of the prisoners' dilemma in certain areas of contemporary philosophical debate,[2] it is somewhat surprising that its use has only just begun to surface in the context of sport philosophy, although Shogans's more recent work refers back to her published use of the dilemma as early as 1981 (23). At first glance the dilemma does seem to represent perfectly the decision making processes involved in choosing whether or not to cheat (or to dope): that is, both parties taking an "if I don't she will, so I ought to just in case" attitude to ensure that neither loses out. However, if such a recognition is to be of any value, then it must be accompanied by the corresponding benefits accrued through the long and detailed expositions of the dilemma in other areas of philosophy. A number of questions concerning the application of the dilemma to sport philosophy immediately spring to mind. If doping in sport is in fact an example of a prisoners' dilemma-structured situation, then does this tell us anything new about doping that might help a future analysis? Having identified it as such, are there "solutions" to the dilemma? What, in fact, *is* a prisoners' dilemma,

---

* Simon Eassom, "Playing Games with Prisoners' Dilemmas," *Journal of the Philosophy of Sport* 22 (1995), pp. 26, 28-31, 36-47.

and what does its exposition tell us about the broader area of the relationship between rational decision making and morality? I could ask numerous others.

The Prisoners' Dilemma

The so-called prisoners' dilemma is just one example of any number of possible scenarios that illustrate what can be called "collective action problems." As Michael Taylor uses the term, "the defining characteristic of a collective action problem ... is very roughly that rational egoists are unlikely to succeed in cooperating to promote their common interests" (27: p. 3). A particularly important class of collective action problems involves conflicts of interest that arise in the use of resources to which there is open access. The textbook example of this is Garrett Hardin's much used "tragedy of the commons" (in which "commons" refers to the British sense of common grazing land).[5] To illustrate, I will translate Hardin's example into a sport-related setting.

Consider a wilderness area, particularly a mountain or lake, that is open to all potential users. Let us assume that each individual user seeks to maximize his or her own gain—whether it be enjoying the tranquility of the setting, the remoteness of the mountain, the opportunity for hunting, fishing, or bird-spotting, and so on. While the total number of actual users and the frequency of their usage is below the optimal capacity of the wilderness area (if such a thing can be measured), individuals can increase their own usage without affecting the potential utility of the area for themselves and others. However, a point will be reached beyond which Hardin's "tragedy of the commons" becomes apparent. There comes a time when each individual's usage begins to entail both a personal gain and a loss: he or she gains the increased pleasure, the extra fish, more stunning wildlife photographs, or whatever, but he or she also begins to notice other users disturbing the tranquility more often, fish stocks are lower, some of the wildlife seems to be disappearing. Yet, the individual benefit still outweighs the individual loss. So, the outdoor recreationist continues to go more often. But for the same reasons all other users begin to do likewise. The net result is that *collectively* the total users bring about a situation where each one *individually* derives less benefit from each visit than they did before the optimum capacity of the area was exceeded. Despite this, most importantly, no individual has an incentive to move unilaterally from his or her position of personal benefit usage.

The ensuing "tragedy," as I have characterized it, is instantly recognizable. At the time of writing, it is at the heart of arguments over Canadian, Spanish, and British fishing rights and quotas. It forms the rationale for control of wilderness areas for skiing developments, mountain climbing permits, and other recreational usage. It affects us all in our decisions to use private rather than public transport. The point of the tragedy is made, most notably, by Mancur Olson in his *The Logic of Collective Action*. Olson considers: Under what circumstances are large groups of people likely to work together to maintain the provision of a public good in which they share a common interest? Olson argues:

> The larger a group is, the farther it will fall short of providing an optimal sup-
> ply of any collective good, and the less likely that it will act to obtain even a
> minimal amount of such a good. In short, the larger the group, the less likely
> it will further its common interests. (18: p. 36)

The implications of Olson's comment, if it is true, have consequences for Schneider and Butcher's desire to galvanize athletes into collective action from within to resolve the issue over doping in sport.

The heart of the problem lies in the rationality account of conflict. For this reason, collective action problems are seen to arise as the necessary result of rational egoists opting for the most individually maximizing strategy regardless of its consequences. More strongly, it is considered that any other action would be illogical, indeed, irrational. The prisoners' dilemma is put forward as the archetypal illustration of this problem.[6]

The prisoners' dilemma simplifies the collective action problem into one of a two-person game in which each "player" can choose one of just two strategies. For reasons that will become clear, these strategies will henceforth be referred to as C and D. Both players must choose their strategy in ignorance of the other (for the simplified game, their choices do not need to be made simultaneously). The possible combination of two players and two strategies yields a strategy vector of four results with individual payoffs that can be represented by a payoff matrix, in which the first letter denotes Player 1's payoff and the second denotes Player 2's payoff (Figure 14.1).

In any given situation, values for all the variables can be substituted. Using the example of political prisoners in jail choosing to confess or remain silent (*Cooperate* or *Defect*), with the ensuing varieties of lengths of prison terms as the payoffs, is what gives the game its identity as the prisoners' dilemma. Schneider and Butcher, following Breivik, presented the "doping dilemma," whereby C and D represent the choices to "not dope" and "dope," respectively (4: p. 237; 22: p. 73). In their payoff matrix the x's and y's refer to the combinations of winning and losing with or without fair competition (I will return to their suggested "payoffs" shortly).

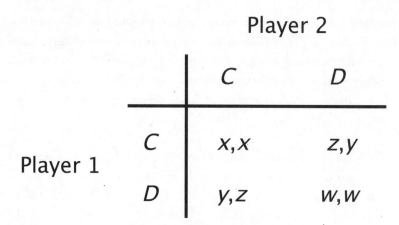

Figure 14.1 Prisoners' Dilemma Payoff Matrix

The distinguishing criteria of the prisoners' dilemma are the relationships between the values of w, x, y, and z, where it is a necessary condition that $y > x > w > z$. Whatever the real values are, it is important to note that the prisoners' dilemma is characterized by a payoff matrix that shows it to be in each individual's best interest to choose D, regardless of which strategy the other player chooses. With option D-C Player 1 gets the big bonanza (y) while Player 2 loses out (z), but if Player 2 defects as well (D-D), at least Player 1 isn't suckered into losing out entirely (both players gaining w). Such are Player 1's supposed thoughts which apply equally to Player 2 with the result that both players defect. Thus, strategy D is said to be the *dominant* strategy.

But, of course, there is a twist that creates the supposed "dilemma." It is clear that if each player chooses the dominant strategy then each receives a payoff (w) that is inferior to the payoff (x) that could be gained if both chose to cooperate. However, it is most important with the prisoners' dilemma that outcome x,x does not yield as great an individual preference to one of the players as some other possible outcome (y) gained at the other's expense (z).

The dilemma becomes more intriguing when various conditions are introduced that at first might appear to aid the prisoners' decision making. Suppose the two prisoners are allowed to communicate and decide on a strategy of cooperation? Suppose one prisoner knows what the other has already chosen? Interestingly, the dominant strategy would still be to defect.[7] Moreover, the rational egoist is more likely to defect under such circumstances. The significance of the dilemma is that the game can be played out under all sorts of varying conditions and yet defection would still be the dominant strategy, but would also produce the *Pareto-inferior* outcome.[8]

Immediately, the translation of the *prisoners'* dilemma into various interesting and speculative *athletes'* dilemmas becomes apparent: to cheat or not to cheat, to dope or not to dope, and so on. With regard to the dilemma of whether to take performance-enhancing substances, as Schneider and Butcher rightly conclude,

> In reasoning about what to do, the athletes, just like prisoners in a prisoner's dilemma, use a form of rational egoism and restrict themselves to independent reasons and so wind up with a less satisfactory outcome than they could have achieved. This is a general point about prisoner's dilemmas. Individual rational self-interest turns out to be self-defeating. (22: p. 72)

The dilemma is not just restricted to the specific instance of doping. In more general terms, just like the "tragedy of the commons," collective action problems have endless exemplars and instances as relevant to sport studies as to anything else. To see this more clearly, Ullmann-Margalit, in *The Emergence of Norms*, simplified the dilemma into what she called "generalised PD-structured situations," with four necessary conditions:

A PD-structured situation is any situation involving at least two persons each of whom is facing a decision as to whether to do A or non-A, such that:
1. If all of them do A the outcome is (and is known to them to be) mutually harmful;
2. If all of them do non-A the outcome is (and is known to them to be) mutually beneficial—or at any rate better than the outcome produced by their all doing A;
3. Each of the persons involved stands to gain most by doing A. That is to say, one's highest pay-off is obtained when one does A while all the others do non-A;
4. One's doing A when the others do non-A is—at least to some extent—at their expense. That is, when all-minus-one do non-A, the outcome to the non-A doers is less beneficial than it would have been had everyone done non-A. (29: p. 23)

That this conceptualization of the generalized prisoners' dilemma appears to amount to a satisfactory description, in one sense, of "cheating" is both interesting and fruitful, and I will return to it later. First, it is necessary to consider in more detail whether or not the "doping dilemma" as constructed by Breivik, and utilized by Schneider and Butcher, is in fact an example of the prisoners' dilemma. Despite the favorable comparisons just made a moment ago, there are some technical hurdles that need to be surmounted before these authors can use the dilemma in the way they would wish. I will deal here with only three: (a) the prisoners' dilemma is a non-zero-sum game, (b) the prisoners' dilemma possesses both "individual instability" and "individual inaccessibility," and (c) the prisoners' dilemma assumes no other benefits gained through any outcome other than those expressed in the matrix. The doping dilemma is unclear about (a), implicitly denies (b) without explicitly recognizing it, and ignores (c).

The Exclusion of Other Benefits Than Strategic Payoffs

Lastly, the remaining significant feature of the prisoners' dilemma, and other rational choice games, is that the benefits accrued by the strategies played out in the game are the *only* benefits that can be considered in determining the decision-making processes involved. No other incentives are included. It cannot be that the players' desires to conform socially, or to obey the law, or to be seen to be moral, or to want to be a martyr, and so on, can be considered as incentives.[12] All altruistic motivations, expressive motivations, and intrinsic rewards are explicitly excluded by rational choice theorists (18: p. 61). The prisoners' dilemma is an examination of the possibility of cooperation in the *absence* of any constraint to cooperate or incentive to cooperate for its own sake. It is by definition a noncooperative game. Without this feature, no "dilemma" would exist.

If the problems associated with cheating in sport are to be conceived in some ways as examples of the prisoners' dilemma, then it must be the case that such problems are seen as intractable; that they cannot simply be solved by rationally persuading athletes to recognize other payoffs as more beneficial. This appears to be ignored by Schneider and Butcher, particularly when utilizing the argument from the internal goods of Olympic sport. Either the guaranteed win with dope is the best payoff or it is not. If it is not, then where is the dilemma? Such a move does not "solve" the dilemma; it simply suggests that there was no dilemma in the first place. This can be seen as a legitimate strategy for dealing with collective action problems, but it is more a denial of the salience of the prisoners' dilemma than a solution to it. However, Schneider and Butcher *do* recognize the problem when talking about "coordination" and "assurance" and the legitimacy of any authority providing these two on behalf of the athletes (22: p. 74). Unfortunately, they do not explore in sufficient depth the significance of this recognition. This brings me onto the second area of concern outlined at the beginning of this paper.

The Prisoners' Dilemma: Rationality and Cooperation

If the prisoners' dilemma has any use at all here (not just for sport philosophers), then it must in some sense be representative of some "truth" about individuals or societies (collective action problems). Are we, in fact, such rational utility-maximizing agents that we are trapped by that very rationality into playing out numerous prisoners' dilemmas, to our own ultimate detriment? As mentioned above, the dilemma allows only rational egoism as a motivating factor in determining the players' strategy. Part of the problem, as far as other commentators are concerned, is just such a pre-eminence given to rationality as the only valid motive in decision dilemmas, stripping away all actual motives, such as compassion and humanity. Of course, as Schneider and Butcher rightly recognize and advocate, the internal goods of a practice may provide sufficient motivation for action regardless of the external goods that could be received by successful engagement in that practice.

At this point it could be suggested that the prisoners' dilemma is a pseudo-problem, that as an abstraction it does not really exist, that its rules and procedures are so rigorous that it is too artificial, or that it can be dissolved by demonstrating how its payoffs and strategies are not the only ones available to rational agents. Perhaps it is a "straw man" to be knocked down, an irresolvable conflict that paradoxically has a resolution. Why persist with it? The answer to this question lies in the assumptions made by rational choice theorists about rationality (and moreover, about morality[13]) and in our general fascination with problems of a certain kind that might be termed "dilemmas." Gauthier presents a typical dilemma (borrowed from Luce and Raiffa's [16] *Games and Decisions*) as an "ideal case" for his treatment of strategic rationality:

> Jane wants very much to go to Ann's party. But even more she wants to avoid Brian who may be there. Brian wants very much to meet Jane. If Jane expects Brian to be at Ann's party she will stay at home. If Brian expects Jane to stay at home so will he. If Jane expects Brian to stay at home she will go to the party. If Brian expects Jane to go so will he. If Jane ... but this is where we began. (9: p. 60)

The decision making problem here is obvious in its comparison to the doping dilemma. Gauthier puts it forward as exemplary of a problem in interaction. The requirement for strategically rational choice only arises in the context of a conflict of interest. The problem for Jane and Brian (or Prisoner 1 and Prisoner 2) is that neither's optimizing response can be combined with any strategy of the other to yield a pair of mutually utility-maximizing responses, "going to the party is Jane's optimizing response, whatever Brian chooses, but it cannot be combined with any strategy of Brian's..." (9: p. 78). In this way, there is no "solution" to the dilemma.

How then do we reconcile the two? Gauthier's answer is an attempt to "solve" the problem by demonstrating that instrumental rationality demands cooperation and not defection. In order to do so he distinguishes between two sorts of maximizers: a straightforward maximizer (SM) and a constrained maximizer (CM). Gauthier argues that the assumption that we are SMs (as exemplified in the presentation of the prisoners' dilemma so far) is mistaken. The constrained maximizer adopts a conditional strategy of cooperating with other constrained maximizers but defecting when interacting with straightforward maximizers. To prove that the instrumentally rational agent would be a CM and not an SM requires a simple calculation of cardinal utilities along the lines presented earlier. Using Schneider and Butcher's cardinal values of 4, 3, 2, 1 for athlete X who is given the combined respective strategies dope/not-dope, not-dope/not-dope, dope/dope, not-dope/dope (22: p. 73), and representing the probability of encountering another CM as p, then:

Payoff for being a CM $= p.3 + (1 - p).2$
Payoff for being an SM $= 2$

The option of gaining 4 utilities is not available to the constrained maximizer, but neither is it to the straightforward maximizer (for all the reasons explained earlier when demonstrating the dilemma). For any given probability of meeting another CM that is greater than 0 it pays to be a CM. For example, suppose that there is a 50:50 chance my opponent is a CM. Calculating out the above sum, the long-term payoff associated with being a CM is 2.5 utilities (0.5 x 3 + [0.5 x 2]) as opposed to 2 utilities for an SM. The possible scenario is actually far more complex than this. CMs may fail to recognize each other, SMs might masquerade as CMs, CMs might not recognize SMs and thus treat them as CMs, and so on. Game theory calculations can allow for all these eventualities. Without demonstrating the conclusion mathematically here, it will always pay to be a constrained maximizer providing the probability of recognizing other CMs is sufficiently greater than the probability of failing to recognize rogue straightforward maximizers.[14]

Gauthier's theory of strategic rationality is an attempt to adjudicate between the claims of "utility-maximization" and "utility-optimization," the culmination of which is a contractarian view of social justice that requires individuals to embrace "morals by agreement." It is fundamental to recognize that, for Gauthier, this is the whole business of moral theory: that it is "essentially the theory of optimizing constraints on utility-maximization" (9: p. 78). Gauthier wishes to maintain that moral principles are nothing other than principles of rational choice, whereby, according to the conventional view of choice, the rational agent chooses that which is most likely to yield the greatest utility (value). Given, as has been shown, that such individual choice under certain circumstances can be detrimental to utility-maximization, Gauthier argues for an agreed basis of cooperation aimed at the achievement of utility optimization. Morality, in the broad determinants of justice and fairness, is thus firmly grounded in rational egoism. It is not so much an alternative account of why we should be moral as an alternative to morality itself. In Gauthier's words the contract provides a "moral" code, "generated as a rational constraint from the non-moral premises of rational choice" (9: p. 4).[15]

If this differs from our traditional conception of morality, then this alone is not its refutation: too bad for morality. But, that this runs contrary to a vast wealth of moral philosophy of sport and discussions of fair play, respect for persons, and the like, must be taken on board by those wishing to use the dilemma and its literature to their advantage.[16] This, for the most part, is what I meant at the beginning by claiming that the use of the prisoners' dilemma does not come "theory-free." Its popularity with game theorists and sociobiologists rests largely in its power to explain the evolution of cooperation in ways that do not require nonanthropological explanations of morality.

While Gauthier begins from a Hobbesian position of natural equality of physical power, making it mutually advantageous for contracting individuals to accept norms and conventions that protect each other's possessions and interests, other theorists have chosen to examine the possibility of altruistic behavior naturally emerging from rationally motivated self-interest. In other words, they wish to suggest that altruistic tendencies and motivations are quite rational, despite our selfish genes. If this is the case, does the dilemma disappear? Clearly not. We are surrounded by innumerable unsolved collective action problems, and we do still recognize the need for state intervention, political entrepreneurs, and other external agents to help in their resolution. I will put forward the idea in the conclusion to this paper that games can possibly serve a purpose in stimulating altruistic tendencies among us, in teasing out our "Humean sympathies" (13).

The incentive to cooperate in the long term is best illustrated by the expansion of the "one-shot" prisoners' dilemma into the "iterated" or repeated prisoners' dilemma. The iterated game is simply the ordinary game repeated an indefinite number of times with the same players. Unlike the simple game, in which defect is the only rational strategy, the iterated game offers far greater strategic scope. It is also more realistic in its application to the games played out among athletes. For example, a particular strategy might be to cooperate most of the time (dope free), but defect on certain occasions. Such a tactic might be used by the athlete wishing to establish trust and a particular public front before moving in for the "sting" on the big occasion. But, of course, all others might be doing likewise. Strategies might also be conditional upon the past history of behaviors among the players on a reciprocal basis: Cooperate with A, B, and C, but always defect against D. The Pareto-optimal strategy over the course of an iterated game turns out to be both surprising and exciting.

The American political scientist Robert Axelrod (working partly in conjunction with W.D. Hamilton) has explored vast numbers of alternative long-term strategies through his computer-simulated competitions for which leading experts in game theory, genetic theory, economics, mathematics, and so on, were invited to submit their choice of utility-maximizing strategy, all to be played out against each other (1). Surprisingly, one of the simplest strategies defeated all the others: More surprisingly, it was one of the "nice" strategies. Submitted by Canadian game theorist Anatol Rapoport, the "tit-for-tat" strategy required the player to cooperate in the first game and thereafter simply copy the previous move of the other player.[17] Furthermore, when subsequent competitions were created with all participants aware of the results of previous strategies, and consequently engaged in producing strategies to exploit tit-for-tat, the results were always the same: Tit-for-tat was the collectively stable strategy.[18]

The net result of the success of tit-for-tat is support for the idea in evolutionary ethics of, what Robert Trivers has called, "reciprocal altruism": a sort of "you scratch my back, I'll scratch yours" morality (28). The implications for our discussion here are found, first, in Axelrod's identification of four properties that tend to make a decision rule successful: (a) avoidance of unnecessary conflict, (b) provocability, (c) forgiveness, and (d) clarity of behavior (2). The first property is reflected in the desire to cooperate as long as one's opponent does. However, if one's opponent does cheat, one must be prepared to retaliate, and yet be forgiving enough to return to the cooperative strategy afterwards. The key is in the clarity of behavior enabling players to adapt to their opponent's patterns of action.

For this reason, following Axelrod in some respects, but also Thomas Schelling's earlier work in *The Strategy of Conflict* (21), salience (or ease of recognizability) becomes a necessary condition of the cooperative "solution" to iterated prisoners' dilemmas. (I will return in the next section to the requirement for salience in connection with rules and game playing.) The further implication for us of reciprocal altruism is the requirement that nonreciprocators are, not only easily identifiable, but also admonished or punished in some way to warn other tit-for-tat strategists to avoid playing with them. Here, I believe, can be found the powerful emotive force of labeling somebody a "cheat." In examining concepts such as cheating in sport, it seems fairly intuitive to accept that one kind of desire or motivation has succeeded over another. To suggest that this is by definition immoral due to that action's possession of some sort of necessary conditions misses the point entirely. If, as Hume (13) wished to suggest, our passions oriented towards sympathy and concern for others are fainter than those based on self-interest, then an important part of maintaining the taboos about cheating and deception in general involves our maintenance of strong social condemnation of them.

To persist in maintaining the issue of cheating as a prisoners' dilemma is to accept that the greatest incentive to cheat exists where there is the greatest assurance that all others do not. In games, as in life, the temptation to cheat is at its highest where there is the greatest dependence on and requirement for trust.[19] For this reason alone, the traditional conceptual approach to the definition of cheating begins the analysis at the wrong end: from its defining conditions rather than its emotive use. I wish to persist with the association between cheating and the prisoners' dilemma, because I believe that it can and will bring to the forefront of discussion some hitherto undiscussed ideas about the relationship between games, rules, and morality. Despite my aim simply to discuss two of the main areas of concern that I have, I do wish to suggest some possible future direction via some concluding remarks.

Games, Rules, and Morality

As I have hinted at various times in this paper, technically speaking, a dilemma has no solution. We often tend to think that it has and hence we ask for advice from others who might see more clearly which choice to make. Usually, the advice we receive does not remove our frustration and, more often than not, is simply a restatement of the dilemma (perhaps a little more clearly) with the imperative that one just has to make a choice. But how do we make that choice? That is the problem, especially if the reasoning behind each choice is the same. It could be that our request for advice is a request for somebody else to actually make a decision for us: to save us from ourselves. The temptation within us all to sometimes do other than we feel we ought to is a tendency that in the main is controlled by sanctions, the fear of detection, social taboos, public or communal rejection, and so on.[20] In this regard, rules (in games, in law, in life) can sometimes act as decisional simplifiers; following the rule, without deploying our rational faculties to ponder its background justification, can itself become a rational decision procedure. In discussing "the force of rules," Frederick Schauer contended that,

> Even the agent willing to take seriously a certain range of decisions, and as a result willing to try to make the best decision she can on a particular occasion, may have prudential epistemic reasons for doubting her own decision-making capacities compared to those of the rule-maker. Again such a decision-maker might (or might not) reconsider that epistemic deference in particular cases when convinced her own judgement was correct, but for the same reasons as just mentioned it may be that the way in which the decision-maker considers this possibility is itself influenced by rules, and once again the consequence would be that the rule provided a reason for action by virtue of the decision-maker's distrust of her own capacities with respect to some family of decisions. (20: pp. 124-25)

The rules of games and sports, more so than laws of the land, are more readily accepted in just such a fashion. Games are first encountered by young children at, what educational psychologists would label, the pretheoretical stage of a child's moral development. A child who asks why the ball is placed in the center of the pitch to start the game might be told that this is simply the way things are done. Beyond the specifics of the game, an important function of such a process is the recognition of rules qua* rules. The encounter with prisoners' dilemma-structured situations through the universal phenomena of game playing might even serve some further purpose in reinforcing the value of rule abidance as a savior from our egoistic selves. Certainly, if the tit-for-tat strategy is to prevail, then any social animal, living in a relatively stable group or community, with the ability to recognize other members of the group and the previous cooperative or uncooperative actions, would need to encounter some recognizable analogue of

---

* = considered just with respect to their status as.

the prisoners' dilemma quite frequently in real life in order to learn that in the long-term "niceness" wins. There are very significant ways in which games can serve as moral educators, regardless of the difficulties that such an idea has faced in recent times.

The simplifying aspect of rules in games and sports provides a high degree of salience (ease of recognizability) with regard to identifying "cheats." Going hand-in-hand with this identifiability must come the necessary rejection from the rest of the game-playing community, or at the very least the public admonition of the defector.[21] For these reasons cheating *does* matter and we *do* want to view it as immoral. Such a way of criticizing another's action is one of our strongest forms of condemnation. It seems absurd to ask a definitional question, "What is cheating?" and *then* debate whether one of its defining conditions is a moral condition (whatever that might mean). Cheating at games is like cheating on one's partner, cheating the tax man, cheating one's parliamentary constituents, cheating the shareholders, and so on. We want to label such actions as cheating and maintain the strong social attitudes towards it in order to deter people from such a course of action, because in a world of numerous prisoners' dilemma-structured situations we must do our utmost to resist the obvious consequence of wholesale defection. For this reason, philosophers such as Peter Singer (25) in *The Expanding Circle* and Edna Ullmann-Margalit (29) in *The Emergence of Norms*, with a bias toward evolutionary ethics, place such an emphasis on norms and conventions (supported by sufficiently severe sanctions) in order to foster the altruistic tendencies that help us avoid the pitfalls of one-shot prisoners' dilemmas:

> It also brought with it something which has not, so far as we can tell, occurred in non-human society: the transformation of our evolved, genetically-based social practices into a system of rules and precepts guiding our conduct toward one another, supported by widely shared judgements of approval for those who do as the rules and precepts require, and disapproval for those who do not. Thus we arrived at a system of ethics or morality. (25: p. 92)

The generalizations of sociobiology might be as distasteful to some as the reduction of morality to Gauthier's "theory of optimizing constraints on utility maximization." But then a spell in prison is meant to reform the character! Gauthier concludes his *Morals by Agreement* quoting Nietzsche, from the second essay of *On the Genealogy of Morals*, "to breed an animal *with the right to make promises*—is not this the paradoxical task that nature has set itself in the case of man? Is it not the real problem regarding man?" (9: pp. 354-55). Such promises arise, in Hume's (13) view (in *A Treatise of Human Nature*) from human conventions. Less pessimistic than Hobbes, Hume felt that strict covenants are not the only escape from the "state of nature." A convention expresses, "a general sense of common interest; which sense all the members of the society express to one another, and which induces them to regulate their conduct by certain rules" (13: p. 490). Conventions are solutions to coordination problems (27: p. 156), where "convention," according to David Lewis, is defined as,

> A regularity R in the behaviour of members of a population P when they are agents in a recurrent situation S is a convention if and only if, in any instance of S among members P,
>
> > (i) everyone conforms to R;
> > (ii) everyone expects everyone else to conform to R;
> > (iii) everyone prefers to conform to R on condition that the others do, since S is a coordination problem and uniform conformity to R is a coordination equilibrium in S. (15: p. 42)

Coordination will only be achieved if players in the game have, what Lewis (15: p. 42) called, "suitably concordant mutual expectations." Gauthier's theory is based on the premise that given the possibility of suitable communication, *agreement* is the basic means of ensuring concordant mutual expectations. Conventions might also arise gradually as more and more people conform to a regular pattern of behavior. Games and competitive sports are illustrative of just such a gradual evolution of convention and rule in the establishment of a commonly accepted social practice. The study of game-playing as a human phenomenon can make a valuable contribution to moral philosophy through an examination of the sorts of need expressed by humans by the need to obey the rules of games. Ask, "Why not cheat?" But first ask, "Why start?" According to the philosophical anthropologist, Mary Midgley, "Man is ... a game-playing animal. The business of moral philosophy starts with the analysis of such concepts" (17: p. 150).

The question with the doping dilemma is whether the athletes do in fact share "suitably concordant mutual expectations," perhaps along the lines of Robert Simon's "mutual quest for excellence" (24: p. 10). Such a precondition is essential if the doping dilemma is to be solved, as Schneider and Butcher suggest, by solving the assurance problem and the coordination problem. My main concern with their analysis is the suggestion that the general will to bring this about can come from rational persuasion of the athletes to act in their own best interests. The main reason that rational choice theorists, such as Olson, deliberately limit the range of decision-making principles available to the players of the prisoners' dilemma is to avoid the regression into such a tautology.

In concluding this meandering overview of the applicability of the prisoners' dilemma to sport philosophy, I want to suggest that games *themselves* are representative of such a dilemma, and not just the doping game. Breivik's and Schneider and Butcher's association of the dilemma with the problem of performance-enhancing substances in elite athletics, paradoxically, does not help resolve the issue. What seems plausible, to me, is that the protracted problem of doping exists because the generalized solutions to prisoners' dilemmas have not worked in this instance. There are numerous possible explanations for this, none of which are new or unique to my analysis here, which have to do with the excessive commercialization of the Olympics, the degradation of Sport, the Lombardian ethic,* and so on. Given these conditions, the prisoners' dilemma prevails.

NOTES

1. The prisoners' dilemma is variously referred to in the singular and the plural (i.e., with the apostrophe denoting possession as prisoner's or prisoners'). I have chosen the latter, less common version, throughout. The whole point about the examination of this type of dilemma is the requirement for strategic rationality, as opposed to parametric rationality (where one party takes his or her circumstances to be fixed such that his or her choice is the only variable element). Consequently, the same dilemma, by necessity, faces both parties: It is the dilemma of both "prisoners," not just "the prisoner." However, in quotation I always defer to the choice of the original author's positioning of the apostrophe.

2. The prisoners' dilemma game was invented around 1950 by Merrill Flood and Levin Dresher, and formalized by A.W. Tucker shortly after. R. Duncan Luce and Howard Raiffa's *Games and Decisions*, first published in 1957, provides one of the earliest in-depth discussions of the dilemma (16). As for its prominence, I will simply point

---

* The idea, associated with football coach Vince Lombardi, that "winning is the only thing"—that it doesn't matter how you win.

to the significance attributed to it in David Gauthier's recognition of the prisoners' dilemma as the motivation for his vastly influential *Morals by Agreement* (1986) as just one example among many of its continued contemporary use (9). Gauthier begins the preface to his book with, "The present enquiry began on a November afternoon in Los Angeles when, fumbling for words in which to express the peculiar relationship between morality and advantage I was shown the prisoner's dilemma. Almost nineteen years later, I reflect on the course of a voyage that is not, and cannot be, completed, but that finds a temporary harbour in this book" (p. i).

...

5. Hardin's (11) article "The Tragedy of the Commons," published in 1968, has been a seminal work in this area. I refer to it here for the benefit of any reader wishing to extend the discussion to more general collective action problems than the prisoners' dilemma.

6. I will not deal with the original presentation of the dilemma in terms of prisoners being interrogated in separate cells. There are various versions, all differing in various ways according to each author's desire to tell a good story. The details of the story are merely stage props used to embellish the drama, the script remains roughly the same in each. One feature is distinctly common to all versions. The protagonists' choices are articulated as "cooperate" and "defect." This one allusion to the original seems to be enough to maintain the dilemma's association with that of prisoners.

7. Playing the prisoners' dilemma game with various groups of students has produced interesting and extremely fertile results, leading to some of the most stimulating group discussions and seminars in my experience of philosophy lecturing. Any number of rules or restrictions can be imposed to vary the game. For example, with one group I assured them that only I would know the results (and they would be anonymous), so only I would know if someone had taken advantage of their classmates' cooperativeness by choosing to "cheat on them." No two groups respond the same, but surprisingly most groups become more self-interested when financial incentives are offered and the "stakes" get higher. It appears to be easier to be altruistic when the consequences matter less!

8. I use the established terminology here simply because Breivik does, as do most other commentators on the dilemma, thus making cross-referencing easier. The terms "Pareto-optimal" and "Pareto-inferior" are named thus after the Italian economist Vilfredo Pareto. Technically speaking, an outcome is Pareto-optimal if (and only if) no other possible outcome affords one player a greater utility and no person a lesser utility. Any other outcome is Pareto-inferior. Thus, in the two-person, two-option prisoners' dilemma, defect-defect is Pareto-inferior, despite still being the dominant strategy.

...

12. While writing this I am reminded of Nien Cheng's *Life and Death in Shanghai* (paperback: Grafton Books): Her harrowing autobiographical account of imprisonment during Maoist-China's cultural revolution on the grounds of her dead husband's association with the "Western imperialist" company Shell Oil. While in prison she and her family endured endless persecution, including the beating to death of her adult daughter by the Red Guard. All she needed to do to end her torment was to confess (to "crimes" that she had not committed). Instead, she maintained her silence and suffered years of torture, purely motivated by her desire to maintain her innocence, her self-esteem, and her dignity.

13. There is not room here, within this paper, to examine this important area. I am simply bringing it to the reader's attention and outlining some ideas concerning Gauthier's treatment of the relationship. For a critique of Gauthier's assumptions concerning rationality and morality, see Joseph Mendola, "Gauthier's *Morals by Agreement* and Two Kinds of Rationality," *Ethics* 97:4 (1987), 765-74: part of the symposium on Gauthier's *Morals*.

14. For those of a mathematical bent, the calculations are as follows. Given the same cardinal utilities of 4, 3, 2, 1, where p is the probability that CMs recognize each other when they meet; where q is the probability that a CM fails to spot an SM; and where r is the probability of encountering a CM; then the payoff for being a CM can be represented by:

$$= rp.3 + r(1 - p).2 + (1 - r).1 + (1 - r)(1 - q).2$$
$$= 2 + rp - (1 - r)q.2$$

In contrast, the overall utility for an SM can be expressed as:

$$= r(1 - q).2 + rq.4 + (1 - r).2$$
$$= 2(1 + rq)$$

The instrumentally rational agent will favor a CM disposition when:

$$= p/q > 2 + [(1 - r).2]/r$$

See Shaun Hargreaves Heap and Yanis Varoufakis, *Game Theory: A Critical Introduction* (London: Routledge, 1995), pp. 162-3 (12).

15. Gauthier is not alone in thinking that an account of rationality is central to moral theory. Recently, see, for example, Richard Brandt, *A Theory of the Good and Right* (Oxford: Oxford University Press, 1986); Alan Gewirth, *Reason and Morality* (Chicago: University of Chicago Press, 1978); Derek Parfit, *Reasons and Persons* (Oxford: Oxford University Press, 1984). In addition, R.M. Hare's *Freedom and Reason*, Thomas Nagel's *The Possibility of Altruism*, and John Rawls' *A*

Theory of Justice have been in publication long enough to have significant secondary literatures surrounding them.

16. It is worth noting here a number of valuable articles in the symposium on rationality and morality contained in volume 96 (1) of *Ethics*, published in October 1985. I have only directly referred to John Elster's article, "Rationality, Morality, and Collective Action" in this paper. Most of the others discuss in some way the failings of Kantian philosophers to adequately account for the prisoners' dilemma, and come down on the side of Utilitarianism. This would most definitely go against the grain with most of the sport philosophy on fair play written in the last twenty years.

17. The mechanics of Axelrod's game are too complex to explain here. The best (briefest and most straightforward) summary of Axelrod's and others' work is found in Richard Dawkins' *The Selfish Gene*, Chapter 12: "Nice Guys Finish First" (6).

18. "Tit-for-tat" is not an Evolutionary Stable Strategy (ESS) as it is possible for it to be "invaded" by another strategy (albeit a "nice" strategy). The significant point is that tit-for-tat cannot be invaded by a "nasty" strategy. Nicer strategies than tit-for-tat are capable of being exploited by nastier strategies and become extinct in the long term, the nastier strategies then eliminating each other. Tit-for-tat remains the collectively stable strategy over the long term.

19. I take the view that the most "successful" cheat is the one who survives totally undetected among rule abiders by strictly maintaining the fronts of rule-abidance himself or herself. The greater trust placed in the cheat by others allows the greater opportunity to maximize his or her own utility. I am thinking, here, of the "trustworthy" honest-looking con-man who successfully embezzles the local community group's charity Christmas Fund, or the marriage partner who secures the spouse's continuing love and affection while carrying on countless undetected extra-marital relationships.

20. I am picturing, here, the classic "candid camera" scenario, in which, for instance, a member of the public enters a store to buy some small item off the shelf (while being filmed by the hidden camera). There is nobody to take the individual's money. Some people leave it on the counter; others leave their goods and walk out. Some call out for the store assistant. When he or she doesn't appear, what do they do? Most walk out without paying (once they're sure there's nobody around); some help themselves to other goods as well; others help themselves to the cash register! That all of them would most likely be law-abiding citizens given the likelihood of some external agency to "help" them, the temptation to do otherwise, just occasionally, seems too great.

21. Just as wayward politicians return to public life after a brief spell in the wilderness (and the public seems to forget that at one time they were considered totally untrustworthy for a position serving their interests), so too do guilty athletes, such as Ben Johnson. It is not a question of whether an athlete is "reformed," but of whether the authorities send out the right signals about our tolerance of such action. Hence, the outcry recently against French soccer star Eric Cantona of Manchester United after he violently assaulted a member of the public on the terraces. The popular opinion was that he should *never* play professional football again.

REFERENCES

1. Axelrod, R., and Hamilton, W.D. "The Evolution of Cooperation." *Science*, 211 (1981), 1390-96.
2. Axelrod, R. *The Evolution of Cooperation*. New York: Basic Books, 1984.
3. Breivik, G. "The Doping Dilemma: Some Game Theoretical and Philosophical Considerations." *Sportwissenshaft*, 17:1 (March 1987), 83-94.
4. Breivik, G. "Doping Games: A Game Theoretical Exploration of Doping." *International Review for Sociology of Sport*, 27:3 (1992), 235-52.
5. Brown, W.M. "Practices and Prudence." *Journal of the Philosophy of Sport*, XVII (1990), 71-84.
6. Dawkins, R. *The Selfish Gene*. Oxford: Oxford UP, 1976.
7. Elster, J. "Some Conceptual Problems in Political Theory." In *Power and Political Theory*. Edited by B. Murray. London: John Wiley, 1976.
8. Elster, J. "Rationality, Morality, and Collective Action." *Ethics*, 96 (1985), 136-55.
9. Gauthier, D. *Morals by Agreement*. Oxford: Oxford UP, 1986.
10. Hampton, J. *Hobbes and the Social Contract Tradition*. Cambridge: Cambridge UP, 1986.
11. Hardin, G. "The Tragedy of the Commons." *Science*, 163 (December 13, 1968), 1243-48.
12. Hargreaves Heap, S., and Varoufakis, Y. *Game Theory: A Critical Introduction*. London: Routledge, 1995.
13. Hume, D. *A Treatise of Human Nature*. Edited by A. Selby-Bigge. Oxford: Clarendon, 1988 (first published 1739/40).
14. Kavka, G. "Hobbes's War of All Against All." *Ethics*, 93 (1983), 291-310.
15. Lewis, D. *Convention: A Philosophical Study*. Cambridge, MA: Harvard UP, 1969.
16. Luce, R.D., and Raiffa, H. *Games and Decisions*. New York: John Wiley, 1957.
17. Midgley, M. "The Game Game." In *Heart and Mind*. Ed. M. Midgley. London: Methuen, 1981.
18. Olson, M. *The Logic of Collective Action*. Cambridge, MA: Harvard UP, 1965.

19. Rawls, J. *A Theory of Justice.* Cambridge, MA: Harvard UP, 1971.

20. Schauer, F. *Playing by the Rules: A Philosophical Examination of Rule-Based Decision Making in Law and in Life.* Oxford: Clarendon, 1991.

21. Schelling, T. *The Strategy of Conflict.* Cambridge, MA: Harvard UP, 1960.

22. Schneider, A., and Butcher, R. "Why Olympic Athletes Should Avoid the Use and Seek the Elimination of Performance-Enhancing Substances and Practices from the Olympic Games." *Journal of the Philosophy of Sport*, XX-XXI (1993-94), 64-81.

23. Shogan, D. "The Prisoner's Dilemma in Competitive Sports." In *Philosophy of Sport and Physical Activity.* Edited by P.J. Galasso. Toronto: Canadian Scholars' Press, 1988.

24. Simon, R. "Good Competition and Drug-Enhanced Performance." *Journal of the Philosophy of Sport*, XI (1984), 6-13.

25. Singer, P. *The Expanding Circle: Ethics and Sociobiology.* Oxford: Oxford UP, 1981.

26. Taylor, M. *Anarchy and Cooperation.* London: John Wiley, 1976.

27. Taylor, M. *The Possibility of Cooperation.* Cambridge: Cambridge UP, 1987.

28. Trivers, R. "The Evolution of Reciprocal Altruism." *Quarterly Review of Biology*, 46 (1971), 35-37.

29. Ullmann-Margalit, E. *The Emergence of Norms.* Oxford: Clarendon P, 1977.

QUESTIONS

1. Is there a difference between winning and being *declared* the winner? Does the cheat want victory or just the spoils of victory?

2. Does the logical-incompatibility thesis imply radical skepticism about sports records? How so, or why not? Is this a mark against formalism?

3. Should tolerance of rule-breaking depend on *how* a rule is broken and what *kind* of rule it is? For any sport, what rule violations or changes would nullify or essentially change it?

4. Is cheating less objectionable when opponents cheat first? Does opponents' bad behaviour somehow license one's own?

5. Whereas the sucker strategy, playing fair no matter what, reflects certain aspects of morality, does the tit-for-tat strategy, in its way, reflect others? What does this imply?

6. Is there a difference between "one-shot" sport cases of the prisoner's dilemma (e.g., doping for the Olympics) and "iterated" cases (e.g., covert dirty play)? A moral difference?

FURTHER READING

Breivik, Gunnar (1987): "The Doping Dilemma: Some Game Theoretical and Philosophical Considerations," *Sportwissenschaft* 17, pp. 83-94.

D'Agostino, Fred (1981): "The Ethos of Games," *Journal of the Philosophy of Sport* 8, pp. 7-18.

Mackie, J.L. (1978): "The Law of the Jungle: Moral Alternatives and Principles of Evolution," *Philosophy* 53, pp. 455-64.

Pearson, Kathleen M. (1973): "Deception, Sportsmanship, and Ethics," *Quest* 19, pp. 115-18.

Reitsma, Regan L. (2007): "What Would Machiavelli Do? Confronting the Strategic Cheater in Pickup Basketball," in *Basketball and Philosophy: Thinking Outside the Paint*, ed. Jerry L. Walls and Gregory Bassham (Lexington, KY: UP of Kentucky), pp. 57-70.

Simon, Robert L. (2010): *Fair Play: The Ethics of Sport* (3rd edition) (Boulder, CO: Westview), especially chapter 3.

FURTHER INQUIRY

If formalism (which implies that winning requires obeying the rules) is true, and an athlete wants to win, then cheating will be irrational. This applies strictly only to constitutive rules, however. Consider what this means for violations of bans on steroids. Unless regulative or auxiliary rules may function constitutively, such cheating (though immoral) will not necessarily be irrational, likewise if an athlete violating constitutive rules prefers the spoils of victory—being *declared* the winner—to an actual win. Because violations often go undetected, formalism implies radical skepticism about sports records, as if all implicitly have asterisks beside them. Many philosophers prefer "broad internalism": a blend of formalism and conventionalism by which a sport has an internal "logic" that determines which rule-violations destroy and which preserve game integrity. When experts disagree on applying this logic in specific cases, that suggests the absence of, or the absence of precision in, such a logic. The prisoners' dilemma might be further applied in specific ways (as to pickup games) or generalized to discuss human nature as Hobbesian-competitive or Lockean-cooperative. Whether sport as outside ordinary life makes the prisoners' dilemma a problematic, or perhaps a *pure*, case for real-life analogy, bears further thought. Too bad the better model is not Pascal's wager, where the potential payoff of clean play (a noble victory) is *so* prized that it is worth accepting the disadvantage of being a so-called sucker. But perhaps we should not hold athletes to standards any higher than those to which we hold ourselves.

Section H

Beyond Rules

In Huizinga's view of ordered play, Suits's formalist theory of games, and just about everywhere else in this book, rules have held a singular place. This is especially true, naturally, of this second part, concerned with rules and values, be they aesthetic, moral, or rational. But values transcend rules, and so it is fitting in this final section to explore two important phenomena in sport that may be called rule-transcendent. Even assuming the rules are followed and judiciously applied, sport ethics still concerns behaviour that is morally blameable despite, or commendable beyond, mere playing by the rules.

Gamesmanship involves the attempt to "psych out" opponents or manipulate officials to gain a competitive advantage without actually cheating. As technically within the bounds of the rules, gamesmanship is perfectly legal, yet even in mild doses it often seems questionable. One reason this is so is that it diminishes the athletic test for the person resorting to it, although it can serve as an excellent challenge for the opponent. As Leslie A. Howe argues, this reveals the gamer, especially in more extreme, clearly immoral cases, to be cowardly. Some gamesmanship, however, appears morally permissible in that it is compatible, rather than at odds, with the purpose of sport.

Participants and spectators often have such a large—sometimes absurd—stake in sport that sportsmanship, the quintessential sport virtue, is far less common than we should hope. The same goes for sportsmanship's anemic cousin, fair play—the bare minimum moral requirement for athletes that we hope they surpass by being truly sporting. In this way, sportsmanship is often seen as *supererogatory*, as morally praiseworthy above and beyond what is morally required. In our last reading, Randolph M. Feezell explores sportsmanship from the perspective of a virtuous character trait at the very heart of sport.

15. GAMESMANSHIP*

LESLIE A. HOWE

"What are you prepared to do to win?" This is a question that any serious competitor will at one time or another have to consider. The answer that one is inclined to make, I shall argue, is revealing of the deeper character of the individual participant in sport as both physical competitor and moral person. To that end, I examine one of the classic responses to the question, gamesmanship,[1] which can be characterized as an attempt to win one game by playing another. I contend that gamesmanship is a deliberate strategy of competition that has certain paradoxical outcomes; although it *might* produce an enhanced competitive environment that calls forth superior performances from participants, its more aggravated manifestations are, in the long term, athletically self-destructive for those who rely on it as a competitive device. I argue the presence of more profound underlying moral failings, as well.

I shall begin by considering what gamesmanship is and what it is not. At this point, the explication of the practice is neutral with respect to its moral value, rather than its efficacy in achieving sport-specific aims. Because gamesmanship is a strategy designed for winning regardless of athletic excellence, I examine the relationship between winning and excellence and how each contributes to the definition of sport. I shall argue that sport is less about results than about the process leading to results and thus that sport is ultimately not about statistics alone but about the athlete who produces those statistics.[2] I defend the view that sport is about the athlete as a person who willingly undergoes various kinds of trial—physical, psychological, and ultimately moral—because he or she is always confronted with the possibility of failure and the choice of how to respond to that possibility.

---

*   Leslie A. Howe, "Gamesmanship," *Journal of the Philosophy of Sport* 31 (2004), pp. 212-25.

Gamesmanship and Fairness

Let us suppose that someone responds to our question "What are you prepared to do to win?" by saying "Whatever it takes." This is, in fact, the sort of thing that many serious competitors are likely to say. It is ambiguous, however. Some, indeed, will mean it literally, but most, perhaps, would take it to mean "everything within the rules." This would rule out cheating in its many and varied forms. There are at least two things that it does not rule out, however: the "professional foul" and gamesmanship. The professional foul is an odd case—it is an action that is explicitly contrary to the rules of the competition, *but* it is an infraction committed openly, with the player accepting (albeit perhaps with much protestation) the legal punishment for it. The term comes from soccer, but it is a tactic practiced as a matter of routine in hockey, where fighting, obstruction, and stick infractions are all prohibited and yet considered "part of the game."[3]

Gamesmanship is harder to pin down in an exact way, but it would seem that the decisive element in gamesmanship is the attempt to gain competitive advantage either by an artful manipulation of the rules that does not actually violate them or by the psychological manipulation or unsettling of the opponent (or sometimes the officials), whether this be by intimidation, nondisclosure of information, outright deception, or the first alternative (instrumental use of the rules). It is important to note that gamesmanship cannot in any straightforward way be prohibited by the rules of competition, for two reasons.

First, violation of the rules is already (necessarily) prohibited by the rules; attempting to violate the rules is cheating (which nullifies the game), and gamesmanship (I am supposing) is not identical with cheating, though it might have much the same end, namely, winning with less strictly athletic effort. Second, gamesmanship, in one sense, relies on the rules in order to exist—it is a testing behavior, testing the rules themselves at times in order to test one's opponent and the officials, but in that case the rules must be in place. Thus, gamesmanship might initially appear at odds with the rules, when it in fact relies on them, as when one appeals to some little-known regulation, takes an unaccustomed but legal time or equipment advantage, delays play in order to obtain a ruling from officials, attempts to catch the opponent off guard by taking an unexpectedly quick start, or deliberately false-starts a race to pressure the opponent into hurrying and thus misexecuting his or her own start.

It is important to stress that the various techniques and strategies employed in gamesmanship are most commonly directed at breaking down or at least interfering with the opponent's psychological preparation or competitive equilibrium and focus. Thus, it is less about obtaining a direct material advantage than about gaining this indirectly, by inducing an overall or momentary competitive failure in the opponent. The gamer (i.e., one who employs gamesmanship) is attempting to break down the on-field athletic competitive threat posed by the opponent by means other than simply running faster, throwing farther or more accurately, and so on.[4]

This is not to say that rule violation might not play an important role in a strategy of gamesmanship or in isolated incidents of it. There are many instances of sporting malpractice and general bad behavior that can certainly contribute to such an overall strategy that might or might not constitute strict instances of gamesmanship per se, rather than something else. For example, fakery intended to deceive officials and gain field advantage (e.g., Rivaldo's mime during Brazil's game against Turkey at the 2002 World Cup),* taking advantage of bad calls that one did not engineer (not admitting that the puck or ball is over the line), ordinary cheating (illegal equipment, doping), attempting to injure an opponent, or overloading the officials with borderline or even flagrant fouls in the knowledge that not all of them will be called (a tactic employed by the Philadelphia Flyers of the mid-1970s). These strategies function best as a variety of gamesmanship if the opposition knows that a violation has taken place but that it has passed without official sanction. These kinds of actions might well be viewed as cheating (and I would not dispute such a description), but they enter into the realm of gamesmanship primarily by virtue of their effect on the opponent's mental poise. One might choose to compete in this way with the expectation that one's behavior will unsettle the opponent's concentration, to get that opponent thinking about you rather than the play. It is a risky strategy but not infrequently a successful one.

Tactics that are more directly performed with the goal of psyching out the opponent and that seem to be more purely examples of gamesmanship would include trash talk and taunting; various forms of intimidation such as throwing inside in baseball, firing slap shots at the goalie's head, and loading the ice with goons (both common tactics in ice hockey); and elaborate delays of procedure, as well as resorting to obscure rules (one of the more celebrated American examples being the George Brett pine-tar incident in a baseball game between the New York Yankees and Kansas City Royals in 1983).† Other variations are basic competitive tactics that might,

---

* He simulated having been fouled and injured.

† Brett's apparent home run in the ninth inning, which would have given the Royals the lead in the game, was nullified by an umpire on complaint by the Yankee manager that the pine-tar on Brett's bat violated a (very obscure and almost never enforced) rule—it went too far above the grip. The American League President reversed this decision, on the grounds that Brett had not violated the "spirit of the rule." The game was resumed much later, and the Royals won.

for example, rely on being unanticipated at a given moment, such as attempting to break your opponent's will by pressing them at specific points during a race—the opponent might know it's coming but not when, or how to respond effectively—or attacking known points of weakness (the other cyclists are poor sprinters, or the opponent collapses after giving up a couple of quick points).

Given that gamesmanship does not violate the *rules* of the game or competition, what exactly is wrong with it, if indeed anything? The target of another's practice of gamesmanship might feel that what has occurred is *unfair*, but, although this might be a common or understandable reaction, I think it is mistaken. Supposing that the gamer has not violated the rules of competition, we cannot say that he or she has taken an unfair advantage. The officials might have failed in some way, but that cannot be laid at the gamer's door. In fact, it is the target who has (been led into having) failed, by allowing him- or herself to become distracted. The appropriate moral parallel here is with seduction: The opponent who directs a strategy of gamesmanship against a competitor constructs an opportunity for the other to fail, but the decisive move, the failure, belongs to the target. If the gamer's behavior is within the rules, it cannot be unfair, and the competitive failure of the target is not the result of unfair advantage. It is because the target did not pass one of the fundamental aspects of competition: the test of psychological strength and preparedness.

Consider, for example, throwing inside. Given that the rules of baseball do not prohibit doing so, a pitcher is entitled to throw inside, that is, close to the batter. He is not entitled to hit the batter, but a "brush-back pitch," a pitch meant to move the batter away from the middle of home plate, is just a "ball." You can't have a good, that is, broadly competitive, game if the pitcher throws nothing but perfect strikes over the plate.[5] The good of competition allows for the tactic and requires that the batter resist the attempt to force him off the plate—because otherwise he will not be able to adequately counter the pitcher's challenge. But what is thereby presented to the batter is just one more mental test, in fact, another manifestation of the mental test that is competition itself. All athletic competition proceeds not simply as a physical test, whether of strength, speed, or technical skill, but also of the will to continue with the test and the training for the test despite fatigue, pain, or indifference, as well as being "up" for the big game, race, and so on. As far as the target of gamesmanship is or perhaps ought to be concerned, the behavior of the opponent is merely more of the same and something else to be mentally prepared for. Training and mental preparation have to include an anticipation of multiple possibilities including things like variable weather and equipment failure, as well as awkward or unpredictable opponents. The better athletes are those who are not fazed by tactics employed to put them off their game.

Thus, whatever else we are to say about the acceptability of the practice of gamesmanship, we cannot say that it is unfair or that it has no athletic or moral value, although, as I shall argue, that value is paradoxical. I shall argue in due course that certain kinds of gamesmanship are indeed wrong because they are athletically self-defeating, as well as morally suspect, whereas others are valuable, possibly even required. To substantiate these claims, however, we also need to consider the importance of winning to athletic endeavor, because the point of gamesmanship is to secure a win and, especially, to do so not by illegal means but by ones that sap the ability of the target to compete on a physical or technical level—in effect to win by removing or diminishing the opposition's capacity to be an athletic threat, narrowly understood, rather than engaging that athletic threat directly.

Winning and Excellence

What is the importance of winning? There is a sense in which winning cannot be separated from the ends of sport. Winning is "written into" most sports by virtue of the fact that those sports define their own terminus as "most points scored within 60 or 90 minutes" or "the first across a 1,000-meter distance," and so on and because the activity and hence skills required of the participants are directed toward such a result.

But there is also a sense in which fixing on this point is rather like the psychological egoist or first-year philosophy student who insists that all our actions must be self-interested because we feel good about having our actions come out the way we wanted. Well, *of course* we do: This is simply to say that our actions are intentional or that we like getting what we want. Likewise, *of course*, winning is a goal of the activity of sport—it could not be otherwise. But this is an explanation of such broad scope that it borders on the vacuous, as well as overlooking the more interesting reasons that people do what they do. Moreover, concentrating on winning generates some counterintuitive assessments. Suppose that a rower, for example, can develop her technique to such a degree that every stroke is perfect, and suppose that her physiological conditioning is measurably superior to all her competitors. Suppose further that 10 strokes from the finish line her oarlock breaks, or a gust of wind hits lane 1 but not lane 6, or.... It seems correct to say here that the best rower does not win. And we can think of any number of other similar "lucky bounce" examples, as well as those in which legal but questionable tactics are deployed to bring about a victory.[6]

It seems, then, that we should say that, although winning is an indicator of excellence, the excellent are not excellent simply because they win. If it is possible for the "wrong team" to win, then we cannot identify excellence in terms of winning alone. In fact, winning frequently depends on many variables external to the winning athlete, including failures both athletic and moral on the part of opponents and officials. So we have to say something more like "the excellent win because they are excellent." Now, this is not on the face of it a very enlightening statement, and I do not wish to argue for the existence of some metaphysical quality of excellence by which the excellent are what they are. Rather, what I want to point to is the circumstance that success on game or race day is normally the result of a great deal of preparation and training, as well as native talent. Likewise, the result of the competition itself is generated by a process of activity that is not equivalent to goals scored, or seconds shaved off, or centimeters measured. Excellence is the description not of a score line but of a deliberately extended activity.

The evidence suggests that excellence and winning are two different goals. Clearly, the excellent do not always win, and winners are at least occasionally inferior to their opponents. Sometimes the excellent are just lucky. A persuasive case can be made, however, for the greater reliability of excellence leading to winning. And herein lies the distinction: Excellence is about developing the means to winning; it is about the athlete and the process involved in getting to the result. After all, a speed skater is excellent not because she wins races but because she skates really well (i.e., has superior technique and physical conditioning, among other things), which *enables* her to win races. As consumers of sport, we concentrate on the product (the result); as participants, we have to concentrate on production, that is, developing excellence.

This is where questions about gamesmanship arise. If the more substantive goal of sport is excellence, and excellence is about process rather than result, and thus the athlete rather than the score line, then we need to consider what effect gamesmanship has on the pursuit and the pursuer of excellence. If and insofar as gamesmanship subverts excellence in favor of winning, it must be considered antithetical to the athletic endeavor. In fact, I want eventually to argue that to resort to gamesmanship demonstrates a failure of self, of self-respect, and of commitment to oneself in sport: an athletic failure that might ultimately be traceable to a moral failure.

The Good of Competition

In the foregoing I referred to the goal or end of sport; by this I do not mean the specific end of *a* sport, as defined by its unique structure (completing a set distance, throwing an object farther, or even winning the game), but the end of *sport* in general; that is, not "why practice this move?" but "why move at all?" I take it that the answer to the latter question is the attaining of some good, other than the numerous contingent goods that might persuade any given individual to take up a particular sport: fitness, stress relief, personal glory, a ticket out of the boonies, and so on. What then might such a good be? The answer to this question is a somewhat roundabout one, but it will also explain what is wrong with gamesmanship as an adopted practice.

I take sport to be a form of structured and artificially constrained play. I use the term "play" because I assume that all athletic activity is, at least ideally, directed to an experience of joy in activity, even though in the real world there can be much more pain and frustration encountered than joy. I use the term "structured" play because any sport is an artificially constrained activity (get a ball in a net of such and such a size *only with your feet*, jump *over a high bar*, walk this distance *without lifting both feet from the ground*, etc.). In fact, it is the structure, and the rules defining that structure, that make each sport a sport, its own recognizable sport. All sports and all games have rules, even if they are vague, flexible, or changeable and whether the pursuit is a team competition or entirely solitary. Thus, I can make a game of mowing the lawn (following a specific pattern or completing the task within a definite time frame, etc.). Here, however, I am concerned with competitions involving at least two persons, whether or not they are games in the conventional sense (e.g., a race). Thus, a sport provides an artificial environment, defined by rules, many of which are essential to nothing other than the sport itself, which allows the individual participant the opportunity to see whether he or she can succeed at the selected activity under the prescribed constraints. After all, any given athletic activity, the movements involved, and so on might or might not be inherently difficult (putting a puck or a ball into a net, rowing a boat, or even walking), but doing so *with specific restrictions on how this can be done* is the whole point of engaging in the activity.[7]

As argued earlier, victory is unavoidably *a* goal in both competitive and recreational athletics, because the definition of what it is to win the game or race is what determines the activities learned and carried out. So this directs the pursuit of skill in the activity, again inevitably—the benefits of cross-training aside, it doesn't make sense to develop kayaking skills in order to succeed at rock climbing. Nevertheless, the preceding description also supposes that the abiding purpose of the game is not the result in the sense of the final score but the successful execution of the skills prescribed as necessary for carrying out the specific activity named by the sport in question—in effect, the *process* of getting to some score line rather than the score line as such. For this reason, the result only "counts" *if* the activity has been performed in the specified manner. It is important to bear in mind that discussions of sportsmanship only make sense if this is assumed, because sportsmanship is precisely about how the activity of sport is carried out by the participants. If all that matters is the score line, it does not matter how you get there. Sportsmanship is, however, all about personal conduct along the road to victory or defeat.

I am supposing a distinction here between the point of *sport* and the point of any given sports *contest*. Although it is a somewhat impoverished view, the point of any given sports *contest* could be and often is taken as simply determining which of two or more opponents is the better at some skill or set of skills: Whoever wins the game is the best. This cannot be the case for *sport* in general, however, because skills can only be assessed or even defined as skills in relation to some given sport or type of contest; that is, there are no such skills, or they have no significance, unless the sport is performed/practiced, and there is no reason otherwise to attempt the assessment, supposing that there is something to assess. So in a contest, I try to see if I am better at *x* than you. But why would I be remotely interested in doing this without some more fundamental motivation? Such a motive could be self-aggrandizement, or money, or some deep project of self-understanding. There are many possibilities, but the measurement of relative abilities in some sports contest is not enough by itself to explain why humans do sports and what they get out of them.[8]

One reason that this is not a good enough explanation is the circumstance that sport is not just about physical abilities. Think of it this way: What would be wrong with a sprint race between a human and an android? *Not* that it would be unfair or hopeless but that it would be meaningless. I think that this might also suggest what among other things is wrong with doping: The contest isn't then between two humans but between a human and a pharmaceutical lab or, in effect, a machine. The steroid body is like the android body in the sense that the machine, mechanical achievement, becomes the focus. But concentrating on the (body as) machine misses the point, just as concentrating on the centimeters or milliseconds does. Sport isn't about mechanical superiority. After all, machines and many animals can lift heavier loads than humans, go faster, propel objects farther, and so on. Sport is about a particular kind of complex organism, an organism with the capacity to fail in nonmechanical ways, completing or attempting a specific and largely unimportant task—an organism with psychological states, reflectivity, and the ability to choose a course of action (to go on, to quit, to cheat). Sport is sport because it is engaged in by beings with these options. And because of this, it is a test, less of the mechanical capacities of a human being than of the choice capacities of that being. Granted, steroid- or EPO-stuffed athletes might still be beings capable of choice, but they have lost the proper focus of their activity—they have seriously missed the point that sport isn't about numbers, it is about character and choices; it is about *them*, not about how fast they go, because a machine could always go faster.[9]

In looking to identify the good of *sport*, the most obvious candidate might well be fitness. Whether or not the purpose of sports *contests* is the determination of relative abilities, it seems clear that *sport* allows for the development of those abilities. As noted previously, however, at least some of those abilities might be in some sense trivial or even frivolous; in some others they might be debilitating. Still, it seems that a notable benefit of sports participation is fitness.

Nonetheless, this cannot be the whole story, for the same reasons just presented against the body-machine model of athletic excellence. Seeing the end of sport as simply fitness is to treat one's body as a device to be tinkered with and either improved or damaged, but as other than one's self. But the human self is neither body nor mind in isolation; it is the production of an embodied consciousness. Consequently, self-development is ideally the development of physical competence in concert with psychic/moral competence. Sport is a means for human individuals to become themselves—to develop physically but also morally (in a broad sense). Depending on my attitude I can become myself, that is, fully develop myself, or I can cheat myself and others out of a valuable experience—I can subvert the process, diminish its possibilities. This is where we can begin to see the value of *competitive* sport and the disvalue of something like gamesmanship as one of many kinds of failure connected with sport that undercut its benefit to the participant. Thus sport is potentially valuable as a means to full human self-development, although it is often used in such a way as to make this less likely to occur.

Competition is a good, from a physical standpoint, for the development of certain skills (though with significant reservations), but more so from the psychological-moral standpoint. I think that there are two main benefits of competition: (a) the experience of ontological wholeness that is not generally available when concentrating on the rehearsal of physical technique, that is, training, but is released as a possibility under the pressure of joint competitors and (b) the psychological trial of the moral self: the response to the question with which this essay began—"What are you prepared to do to win?" Thus, competition presents the opportunity for self-revelation, in both an ontological and a moral dimension.[10] (Of course, I am also assuming that a person is motivated toward self-development and improvement; I shall pretend, utterly contrary to fact, that this point is unproblematic.)

Competition in sport is valuable because it compels a response to various kinds of challenge, whether to one's level of physical competence or to one's sense of self. This puts sports in familiar moral territory. I'm not as good—physically, intellectually, morally—as I thought I was; A is better than me. What am I going to do about it? Improve? Wallow in envy? Give up? What if A does things that are wrong; shall I do the same just because A does? The whole gamut of traditional virtues and vices enter into play here; industry and humility on the one side, envy, apathy, sloth, and wrath on the other. Just as we are all paragons of virtue so long as we are not tried, and we are all Pele or the Rocket in our backyards, it's only when we are confronted with the real possibility of failure or defeat that we know how good we are. The bad sport or devious competitor, like the seducer, is perversely significant for the one with pretensions to superiority as proof for the claim.

The good of competitive sport is that it is a test of the whole athlete—not just his or her physical skills, which could be tested just as well in training or in the lab, but their psychological and moral skills, as well. Competitive sport is supposedly about athletes doing their very best—the pursuit of excellence[11]—but this can only happen *if* a certain psychological attitude is present. Competition is very much directed to the psyche of competitors: Can they do their best *now*. It has become a commonplace criticism of some sports that far too much emphasis is placed on competition in the form of games and tournaments and not enough on practice, to the detriment of skill development, and even informal games of shinny[12] or kick around are often better for developing physical skills than formal games. You train for games; games only minimally train the body. It is only on race day or game day, however, that you find out how good you really are.

Competition generally involves winners and losers, and to enter into competition is to risk losing. Ordinarily, we want competitive opponents to be of *comparable* strength, ability, and so on, but we do not want an endless succession of draws—the ideal is some combination of two situations: The best athlete or team always wins, and on any given occasion anyone can win. But note that in both cases there is a *win*—which also means that someone loses.[13] Now, another (though not strictly equivalent) way of phrasing our opening question could be "Are you willing to accept defeat?" The possible answers to this question would be just as revealing. One way of thinking about gamesmanship is to see it as a refusal to accept defeat, and this might be why it is sometimes admired. But when that defeat is legitimate—that is, within the rules and by an athletically superior opponent—the reasonable and,

I suppose, "sporting" reaction must be to acknowledge that one has been bettered and resolve to be better oneself. One could then see the relationship between gamesmanship and sportsmanship in terms of their attitude toward defeat: Sportsmanship admits when the best athlete has won, even if that isn't me; gamesmanship refuses to risk that this might not be me. And that is a problem, because I cannot improve if I do not allow the evidence that I must.

Part of the common understanding of sportsmanship includes losing graciously, which is not to say indifferently. We might say that being a "good sport" implies accepting defeat by the superior opponent, but this is not accepting failure as such. I need to accept my defeat and acknowledge the other's superiority if I am to learn from my defeat and improve my own skills (including mental preparation and attitude). This is entirely compatible with refusing to accept defeat in the sense of being determined not to be defeated in the future. This is the difference between a mature individual/athlete and the classic "sore loser." It is the difference between making excuses for yourself versus analyzing why you lost, all other things being equal. But what if other things are not equal and the other won by cheating or using borderline tactics? Again, the mature competitor distinguishes between what the other's behavior says about her and what she herself did or failed to do.

Thus, sport is an artificial environment in which the participant *can*, though by no means *must*, develop certain personal virtues such as confidence, fortitude, generosity, cooperativeness, humility, and so on. Participation in sport implies a willingness on the part of the participant to accept the risk of losing. Insofar as gamesmanship is the refusal of this risk, it implies cowardice.

Gamesmanship and Selfhood

Gamesmanship is a category fraught with ambiguities and seeming paradoxes. The paradoxes, I believe, can be resolved; the ambiguities are perhaps too deeply rooted. I will first consider the athletic ramifications of the practice.

I have already suggested that the gamesmanship of an opponent presents an additional level of psychological test for its target. I also contend that resorting to the strategy (if it succeeds) lessens the athletic test for the gamer. If so, what would seem to follow from this is that gamesmanship is a detriment to the gamer if it succeeds and a benefit to the target if it fails, that is, insofar as the target of the practice becomes stronger by resisting the attempt. We are left then with the peculiar consequence that gamesmanship, which is a strategy for ensuring victory, is ultimately a self-defeating practice for the person engaging in it but not necessarily bad for sport in that it provides an additional opportunity for (self) testing. Thus, it is good if it fails and bad if it succeeds, but either way, it might be better that it occur, though especially if it occurs and fails.

In that case, it would seem to follow that gamesmanship ought to be encouraged. To do so has undesirable consequences, however, not for those who survive it but for those relying on it. Because they never get properly tested, their skills might be expected to eventually deteriorate. Moreover, encouraging gamesmanship makes the gamer instrumental for the sporting athlete, at a cost to the gamer of some athletic development. And it seems odd that sporting athletes should be so described if they are using the gamer to benefit themselves at a cost to the other. In addition, sporting players should object to gamesmanship they can themselves withstand because it diminishes (in the long run) their opponent, and this eventual outcome will negatively affect their own development by giving them poorer competition. So, no matter what, gamesmanship diminishes both parties to the contest, regardless of the target's response.

How do we make sense of this nest of ambiguity? Although it is not a completely satisfactory solution, I think that we have to make a distinction between "weak" and "strong" forms of gamesmanship, the former designating the forms of gamesmanship that are compatible with an ideal of sport as a "mutual challenge to achieve excellence" (2: p. 112) and the latter marking out those that are not.[14] Actions such as throwing inside, the fast break, hard tens,[15] and withholding line-up and injury information would fall into the weak category; deception with regard to line calls and fouls ("simulation"), gross acts of intimidation such as physical abuse (especially where this is above the norm expected in that sport), mobbing officials, and disrupting players' preparations would count in the strong category. The criterion we need to apply, then, in attempting to distinguish between appropriate and inappropriate forms of gamesmanship is whether the practice *improves both* participants or not.

Provided that a tactic is compatible with the rules of a given sport and with the aims of sport in general, there seems no prima facie reason to discourage it. If it enhances or furthers these aims, including the athletic development of the participants, that seems prima facie a good reason to encourage it.

Whether that means, however, that any reasonable, much less moral, individual should willingly adopt such a tactic or participate in a sport that includes it is a distinct issue—that is, distinct in theory, not in actuality; athletic practice and moral practice are not separate worlds. Consequently, although I have so far attempted to distinguish the instrumental value of gamesmanship for athletic ends, we must also consider its specifically moral dimensions while recognizing that the moral and the athletic are, in actuality, intertwined.

A case can be made that certain forms of (weak) gamesmanship are indeed *required*—it would be wrong not just athletically but also morally not to employ them, because to withhold such actions is disrespectful of the opponent—it implies that the other competitor is not significant enough to warrant one's full attention. A pitcher who refuses to send his best stuff, or to pitch inside, not only does not provide an adequate challenge but also is telling the batter that he is of no concern, that he doesn't matter. Although being blown out can be humiliating, it is insulting to be dismissed by an opponent as not worth their full effort. The weak forms listed previously all enhance—contribute to—the contest for both parties. They involve recognizing the other as an engaged participant in the contest and as such acknowledging indirectly the fact that you need the opponent, rather than, as the strong forms of gamesmanship do, attempting to eliminate the opponent in such a way that one is never really tested.[16] Weak gamesmanship is a challenge to the other to "bring it on," an invitation to compete fully, which is a vitally different attitude than the strong one that attempts to get the other ejected, literally or figuratively.

In summary, the "strong" sort of gamesmanship certainly can bring one profit, in terms of victories scored, but it closes off the participant to the other benefits of sport, specifically, those that concern personal growth and development, and conceivably athletic development, as well. If you can get your opponent to cave mentally, you don't get pushed as hard as you might. This lessens the competitive situation and your own opportunities for improvement and achievement, whether on that day or in the future. In this respect, gamesmanship undercuts the benefit of sport to the player who employs it. We might ask this player, If you can win anyway, why do you have to do this? And if you can't, wouldn't it be better to face up to the fact and start working on improving? If you have to taunt or physically intimidate your opponent in order to win, if you need to make him small, it suggests a lack in you, specifically, a lack of confidence or self-respect, and possibly of the necessary skills as well—after all, can't you beat him on your own?

The resort to gamesmanship suggests a deeper and already present failure of self on the part of those who use it. They are not simply "unsporting"; they lack the attitude toward themselves that makes effective participation in sport possible for themselves. Thus, athletes who practice strong gamesmanship demonstrate a pre-existing defect of moral character that makes them less able to improve as athletes or even to know their present level of ability. This means that it is an athletic failing that issues from a moral one. What is, at the least, ironic about it is that it perpetuates athletic deficiency for the gamers. As they win, their own capacity for losing is reinforced; they become or remain less competent. In this way, gamesmanship constitutes both a moral and an athletic failing.

In contrast, sportsmanship, which in the competitive context includes weak gamesmanship, involves recognizing the opponent as essential for one's own growth and as the condition for the game or competition. Hence the importance of respect for one's opponent. Failure to respect your opponent suggests that he or she is not needed for your own exalted status, which, aside from being rude, is simply false. Without an opponent you don't compete, and without competition you have no knowledge about your own expertise, nor are you challenged to improve. Hence, competitors who take their own athletic development seriously want their opponents to do as well as they possibly can—because that makes themselves better.[17] Strong gamesmanship prevents this or, at least, interferes with its realization.

Conclusion

One of the problems with looking at athletic competition strictly in terms of its structural elements is that the existential actuality of the athlete is inadequately acknowledged. By this I mean that the athlete is not merely a piece on the board, or even a perfectible body-machine, but a person, capable of and required to make self-defining choices, who exists off, as well as on, the playing field. When we say that sport builds character we must remember that it does not invent it; sport reveals it and then either rewards or punishes it. Certain ways of doing sport encourage the worst in a human being and hobble the best. It is no use saying "that's the way it's played," any more than "the poor will always be with us," or "war is inevitable"; we can always *choose* to play differently than we do.

Thus, the question with which we began—What are you prepared to do to win?—goes to the core of what it is to be an athlete and a responsible being. If one of the principal benefits of sport is the development of the participant's physical and personal skills (including self and moral development), then certain attitudes and behaviors on the part of the participant are necessary for this to be a success. The ideal of sportsmanship might well capture at least some set of the necessary virtues, in particular the requirement that competitors practice an openness to the game and to learning about themselves in the game, as well as a respect both for themselves and their opponents, which can then enable the competitors to improve athletically, competitively, and morally. Gamesmanship, on the other hand, can be a useful thing if its practice in any given case is compatible with these ends, but if not it is destructive of sport and its practitioners.

NOTES

1. Some will find the terms "gamesmanship" and "sportsmanship" to be gender biased. As a woman who has and continues to participate in traditionally male sports on male, female, and mixed teams, I am hardly indifferent to gender bias in the cultural definition of sport and its language (see also Howe [12]). However, although there might be some important deconstruction to be done regarding historical and normative assumptions behind the apparently masculine bias of these terms, for the purposes of the present discussion I shall employ them as is for the fairly practical reason that they correspond to the common usage of sports participants (rightly or wrongly) and because I here take the "man" in "gamesmanship" to have the same gender-indifferent marker quality that it has in a directive such as "cover your man," to which an entirely appropriate response might be "I've got her."

2. I do not intend to argue that it's not whether you win or lose, but how you play the game ... exactly. "It's just a game" can be the favorite excuse of the willfully mediocre (cf. Simon's comments, 17: pp. 33-34). However, suppose two athletes with exactly similar stats; it does not follow that we could not reasonably ask which of the two was the better athlete—*how* they each achieved their results would be a deciding factor. I am arguing for the inclusion of that factor and for a greater weight to be placed on it than is the current norm.

3. The "oddity" of professional fouls stems from the circumstance that, from the point of view of an instrumental model of rationality, their commission can be described as rational (a possible penalty traded off against an otherwise certain goal). Nonetheless, because it is a deliberate violation of the same rules that define and make possible the contest in which the violation occurs, the perpetrator appears, by another way of thinking, to be acting irrationally. The rationality and indeed the sportsmanship of professional fouls, however, fall outside the scope of this article.

4. For an extensive, and somewhat hilarious, catalogue of such techniques see Potter (16); the subtitle of this slim volume captures the point well: *The Art of Winning Games Without Actually Cheating* or, it can be added, being particularly good at any of them.

5. Besides, as remarked in the movie *Bull Durham*, it is "undemocratic."

6. See Dixon (6).

7. See Suits (18), especially pp. 20–34. Although Suits's emphasis on the formal quality of games is basically right, the point is somewhat overstated, for at least two
reasons. One, rules are often vague or fluid; this is especially the case when we have
informal games, which are no less games for being informal. Two, rules define
the outside limits of games but not their content, which is, after all, *play*—that is,
everything that happens in between the rules and that is not determined to occur
by the rules. Thus, when rules are changed, it is (one hopes) in order to enhance
play. Game rules are like laws but in the sense that even the most law-abiding of
us do not live by following the law—we *live*, and try not to break the law (or to get
caught). The game as it is played is not the rules; the game is the play that happens
inside the rules, and games that are not played are empty forms.

8. Compare Fraleigh (10) on this question, especially chapter 7.

9. A very awkward set of problems is raised by sports in which equipment, and its
technological perfection, is paramount for both participation and competitive
success, from archery and canoe-kayak at one end to cycling in the middle and
motor sports at the far end. I cannot adequately explore these issues here, save to
observe that I take the point of standardizing equipment precisely to ensure that
it is the athletes who decide the event rather than the manufacturers. When the
equipment dominates the event, I suspect that we do indeed have a contest of
designers and their machines, not of athletes. But where this balance shifts from
one side to the other is a very tricky question.

10. I have argued elsewhere (13) that athletic activity is a means of developing
the sense of embodiment and the understanding of the self as embodied; in
that article I was concerned with the encountering of physical boundary in
activity, which does not *necessarily* require what most of us would recognize
as competition. Here I want to concentrate on what role sport *as competition*
has on the development of the embodied self, in particular the question of
how athletic competition can enhance the development of moral selfhood
and personality.

11. Cf. Simon (17: ch. 2).

12. Shinny is hockey with minimal equipment (skates and sticks) and minimal and
largely consensual, sometimes fluid, rules.

13. I disagree, however, with Fraleigh's suggestion that ties diminish the value of a
sports contest. He enumerates in ref. 9 six criteria for a *bad* sports contest, the
last of which is incompleteness because of a tied score, and goes on to state that
a *neutral* contest is one that is deficient because of its ending in a tie, that is, by
virtue of being "incomplete by nondetermination of winners and losers" (9: p.

57)—even though the other requirements for a *good* contest are met. The point (admittedly simplified) is that if a central purpose of a good sports contest is to determine relative abilities, and if this requires winners and losers, then ties fail to be good contests because they fail to meet this end (see also 10: ch. 7, esp. pp. 98-99). In opposition to this view, it must be said that sometimes a draw is exactly the right result, and the contest is in no way diminished by the nondecision; no one who witnessed the game between the Montreal Canadiens and Central Red Army hockey teams on 31 December 1976 (widely considered to be one of the best hockey games ever played) thought that the 3-3 score was anything but just and satisfying, not least because it demonstrated just how good both teams were. For a detailed and convincing discussion of this issue, see Torres and McLaughlin (19).

14. The terminology is not compelling, but because I will make certain moral evaluations of these types of gamesmanship in the following I hope it will be less confusing, not to mention question begging, than calling them good and bad.

15. A "hard ten"—pulling an extra-hard 10 strokes—is a tactic employed as the rowing equivalent of a fast break, the intent of which is to gain distance and demoralize the crew of the boat next to yours.

16. See Boxill (2: p. 112).

17. This is why competitors shake hands after a hard-fought game: It is an acknowledgement of a shared experience between them as competitors and respect for the other as a contributor to it. And although coaches, trainers, managers, and others might be continually involved in athlete *preparation*, the moment of *competition* is the one pure experience that belongs to the athlete(s) alone; hence, the handshake is a symbolic but also an essentially private exchange. However, see also Boxill's comments (2: p. 113). She suggests that competition leads to friendship, which is characterized by the postgame handshake. This would be to suppose too much: Respect and acknowledgement of the other do not entail the positive feeling involved in friendship; there might be and often is a fair degree of animosity and simple dislike between opponents (centered in each other's on-field conduct), but this is separable from acknowledgement of the other as a valued opponent.

REFERENCES

1. Arnold, Peter J. "Three Approaches Toward an Understanding of Sportsmanship." *Journal of the Philosophy of Sport*. 10, 1984, 61-70.

2. Boxill, Jan. "The Ethics of Competition." In *Sports Ethics*, Jan Boxill (Ed). Oxford: Blackwell, 2003, 107-15.

3. Butcher, Robert, and Schneider, Angela. "Fair Play as Respect for the Game." In *Sports Ethics*, Jan Boxill (Ed.). Oxford: Blackwell, 2003, 153-71.

4. Delattre, Edwin J. "Some Reflections on Success and Failure in Competitive Athletics." *Journal of the Philosophy of Sport*. II, 1975, 133-39.

5. Dixon, Nicholas. "On Sportsmanship and 'Running Up the Score.'" *Journal of the Philosophy of Sport*. XIX, 1992, 1-13.

6. ———. "On Winning and Athletic Superiority." *Journal of the Philosophy of Sport*. XXVI, 1999, 10-26.

7. Feezell, Randolph M. "Sportsmanship." *Journal of the Philosophy of Sport*. XIII, 1986, 1-13.

8. ———. "Sportsmanship and Blowouts: Baseball and Beyond." *Journal of the Philosophy of Sport*. XXVI, 1999, 68-78.

9. Fraleigh, Warren P. "An Examination of Relationships of Inherent, Intrinsic, Instrumental, and Contributive Values of the Good Sports Contest." *Journal of the Philosophy of Sport*. X, 1984, 52-60.

10. ———. *Right Actions in Sport: Ethics for Contestants*. Champaign, IL: Human Kinetics, 1984.

11. Hardman, Alan, Fox, Luanne, McLaughlin, Doug, and Zimmerman, Kurt. "On Sportsmanship and 'Running Up the Score': Issues of Incompetence and Humiliation." *Journal of the Philosophy of Sport*. XXIII, 1996, 58-69.

12. Howe, Leslie A. "Being and Playing: Sport and the Valorization of Gender." In *Philosophy and Everyday Life*. Laura Duhan Kaplan (Ed.). New York: Seven Bridges Press, 2002, 108-26.

13. ———. "Athletics, Embodiment, and the Appropriation of the Self." *Journal of Speculative Philosophy*. 17(2), 2003, 92-107.

14. Keating, James W. "Sportsmanship as a Moral Category." *Ethics* 75, 1964, 25-35.

15. Pearson, Kathleen M. "Deception, Sportsmanship, and Ethics." In *Sports Ethics*, Jan Boxill (Ed.). Oxford: Blackwell, 2003, 81-83.

16. Potter, Stephen. *The Theory and Practice of Gamesmanship*. London: Rupert Hart-Davis, 1947.

17. Simon, Robert L. *Fair Play: Sports, Values, and Society*. Boulder, Co: Westview, 1991.

18. Suits, Bernard. *The Grasshopper: Games, Life, and Utopia*. Toronto: U of Toronto P, 1978.

19. Torres, Cesar R., and McLaughlin, Douglas W. "Indigestion? An Apology for Ties." *Journal of the Philosophy of Sport*. XXX(2), 2003, 144-58.

16. SPORTSMANSHIP*

RANDOLPH M. FEEZELL

A movement in contemporary moral philosophy is attempting to return our attention to thinking about the centrality of virtue in the moral life. Until recently the language of virtue had seemingly fallen into disfavor in twentieth-century philosophizing about moral matters. We heard much talk about the naturalistic fallacy, verificationism, the expression of attitudes, prescriptivity, universalizability, the principle of utility, and the like, but little talk about *being* a certain kind of person, having certain dispositions or characteristics that we have always thought to be central to living life in a civilized moral community. In the move toward thinking about lived moral experience, philosophers began talking about issues of pressing social concern, such as abortion, euthanasia, and war. The mistaken impression occasioned in our students and in the community may have been that the return to relevancy, to "real" moral concerns, involved the necessary connection between applied ethics and social ethics. Again, one wonders what happened to the texture of individual moral experience, moral discourse, and moral education, where we stress the importance of friendliness, compassion, fairness, truthfulness, and reliability. Perhaps an important part of applied ethics involves trying to understand individual virtues; for example, what do we mean or what are we recommending when we speak of aspects of the virtuous life such as compassion or boldness?

In this context I believe it is relevant to think about the value of sportsmanship. Sports have a prevalent place in American cultural life, as well as in numerous foreign countries. Spectator sports set attendance records, yet crowd behavior is often atrocious. More adults participate today in sports with differing degrees of seriousness. Vast numbers of young people play sports, coming of age mor-

---

* From Randolph M. Feezell, *Sport, Play, and Ethical Reflection* (Urbana, IL: U of Illinois P, 2004), pp. 83-96, notes 159-60.

ally as they devote a large amount of time to their athletic endeavors. Impressive claims are made about the role of sports in the development of character and how important sports are as a preparation for later competitive life. It should be important to understand what it means to be a good sport. Parents often stress to their children the importance of being a good sport, but it is not apparent what that means.

It is helpful to start with a few examples before turning to the main arguments of this chapter. The paradigm case of a bad sport is the cheater. Consider a high school basketball game. At the end of a close game, a flurry of activity takes place beneath the basket. A foul is called and the coach sees that the referees are confused about who was fouled. He instructs his best foul shooter to go to the free throw line to take the shots although he knows, as does his team and most of the crowd, that another player, a poor foul shooter, was actually fouled. The wrong player makes the free throws and his team wins.[1] In this case the coach has cheated. He has instructed or encouraged his players to cheat, and we would say he is a bad sport or, in this instance at least, whether acting out of character or not, he has acted like a bad sport.[2] He has displayed poor sportsmanship.

Why is the cheater a bad sport? What is wrong with cheating? The answer is not difficult to find. Two teams agreed to play the game of basketball, defined by certain rules that constitute what it means to play basketball. By cheating, the coach intentionally broke a rule, thereby violating the original implied agreement. In this sense, cheating is a kind of promise breaking or violation of a contractual relationship. Notice that the moral reason that explains the wrongness of cheating is not unique to playing basketball; an ordinary moral rule has been broken. In the language of virtue, the coach has been found lacking in trust and integrity. He has attempted to gain an unfair advantage by breaking a rule. Perhaps being a good sport is simply an extension of being a good person—in one sense, this is an obvious truism—and the meaning of the virtue of sportsmanship is not unique to the activity in question.

Consider some other examples. The intent to injure would usually be a serious moral violation, but acting in such a way that one *might* injure an opponent is often morally ambiguous. Think of a hockey player fighting or a pitcher in baseball throwing one "under the chin." Should one yell at an opponent in hopes of rattling him? Certainly how one responds to defeat or victory is often thought to be an important part of sportsmanship. Should one ever refuse the traditional handshake after the contest? What about running up the score on an opponent or refusing to give credit due to an opponent who has defeated you? In such cases our judgments are more ambiguous and our explanations less obvious. Certainly no rule is violated when one team runs up the score on another, or when a tennis player continually whines, complains, throws his racket, interrupts play, and questions calls. But we want to say this type of behavior is bad form, somehow inappropriate because it violates the nature of what sport is about.

Is there some essential meaning of the virtue of sportsmanship? How can we unify our concept of sportsmanship? Are some aspects of it more central than others? In this chapter I attempt to respond to these questions. First I critically discuss James Keating's views. Keating first published his analysis of sportsmanship in 1964, and it has become a standard part of the literature in philosophy of sport.[3] Later, he published a revised version of his original paper.[4] Because of the significance and influence of Keating's seminal work, it is appropriate to begin our reflections on ethics in sport with a consideration of the framework within which he attempts to understand sportsmanship. Moreover, his fundamental distinction between sport and athletics is still very much with us; it is often either explicitly or implicitly used to reinforce the notion that the behavior and attitudes appropriate for playful, recreational activities are quite different from the norms and responses appropriate for participation in the deadly serious world of competitive athletics. Keating has offered an important framework within which to initiate an understanding of sportsmanship, just as Weiss's seminal work provided a useful starting point for reflecting on the nature and attraction of sport. I do not believe that Keating is correct in radically separating sport and athletics, and to the extent that this type of view is still prevalent when people talk about sport and what is and is not appropriate behavior in sports, a correction is needed. The chapter is not wholly critical, however. Emerging from the friendly engagement with this type of approach to sport and sportsmanship will be a positive view that attempts to preserve the precarious balance between the seriousness of competition and the nonseriousness of playful activities.

Keating's paper is a valuable resource for a number of reasons, not the least of which is his overview of the many and varied claims made about the nature of sportsmanship. Some have made extraordinary assertions about the importance of this notion, as if it is *the* most important virtue in American cultural life. The interpretations of the essence of sportsmanship have included numerous other virtues: self-control, fair play, truthfulness, courage, endurance, and others.[5] Keating attempts to unify our understanding by providing a tidy scheme that shows which virtues are essential and which are of only accidental importance. His argument is simple and compelling. Sportsmanship is the conduct that is becoming to a sportsman, or one who engages in sport, so we simply have to understand what sport is. Here we have the crux of the argument, because the term refers to "radically different types of human activity."[6] Keating could not be more emphatic stressing the extreme separation of sport as playful activity and sport as competitive athletic contests. On three different occasions he speaks of them as "radically different types of human activity," and at one point says that "a drastic change takes place" when we move from playful activity to athletics.[7]

What, more precisely, is the distinction? Taking hints from dictionary definitions and etymology, Keating argues that "sport" refers both to the pleasant diversion of play and to spirited competitive athletic contests. To understand the true meaning of sportsmanship, we must carefully distinguish conduct and attitude appropriate to play and conduct and attitude appropriate to athletics. "In essence, play has for its direct and immediate end joy, pleasure, and delight and which is dominated by a spirit of moderation and generosity. Athletics, on the other hand, is essentially a competitive activity, which has for its end victory in the contest and which is characterized by a spirit of dedication, sacrifice, and intensity."[8]

Thus the virtues of the player are radically different from the virtues of the athlete. Insofar as the activity determines the conduct appropriate to it, the player should conduct himself with an attitude of "generosity and magnanimity," keeping in mind his obligation to maximize the pleasure of the event and reinforce the ludic character of the activity. Play is essentially cooperative. On the other hand, the athlete is engaged in a competitive struggle whose end is exclusive possession of victory. In the words of G.J. Warnock, this is a situation in which things have the "inherent tendency to go badly"[9] unless moral restraints are put on the rigors of competition. "Fairness or fair play, the pivotal virtue in athletics, emphasizes the need for an impartial and equal application of the rules, if the victory is to signify, as it should, athletic excellence."[10] In athletics, generosity and magnanimity are misplaced, as they supposedly are in other areas of life that are essentially competitive. Your opponent expects only that you fairly pursue your self-interest, not that you are to be interested in his goal, for you cannot be. Victory is the telos* of the activity and an exclusive possession. Once the contest ends, the athlete, like the victor or vanquished in war, should face victory or defeat with modesty or a strength of composure.

---

* = the defining, essential aim, end, purpose.

Since Keating's view of sportsmanship depends so heavily on the sharp distinction between sport as playful activity and sport as athletic competition, we should look more closely at that distinction. How does Keating arrive at it? He begins by citing Webster's definition of sport as "diversion," "amusement," and "recreation." However, since so many sporting events (he mentions, among others, the World Series, the Davis Cup, and even a high school basketball tournament) would be inaccurately described in these terms, there must be another important sense given to this notion. Etymologically, the English forms of the word "athlete" suggest the centrality of contest and the struggle for excellence and victory, so "sport," he concludes, must refer to "radically different types of human activity." Although there might already be something misleading about placing such emphasis on etymology and dictionary definitions, the distinction ultimately is a phenomenological one. We should look at lived experience for the basis of the distinction, for play and athletics are radically different "not insofar as the game itself or the mechanics or rules are concerned, but different with regard to the attitude, preparation, and purpose of the participants."[11] Now curiosities arise, of a logical, psychological, and moral nature.

Consider one of Keating's own examples, a high school basketball tournament. Suppose Team A is coached by Smith, who views sport as little short of war. The opponent is the enemy, who must be hated in order to produce maximum intensity and effort. Practices and games are pervaded by a spirit of overarching seriousness. He yells at his players and at referees. He never lets up because he views sport as real life, or, if not quite like real life, of great importance as preparation for the harshness of the "real" world. There is a certain ruthlessness in his pursuit of victory, and anything goes, short of outright cheating, although even here he is inclined to think that it's alright if you don't get caught. For example, he wouldn't hesitate to run up the score if it might enhance his team's rating and its future tournament seeding. He expects no less from his opponent.

On the other hand, Team B is coached by Jones, whose whole approach to basketball is fundamentally different. He is also a spirited competitor who instills in his player-athletes the value of excellent performance, victory, and fair play. However, he never forgets that basketball is a game, an arbitrary construction of rule-governed activities invented in order to make possible an intrinsically satisfying activity.[12] For Jones there is always something magical about the world of basketball, with its special order, its special spatial and temporal rhythms. It is set apart from the concerns of ordinary reality. To play and coach basketball is to engage in joyful activities, and the pleasure is increased by improving skills, being challenged to perform well, inventing strategies, and achieving one's goals. He sees the opponent not as an enemy but as a friendly competitor whose challenge is necessary to enhance the pleasurable possibilities of his own play. He realizes it is difficult to sustain the spirit of play within spirited competition, but that is his goal. His seriousness about the pursuit of victory is always mediated by an awareness that basketball is "just a game," valuable for the moment, whose value consists primarily in the intrinsic enjoyment of the activity. Fun is an essential element in his understanding of sport.

Are these two coaches engaged in fundamentally different human activities? The example suggests that Keating's distinction is plausible. In one sense, the coaches' attitudes are so dissimilar that we want to say they are engaged in different activities. But the most important question here is moral, not psychological. I see no reason to take Smith's attitudes as normative. Although the picture of Smith may appear to be overdrawn, it is undoubtedly a correct description of the understanding and attitudes some people have regarding sports. However, it doesn't follow that their attitudes are correct. Keating's argument is logically curious. Recall that play and athletics have been characterized as being radically different with regard to attitudes, but later he states that "the nature of the activity determines the conduct and attitudes proper to it."[13] Without further clarification, this appears to be circular and uninformative concerning how our original attitudes toward sport should be formed. I would say that Smith has an impoverished view of sport, an impoverished experience of sport, and it is just such views and attitudes that tend to generate unsportsmanlike behavior in sport.

There are two main problems with Keating's analysis, vitiating his account of sportsmanship. First, because he takes his understanding of play simply from Webster's definition of sports as "diversion," "amusement," and "recreation," he fails to describe adequately the nature of play so as to understand how sport could be seen as an extension of play. Second, and probably because of his limited clarification of play, he incorrectly ascribes a false exclusivity to the psychology of the player and the athlete.

The player and the athlete are to be radically distinguished supposedly on the grounds that they differ with regard to attitude, preparation, and purpose. The previous example made such a distinction plausible but failed to show why one set of attitudes should be normative. In numerous other cases, however, the distinction is difficult if not impossible to make, precisely because the attitudes of the participants are mixed. Consider an ex-college basketball player engaged in a pickup game. Is this person a player or an athlete? What virtues should characterize his conduct? On Keating's model it would be difficult to say. Suppose the basketball player intends to play well, puts out maximum effort, competes hard, pursues victory and attempts to play fairly. Why? Because he still loves the game; he still enjoys the competitive play, the very feel of the activity. Each game is a unity, the development of a totality with its own finality. Something is at issue, and this is an arena in which the issue at hand will be decisively resolved. He finds the dramatic tensions satisfying, as well as the frolicking nature of running, jumping, and responding to the physical presence of other players. He enjoys the sheer exuberance of the experience. He is serious about his play because such seriousness enhances the activity and heightens the experience. He is serious because the internal logic of the activity demands the pursuit of victory and he both loves and respects the game of basketball. Yet he realizes that in a profound sense, his seriousness is misplaced. It doesn't really matter who wins the game, although it does matter that the festivity occurs. Such an attitude toward the pursuit of victory acts as an inner negation of his original seriousness and produces moderation. One might go on here with an extended phenomenological account, but the point is already clear. His attitudes and purposes are extraordinarily complex. He is simultaneously player and athlete. His purpose is to win the contest *and* to experience the playful and aesthetic delights of the experience. His attitudes are at once both playful and competitive, and these color his relationship with his fellow participants. He sees his opponent as both competitor and friend, competing and cooperating at the same time. These are the attitudes that guide his conduct.

Such a fusion of attitudes and purposes may be unsatisfying to some, but I think such a picture of the player-athlete is a truer one than the one offered by Keating. His radical distinction between play and athletics is an excellent example of what Richard Taylor calls polarized thinking. In the context of showing how such thinking leads to metaphysical puzzlement or confusion, Taylor says the following:

> There is a common way of thinking that we can call *polarization*, and that appears to be the source of much metaphysics. It consists of dividing things into two exclusive categories, and then supposing that if something under consideration does not belong to one of them, then it must belong in the other. "Either/or" is the pattern of such thought, and because it is usually clear, rigorous, and incisive, it is also often regarded by philosophers as exclusively rational.[14]
>
> Such sharpness and precision are sometimes bought at the expense of truth, for reality is far too loose a mixture of things to admit of such absolute distinc-

tions, and sometimes, both in our practical affairs and in our philosophy, we are led into serious errors, which are fervently embraced just because they seem so clearly to have been proved.[15]

Keating offers only one extended example to show what his polarized view of sportsmanship would look like in practice, and his conclusions are odd.

> It is the contestant's objective and not the game itself which becomes the chief determinant of the conduct and attitudes of the players. If we take tennis as an example and contrast the code of conduct employed by the player with that of the athlete in the matter of officiating, the difference is obvious. The player invariably gives the opponent the benefit of any possible doubt. Whenever he is not certain, he plays his opponent's shot as good even though he may believe it was out. The athlete, however, takes a different approach. Every bit as opposed to cheating as the sportsman, the athlete demands no compelling proof of error. If a shot seems to be out, the athlete calls it that way. He is satisfied that his opponent will do the same. He asks no quarter and gives none. As a result of this attitude by comparison with the player, the athlete will tend toward a legal interpretation of the rules.[16]

I have played tournament tennis and find this example not only unconvincing, it is simply inaccurate in some respects. It bears little resemblance to my own experience and that of those with whom I play. First, based on Keating's model, it would be impossible for me to know whether I am a player or an athlete in the context of my tennis playing. I should say I am both, since I compete for victory, but also find great fun in the activity and recognize my opponent as a partner of sorts. Moreover, the conventions of tennis render Keating's example misleading and of little value in helping us to understand sportsmanship. If one is not certain that a ball is out, one plays it. Only if one is sure the ball is out is it to be called out. If a call is made but disagreement arises, a let is called and the point is replayed. Giving the benefit of the doubt to the opponent isn't generosity here; it is simply recognizing the relevant conventions. Actually, Keating's description of the so-called "athlete" sounds suspiciously like an example of bad sportsmanship, since such a person's zeal in the pursuit of victory ignores the unwritten rules of playing without officials and tends to destroy the spirit of play. A more playful spirit would mediate against a zealousness that fuels inappropriate conduct and ignoring the rules.

The other main problem with Keating's view of sportsmanship is his account of the nature of play and its relationship to sport. Such a topic demands an extended treatment, and I have attempted to do this in the previous chapters [of *Sport, Play, and Ethical Reflection*]. Briefly, the most accurate and inclusive phenomenological accounts of experience in sport are those that focus on the nature of play and which show, either explicitly or implicitly, that sport is a formal, competitive variety of human play. I agree with Kenneth Schmitz when he says that "sport is primarily an extension of play, and that it rests upon and derives its central values from play."[17] Huizinga's classic account of play stresses that it is an activity freely engaged in when someone metaphorically "steps out" of ordinary life and becomes absorbed in an alternative world of play, with its own order and meaning, constituted by its own rules, experiential rhythms, traditions, tensions, and illusory quality. He also stresses the element of fun as essential. He sums up his account in the following passage:

> Summing up the formal characteristics of play we might call it a free activity standing quite consciously "ordinary" life as being "not serious," but at the same time absorbing the player intensely and utterly. It is an activity connected with no material interest, and no profit can be gained by it. It proceeds within its own proper boundaries of time and space according to fixed rules and in an orderly manner.[18]

Schmitz strengthens the analysis of play by distinguishing four types: frolic, make-believe, sporting skills, and games.[19] The movement from frolic to sport is a continuum from less formal, spontaneous, animal-like behavior to more formal activities guided by rules, in which knowledge, preparation, and understanding are called for. In all forms, Schmitz, like Huizinga, stresses the movement from the ordinary to the world of play by a free decision to play. "Such a constitutive decision cannot be compelled and is essentially free. Through it arises the suspension of the ordinary concerns of the everyday world."[20] This decision constitutes an act of transcendence beyond the natural world, in which a new totality is opened and experienced with a sense of exhilaration and celebration. Schmitz compares the transcendence of play with religion and art. Also akin to Huizinga's account, Schmitz stresses, especially for the more formal varieties of play, the new order of the world of play with its new forms of space, time, and behavior. It is a "transnatural, fragile, limited perfection... delivering its own values in and for itself, the freedom and joy of play."[21] Finally, it is a "distinctive mode of being. It is a way of taking up the world of being, a manner of being present in the world... whose existential presence is a careless joyful freedom."[22]

The problem for the play-theorist of sport is how to connect such a striking description of play with sport. Many think, as Keating seems to, that this account necessarily excludes essential elements of sport, including the striving for excellence and good performance and contesting for victory. But the strength of the play theory of sport is the way in which it can provide both a rich phenomenological account of the experience of play within sports and an explanation of the prominence and appropriate value of good performance and victory. No one would deny that the pursuit of victory is essential in sport; after all, a contest is not mere frolic. But why *do* so many engage in sport? Why do we create our games and begin and continue to play them? The critics of sport give us an important perspective here when they wonder why so many people become obsessed with things like hitting a ball with a wooden club, throwing a ball into a hoop, or smashing a little ball around expansive fairways. They can understand why children, lacking maturity and experience, could enjoy the exuberance of such activities. But grown people? Compared with suffering, friendship, and possible catastrophes because of deep-rooted human conflicts, playing games and treating them with utmost seriousness seems silly. Bernard Suits brings this out well in attempting to define game playing:

> It is generally acknowledged that games are in some sense essentially nonserious. We must therefore ask in what sense games are, and in what sense they are not, serious. What is believed when it is believed that games are not serious? Not, certainly, that the players of games always take a very light-hearted view of what they are doing. A bridge player who played his cards randomly might justly be accused of failing to play the game at all just because of his failure to take it seriously. It is much more likely that the belief that games are not serious means what the proposal under consideration implies: that there is always something in life more important than playing the game, or that a game is the kind of thing that a player could always have reason to stop playing.[23]

The important insight here is that the nonseriousness at the heart of play is based on the recognition that there are more important values in life than the value of improving sporting skills and winning games. A correct and wise attitude concerning sport would place these values in an appropriate hierarchy. Suits goes on to deny such nonseriousness as the essence of game playing on the grounds that one could take a game so seriously as to consider it supremely important, taking over one's whole life and forcing one to avoid other duties. But his point is psychological, not moral. Undoubtedly someone *could* have such an attitude, but he ought not. Suits sees this clearly. "Supreme dedication to a game... may be repugnant to nearly everyone's moral sense. That may be granted, indeed insisted upon, since our loathing is excited by the very fact that it is a game which has usurped the place of ends we regard as so much more worthy of pursuit."[24] Suits concludes his attempt to define game playing by arguing that when we play a game we accept the arbitrary way in which means are used to achieve certain ends—for example, in golf our goal is not just to put the ball in the hole but to do it in an extraordinarily limited way—because we simply want to make the activity possible.[25] Evidently, such activity, without external practical ends, must be intrinsically satisfying.[26]

This analysis leads us to a point where we can see the paradoxical attitudinal complexity of the player-athlete. We might distinguish between internal and external seriousness. The activity of playful competition calls for pursuit of victory. As Suits suggested, if someone isn't serious in this sense he might be accused of not playing the game at all. On the other hand, there is an external perspective from which the internal seriousness of competition is mediated by an awareness that the activity is a form of play, infused with its own values and qualified by the values of life outside the play world. The activity engaged in is both competition and play, serious and nonserious. This is the understanding of the activity that gives rise to a more adequate understanding of sportsmanship. The spirit of play may be absent within sport, but it ought not to be if, as has been argued, sport is intimately and in some sense originally related to the playful activity of game playing. Once again, Schmitz offers helpful comments:

> Sport can be carried out without the spirit of play. Nevertheless, in the life of individuals and in the history of the race, sport emerges from play as from an original and founding posture. Sport is free, self-conscious, tested play which moves in a transnatural dimension of human life, built upon a certain basis of leisure.... There is certainly a return to seriousness in the discipline of formal sport. There is training, performance and competition. But the objectives of sport and its founding decision lie within play and cause sport to share in certain of its features—the sense of immediacy, exhilaration, rule-directed behavior, and the indeterminancy of a specified outcome.[27]

Let us turn now to a positive account of the virtue of sportsmanship.

In my view, instead of a rigid and precise distinction between play and athletics, we must be content with a fuzzy picture of the fusion of these activities, a picture in which edges are blurred and paradox is retained. Keating's view embraces tidiness at the cost of truth. Still, we want to ask, What is the essence of sportsmanship? I tend to think that the question is misleading and the phenomenon is dispersed in our experience in innumerable particular instances. We ought to be hesitant about attributing to this notion an abstract unity that is not found in experience. Wittgenstein's admonition that we ought to be suspicious of such talk and appeal to particular cases is well taken here, as always. However, if we view sport as an extension of human play, competitive play, we can offer an understanding of the virtue of sportsmanship that will be somewhat more satisfying intellectually, although it will not always generate easily purchased moral recommendations. This shouldn't surprise us.

Keating is right to see that we must understand sportsmanship as conduct arising from our attitudes, and he is correct in attempting to describe the attitudes appropriate to sport. He is simply incorrect about the attitudes. If sport is understood as an extension of play, then the key to sportsmanship is the spirit of play. Within the arena of competition the spirit of play should be retained. It would be helpful to think of this in Aristotelian terms. Recall Aristotle's description of virtue:

> By virtue I mean virtue of character; for this pursues the mean because it is concerned with feelings and actions, and these admit of excess, deficiency and an intermediate condition. We can be afraid, e.g., or be confident, or have appetites, or get angry, or feel pity, in general have pleasure or pain, both too much and too little, and in both ways not well; but having these feelings at the right times, about the right things, toward the right people, for the right end, and in the right way, is the intermediate and best condition, and this is proper to virtue. Similarly, actions also admit of excess, deficiency and the intermediate condition.[28]

In fact, Aristotle's description of the virtuous person reinforces my previous attempt to ascribe a certain psychological complexity to the player-athlete. The courageous or brave person, according to Aristotle, is neither excessively fearful, else he would be a coward, or excessively confident, else he would be foolhardy and rash.[29] He feels appropriately fearful, which moderates his confidence, and he feels appropriately confident, which moderates his fear. His virtuous acts are expressions of such moderation and a result of experience and habit. Likewise, the good sport feels the joy and exuberance of free, playful activity set apart from the world, and he feels the intensity of striving to perform well and achieve victory in the context of playing fairly according to the rules and traditions of his sport. Sportsmanship is a mean between excessive seriousness, which misunderstands the importance of the spirit of play, and an excessive sense of playfulness, which might be called frivolity and which misunderstands the importance of victory and achievement when play is competitive. The good sport is both serious and nonserious.

Many, if not most, examples of bad sportsmanship arise from an excessive seriousness that negates the spirit of play because of an exaggerated emphasis on the value of victory. Schmitz has a superb comment on such exaggeration:

> The policy of winning at all costs is the surest way of snuffing out the spirit of play in sport. The fallout of such a policy is the dreary succession of firings in college and professional sport. Such an emphasis on victory detaches the last moment from the whole game and fixes the outcome apart from its proper context. It reduces the appreciation of the performance, threatens the proper disposition toward the rules and turns the contest into a naked power struggle. The upshot is the brutalization of the sport. And so, the sport which issued from the play-decision, promising freedom and exhilaration, ends dismally in lessening the humanity of players and spectators.[30]

Such exaggeration of victory goes hand in hand with the way we view our relationship to our opponents. The spirit of play moderates, not negates, the intensity with which we pursue victory and introduces a spirit of friendship and cooperation in what would otherwise be a "naked power struggle."[31] Thus, the good sport doesn't cheat, attempt to hurt the opponent, or taunt another. A certain lightness of spirit prohibits uncivil displays of temper, constant complaints to officials, and the like. Throughout the activity, self-control and kinship with others are necessary to maximize the possible values of the play world.

What does all this mean in more particular instances and over a wider range of examples? Once again Aristotle is helpful. First he insists that it would be misguided to expect an extreme degree of exactness, clarity, or precision in our present moral inquiry. We should expect a degree of precision appropriate to the inquiry, and in ethical theory, "it will be satisfactory if we can indicate the truth roughly and in outline."[32] In addition, when speaking of moral virtue we seek the mean "relative to us." Virtue is not alike to all people in all situations. Terrence

Irwin comments:

> Aristotle warns against any misleading suggestion that his appeal to a mean
> is intended to offer a precise, quantitative test for virtuous action that we can
> readily apply to particular cases—as though, e.g., we could decide that there
> is a proper, moderate degree of anger to be displayed in all conditions, or in
> all conditions of a certain precisely described type. The point of the doctrine,
> and of Aristotle's insistence of the 'intermediate relative to us,' is that no such
> precise quantitative test can be found.[33]

To see the virtue of sportsmanship as a mean between extremes is not to be
given a precise formula for interpreting whether acts are sportsmanlike, but to
be given an explanatory and experiential context within which we can learn
and teach how we ought to conduct ourselves in sports. From the standpoint
of teaching and moral education, an appeal to exemplars of this virtue will
always be useful, for they show us what it means to be playful and cooperative
in our sport experience. I cannot see that the moral philosopher is required to
do more.

NOTES

1. There is some dispute whether we should say that the cheating coach's team won.
   Bernard Suits, in "What Is a Game?" in *Sport and the Body*, ed. Gerber and Morgan,
   12-13, argues that in a strict or logical sense one cannot win by cheating. The game is
   defined by its rules, so one cannot win the game by breaking the rules, since, in that
   case, one would not be playing the game at all. On the other hand, Craig K. Lehman,
   in "Can Cheaters Play the Game?" *Journal of the Philosophy of Sport* 7 (1981), 41-46,
   argues that the conventions of sport may allow some breaking of the rules (e.g., Gaylord
   Perry throwing a spitball or an offensive lineman holding) without thinking that the
   violator has ceased to play the game because of such nonobedience. I am sympathetic
   to Lehman's arguments, but the so-called "incompatibility thesis" is not crucial to my
   arguments in this chapter. I simply start with a paradigm example of unsportsmanlike
   behavior, and the cheating coach is a good place to start since such behavior violates
   the rules of basketball and the unwritten conventions of proper conduct in the sport.
2. Here I am using the term "bad sport" to describe the cheater as someone who displays
   poor sportsmanship. In *The Grasshopper: Games, Life and Utopia* (Toronto: U of Toronto
   P, 1978), chapter 4, Bernard Suits distinguishes the trifler, the cheater, and the spoilsport.

What I mean by "bad sport" is not what Suits means by "spoilsport." In the broad sense in which I am using the notion, the trifler, cheater, and spoilsport are all bad sports.

3. James Keating, "Sportsmanship as a Moral Category," *Ethics* 75 (Oct. 1964): 25-35. Keating's views are extensively discussed in *The Philosophy of Sport*, ed. Osterhoudt. His views are noted by Carolyn Thomas in *Sport in a Philosophic Context* (Philadelphia: Lea and Febiger, 1983), and by Warren Fraleigh in *Right Actions in Sport: Ethics for Contestants* (Champaign, IL: Human Kinetics, 1984). The paper is anthologized in *Sport and the Body*, ed. Gerber and Morgan; in *Philosophic Inquiry in Sport*, ed. Morgan and Meier; and in *Ethics in Sport*, ed. Morgan, Meier, and Schneider.

4. James Keating, *Competition and Playful Activities* (Washington, DC: UP of America, 1978).

5. Ibid., 39-42.

6. Ibid., 43.

7. Ibid., 47.

8. Ibid., 43-44.

9. See *The Object of Morality* (London: Methuen, 1971), chapter 2. Warnock's comments attempt to describe generally "the human predicament" and the way in which morality serves to better the human predicament by countervailing "limited sympathies."

10. Keating, "Sportsmanship as a Moral Category," 52.

11. Ibid., 43.

12. See Suits, "What Is a Game?"

13. Keating, "Sportsmanship as a Moral Category," 44.

14. Richard Taylor, *Metaphysics*, 3rd ed. (Englewood Cliffs, NJ: Prentice-Hall, 1983), 106.

15. Ibid., 107.

16. Keating, "Sportsmanship as a Moral Category," 50.

17. Schmitz, "Sport and Play," 22.

18. Huizinga, *Homo Ludens*, 13.

19. Schmitz, "Sport and Play," 23.

20. Ibid., 24-25.

21. Ibid., 26.

22. Ibid.

23. Suits, "What Is a Game?" 14.

24. Ibid., 15.

25. Ibid., 17.

26. The conclusion concerning intrinsic satisfaction is mine, not necessarily Suits's. I leave open the question whether his account of "lusory attitude" would agree or disagree with this conclusion. See his discussion in *The Grasshopper*, 38-40 and 144-46. His

comments on page 40 seem close to the conclusion I offer, but his later comments on professional game-playing lead elsewhere.

27. Schmitz, "Sport and Play," 27.

28. Aristotle, *Nicomachean Ethics*, trans. Terence Irwin (Indianapolis: Hackett, 1985), 1106b.

29. Ibid., 1107.

30. Schmitz, "Sport and Play," 27-28.

31. Drew Hyland's "Competition and Friendship," in *Sport and the Body*, ed. Gerber and Morgan, 133-39, offers an excellent analysis of how competition always involves the risk of degenerating into an alienating experience, but it need not. Competitive play can be a mode of friendship. This essay also appears in *Philosophic Inquiry in Sport*, ed. Morgan and Meier, 231-39.

32. Aristotle, *Nicomachean Ethics*, 1094b.

33. These comments are from Irwin's translator's notes, 313.

QUESTIONS

1. Is Howe's weak/strong gamesmanship distinction plausible? Is it a difference of *kind* or a difference of *degree*, and does this matter?

2. Do you agree with the contention that sportsmanship implies (weak) gamesmanship? Are there certain cases of weak gamesmanship that, if effective, tarnish one's victory?

3. Many philosophers of sport swim against the current in using the gendered 'games*man*ship' and 'sports*man*ship.' Is this a problem, or merely a lack of elegant neutral substitute terms?

4. What advantages are there to Keating's dichotomy between sport and athletics? Should we defend the dichotomy from Feezell's critique, and if so, how?

5. Is sportsmanship a virtue, as Feezell proposes? Are there other ways, either complementary or competing, of understanding sportsmanship?

6. Do questions of what sport essentially is and what it ideally ought to be ultimately overlap? How so, or why not?

FURTHER READING

Arnold, Peter J. (1983): "Three Approaches Toward an Understanding of Sportsmanship," *Journal of the Philosophy of Sport* 10, pp. 61-70.

Butcher, Robert and Angela Schneider (1998): "Fair Play as Respect for the Game," *Journal of the Philosophy of Sport* 25 (1), pp. 1-22.

Dixon, Nicholas (1992): "On Sportsmanship and 'Running up the Score,'" *Journal of the Philosophy of Sport* 19, pp. 1-13.

Hyland, Drew (1978): "Competition and Friendship," *Journal of the Philosophy of Sport* 5, pp. 27-38.

Keating, James W. (1964): "Sportsmanship as a Moral Category," *Ethics* 75, pp. 25-35.

Simon, Robert L. (2010): *Fair Play: The Ethics of Sport* (3rd edition) (Boulder, CO: Westview).

FURTHER INQUIRY

Permissible gamesmanship seems compatible not only with sportsmanship and the end of sport as a test of the whole person but also with the means of participating itself: hard sprints or brush back pitches are in this sense similar to strenuous play generally and other opponent-unsettling moves like dekes. Such gamesmanship however is less clearly gamesmanship (as a dispensable tactic) than an essential part of the game. How should we interpret gamesmanship that is neither strong nor weak—perhaps "medium" gamesmanship—cases of razzing as much as mild trash or smack talk? Perhaps an opponent's poor play is a less objectionable target for razzing than, say, their private life—or do such manoeuvers always edge too close to the unsporting? Also, should we conscientiously seek gender-neutral alternatives to 'gamesmanship,' 'sportsmanship,' and so on? Should we prefer the inelegant 'sportspersonship,' or opt instead for more creative attempts, 'playership,' 'sportitude': that sort of thing? If fair play really is more basic, perhaps it is simply what we mean by sportsmanship in more competitive settings, a variety, not an alternative. As a virtue in life, sportsmanship involves both Aristotelian balance and stoic serenity. As a virtue in play, in *how* one plays the game, sportsmanship has an aesthetic as well as moral dimension, one well worth exploring, and which might help bring closer, if only in our minds, what sport really is and what it really ought to be.

PERMISSION ACKNOWLEDGMENTS

Peter J. Arnold. "Sport, the Aesthetic and Art: Further Thoughts." *British Journal of Educational Studies* 38 (2), 1990; pp. 160-79. Reprinted by permission of the publisher (Taylor & Francis Ltd, http://www.tandf.co.uk/journals).

David Best. "The Aesthetic in Sport." *Philosophy and Human Movement*, copyright © Allen & Unwin 1978 (Unwin Hyman 1979). Reprinted by permission of Taylor & Francis Books UK.

W.M. Brown. "Paternalism, Drugs, and the Nature of Sports." *Journal of the Philosophy of Sport* 11 (1), 1984; pp. 14-22. Reprinted by permission of the publisher (Taylor & Francis Ltd, http://www.tandf.co.uk/journals).

Simon Eassom. "Playing Games With Prisoners' Dilemmas." *Journal of the Philosophy of Sport* 22 (1), 1995; pp. 26-31; 36-47. Reprinted by permission of the publisher (Taylor & Francis Ltd, http://www.tandf.co.uk/journals).

Randolph M. Feezell. "Sportsmanship." *Journal of the Philosophy of Sport* 13 (1), 1986; pp. 1-13. Reprinted by permission of the publisher (Taylor & Francis Ltd, http://www.tandf.co.uk/journals).

Dennis Hemphill. "Cybersport." *Journal of the Philosophy of Sport* 32 (2), 2005; pp. 195-207. Reprinted by permission of the publisher (Taylor & Francis Ltd, http://www.tandf.co.uk/journals).

Jason Holt and Laurence E. Holt. "The 'Ideal' Swing, the 'Ideal' Body: Myths of Optimization." *Golf and Philosophy: Lessons from the Links*, edited by A. Wible. Lexington, KY: University Press of Kentucky, 2010; pp. 209-20. Reprinted with the permission of the University Press of Kentucky via Copyright Clearance Center.

Leslie A. Howe. "Gamesmanship." *Journal of the Philosophy of Sport* 31 (2), 2004; pp. 212-25. Reprinted by permission of the publisher (Taylor & Francis Ltd, http://www.tandf.co.uk/journals).

Johan Huizinga. "The Nature and Significance of Play." *Homo Ludens: A Study of the Play-Element in Culture.* Copyright © 1950 by Roy Publishers. Reprinted in North America by permission of Beacon Press, Boston.

Craig K. Lehman. "Can Cheaters Play the Game?" *Journal of the Philosophy of Sport* 8 (1), 1981; pp. 41-46. Reprinted by permission of the publisher (Taylor & Francis Ltd, http://www.tandf.co.uk/journals).

John W. Loy, Jr. "The Nature of Sport: A Definitional Effort." *Quest* 10 (1), May 1968; pp. 1-15. Copyright © 1968, John W. Loy, Jr. Reproduced by permission of Taylor & Francis Group, LLC (http://www.tandfonline.com).

Klaus V. Meier. "Triad Trickery: Playing With Sports and Games." *Journal of the Philosophy of Sport* 15 (1), 1988; pp. 11-30. Reprinted by permission of the publisher (Taylor & Francis Ltd, http://www.tandf.co.uk/journals).

Robert L. Simon. "Good Competition and Drug-Enhanced Performance." *Journal of the Philosophy of Sport* 11 (1), 1984; pp. 6-13. Reprinted by permission of the publisher (Taylor & Francis Ltd, http://www.tandf.co.uk/journals).

Margaret Steel. "What We Know When We Know a Game." *Journal of the Philosophy of Sport* 4, 1977; pp. 96-103. Reprinted by permission of the publisher (Taylor & Francis Ltd, http://www.tandf.co.uk/journals).

Bernard Suits. "The Elements of Sport." *The Philosophy of Sport: A Collection of Essays*, edited by R.G. Osterhoudt. Springfield, IL: Charles C. Thomas, 1973. Reprinted with the permission of Cheryl Ballantyne.

Iris Marion Young. "Throwing Like a Girl: A Phenomenology of Feminine Body Comportment, Motility, and Spatiality." *Human Studies* 3 (1), 1980: pp. 137-56. Reprinted with kind permission from Springer Science and Business Media.

INDEX

Adderall, 228
the aesthetic, 8, 161
  distinction between means and end is
    inapplicable, 158
  non-functional or non-purposive
    concept, 157-59
  wider than notion of art, 180
the aesthetic/artistic distinction, 73, 155,
  169-73
the aesthetic and art, 179-83
aesthetic appreciation of purposive sports,
  162-64
aesthetic approach to establish sport as
  art, 188
aesthetic attitude, 167, 180-81
aesthetic biases in golf, 100-01
aesthetic content, 155-57
aesthetic criteria, 154, 166, 172, 182
aesthetic experience, 181, 183
aesthetic experience in sport, 166
aesthetic feelings, 166-68
aesthetic objects, 181
aesthetic perception, 180
aesthetic sports, 36, 100, 110. *See also*
  performative sports
  aesthetic criteria for scoring, 154, 172
  aim, 160, 162, 169
  as art, 171-72, 176-77, 179
  means and ends in, 161-62, 169, 184, 186
  scope for art work to emerge, 193
  as vignette art forms, 179
'aesthetic' (usage), 156
aesthetics, 11-12, 153
AFL Live: Premiership Edition, 119
alcohol, 204, 215
Ali, Muhammad, 165
altruism, 247-49, 251
amateur sports in America
  government of, 45

ambiguous transcendence, 134-35, 137
American College of Sports Medicine,
  203
American wrestling, 47
amphetamines, 204-05
analogous approach to establish sport as
  art, 188
Anthony, W.J., 172
anthropology, 16
applied ethics/social ethics connection,
  281
architecture, 191-92
Aristotelian *animal ridens*, 7
Aristotle, 29-30, 293-94
  description of virtue, 292
Arnold, Peter J., 154
art, 174, 182, 186, 191
  abstract, 192
  the aesthetic and, 159
  comment on life issues, 171-72, 177,
    183, 190-92
  definitions, 181-82
  ends and means cannot be
    independently specified, 159, 187
  work of art is *sui generis*, 182, 186
art forms, 73, 173
art objects, 181, 187
'art' (usage), 177
artificiality, concept of, 227
the artistic, 169. *See also* the aesthetic/
  artistic distinction
assurance problem, 253
athletic games, 63, 74
athletic performances and athletic games
  (Suits's distinction), 74
athletic teams, 45, 49-50
athleticized golfer, 94, 97-100
athletics, 283. *See also* sports
  competition in, 12, 284

fairness or fair play, 284
  generosity and magnanimity misplaced
    in, 284
augmented reality computer games, 114-15
Australian Rules Football (AFL), 119
auto-racing computer games, 117
auxiliary personnel (managers, physicians,
  trainers), 49
auxiliary rules, 36, 64, 201
averaging model of the golf swing, 94-97,
  100-01
Axelrod, Robert, 248-49

bad sport, 282
Bale, J., 110
Bannister, Roger, 174
Barber, Miller, 96
baseball, 73, 102, 184, 234-35
basketball, 184, 285
Beardsley, Aubrey, 181
Beardsley, Monroe C., 181
beatification, 15
Beauvoir, Simone de, 128-31
Best, David, 154, 183
Best's view that sport is not art, 179
  Arnold's account of, 190-92
bicycle ergometers, 116
billiards, 102
biomechanics, 95
blood doping, 204-05, 227
Blood Wedding, 194
bodily self-image, 131
body as first locus of intentionality, 135
Body Experience in Fantasy and Behaviour
  (Fisher), 146n13
body-machine model of athletic
  excellence, 271
Bolero (Ravel), 195
borderline cases (rule violation), 234
Borzov, Valeriy, 156
bowling, 102
Boxill, J.M., 188, 190
boxing, 69
Boyle, Robert H., 49
brain, 108
Brandt, Richard, *A Theory of the Good and
  Right*, 255n15
breast, 128
Breivik, Gunnar, 239, 241, 243, 253
Brett, George, 265
bridge, 28, 58, 60, 113

Brown, W.M., 201, 211
"brush-back pitch," 266
Butcher, Robert B., 239, 241, 243-46, 252
Buytendijk, F.J.J., *Woman: A
  Contemporary View*, 145n2

Caddy Shack, 110
caffeine, 204, 215, 228
Caillois, Roger, 38, 40, 46
card and board games
  combination of strategy and chance, 42
Carlisle, R., 172
Carmen (Bizet), 194
carnival, 14
Case of the Dedicated Driver, 31
categorical imperative, 236
ceremonial games, 13
ceremony, 16
chance, 27, 35, 37, 40, 42, 112, 118
cheater, 12, 47, 249, 251, 282
cheating, 66, 201, 219, 229. *See also*
  logical-incompatibility thesis;
    performance-enhancing drugs
  moral arguments about, 235, 251
  as unethical and/or unsportsmanlike, 235
chess, 28, 42, 58, 60, 112-13
childhood obesity, 110
children and youth in sports
  paternalistic control of drug use, 216-
    17, 220
  restrictions on what young athletes may
    do, 217-18
"child's play," 11
child's world, imagination in, 15
Chung, Kyung-Wha, 161
Clarke, Darren, 99
climbing, 160
coaching, 29, 89-90
  best coaches not always good players, 89
  correcting unfair, dishonest, or
    unsportsmanlike actions, 219
  facilitating student's process of
    discovery, 90
  instilling values of fairness and honesty,
    220
cocaine, 215
coercion, 206-07
"A Cognitive-Developmental Analysis of
  Children's Sex-Role Concepts and
  Attitudes," 148n21

cognitive enhancers, 228
coin flip, 43
collective action problems, 241, 243
collegiate athletic teams, 45, 50
collegiate football, 40
Comaneci, Nadia, 162
comic, 7-8
comparative religion, 16
competence (vs. acting voluntarily), 216.
   See also coercion
competition, 12, 41-42, 161
   contrasting the competitive with the
      aesthetic, 161
   the good of, 268-73
   involves winners and losers, 272
   moral restraints on, 284
   opportunity for self-revelation, 271
   playful competition, 38, 46
   prohibition of performance-enhancing
      drugs, 209
   spirit of play retained, 283, 292
competitive music festivals, 161
competitive pressures to use performance-
   enhancing drugs, 207-09. *See also*
   cheating
competitive sport, 63, 284. *See also* sports
   comparable strength, ability in
      opponents, 272
   establish commonly accepted social
      practice, 252
   pursuit of excellence, 203, 209-10, 272
   respect for opponents as persons, 210, 212
   test of persons, 210, 212
   test of the whole athlete, 272
Composition VII (Mondrian), 191
computer games, 107, 110, 116
   augmented reality, 114-15
   auto-racing, 117
   game player/game character merge in
      the lived experience, 120
   head-up displays, 115
   sport simulations, 107, 114
   tactile or haptic user interfaces, 115
   using bodies as an interface, 118
   in which players are positioned as first-
      person agents, 116
computer games as sport, 114-18, 120-21
   arguments against, 109-11
   supporting arguments, 111-14
computer games as virtual, 111
computerized downhill ski racing, 117

constitutive rules, 22-23, 25, 36, 64, 66,
   69, 201
constrained maximizer, 246
contemplation, 167-68
context in which movement occurs, 166-67
contractarian views of social justice, 247
cooperation, 246-47
cooperative solution to iterated prisoners'
   dilemmas, 249
cooperativeness, 273
coordination problem, 252-53
Cordner, C.D., 188, 191
costume, 194-95. *See also* dressing up
courage, 12, 210, 212, 283, 292
Cranston, Toller, 176-77, 188-89
crap games, 42
craze, 28-29, 62
cricket, 61, 102
criticism (sport pundits), 29
croquet, 102
cross-training, 97-98, 102
"cult of conditioning," 99
curling, 61
Curry, John, 176-77, 188-89
cybersport, 114, 120-22. *See also* computer
   games

Daly, John, 99, 101
dance, 103, 166, 169
dance as art, 172, 186
dance as art object, 187
darts, 102
data gloves, 116
Dean, Christopher, 194
"death of play" in contemporary sport, 75
defeat, acceptance of, 272-73. *See also* failure
degradation of Sport, 253
Delattre, Edward, "Some Reflections on
   Success and Failure in Competitive
   Athletics," 232-33
Deleuze, G., 121
Descartes' mind/body dualism, 107
Dewey, J., 194
Dickie, G., 189-90
"Differential Sex Role Socialization
   toward Amplitude Appropriation,"
   147n19
"disciplinary matrix," 84
display, 46-48
diving, 63, 100, 103, 160-62, 167, 171, 185
   aesthetic criteria, 172

diving competitions, 63
  as game, 67, 70
  rules, 65, 67
  unnecessary obstacles, 68
doping, 224, 270. *See also* performance-enhancing drugs
doping dilemma (version of prisoners' dilemma), 239, 241, 243-45, 252
drama, 7, 15, 192
Dresher, Levin, 253n2
dressing up, 14, 47
dribbling or heading the ball in soccer, 85
drug use. *See also* performance-enhancing drugs
  effectiveness of, 215
  paternalistic control of, 215, 220, 225
drug use in sports by children and young people
  paternalistic control, 216-17, 220
drugs and tests of ability, 210-11
Duquin, Mary E., 147n19
Dworkin, Gerald, 216
Dwyer, Fred, 207

Eassom, Simon, 230
educational sphere of sports, 48, 219
"Effect of Guided Practice on Overhand Throw Ball Velocities on Kindergarten Children," 145n2
electronically extended athletes in digitally represented sporting world, 114
elements of game, 19-25
  goal, 20-21
elements of sport, 19
"The Elements of Sport" (Suits), 59
eligibility rules, 201
elite players (golf), 96, 98
  ideal swing and, 95-96
Els, Ernie, 100
embodiment, 107-08, 120
The Emergence of Norms (Ullmann-Margalit), 243, 251
EMFi (Electro Mechanical Film) sensors, 118
English, J., 110
epistemology, 81, 83
Erasmus, *Laus Stultitiae*, 8
Erikson, Erik, 139
"Estimated versus Actual Physical Strength in Three Ethnic Groups" (Gross), 146n11
event rules, 67

evolutionary ethics, 248, 251
excellence, 57, 93, 101, 175, 272, 284-85, 290
  in art, 182
  body-machine model, 271
  gamesmanship and, 263, 268
  mutual quest for, 201, 209-10, 227, 252, 274
  use of drugs and, 203, 205, 224
exemplar, 84-85, 89
  learning a physical skill, 84-88
  learning science, 84, 90
  standard scientific experiment or problem, 84
existential phenomenology, 129
The Expanding Circle (Singer), 251
extrinsic rewards, 74

failure, 263. *See also* defeat, acceptance of
fair play, 261, 283
fairness, 12, 221, 224
  gamesmanship and, 264-67
fan, the, 52. *See also* spectator sports
feelings as criteria of aesthetic quality, 166-68
Feezell, Randolph M., 262
Feinberg, Joel, 216
females as "field-dependent," 141
feminine being-in-the-world, 131
feminine bodily existence, 130, 142
  ambiguous transcendence, 134-35, 137
  body frequently is both subject and object, 137
  discontinuous unity with surroundings, 134, 137
  experiences itself as *positioned* in space, 140
  inhibited intentionality, 136
  overlaid with immanence, 135
  as rooted in place, 141
  self-referred, 138, 140
  spaces as enclosed or confining, 139
  underuses real capacity, 136
feminine body comportment and movement, 131-39, 141-43
  fear of getting hurt, 133, 142
  growing up as a girl and, 143
  timidity, immobility, and uncertainty, 139
"feminine essence," 128-29
feminine spatiality, 139-40
feminist attitude, 128
feminist theory, 129

festival and ritual, sphere of, 10
figure skating, 100, 103, 160-62, 171, 184
  aesthetic criteria, 172
  as art form, 176-77
  event rules, 67
  judged on artistic impression as well as
    technical merit, 194
  performative in nature, 193
  as vignette art, 193
"A Fine Forehand" (Ziff), 83
fine motor activities, 114
fine-motor-skill sports (archery), 110
Fischer, Bobby, 29
Fisher, Seymour, *Body Experience in
  Fantasy and Behaviour*, 146n13
fitness, 271
Fleming, Peggy, 189
Flood, Merril, 253n2
Fogelin, Robert, 112
following, 25-26
  stability of, 26, 29
  wide following, 28-29, 61
folly, 8
football, 40, 160-61, 176, 183, 234
  "more than a game" claim, 111
  offside rules, 66
  technological elements, 46
football games, 63
football teams, clandestine action, 47
football teams, organization of, 44
fouls (professional fouls), 229, 264
free style skating, 193, 195
freedom, 9, 38. *See also* liberty (individual
  liberty)
Freedom and Reason (Hare), 255n15
freedom for athletes to experiment with
  drugs, 211
Friessen, J., 186
Frobenius, Leo, 16
frolic, 289
Fugard, Athol, 173
"fun" (current usage), 5
fun of playing, 4-5
Furyk, Jim, 96, 100

game as unique event, 43
game occurrences, 35, 51
game playing
  Suits's definition, 56-57, 67, 74, 112, 290-91
game theory, 246
GameBike, 117-18, 120

games, 58, 289
  athletic (*See* athletic games)
  ceremonial, 13
  competition, 41
  creative endeavours, 88, 90. *See also*
    exemplar
  encountered at pretheoretical stage of
    child's life, 250
  equality between opposing sides in, 39, 272
  essentially different from ordinary
    activities of life, 24, 26
  establish commonly accepted social
    practice, 252
  "it's only a game," 111
  knowledge acquired by demonstration,
    89-90
  less than the real thing, 111
  limitations on means the players may
    employ, 25, 31-32, 41, 67-68, 290-91
  means in, 21
  new skills developed, 26, 48
  playful, 41
  purpose, 236-37
  rational choice games, 244
  as refereed events (Suits's view), 64
  rules, 1, 12, 39, 44, 69, 88, 236, 251,
    266
  seriousness/unseriousness of, 290
  subordinate to other ends, 29
  transmission of skills and knowledge, 48
  uncertain outcome of, 38-39
Games and Decisions (Luce and Raiffa),
  253n2
games and play
  associated with childhood, 111
games and sports, 25-29
  criteria for determining the winner, 39-40
games denominated as sports
  requirements, 25-29
games of chance, 27, 42
games of skill, 25-27
games of strategy, 42
gamesmanship, 261, 264
  both moral and athletic failing, 276
  diminishes both parties, 274-75
  disvalue of, 271
  does not violate the rules of the game, 266
  failure belongs to the target, 266
  implies cowardice, 273
  instrumental value of, 274
  psyching out the opponent, 265

refusal to accept defeat, 272-73
relies on rules in order to exist, 264
strategy for winning regardless of
   athletic excellence, 263
subversion of excellence in favour of
   winning, 263, 268
test of psychological strength and
   preparedness, 266
gamesmanship and fairness, 264-67
gamesmanship and selfhood, 273-76
Gauthier, David, 245-47, 252
   Morals by Agreement, 251
general fitness conditioning, 97
generosity, 273
generosity and magnanimity, 284
gestalt, 86, 89
Gewirth, Alan, *Reason and Morality*, 255n15
Gloucester in *King Lear*, 173-74, 191
Goffman, Erving, 48
golf, 40, 93-94, 290-91
   athleticized golfer, 94, 97-100
   head-up displays, 115
   undue athleticization, 101-02
   walking regimen for, 98
   weight-training for, 98
golf as a sport (question), 94, 101-02
golf swing
   "deviant" swings, 96
   multiple realizability, 102
good sport, 273, 282, 293. *See also*
   sportsmanship
   extension of being a good person, 282
Goodman, Paul, 31
Gopal, Ram, 171
Gore, Jason, 99
government of games and sports, 45
Grand Prix automobile racing, 61
The Grasshopper (Suits), 56, 59, 65, 71
Graves, H., 55
"Green Table" (Jooss), 183
Gross, A.M., "Estimated versus Actual
   Physical Strength in Three Ethnic
   Groups," 146n11
gross motor activities, 114
gross physical skill, 102
Guattari, F., 121
Guernica (Picasso), 173, 191
guitar duels, 102
gymnastics, 63, 100, 103, 160, 167, 169,
   171, 184
   as game, 67, 70

limiting characteristics, 68
Modern Educational Gymnastics, 160
Olympic gymnastics, 161-62, 172, 184
partially aesthetic activity, 187
rules, 65-67
Seoul Olympic Games, 70
technical and aesthetic evaluations, 185

Hagen, Walter, 96
Hamilton, W.D., 248
handball, 184
hang-gliding, 224
hard paternalism, 216-17, 224
Hardin, Garrett, 240
Hare, R.M., *Freedom and Reason*, 255n15
harm principle, 206, 209
head-tracking devices, 116
head-up displays, 115
health issues
   for children and youth in sports, 218
Heim, M., 109-10
Hemphill, Dennis, 107
Herron, Tim, 99
higher forms of play, 11, 14
Hobbes, Thomas, 252
Hobbesian position, 247
hockey, 66, 183, 264
Hogan, Ben, 95-97
Hogarth, William, 191
Holt, Jason, 82
Holt, Laurence E., 82
homogenized technique. *See* averaging
   model of the golf swing
honesty, 221
Howe, Leslie A., 261
Howell, Charles, 99
Huizinga, Johan, 1, 38, 40, 46-47, 75,
   111, 261, 289
hula-hooping, 61
   craze, 29, 62
human-computer interface in computer
   games, 114-15
Hume, David, 249
   A Treatise of Human Nature, 252
Humean sympathies, 247
hurling, 61

ice dancing as art, 189
ideal swing in golf, 95-96
   aesthetic bias, 100
illusion as convention of art, 175

imagination, 6, 16, 174, 192
  in child's world, 15
immanence, 131, 135, 138
Immelman, Trevor, 95
immersion (in human-computer interface),
  114-17, 120
"incoherence of causality," 116
"incoherence of space," 116
Indian classical dance, 171
individual liberty, 205, 216-17. *See also*
  freedom
inductive learning, 83
informed consent, 206-07
inhibited intentionality, 134, 136-37, 140
institutional theory of art, 189-90
institutionalization as component of
  sports, 60-63
institutionalized games, 35, 37
instrumental rationality, 246
intensional object, 176
intentionalist approach to establish sport
  as art, 188
intentionality in motility, 135-36
interactivity (in human-computer
  interface), 114, 116-17
International Olympic Committee (IOC),
  61, 215
international organizations governing
  sports, 45
intrinsic goods, 30-31
Irwin, Terrence, 294
iterated or repeated prisoners' dilemma,
  248-49

Jacklin, Carol N., 147n18
jai alai, 61
"The John Curry Theatre of Skating," 177
Jones, Bobby, 96-97
Jooss, Kurt, 183

Kahn, Roger, 40
Kalverson, Lolas E., "Effect of Guided
  Practice on Overhand Throw Ball
  Velocities," 145n2
Kansas City Royals, 265
Kant, Immanuel, 137, 236
Keating, James, 283-85
  on the nature of play, 289-90
  polarized view, 287-88
Keenan, F., 174-75
Kierkegaard, Søren, 28

kinesiology, 95
King Lear, 173, 191
know-how, a species of knowledge, 107
knowing a game, 83, 88
knowing how, 81. *See also* learning a
  physical skill
knowing how rather than knowing that, 86
knowledge, Plato's definition, 81
knowledge as technological aspect of
  games, 83
knowledge of the rules and procedures of
  a game, 88
Kolberg, L., 148n21
Kovich, M., 188
Kretchmar, R.S., 120
Kuhn, T.S., 84-85, 90

language, 6
language of science, 84
laughing as exclusive to man, 7
Laus Stultitiae (Erasmus), 8
Leach, E.R., 48
learning a physical skill, 84-87. *See also*
  knowing how
  by exemplars, 84, 86
  unconscious, 87
  what it feels like, 86-87
  whole integrated action, 87-88
learning science, 90
Lehman, Craig K., 229
Lehman, Tom, 96
leisure ethic, 30-31
Lewis, David, 252
libertarianism of sport, 208
liberty (individual liberty), 205, 216-17.
  See also freedom
limitedness of play, 11, 38
Locke, John, 234
The Logic of Collective Action (Olson), 241
"The Logic of Tacit Inference" (Polanyi), 87
logical-incompatibility thesis, 229, 231-
  32, 234-36
Lombardian ethic, 253
losing graciously, 272-73
Low, G., 116
Lowe, B., 172, 178
Loy, John W., 35
  "The Nature of Sport," 83
  sports are games view, 35
Luce, R. Duncan, *Games and Decisions*, 253n2
luge, 224

LumePong, 118, 120
Lumetila project, 118
lusory attitude, 19, 25, 69
lusory goal of a game, 21
lusory means, 21, 25

Maccoby, Eleanor E., *The Psychology of Sex Difference*, 147n18
Maheu, R., 174
make-believe, 289
make-believe in sports, 40-41
masculinity, used to define "real" sport, 110
masks and disguises, 14. *See also* costume; dressing up
McBride, Frank, 71
Mediate, Rocco, 99
medication, 220
Meier, Klaus V.
  on Suits's definition of sport, 36, 57, 59-60, 63-75, 112-13
Merleau-Ponty, Maurice, 130, 135-37, 139-41
  distinction between phenomenal space and objective space, 138
  The Phenomenology of Perception, 131, 134
Midgley, Mary, 252
Mill, J.S., 206, 216, 224
mime as art, 186-87
mind, 5
mind/body dualism, 107
Modern Educational Gymnastics, 160
Mondrian, Piet, 191
moral failure
  gamesmanship traceable to, 268
moral philosophy, 252, 281
moral theory, 233, 247
morality grounded in rational egoism, 247
Morals by Agreement (Gauthier), 251
Morgan, William J., 57
mountain climbing, 61, 224
multiple realizability, 94, 97, 102-03
Munich Olympics, 185, 215
Murray, Thomas, 203
music, 191-92
mystical (sacred performances), 15
myth, 6

Nagel, Thomas, *The Possibility of Altruism*, 255n15
NAIA (National Association of Intercollegiate Athletics), 45
Narveson, Jan, 27

National League baseball, 73
natural phenomenon such as sunsets (not art), 170
"The Nature of Sport" (Loy), 83
NCAA (National Collegiate Athletic Association), 45
Nelson, Byron, 96
New York Yankees, 265
Nicklaus, Jack, 99
Nietzsche, Friedrich, *On the Genealogy of Morals*, 251
non-aesthetic sports, 183-84. *See also* purposive sports

objectified bodily existence, 143
objets trouvés, 169-70, 180
offensive holding, 233, 237
offside rules in football and hockey, 66
O'Hair, Sean, 99
Olson, Mancur, 251
  The Logic of Collective Action, 241
Olympic Games, 40, 59, 61, 63, 173, 175, 198, 244
  commercialization, 253
  performance-enhancing drugs, 203, 215, 239
Olympic gymnastics, 70, 161-62, 172, 184-85
On the Genealogy of Morals (Nietzsche), 251
One Day in the Life of Ivan Denisovich (Solzhenitsyn), 159
100-yard dash as game, 70
optimal performance, 93-95, 97, 103. *See also* multiple realizability
organizational sphere of game or sport, 44-45
orgies of young men of rank, 14
orienteering, 160
Osborne, H., 181
Osterhoudt, Robert, 61, 112
Othello, 174
"others," 13
Oxford English Dictionary, 14

Paddick, Robert J., 112
paranoia, 27
Pareto-inferior outcome, 242
Pareto-optimal strategy, 248
Parfit, Derek, *Reasons and Persons*, 255n15
partially aesthetic physical activities, 186-87
partially aesthetic sports, 192
partially athletic sports, 184-86

patriarchal culture, 141, 143
payoff matrix, 242
Pearson, Kathleen, 126, 234-36
performance, 14-15, 36, 63-64, 193. *See also* performative sports
performance-enhancing drugs, 201, 203, 243, 253. *See also* doping
  arguments against the use of, 206-09
  borderline cases, 204-05
  capacity to benefit from, 211
  damaging effects, 220-21
  drug use is inconsistent with the nature of sport argument, 224
  effectiveness, 211, 215
  equal access and information, 224
  ethical issues, 204-05
  freedom to experiment with, 211
  harm to other competitors, 206-08
  harm to the user, 206, 215
  informed consent, 206-07
  paternalistic control of, 215, 220, 225
  prohibition of, 209, 220-21
  protection of the young, 209, 220-21
  what counts as, 204-05
performative sports. *See also* aesthetic sports
  rules, 63-67, 74
Perry, Gaylord, 232, 236-37
Perry, Kenny, 96
Le Petit Prince (Saint-Exupéry), 176
"phatria," 13
Phenix, P.H., 187
The Phenomenology of Perception (Merleau-Ponty), 131, 134
Philadelphia Flyers, 265
philosophy as a skill, 90-91
philosophy as "the discipline that involves *creating* concepts," 121
philosophy of kinesiology, 82, 93, 103
philosophy of mind, 107
philosophy of science, 84
physical prowess, 35, 43, 58, 72, 102, 107, 113, 118
  essential characteristic of sport, 112
physical requirements necessary to play golf, 98
physical skills, 25, 27-28, 43
  example of knowing how, 81
  games of, 42
  not a defining characteristic of sport (Meier), 58
physical skills needed for sports, 85

physicality, 112
  an internal good of sport, 112
Picasso, Pablo, 173, 191
pickup sticks, 102
Pietri, Dorando, 175
Plato, 81
play, 9
  animal level, 3, 5, 7
  as autotelic activity, 72-73
  biological function of, 4
  boundaries of time and space, 14. *See also* play-ground
  Caillois's definition, 38
  cooperative, 284
  culture function, 5, 9-11
  "death of play" in contemporary sport, 75
  differentness and secretiveness, 14
  disinterestedness, 10
  dressing up, 14
  ethical value, 12
  formal characteristics of, 14
  higher forms of, 11, 14
  Huizinga's definition, 1, 38, 289
  "imagination" of reality, 6
  Keating's account of, 289
  limitedness, 11, 38
  Meier's definition, 72
  not "ordinary" or "real" life, 5, 9-11, 13-14, 40-41, 111
  "only pretending" quality of, 10, 40
  play-element in archaic ritual, 16
  "playing at nature," 16
  primordial quality of, 4
  Schmitz's four types, 289-90
  secrecy, 13-14
  seriousness/nonseriousness, 7, 10, 14, 290
  as a significant form, 6
  significant function, 3
  as social construction, 6
  subordinate social status, 111
  subordinate to other ends, 111
  tendency to be beautiful, 11
  as a transitive verb, 1
  voluntary activity, 9, 38
play, game, sport interrelationship, 72-73, 75
  Venn diagrams, 71, 74
play, game, sport on a continuum, 111, 113
play-community, 13
play-concept, 7-8, 12
play-ground, 11, 15
play theory, 111

play theory of sport, 290
player and athlete distinction (in Keating's account), 284-88
player-athlete
    paradoxical attitudinal complexity, 291
    psychological complexity, 292
playful competition, 38, 46
Polanyi, M., 88
    "The Logic of Tacit Inference," 87
The Possibility of Altruism (Nagel), 255n15
practical attitude, 180
pre-lusory goal of a game, 20-22, 25, 32
primary consumers, 51-52
primary producers (of a game), 51
    prisoners' dilemma, 230, 240-43, 250-51. *See also* doping dilemma (version of prisoners' dilemma)
    noncooperative game, 244
    not "theory-free," 247
    pseudo-problem, 245
"Problems of Sex Differences in Space Perception and Aspects of Intellectual Functioning," 147n18
professional athletes, 40, 64, 94, 97
    performance-enhancing drug use, 206, 215, 223
professional-automobile-racing helmets head-up displays, 115
professional foul, 229, 264
professional wrestling
    rules are routinely violated, 234
psychology, 16
The Psychology of Sex Difference (Maccoby), 147n18
Puritanism, 30-31
purposive and aesthetic sports (gap between), 160-66
purposive sports, 153, 183
    aesthetic is not central to the activity, 160
    looked at aesthetically, 162-64
    variety of ways of achieving the end, 161

racquetball, 58
Raiffa, Howard, *Games and Decisions*, 253n2
rape, 143
Rapoport, Anatol, 248
rational choice, 251
rational choice games, 244
rational egoism, 241-43, 245, 247
rational self-interest, 230

rationality account of conflict, 241
Rawls, John, *A Theory of Justice*, 255n15
Reason and Morality (Gewirth), 255n15
Reasons and Persons (Parfit), 255n15
reciprocal altruism, 248-49
recreational use of drugs, 220
refereed games, 63-64
regulative rules, 36, 66, 201
regulatory bodies, 45
Reid, L.A., 161, 167-68, 170-72, 174
representation, 14-16, 47
research and development, 29
Rice, Grantland, *The Tumult and the Shouting*, 233
risk in sports, 207-09, 221, 224-25
Ritalin, 228
rites or ritual act, 6, 15-16, 46, 48
Rivaldo, 265
Roberts, W., 145n2
Robertson, Mary Ann, 145n2
Robson, Bobby, 191
rowing, 164, 167
rugby, 61, 183
rule of practice, 66
rule types, 36
rule violation, 229, 231
    context, 233, 235
    deliberate, 229, 231-32, 234
    tolerated by convention, 229, 234
rules, 14, 65-67
    auxiliary. *See* auxiliary rules
    constitutive. *See* constitutive rules
    decisional simplifiers, 250-51
    easing up on, 22
    eligibility rules, 201
    event rules, 67
    pre-event rules, 64
    regulative rules, 36, 66, 201
    for which there is a fixed penalty, 22
rules in games, 1, 12, 39, 44, 69, 236, 251
rules in sports, 39, 44, 251
Russian roulette, 27
Ruth, Babe, 101

Saint-Exupéry, Antoine de, *Le Petit Prince*, 176
salience (or ease of recognizability), 249, 251
sanctions, 39, 250-51
Sanders, Doug, 96
sandlot game of baseball, 73
Sartre, Jean-Paul, 135
saturnalia, 14

Schauer, Frederick, 250
Schelling, Thomas, *The Strategy of Conflict*, 249
Schlesinger, G., 181
Schmitz, Kenneth, 111, 289, 291
Schneider, Angela J., 49, 239, 241, 243-46, 252
science, Kuhn's view of, 84
scientific achievement in sport, 228. *See also* technological sphere in sport
scientific revolutions, 84
Scruton, R., 175
secrecy, 14, 46
    Huizinga's meaning of, 46-47
    play, 13
self-consciousness, 143
self-control, 283
self-development, 271-72
self-image, 131
self-interest, 249
self-reference, 138
self-reliance, 221
selfhood
    gamesmanship and, 273-76
Seoul Olympic Games, 70
seriousness
    derivative seriousness, 30
    sport and, 29-32
seriousness/nonseriousness, 32
    of play, 7, 10, 14, 290
seriousness/nonseriousness of games, 290
serving or volleying in tennis, 85-86
Sherman, Julia A., 147n18
Shogan, 239
Shorter, Frank, 215
similarity classes, 84
Simon, Robert L., 201, 252
Simpson, A., 188
Singer, Peter, *The Expanding Circle*, 251
situatedness of human experience, 128-29
situation of women within a given sociohistorical set of circumstances, 129-30, 141
ski jumping, 184, 187, 192
skiing, 164, 167, 224
skill in games, 25-27. *See also* learning a physical skill
skillful play as form of sporting intelligence, 120
skillful play in computer-simulation games, 118-20
Sluman, Jeff, 99

Smart Golf, 110, 117, 120
soccer, 85, 174, 264
social condemnation of cheating, 249-51
social justice, contractarian views of, 247
Socrates, 91
soft paternalism, 216-17, 222-23
softball, 102
Solzhenitsyn, Aleksandr, *One Day in the Life of Ivan Denisovich*, 159
"Some Reflections on Success and Failure in Competitive Athletics" (Delattre), 232-33
sore loser, 273
Spassky, Boris, 28
spatial perception
    differences between the sexes, 141-42
spatiality, 131-33
    feminine spatiality, 139-40
    lateral space, 127
speccie example, 119-20
spectacular element of sport, 47
spectator sports, 52, 281
spitballs, 232-33, 235-37
spoil-sport, 12-13, 47. *See also* bad sport; sportsmanship
sponsorship for sport teams, 45
sport/athletics distinction (Keating), 283-86
sport aesthetics, 153
sport and seriousness, 29-32
sport-art, free style skating as, 195
sport as a game occurrence, 35, 37-43
sport as a social institution, 35, 37, 49-50
sport as a social situation, 50-52
sport as a social situation or social system, 35, 37
sport as drama, 174
sport as extension of play, 289, 292. *See also* play, game, sport interrelationship
sport as institutional game, 35, 37
sport as institutional pattern, 43
sport as institutionalized game, 44-48
sport as structured and artificially constrained play, 269
sport clubs, 49
sport is art debate, 153-54, 157, 174, 178, 192
    artistry and art within sport, 192-95
    opposition, 179, 190-92
    sport as art form, 170, 172, 176, 179-80
    unsuccessful attempts to establish, 187-90
sport occurrence, 60
sport order, 49-50

sport simulations. *See under* computer games
sport situation, 50-51
sport-specific conditioning, 102
sporting goods manufacturers, 49
sporting skills, 289
sportniks, 50
sports, 19. *See also* competitive sport;
  games and sports
  about the athlete as a person, 263, 271
  from aesthetic point of view, 155-57
  aesthetic terms applied to, 73
  athletic achievement replaced by
    scientific achievement (fear), 228
  attendant roles and institutions (or
    ancillary functions), 29
  auxiliary personnel, 49
  chance in, 42
  character development, 273, 276, 282
  coded as masculine activity, 110
  competitive games of inclusively gross
    physical skill, 101
  confined to class of physical games, 28
  definitions, 57, 59-60, 63-75, 101
  "dressing-up" element, 47
  essential shallowness of, 40
  following, 25-26, 28-29, 61
  formal instruction, 48
  formally codified rules enforced by a
    regulatory body, 44
  games of physical skill, 36, 58
  games of skill rather than games of
    chance, 27, 112
  knowledge acquired by demonstration,
    89-90
  Loy's account of, 35
  as means to full human self-
    development, 271
  multipurpose, 237
  performative. *See* performative sports
  physical prowess, 35, 43, 58
  play characteristics, 38, 291
  purposive. *See* purposive sports
  require limitation on means the players
    may employ, 31
  spectacular element of, 47
  spectator. *See* spectator sports
  a type of intrinsic good, 32
sports are games (view), 74, 102. *See also*
  play, game, sport interrelationship
sports that are not games (assertion), 43,
  71-72, 112

sportsmanship, 221, 237
  about personal conduct on road to
    victory or defeat, 270
  accepting defeat by a superior
    opponent, 273
  bad sport, 282
  bad sportsmanship, 293
  Keating's account of, 283-86, 288-92
  recognizing opponent as essential for
    one's own growth, 276
  as supererogatory, 261
  virtue of, 262, 282-83, 292, 294
sportworld, 35
squash, 160, 167
Stadler, Craig, 96
stage, comparison of life to a, 7
Steel, Margaret, 82
steroids, 64, 201, 204-05, 221, 228,
  271. *See also* performance-enhancing
    drugs
  risks, 204
  side effects, 203
Stewart, Mario, 31
Stolnitz, J., 180-81
Stone, A., 109
Stone, Gregory P., 47-48
straightforward maximizer (SM), 246
strategic rationality, 245-46
strategy and tactics (knowledge or
  learning), 88, 90
The Strategy of Conflict (Schelling), 249
Straus, Erwin, 127-28, 131
strong form of gamesmanship, 274-75
Suits, Bernard, 1-2, 36, 57, 102, 112-13,
  231, 261, 290-91. *See also* logical-
    incompatibility thesis
  distinction between autotelic and
    instrumental, 73
  distinction between game rules and
    performance ideals, 69
  "The Elements of Sport," 59
  The Grasshopper, 56, 59, 65, 71
  on performative sports, 66-67
  "Tricky Triad," 56, 75
  "What Is a Game?," 32-33
Suitsian formalism, 229
surfing, 184
Sutton-Smith, Brian, 42
Sweat-Bead, 28-29, 62
symbolic sphere of sport, 46
Symphonic Variations, 194

synchronized swimming, 110, 160, 162, 171, 184
   aesthetic criteria, 172
   performative in nature, 193
   as vignette art, 193, 195
systematized training, 48

"tacit knowing," 88
tactical rule, 66
Tamboer, J., 120
Taylor, Michael, 240
Taylor, Richard, 287
teams. *See* athletic teams
technological sphere in sport, 46, 222, 224-25, 228. *See also* scientific achievement in sport
tennis, 85-86, 88, 167
testosterone, 203-04, 221
theories of art, 181-82
theories of science, 84
A Theory of Justice (Rawls), 255n15
A Theory of the Good and Right (Brandt), 255n15
Thomas, Carolyn, 206
Thorpe, Jim, 96
throwing inside in baseball, 265-66, 274
"throwing like a girl" concept, 108, 127-28, 133
tit-for-tat strategy, 248, 250
Torvill and Dean, 194
Tourischeva, Ludmilla, 162, 185
track and field, 160, 183
tragedy in a play, 173-74, 191
tragedy in sport, 173, 175, 191
"tragedy of the commons," 240, 243
'tragic' (uses of the term), 174-75
training techniques with risk to health, 207-09, 221, 225
trampolining, 160, 162, 171, 185
transcendence, 131
transcendence of play, 289
transcendental subjectivity, 137
trash talk and taunting, 265
A Treatise of Human Nature (Hume), 252
Trevino, Lee, 96, 100
"Tricky Triad" (Suits), 56, 63, 75
Trivers, Robert, 248
Tucker, A.W., 253n2
The Tumult and the Shouting (Rice), 233

Ullmann-Margalit, Edna, *The Emergence of Norms*, 243, 251
U.S. Open, 99

Valéry, Paul, 12
Veblen, Thorstein, 40, 47
Vedic sacrificial rites, 16
Venn diagrams (of play, game, sport interrelationship), 71
victory. *See* winning and victory in sport
videogames. *See* computer games
vignette art forms, 193
   choreographed music, 193-95
virtual reality, 109-10, 114-16
virtue, 281
   Aristotle's description of, 292
   not alike to all people in all situations, 294
virtue of sportsmanship, 282-83, 292
   a mean between extremes, 293-94

Waldorf, Duffy, 96
Warnock, G.J., 284
Watson, Tom, 99
weak gamesmanship, 274-75
weight-lifting contests, 42
Weiss, Paul, 43, 112, 283
Weitz, M., 182
Wertz, S.K., 188-89
"What Is a Game?," (Suits), 32-33
whole-body movement
   in computer games, 117-18
   girls/women tend not to use, 133, 135, 142.
      See also feminine body comportment
         and movement women typically
         refrain from, 135-37, 140
winner, criteria for determining, 39-40
winning and excellence relationship, 263, 267-68. *See also* excellence
winning and victory in sport, 75, 269, 284
   exaggerated emphasis on, 221, 293
Witt, Katarina, 194
Wittgenstein, Ludwig, 165-66, 292
Woman: A Contemporary View (Buytendijk), 145n2
woman as Other, 131
women's sports, devaluation, 110
Woods, Tiger, 96, 98-99
wrestling, 47, 234

Young, Iris Marion, 108

Zátopek, Emil, 163
Ziff, Paul, "A Fine Forehand," 83

from the publisher

A name never says it all, but the word "broadview" expresses a good deal of the philosophy behind our company. We are open to a broad range of academic approaches and political viewpoints. We pay attention to the broad impact book publishing and book printing has in the wider world; we began using recycled stock more than a decade ago, and for some years now we have used 100% recycled paper for most titles. As a Canadian-based company we naturally publish a number of titles with a Canadian emphasis, but our publishing program overall is internationally oriented and broad-ranging. Our individual titles often appeal to a broad readership too; many are of interest as much to general readers as to academics and students.

Founded in 1985, Broadview remains a fully independent company owned by its shareholders—not an imprint or subsidiary of a larger multinational.

If you would like to find out more about Broadview and about the books we publish, please visit us at **www.broadviewpress.com**. And if you'd like to place an order through the site, we'd like to show our appreciation by extending a special discount to you: by entering the code below you will receive a 20% discount on purchases made through the Broadview website.

Discount code: **broadview20%**

Thank you for choosing Broadview.

Please note: this offer applies only to sales of
bound books within the United States or Canada.

The interior of this book is printed on 100% recycled paper.

PERMANENT

BIO GAS
ENERGY